THE NAZIS

THE RISE AND FALL OF HISTORY'S MOST EVIL EMPIRE

PAUL ROLAND

This edition published in 2024 by Arcturus Publishing Limited
26/27 Bickels Yard, 151–153 Bermondsey Street,
London SE1 3HA

AD006191UK

Printed in the UK

MIX
Paper | Supporting
responsible forestry
FSC® C171272

CONTENTS

INTRODUCTION:
A Question of Evil

This book differs from most conventional histories of the Third Reich in that it argues that the Nazi state was more than a sociopolitical phenomenon. Instead, it was the manifestation of its Führer's fatally flawed personality.

Sadistic criminals, serial killers and brutal dictators are routinely referred to as 'evil' and Adolf Hitler is often cited as the personification of the malevolent spirit manifest in man. But malicious spirits are a creation of the primitive, irrational mind, and common sense contends that evil is entirely man-made – a deliberate, wilful act by individuals who seek satisfaction in destruction out of cruelty and a lack of empathy for their victims.

We may not believe in the devil these days, but we continue to demonize dictators. This is to avoid being forced to see them for what they really are – a shadow of ourselves, the embodiment of our darkest fears, a reflection of what we could become if we abandoned the conventional rules of conduct and indulged our basest instincts.

Some historians argue that Hitler was an aberration, the product of a violent, unstable era in European history which could only have come about in the aftermath of the First World War. They seek to reassure us that the milieu from which he emerged was a form of collective shell-shock and is unlikely to occur again. There will always be tinpot dictators throwing their weight around, suppressing their own people and threatening their neighbours, they say, but Hitler and 'Uncle' Joe Stalin, his equally bloodthirsty ally, were the last in a line of conquerors going all the way back to Genghis Khan. These historians would have us believe that such men will be obsolete in the 21st century.

Opposite page: *Was Hitler the main architect of the Nazi state or simply its figurehead? Did his turbulent nature compel him to forge a new order?*

The same historians have suggested that the Nazi party's rise to power was exclusively because of sociopolitical factors. It is the purpose of this book to present the argument that Hitler did not wage war solely to avenge Germany's humiliating defeat in 1918. It will be shown that his insatiable appetite for conquest was not driven by territorial ambition alone nor by the desire to restore German honour and pride. Instead, the former Austrian corporal was consumed by the belief that divine providence had entrusted him with a sacred mission, which was to subjugate all 'inferior' races and eradicate the Jewish people from the face of the earth.

Hitler created and nurtured a climate of suspicion, fear and deceit which pitted his own ministers against one another. He hoped they would be too occupied with squabbling among themselves to plot against their Führer. But once the initial euphoria of swift and easy victory over France and the Low Countries died down, and the reality of a protracted war with Russia filtered through, the German people woke up to the fact that they were living in a fascist police state. Anyone with a grudge could anonymously inform on a family member, friend or neighbour. German civilians knew that these suspicions would be ruthlessly acted upon by the Gestapo, who routinely resorted to torture to extract a confession. Such conditions are not created by a unique combination of random historical events. Nazi Germany was one man's nightmare made manifest.

So if we are to understand how the Third Reich came into being – and why the German people worshipped Hitler as their saviour, even as their cities crumbled around them in the last days of the war – it is necessary to appreciate what kind of a mind conceived the Nazi state.

The mind of Adolf Hitler

Hitler was a neurotic, unstable, paranoid personality whose infamous rages were a manifestation of his malignant narcissism and megalomania – and which prohibited anyone from questioning his authority. Malignant narcissism is a comparatively common psychosis exhibited by violent criminals and tyrants who have a distorted view of reality and failed to develop a sense of morality. The core components are pathological self-absorption, antisocial behaviour, a persecution complex and unconstrained aggression.

One of the characteristics of pathological narcissists is a lack of empathy for others. Unable to feel genuine emotion, they fake it by mimicking the facial expressions and language of those around them. Such people are psychologically unstable because they suffer from 'identity diffusion', meaning that they don't have a real sense of self. Instead, they exhibit aspects of themselves as if playing a role. They have not completed the process of integration which characterizes healthy individuals whose self-image is formed from interaction with other people.

The chameleon-like character of pathological narcissists betrays the fact that they are acting out the role which they consider suitable to their situation. Their condition typically manifests as over-confidence and self-absorption, and their lack of empathy desensitizes them to such an extent that they can commit violent acts without any sense of guilt.

Malignant narcissists are devoid of conscience and driven by self-interest. Their amorality can lead them to exploit the beliefs and convictions of others in order to consolidate their own power. They are not deterred by the threat of punishment or retribution, which makes them resistant to condemnation, censure and – in the case of tyrants – economic sanctions. Only the threat of force can deter them, because it makes them question their belief in their own supremacy.

> *'It was not only Hitler, the madman, who created German madness, but German madness which created Hitler. Having created him as its spokesman and leader, it has been carried along by his momentum . . . it continues to follow his lead in spite of the fact that it must be obvious to all intelligent people now that his path leads to inevitable destruction.'*
>
> *Psychoanalyst Walter C. Langer*

According to leading American political psychologist Aubrey Immelman, the malignant narcissist harbours a siege mentality behind his grandiose facade:

'They are insular, project their own hostilities on to others, and fail to recognize their own role in creating foes. These real or imagined enemies, in turn, are used to justify their own aggression against others. Malignant narcissists are cold, ruthless, sadistic, and cynically calculating, yet skilled at concealing their aggressive intent behind a public mask of civility or idealistic concern.'

A 'right man'

Hitler was what is known in clinical psychology as a 'right man': that is, someone who stubbornly believes himself to be in the right at all times and cannot conceive that his perspective may be distorted or that someone else may have a valid opinion. It is said that such people would 'cut off their nose to spite their face'. Such blinkered perception and stubbornness proved an asset in Hitler's early days because his fanaticism was focused on a single objective. But such an intensely blinkered view, when allied with inflexibility, can only lead to inner conflict and ultimately to psychological disintegration and self-destruction.

Hitler could not accept defeat, and when it came he ranted and raged that he would drag the nation down with him, because the German people were evidently 'unworthy' of the sacrifices he had made for them. His solution to all problems was to use threats and violence. He was devoid of conscience and had no conception of morality. 'Conscience', he said, was a Jewish invention and therefore it was the duty of the Germans to distrust it and free themselves of the 'dirty and degrading [idea of] conscience and morality'.

Even as a youth, Hitler was in a state of constant denial and his grip on reality was tenuous at best.

Nature or nurture?

The question of whether an individual's character is determined by nature or nurture continues to be the subject of fierce debate among psychologists, sociologists and criminologists the world over. Namely, whether evil-doers act according to their nature, are compelled by some physiological impulse to seek satisfaction in antisocial acts, or whether they are conditioned to do so by their upbringing.

And while it has been proven that the brains of sociopaths and psychopaths exhibit certain physical anomalies which contribute to their aberrant behaviour, there is no definitive study proving that criminal tendencies are the direct result of a genetic fault or some other abnormality.

However, there is compelling empirical evidence which shows that individuals who were subject to abuse in their early years are more likely to demonstrate abusive behaviour towards others when they reach their teens and adulthood. Moreover, they will commit those acts knowing they are wrong and in spite of the consequences.

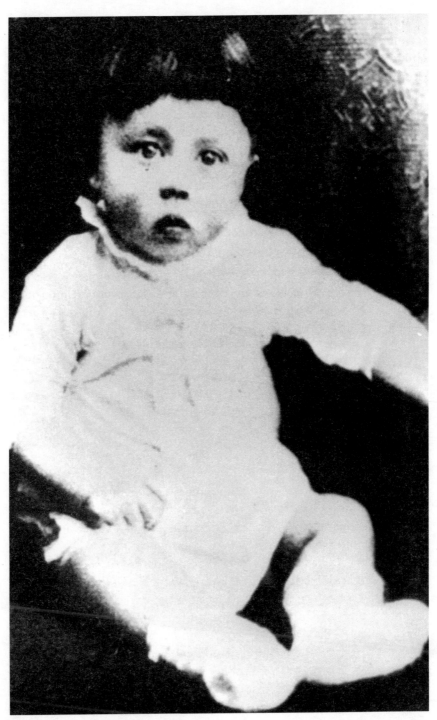

Adolf Hitler at about one year old

Whether Adolf Hitler had suffered an abusive childhood to the extent that his many biographers have described, or whether he was simply a product of the turbulent times in which he lived, is debatable. However, he evidently lacked the strength of character to come to terms with his early experiences and the temperament to exorcise, or at least subdue, his personal demons. He appears to have been bedevilled by his upbringing and his own perverse nature, which saw him nurture his resentments until they consumed him – but not before he had taken his rage out on the world.

> 'To say the least, he was considered argumentative, autocratic, self-opinionated and bad-tempered and unable to submit to school discipline. Nor was he industrious, otherwise he would have achieved much better results, gifted as he was.'
>
> Professor Huemer, one of Hitler's school teachers

CHAPTER 1
Hitler's Early Life

Of the many odd twists of fate that affected the life of the future Führer, perhaps none is more significant than that which occurred 13 years before his birth. His paternal grandfather belatedly legitimized his own 39-year-old bastard son Alois (Adolf's father) by changing his name from Schicklgruber to Hitler in order that Alois could share in an inheritance bequeathed by an uncle. Had he not done so it is conceivable that Hitler might never have come to prominence, for there is power in a name and it is hard to imagine the German people venerating Adolf Schicklgruber as they did Adolf Hitler. ('Heil Schicklgruber' does not have quite the same impact!)

Various authors have speculated that the name change was effected for a more sinister reason. That is, in order to silence persistent local rumours that Alois' real father was a Graz Jew named Frankenberger who had employed Adolf's grandmother, Maria Anna Schicklgruber, as a domestic servant. This might explain why Hitler ordered four secret investigations into his ancestry between 1932 and 1940 and why the findings were never disclosed. It would also account for his otherwise inexplicable destruction of his father's birthplace, Dollersheim, and the levelling of the graveyard in which his grandmother was buried, as well as the burning of the parish records. It has even been argued that Hitler grew his Chaplinesque moustache to disguise what he believed was his characteristically Semitic nose.

> 'These people [journalists] must never find out who I am. They mustn't know where I come from or my family background.'
>
> Adolf Hitler, quoted in Hitler: A Biography, Joachim Fest, 1973

Whatever the truth of these rumours, Adolf's forebears on his father's side were clearly not the sturdy stock that would produce the future Master Race. They were itinerant farm labourers and work-shy peasants, whose habitual intermarriages produced an uncommonly high number of physically disabled or imbecile children. Secret Gestapo files now stored in the US Library of Congress and in the Institut für Zeitgeschichte Archiv in Munich record several stunted branches on the family tree including that of Josef Veit, a cousin of Hitler's father who bore three mentally retarded children, one of whom was to commit suicide in a mental institution. According to an affidavit signed by Dr Edward Kriechbaum and stored in the Linz archives, Adolf's aunt Johanna was said to be schizophrenic, while his cousin

Edward Schmidt was a hunchback who also suffered from a speech impediment.

The family practitioner Dr Bloch testified to the OSS (Office of Strategic Services) in 1936 that Hitler had a sister whom he suspected was mentally retarded because she was always hidden away whenever he visited her parents' home. He also said that Adolf's younger sister, Paula, was a 'high grade moron'. The inbreeding which appears to have been characteristic of the Hitler line could account for his infamous rages. It would also explain his fear of inherent insanity, his repugnance for physical deformity and his belief that if he married he risked producing 'feeble-minded' children.

By comparison, Hitler's maternal ancestry was slightly more stable. His mother's family had been smallholders in the village of Spital in Lower Austria, near Vienna, for four generations, but were considered by the inhabitants of the capital to be no better than peasants. They were despised as much for their ignorance as for their lowly origins and their humourless, suspicious nature.

Hitler's mother

Klara Pölzl, Hitler's adored mother, was a simple, fastidiously neat young woman with a somewhat boyish face and piercing blue eyes. They were a feature that her only surviving son was to inherit and with which he would later enthrall his admirers. Klara had little expectation of improving her situation until, at the age of 16, she moved in with her 'Uncle' Alois and his first wife Anna Glassl as their unpaid domestic servant. Alois apparently wasted little time in pursuing both Klara and the maid Franziska Matzelberger until Anna got wise and insisted on a separation. Alois then set up home with Franziska (or 'Fanni' as she was called) who demanded that her rival, Klara, be packed off to Vienna. Alois and Franziska married three years later when he was 46 years old and she was just 22. The couple had two children – a son, Alois jnr., and a daughter, Angela – before Franziska succumbed to a fatal bout of tuberculosis, prompting her husband to summon Klara back from the city to look after the children.

Alois Matzelberger (who later took the surname Hitler) grew up to become an embarrassment to his famous half-brother. He was twice convicted of theft and once jailed for bigamy. After a brief spell in Britain he deserted his family and returned to Berlin where he ran a beerkeller and stubbornly refused to discuss his family history for fear of angering

Adolf. Angela, Hitler's half-sister, fared better. She married well and after her husband's death went to live with Adolf in Berchtesgaden as his cook and housekeeper. But when she left him in 1936 to remarry, Hitler exhibited his infamous vindictiveness and refused to send her a wedding present.

Klara appears to have harboured no ill feeling towards Franziska for she nursed her during her final illness. However, while his wife lay dying, Alois pressed his attentions upon his adopted 'niece' and succeeded in getting her pregnant. After Fanni's death he then attempted to 'put things right' by marrying Klara when her condition aroused the attention of the village gossips.

Klara was a simple, fastidiously neat young woman with piercing blue eyes

Klara Hitler

Klara Pölzl was a simple, modest girl of Austrian peasant stock and was just 24 when she married her twice-widowed husband Alois, a customs official to whom she was related by blood. She became pregnant with their first child while serving as a housemaid to Alois and his second wife Franziska, who was then dying of tuberculosis. When her first three children died, Klara saw this as divine punishment for her infidelity and became neurotic about hygiene. She would scrub their modest house from morning to night as if exorcizing a curse that had been placed on the family. And so, when her fourth child, Adolf, was born she became over-protective, fearing for his safety and believing that if he survived he must be destined for great things and that his achievements would compensate for the loss of his siblings.

Klara became even more neurotic whenever Adolf fell sick, which was frequently. When he finally grew into a sullen but healthy child Klara, Adolf's younger sister Paula and his stepsister Angela would come between the boy and his strict, brutish father, who beat him on an almost daily basis. According to a friend, through this intervention 'Hitler must have seen women and girls as guardian angels from an early age'.

The eminent Harvard psychologist Henry Murray analyzed the metaphors in *Mein Kampf* (1925) and concluded that Hitler's aversion to a physical relationship with the opposite sex was the result of his 'over-identification' with his mother, which 'severely compromised his masculinity' and may have led to him becoming a 'passive homosexual'. It was Murray's opinion that Hitler was both impotent and a 'fully fledged masochist' and that the dictator was driven to overcompensate for his sexual inadequacy through aggression.

Whether that is true or not, Klara's almost suffocating affection and her encouragement of her son's fantasies undoubtedly contributed to his narcissistic personality.

Because Klara was Alois' second cousin, the couple had to apply for an episcopal dispensation in order to marry. The wedding took place at the parish church of Braunau in January 1885, at 6 o'clock on an overcast winter's morning. Four months later their first child, Gustav, was born, followed by a daughter Ida in 1886 and then a second son, Otto, who died within days of his birth.

Adolf was their fourth child and their only surviving son. A third son, Edmund, was born to the couple in 1894, but he died at the age of six. Only Adolf and a younger sister, Paula (born in 1896) survived.

Klara was a devout Catholic and must have been wracked with guilt at having deceived Alois' former wives. She considered herself to have sinned against them and survived and her guilt must have been compounded by the death of her first two children from diphtheria the year before Adolf was born. It is likely that she might have seen their painful and protracted deaths as divine punishment. For the same reason she might have borne her husband's alleged beatings without protest, as penance for her imagined sins.

Mother love

Adolf Hitler was born at half past six in the evening of 20 April 1889 in the village of Braunau am Inn in Austria, within sight of the Bavarian mountains. Hitler considered the location to be highly significant and later wrote that he believed fate had chosen Braunau as his birthplace so that he would make it his life's mission to reunite the German-speaking peoples on both sides of the border.

Adolf was by all accounts a sickly, demanding child whose condition must have increased his mother's innate anxiety while helping to assuage her guilt. If he survived, she could see it as proof that her penance had been paid so she doted on him to the detriment of the boy's emotional and psychological development. Her compulsive cleaning of their home and her obsessive attention to the cleanliness of her children were further indications of her need to scrub the shame and guilt away. Hitler's own fastidiousness and his obsession with personal hygiene in adulthood were perhaps the direct results of his mother's neurosis. It also led to his unnatural obsession with bodily functions and his belief that germs were targeting him specifically. But for all his mother's care and attention, she could not protect him from repeated beatings at the hand of her husband. Her failure to intervene rankled with her son, who must have resented her weakness as much as he cursed his father's cruelty.

Dr Bloch, the family doctor, described the relationship between mother and son as uncommonly close.

Roots and Rumours

It was rumoured that Hitler's paternal grandfather might have been a Jew from Graz called Frankenberger, who seduced his paternal grandmother Maria Anna Schicklgruber while she was employed as a maid in his household.

It is suggested that this is why Hitler ordered his grandmother's tombstone to be removed, and all trace of her grave destroyed after he came to power. Even the parish records were burnt on his orders, to erase all documented proof of his father Alois' birth.

If there was no truth in the rumour, then why did Hitler order four separate investigations into his ancestry between 1932 and 1940 and why did he have his father's birthplace of Döllersheim levelled to the ground? It has also been claimed that Hitler subjected himself to periodic bleeding to 'purge' his 'contaminated' Jewish blood.

One symptom of Hitler's neurosis was 'transference', in which subjects unconsciously offload their internal conflicts on to other individuals. This tendency to blame others for one's personal failings is typical of neurotic paranoid personalities. As psychoanalyst Walter C. Langer noted, 'By this process, the Jew became a symbol of everything which Hitler hated in himself.'

Adolf grew up hating his father and revering his mother, creating in his mind a syndrome known as primitive idealization whereby a child imagines that one parent is wholly virtuous and the other is entirely bad. Many children who are conditioned in this way adjust their distorted perspective when they realize that the idealized parent has failings and the other has redeeming qualities. But Hitler's childhood world of absolutes remained with him to the end. His worldview was distorted through the mirror of his own warped ego and he would not be reasoned with. That is why he flew into a rage whenever his authority was questioned.

A brutal upbringing?

According to those who knew him, Alois Schicklgruber was a strict, domineering, officious, hot-tempered and humourless man who ruled his household with a rod of iron. He insisted that he be obeyed without question and that his children address him formally as 'Herr Vater'. They were not to speak until given permission to do so and his son, Adolf, was often summoned with a whistle, like a dog, rather than being called by name. It must have been demeaning for the boy to have the pet Alsatian named after him and be treated no better than the animal. The only known photo of the father portrays a portly and proud provincial official. In his Austrian customs service uniform, with his close-cropped hair and long, bushy handlebar moustache, he looks every inch the old Prussian aristocrat he aspired to be.

As a child, Adolf elicited sympathy from other children by claiming to have dragged his drunken father from the village inn on many occasions. Later in his life he recalled: 'That was the most shameful, humiliating experience I have ever had. How well I know what a devil alcohol is. It was – because of my father – the greatest enemy of my youth!'

But it seems unlikely that Alois was an alcoholic. He was much

Alois Schicklgruber was a strict and domineering father who ruled his household with a rod of iron

respected in the customs service, in which he had attained a high rank. His position had given him sufficient income to buy a pleasant house in the village of Fischlham near Linz, which boasted nine acres of land, fruit trees and a splendid view of the surrounding countryside. His wages were on a par with that of a country lawyer and even after his retirement in 1895, when Adolf was six years old, he benefited from a generous pension of 2,660 kronen, on which the family could live very comfortably. It is true, however, that Hitler's childhood was unsettled, as the family moved repeatedly for no apparent reason.

> 'No matter how firm and determined my father might be, his son was just as stubborn and obstinate.'
>
> Adolf Hitler, Mein Kampf

By the time Adolf was 15 years old he had attended five different schools and could recall seven different homes, including a renovated mill and a period when the family were guests at a local inn. After that they finally settled in the village of Leonding, where they purchased a modest furnished apartment, by which time the volatile relationship between father and son had become a battle of wills. Alois, now in his 60s, insisted that his son follow him into the civil service, but Adolf stubbornly refused to study in the hope of forcing his father to allow him to follow his ambition to become a painter.

It is clear from Hitler's remarks in later life that he both respected and feared his father, but he was determined to distance himself from the old man by his actions. Adolf's aversion to tobacco stemmed from memories of his father's habit of smoking in the house from morning to night. In the meantime, his mother would invoke his father's unimpeachable authority by pointing to the row of pipes on the kitchen shelves.

Hitler also grew to detest his father's obsession with punctuality, which he sneered at in later life by lying in bed until lunchtime – to the frustration of his ministers and visiting dignitaries. Even Alois' rule forbidding idle talk was to influence his son's behaviour: Adolf would often indulge in rambling reminiscences with his guests (the so-called 'table talks') and aimless all-night monologues with his long-suffering valet. But ultimately he could not help becoming that which he had detested. Like his father before him, Hitler was humourless and hot-tempered and he would not tolerate his orders being questioned or his opinions contradicted.

Childhood trauma

The arrival of Adolf's brother Edmund in 1894, when Adolf was six, prompted Klara to entrust her elder boy to his then married half-sister Angela, thus robbing him of his mother's undivided attention at a critical age. It is said that Hitler prayed for God to take the infant as he had his deceased brother and sister. Although it was to be six years before Edmund died of complications following a bout of measles, the belated fulfilment of this childish curse is likely to have left an indelible psychic scar on the surviving sibling. Edmund's premature death may have reinforced Adolf's conviction that he alone had been spared because he was special. His mother had made this assertion so often that it was imprinted on his mind to the extent that he could not fail to believe that he was protected by Providence, singled out to fulfil some special mission.

Although Adolf had prayed for Edmund's death, he would have suffered extreme guilt when he witnessed the grief it caused his mother. And his feelings would have been compounded by the manner in which Edmund was laid to rest. His parents flatly refused to attend their son's funeral and instead spent the day in Linz, leaving the 11-year-old Adolf to grieve alone.

It is thought that Alois had forbidden his wife to attend the funeral merely because he had fallen out with the local priest. He is known to have argued with the priest over 'political' differences and Klara was too submissive to defy him. One can only wonder at Hitler's state of mind as he stood watching his brother's body being lowered into the frozen ground while a blizzard whipped around the mourners at the graveside.

However, it was not long before Adolf witnessed an event that must have seemed like divine retribution for his father's cruel and unfeeling act. On the morning of 23 January 1903 Alois Hitler died from a massive haemorrhage while taking his daily beaker of wine at the local inn. He was 66. His son did not mourn his passing.

> 'No person manifesting Hitler's pathological personality traits could possibly have grown up in the idyllic home environment Hitler himself has described.'
>
> *Walter Langer, US Office of Strategic Studies Report*

School life

The period immediately following his father's death was one of liberation for the sullen adolescent, who was finally free of the suffocating shadow of his overbearing parent. And yet Hitler's new-found freedom did not produce an improvement in his school work. He later claimed that his poor grades were caused by the fact that he had deliberately neglected his studies in the hope that his father would relent and allow him to pursue his ambition to become an artist. But after his father's death his report cards continued to record a steady decline. Instead, his increasing arrogance, lack of attentiveness and poor marks prompted his expulsion from the Realschule in Linz at the age of 15, forcing his widowed mother to send him to the state high school in Styr 15 miles (24 kilometres) away, where he was to continue his education.

Although Hitler later claimed that Klara was destitute at this time, in fact she was far from it. She received a widow's pension which was roughly two-thirds of her late husband's income, plus a generous lump sum of 650 kronen from his former employer. With the sale of the family home in June 1905 she was able to pay for Adolf's lodgings in Styr and move into a spacious apartment in the Humboldtstrasse in Linz, in order to be near her married stepdaughter, Angela.

Hitler's academic failure could possibly be attributed to a normal adolescent aversion to authority and an unwillingness to work at subjects in which he had little interest. He might also have hoped that the generous widow's pension his mother received would make it possible for him to pursue the bohemian lifestyle he had long dreamt of. If so, her insistence that he should continue to attend school must have seemed like an act of betrayal, but it is likely he would have vented his frustration on his teachers rather than his adored mother. That would explain his lifelong distrust of academics and experts of all kinds. To the end of his life he was intimidated by intellectuals and chose to surround himself with shallow admirers who would reassure him of his genius.

With the exception of his history teacher at Linz, who described Adolf's grasp of the subject as no more than 'fair', and a science master who admitted that his former pupil was unremarkable, Hitler was disparaging of his masters, seeing them as his 'natural enemies'. He described them as 'erudite apes', 'slightly mad', 'effete', 'abnormal' and 'mentally deranged' – which probably reveals more about Hitler's state of mind than it does about the academic abilities of his teachers.

Physical abnormality

There is another explanation for Hitler's poor academic record which merits consideration. It has been suggested that Hitler was a monorchid: that is, he had only one testicle, a condition which can produce a number of characteristic behavioural disorders. These are the very aberrations that he exhibited. He had learning difficulties; a lack of concentration; the compulsion to fantasize and lie; social and sexual inadequacy; an attraction to physical danger; an aversion to criticism; and a feeling of being in some way 'special' (this is presumably a defence mechanism to explain the 'abnormality').

Hitler's monorchidism was discovered during a Soviet autopsy on the Führer's charred remains, conducted in 1945. Although the identity of the body found in the grounds of the Reichschancellery has been disputed, an independent team of Norwegian and American dental experts has now confirmed that it was Hitler's corpse.

A monorchid child does not automatically exhibit the neuroses that Hitler displayed, and can be expected to overcome the fear that his condition makes him somehow

A rare photo of the young Hitler, aged ten, at school in Lambach: he was not an outstanding pupil

less of a man. However, if a boy is already psychologically disturbed, this uncommon condition can intensify his psychosis. Such symptoms typically manifest themselves in pre-pubescence, the period in which Hitler's academic achievements went into decline.

An early sketch by a classmate depicts the 15-year-old Adolf as an unimposing youth, but one who would presumably have had as much luck with the local girls as any of his contemporaries. The fact that Hitler avoided romantic entanglements of any kind, preferring to fantasize about girls he never had the courage to talk to, suggests something more than the usual adolescent awkwardness. He could have experienced a fear of intimacy that may have had a physical and a psychological basis.

It would not be unreasonable to imagine that Hitler, in his ignorance, would have blamed his mother for his condition. Her repeated assurances that all would be well were to prove unfounded, and this would have served to intensify his anxiety, adding to his catalogue of violently conflicting emotions.

Castration complex

It is not uncommon for monorchid boys to develop a castration complex. The more disturbed children among them might even compensate for this feeling by indulging in violent fantasies involving the emasculation of their enemies. It is significant that in adulthood Hitler repeatedly talked of castrating those artists who displeased him and that he reintroduced beheading as a form of execution in place of a firing squad.

It has been noted that boys who are missing a testicle, or whose testicles have not descended, often exhibit their anxiety concerning their sexual identity by clutching their genitals for reassurance or by putting a hand over their crotch. It cannot be coincidence that this is precisely the gesture that Hitler can be seen making repeatedly in newsreel footage, in countless photographs and even in official portraits. Whatever the situation, he is frequently seen with his hands folded over his crotch in a protective gesture. His hands are only fleetingly placed behind his back and they are rarely visible at his sides.

Hitler was also known to indulge in infantile displays of what he believed were masculine feats of strength and endurance – but they were clearly sexual substitutes. On one occasion he attempted to impress a female guest at his mountain retreat in the Obersalzberg by keeping his arm in the Nazi salute position for a long period of time. After assuring her that he could keep it up longer than Goering, he said, 'I can hold my arm like that for two solid hours. My arm is like granite – rigid and unbending. . . . It's an amazing feat. I marvel at my own power.'

It has been noted that monorchid men invariably transfer their sexual energy to their eyes. Hitler is said to have practised and perfected his penetrating stare in the mirror, no doubt as a substitute for sexual gratification.

As unlikely as it might sound to those not steeped in Freudian psychology, it would certainly explain Hitler's infamous and otherwise inexplicable hypnotic power. It will be remembered that many of those who found themselves in Hitler's presence commented on the hypnotic quality of his piercing blue eyes.

A boyhood friend, August Kubizek, recalled in his biography *The Young Hitler I Knew* (Boston 1955) that his mother was frightened by Hitler's penetrating gaze: 'I remember quite distinctly that there was more fear than admiration in her words. . . . Adolf spoke with his eyes. . . . Never in my life have I seen any other person whose appearance . . . was so completely dominated by the eyes.'

> *'He saw everywhere only obstacles and hostility. He was always up against something and at odds with the world . . . I never saw him take anything lightly.'*
>
> August Kubizek,
> a childhood friend of Hitler

Hitler's mesmerizing gaze

When Hitler ranted against those who failed to recognize his genius, his friend remembers that his face was livid and his lips were clenched white with fury. 'But the eyes glittered. There was something sinister about them. As if all the hate of which he was capable lay in those glowing eyes.'

Even at the very end, as he shuffled through the Berlin bunker in April 1945, a shell of his former self, his eyes retained their power. A young adjutant recalled that in the last hours of Hitler's life his eyes were still 'strangely penetrating'.

Psychological Tests

The first attempt to understand the minds of the Nazi leaders came in the immediate aftermath of the war in Europe, when 21 members of Hitler's inner circle were incarcerated at Nuremberg awaiting trial for crimes against humanity. The Allied prosecution hoped that if some of the defendants were willing to submit to a series of psychological tests, they might learn what had made such apparently ordinary men commit such unspeakable crimes. With little to occupy them in the months leading up to the trial, Hermann Goering, Joachim von Ribbentrop, Rudolf Hess and Albert Speer agreed to take the tests under the supervision of two American experts – psychologist Gustave Gilbert, PhD and psychiatrist Douglas Kelley, MD.

Both Kelley and Gilbert concluded that all of the accused were legally sane, but they disagreed on their interpretation of the data. Gilbert declared that there were three distinct psychopathic types in the group, whom he categorized as schizoid, narcissistic and paranoid. He argued that they had been conditioned to defer to authority without question and so had not developed any critical faculties. In contrast, Kelley contended that the defendants were the pathological product of a 'socio-cultural disease' and had been encouraged to commit criminal acts by their psychotic leader, like the brainwashed members of a religious cult. Once Hitler was gone, they reverted to their original unprepossessing personalities.

This well-intentioned attempt to understand the criminal mind was, however, fundamentally flawed. It was rather naive to assume that a series of simple and highly subjective psychological tests could identify the various contributing factors that led to the development of such complex personality disorders and extreme aberrant behaviour.

Portrait of the Tyrant as a Young Artist

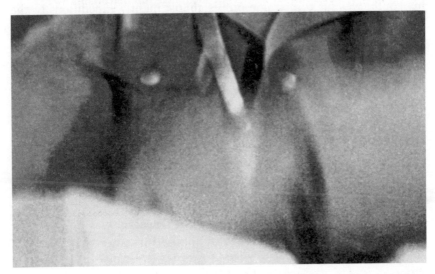

Hitler's frustration at not being allowed to pursue his artistic ambitions came to a head when he succumbed to what he later claimed was a serious lung infection (quite possibly a psychosomatic disorder) in his final year at Styr. He appealed to his mother to allow him to return home to convalesce and to his relief she relented. She was not in the best of health at the time, so she insisted that he stay with his Aunt Theresa in Spital. Curiously, the family doctor, Dr Bloch, dismissed the entire episode as a figment of Hitler's fevered imagination and implied that he was simply malingering to elicit his mother's sympathy.

As he recalled, 'I cannot understand the many references to his lung trouble as a youth. I was the only doctor treating him during the period. . . . My records show nothing of the sort. . . . There was never anything seriously wrong with Hitler.'

After making a miraculous recovery Hitler persuaded his mother to purchase a piano so that he could write his own operas, but he quickly tired of his teacher, who demanded that he practise his scales rather than rely on his natural genius. Undaunted, he threw himself into what he later called the 'hollowness of a comfortable life'. He indulged his passion for attending the opera, museums and art galleries in Linz and he dressed in style – all, of course, at his mother's expense.

In his black silk-lined overcoat, tweed jacket, cravat and kid gloves Hitler was every inch the young man about town, but no matter how hard he affected the air of a gentleman he must have known he was only playing the part. August Kubizek, the only close acquaintance of his youth, was his companion on his almost nightly expeditions to the city during those carefree years. Although it was clear that he was the truly talented one, Kubizek patiently endured Adolf's rambling sermons on the merits of true German art. He also tolerated his embittered political rants against the decadent Hapsburg monarchy, which was fast becoming an obsession.

Destiny calling

In 1906, in the early hours of a chill November morning, Hitler and Kubizek emerged from the opera house in Linz with the last strains of Wagner's *Rienzi* still ringing in their ears.

For Kubizek, the music student, the evening was to prove a memorable one and not because of the performance they had just enjoyed. That night he was treated to a performance of an entirely different nature, quite possibly the first evidence of Hitler's gift for oratory, as he delivered an impassioned speech under the stars on the deserted road leading up to Freinberg.

Hitler's earlier monologues, witnessed at a distance by his Realschule professor and other children, had been addressed to the trees on a hill in Leonding, but this night was different. He had grown tired of imagining and now demanded a real audience. Wheeling around, he took his startled friend by the hands and stared fixedly into his eyes as if willing the boy to submit. Kubizek could not remember what was said that morning, but he would never forget the intensity with which the 17-year-old Hitler poured forth his diatribe against society and his determination to dedicate his life to saving the German people.

'It was as if another being spoke out of his body and moved him as much as it did me. It was not at all a case of a speaker carried away by his own words. On the contrary; I rather felt as though he himself listened with astonishment and emotion to what burst forth from him with elemental force . . . like floodwaters breaking their dykes, his words burst from him. He conjured up in grandiose inspiring pictures his own future and that of his people. He was talking of a mandate which, one day, he would receive from the people to lead them from servitude to the heights of freedom – a special mission which would one day be entrusted to him.'

Power over the masses

Clearly Hitler had a sense of his own destiny, but it was one in which Kubizek was to play no part. That night he realized that Hitler only sought his company because he needed an audience.

The compulsion to talk appears to have come from Hitler's need to dominate others with the power of his voice and the force of his argument. In time, it has been said, his speeches would take on a decidedly sexual quality. He would begin in a low, seductive tone and build up to an ecstatic climax after which he would retire from the podium drained of strength and drenched in sweat, with a glazed look of satisfaction in his eyes.

The Polish journalist Axel Heyst witnessed Hitler's power over the masses, but remained

> 'I came to understand that our friendship endured largely for the reason that I was a patient listener. . . . He just HAD TO TALK.'
>
> August Kubizek

unmoved. 'In his speeches we hear the suppressed voice of passion and wooing, which is taken from the language of love. He utters a cry of hate and voluptuousness, a spasm of violence and cruelty. All those tones and sounds are taken from the back streets of the instincts; they remind us of dark impulses repressed too long.' The poet René Schickele was more direct. He damned Hitler's speeches as oral 'rape and murder'.

The intimate nature of the relationship between orator and audience was not lost on the Führer himself who said, 'One must know exactly when the moment has come to throw the last flaming javelin which sets the crowd afire.'

For people such as Hitler, verbal intercourse is often a substitute for sexual relations, which they avoid for fear of ridicule. Oral discharge, as the psychoanalysts would term it, keeps the object of desire at a distance. There may be some truth in this Freudian analysis of Hitler's powers of oratory, but those who have seen newsreel footage of the Führer in full flight have often gained the impression that Hitler was merely a man who was seduced by the sound of his own voice.

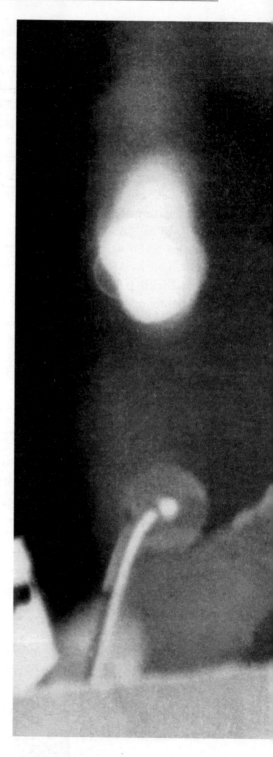

Hitler instilled a quasi-religious fanaticism in his audience through his power of oratory

32

Unrequited love

Hitler's oratory was clearly powered by an unbridled animal passion and for that reason he had an extraordinary effect on a live audience. At the same time, his speeches made no lasting impression, unlike the speeches of Winston Churchill, for example, whose eloquent words appealed to the intellect.

It is arguable that Hitler might have channelled his energy to less destructive ends if he had allowed himself to indulge in an intimate relationship in his youth. But he was incapable of relating to other people. Aside from his innate distrust and paranoia, he also manifested symptoms of a form of erotomania, the belief that he was involved in a romantic relationship which did not exist.

In the winter of 1906, Hitler came across a girl named Stefanie. She was window-shopping in the Landstrasse in Linz with her mother and he became infatuated with her. Typically, he preferred to worship her from afar, so every afternoon at precisely 5 o'clock he waited where he had first seen her, hoping for a fleeting glimpse of his beloved. Every gesture would be analyzed in the hope of finding a sign of approval. His only concession to convention was to write reams of absurdly romantic poetry in which he envisaged her as a pure Wagnerian heroine, none of which he thought to send her. He could not summon up the courage to speak to her and therefore was able to avoid the risk of rejection. So long as he didn't approach her he could continue his fantasy, for what if this symbol of Germanic virtue spurned him? The prospect was too hideous to contemplate.

After months of martyrdom he wrote her an earnest, anonymous letter. He began by declaring his love and ended by begging her to wait four years until he had made his name and could marry her. Until then he would make what he considered to be the supreme gesture. He would leave home to live the life of an impoverished artist in Vienna. But there may have been more mundane reasons for his departure. Relatives were asking uncomfortable questions – when was he going to earn his own living and not be entirely dependent on his mother?

Vienna

And so it was that in the spring of 1906, just after his 17th birthday, Hitler turned his back on Linz and set out for Vienna, the bustling cosmopolitan capital of culture and the jewel in the crown of the old

Infatuation

Hitler's volatile and turbulent nature manifested itself after he became infatuated with a pretty young blonde he had seen window-shopping in Linz with her mother in 1906. Her name was Stefanie Jansten. She was 17 and the very image of the pure Aryan girl that Hitler had imagined he would fall in love with.

From that first day, Hitler kept a vigil at the Landstrasse bridge where he had first seen her, with the devoted Kubizek at his side. He silently seethed whenever he witnessed the object of his obsession flirting with the army officers and cadets who strolled along the promenade. Hitler consoled himself with the notion that Stefanie was only pretending to be interested in these eligible bachelors in order to disguise her true feelings for her shy suitor. It was Kubizek's opinion that the experience of having to suffer silently while these young aristocrats charmed the girl he desired led to Hitler's lifelong hostility towards the officer class, whom he despised for their haughty arrogance and inherited privilege.

According to Kubizek, Stefanie was totally unaware of his friend's intentions and therefore rarely acknowledged them when she passed. Occasionally she would offer a polite smile and on those occasions Adolf would be beside himself with joy. 'But when Stefanie, as happened just as often, coldly ignored his gaze, he was crushed and ready to destroy himself and the whole world.'

Hapsburg Empire. As he strolled through the historic centre, gazing up at the imposing imperial symbols of power, he visualized himself presenting the treasures of the Reich in a new setting with himself as its chief architect.

In Hitler's deluded mind, the years he spent in Vienna were a time of martyrdom, of intolerable suffering in body and soul. He imagined himself being forced to take a succession of manual labouring jobs, like shovelling snow or breaking his back on building sites. In fact, he didn't do an honest day's work during that period, but lived very comfortably on the generosity of his relatives. The only exception was a 15-month period from September 1908 to December 1909, when he depended on the charity of Jewish welfare organizations, a helping hand he must have accepted begrudgingly, to say the least. Only when he found himself needing extra money did he paint a few postcards of the sites. They were bought mainly by Jewish gallery owners who were later forced to return them when the Nazis sought to erase the Führer's past.

Disillusionment

It was not until a year later, in October 1907, that Hitler's illusions of imminent fame and fortune finally came crashing to the ground. That autumn he was rejected by the Vienna Academy of Fine Arts, whose examining board considered his drawings 'unsatisfactory'.

Determined to prove the Academy's experts wrong he persuaded his crippled aunt, Johanna, to become a patron of the arts by supporting his ambitions from her life savings. Her contributions were supplemented by an orphan's pension of 25 kronen per month, obtained by deception from the state. The money should have been paid to his sister Paula, but Hitler had made a false declaration stating that he was a student at the Academy, which entitled him to her share. A court order corrected the situation in May 1911.

Added to that sum, he received a small inheritance from a great aunt, Walpurga Hitler, and on his 18th birthday, in 1907, he became legally entitled to his share of his father's savings which had been accumulating interest for over three years and now amounted to 700 kronen. In total, he received the equivalent of a school teacher's salary during those aimless years in Vienna and did not put in a day's work to earn it. Instead he spent the afternoons in idle daydreaming. He planned new buildings for the capital that, he assured the doggedly loyal Kubizek, he would be commissioned to build once the city fathers recognized his genius. When he tired of sketching, he made plans for a Reich Orchestra which would tour the country bringing German culture to the masses. He would personally select the programme from works he judged to be suitable. That is, music he had heard while accompanying his friend to concerts on an almost nightly basis, thanks to the allocation of free tickets from the Conservatory, where Kubizek was then studying composition.

While Kubizek pursued his studies he and Hitler were amiable companions, though it was evident that Hitler considered his friend his inferior. They even shared a room together for a time in the Sixth

District, which was large enough to house Kubizek's grand piano. But after Kubizek graduated with honours from the Vienna Conservatory, Hitler felt increasingly uncomfortable. Kubizek's presence reminded him of his own unfulfilled ambitions. From that moment on, he and Kubizek were barely on speaking terms.

The death of Hitler's mother

In December 1907, Hitler's life of idleness was interrupted by the death of his mother. Klara had been diagnosed with breast cancer and hospitalized in January of that year. A mastectomy was performed by the house surgeon, assisted by Dr Bloch who continued to care for her after she returned home. She recovered well enough to take short walks through the village that summer, but in November she suffered a relapse and Dr Bloch had to administer large doses of morphine to ease the pain.

Dr Bloch, Hitler's sister Paula, August Kubizek and the local postmistress have all testified that Adolf hurried home from Vienna to be at his mother's bedside. But their stories of the dutiful son scrubbing floors and attending to her every need are contradicted by Franz Jetzinger in his biography *Hitler's Youth*. Jetzinger quotes a neighbour who claimed to have tended Klara in those final weeks. Her version of events sounds more plausible because she shared her recollection of Klara's last days with others at the time and was able to produce a letter written by Hitler thanking her for having tended his mother in his absence. Her story also appears to be substantiated by the fact that when she herself was ill her hospital care was paid for by a grateful Führer.

It has been suggested by some that Hitler's anti-Semitism began when he blamed the Jewish family physician for not saving his mother, or for prolonging her agony by administering the wrong treatment. Others say that if Hitler had been too preoccupied with his own pleasure to attend his dying mother, or had deliberately stayed away because he could not bear to see her suffer, he would have bitterly resented Dr Bloch for assuming the role of dutiful carer – a role that was rightfully his.

But this is not supported by the evidence. Dr Bloch received several hand-painted postcards at the time of Klara's death, in which Hitler expressed his profuse gratitude for the compassion and care with which his mother's passing had been eased. Also, the physician continued to speak of Hitler as a doting son after he had emigrated to America and was safe from the attentions of the Gestapo.

Perhaps the most intriguing question, and one which will doubtless remain unanswered, is why Hitler refused to mark his mother's grave with a headstone. It was only after he became chancellor of Germany that local Nazi party activists noted the omission and erected a gravestone at their own expense. When Hitler visited the cemetery in 1938 for the first and last time, he stood for only a few seconds and then turned and walked briskly back to his waiting car. If he loved his mother as much as he professed to do and the affection had been mutual, why did he deny her a memorial? What dark and disturbing secret had died with her?

Opposite page: *The rabid anti-Semite Julius Streicher – 'real Nazi trash'*

CHAPTER 3

Insidious Influences

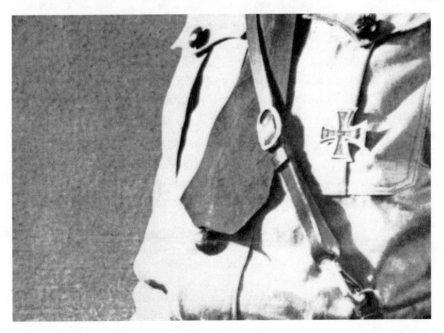

It is arguable that Hitler's ambivalent feelings towards Dr Bloch sowed the seeds of the virulent anti-Semitism that surfaced just months later. His feelings towards the Jewish physician must have been a mixture of gratitude and resentment, for the doctor possessed the compassion and medical knowledge to be a comfort to Hitler's mother when her son could only stand helplessly by, if indeed he was there at all. A neurotic, morose, self-centred person like Hitler would have been eaten up by such conflicting emotions, unless he could have found a substitute to blame for all his troubles. Unable to confront Dr Bloch with his true feelings, he would in all likelihood have turned on the Jews in general. As a good Catholic, he could not reproach God for his loss. Instead he would have internalized his anguish and, when it threatened to consume him, he would have spewed it out like an overflowing volcano. The Jews were a target he had cynically sized up in the knowledge that they would not fight back.

Jew-baiting was widespread in Europe at the time and the pernicious influence of the Jews would have been an accepted topic of conversation at all levels of Austrian society. Several anti-Semitic societies and periodicals openly promoted the disenfranchising of the Jews and spread vicious lies regarding Jewish religious rites, which were said to involve the sacrifice of Christian children. Even 'respectable' politicians felt safe in voicing their irrational prejudices in a public forum. In a speech to the Vienna parliament in 1887, the political extremist Georg Schonerer sought to justify his views: 'Our anti-Semitism is not directed against the Jews' religion. It is directed against their racial characteristics . . . everywhere they are in league with the forces of rebellion. . . . Therefore every loyal son of his nation must see in anti-Semitism the greatest national progress of this century.'

In Hitler's case, it would appear that he also had the Jews to blame for his rejection at the Academy of Art in Vienna. This happened on two separate occasions, for he reapplied in October 1908 and was rejected out of hand. On the second attempt, the board took a

> *The dragon of international Jewry must be slaughtered so that our dear German people can be freed from their prison.'*
>
> Dr Karl Lueger (1844–1940), mayor of Vienna

cursory glance at his sample sketches and refused to allow him to take the entrance test. He still nurtured the hope that he might be allowed to apply for a place at the School of Architecture, but that faded with

the realization that he couldn't fulfil the minimum requirements for entry because he hadn't completed his formal education. It must have been a shattering blow to his inflated ego when he discovered that all his plans were to be frustrated by petty officials. He was perhaps reminded of his father's earlier objections to his artistic ambitions. Unable to accept the fact that he lacked the abilities he thought he possessed, he blamed the Academy for being blind to his genius.

He admitted many years later that he had investigated the racial origins of the admissions committee and discovered that four of the seven members were Jewish. He doesn't say how he arrived at this conclusion. It might have been mere bravado on his part, or he might simply have assumed that those whose surnames sounded Jewish must have been Jews. He then claimed to have written a spiteful letter to the director ending with the threat, 'For this the Jews will pay!'

Seething with resentment, Hitler now turned his energies on those he imagined had denied him his calling and in doing so, ironically and tragically, secured his place in history.

Europe's Jews became the scapegoat for discontent in many countries, especially Austria and Germany

Perverted philosophy

Hitler's first encounter with an orthodox Jew in Vienna awakened his innate paranoia and provided him with an entire race of people on to whom he could project his feelings of unworthiness.

'Wherever I went I began to see Jews and the more I saw, the more sharply they became distinguished in my eyes from the rest of humanity ... I began to hate them ... I had ceased to be a weak-kneed cosmopolitan and became an anti-Semite.'

It is a mistake to imagine that Hitler formed his racist ideology after studying the great German philosophers such as Nietzsche, Hegel and Luther. He lacked the intellectual capacity to follow their arguments and was certainly incapable of formulating philosophical theories of his own. Moreover, he had no patience for literature, preferring to amuse himself with the children's adventure stories of Rabautz the horse and the popular westerns of Karl May. Contrary to claims by Kubizek that Adolf was an avid reader (a claim he subsequently retracted), there were no books of 'humane or intellectual value' in his library, according to Christa Schroeder, one of the Führer's private secretaries.

Nor did Hitler quote from the likes of Hegel and Nietzsche in his memoirs, speeches or informal table talks, an omission which betrayed the fact that he simply wasn't familiar with them. All of his ideas were obtained second-hand from the most specious of sources – the anti-Semitic pamphlets and racist periodicals 'bought for a few pennies' during his Vienna days, which served to reinforce his prejudices and gratify his craving for pornography. It is clear from the hysterical nature of the texts, from the crude cartoons and lurid illustrations, that these publications were not political tracts but were intended to satisfy the sadistic and sexual appetites of their male readers.

It has been argued that Hitler was also influenced by the *völkisch* 'mystics' Lanz von Liebenfels (1874–1954) and Guido von List

> *'I suddenly encountered an apparition in a black caftan and black sidelocks. "Is this a Jew?" was my first thought. ... I observed the man furtively and cautiously, but the longer I stared at this foreign face, scrutinizing feature for feature, the more my first question assumed a new form. "Was this a German?"'*
>
> Adolf Hitler, Mein Kampf

(1865–1919), as well as the other pseudo-intellectuals who adopted aristocratic names to hide their working class origins. But he doesn't appear to have understood their convoluted reasoning – he merely regurgitated it. The parallels between List, Liebenfels and Hitler are strikingly similar, so much so that there can be little doubt that Hitler simply used his impressive facility for retaining facts to commit to memory whole passages from his mentors' manifestos.

Prejudice and plagiarism

In 1934, for example, Hitler first considered the ways in which Germany could prevent 'racial decay' and then suggested, 'shall we form an Order, the Brotherhood of Templars round the Holy Grail of the pure blood?' It was a phrase which echoed almost word for word that of his dark guru Liebenfels, who had written in 1913 of: 'The Holy Grail of German blood that must be defended by the Brotherhood of the Templars'. Hitler also stole key phrases from List and Liebenfels such as 'the Hydra-headed international Jewish conspiracy', which appeared with monotonous regularity in his speeches and informal rants.

Liebenfels' anti-Semitic and *völkisch* theories were spread all over the pages of his magazine *Ostara*, and Hitler was an avid reader. The anti-Semitic Viennese newspaper, *Deutsche Volksblatt*, also fuelled Hitler's rhetoric of hatred. But he found more than political and racist doggerel in the rancid pages of *Ostara* and the *Volksblatt*. Hysterical, ill-informed articles on the subjects of women's rights, homosexuality, syphilis and castration provided him with the justification for his fear of intimacy. 'Evidence' in the form of cranial diagrams was presented in support of the pamphleteer's belief that women were intellectually inferior and that 'over-educated race murdering educational idiots and characterless professors' could be identified by the shape of their skulls.

Readers were encouraged to take *Ostara*'s racial biology test which allotted points according to physical characteristics. There were 12 points to be had for blue eyes, while, predictably, points were deducted for dark eyes. Tall, blond, white-skinned males with the 'right shaped nose' earned top marks (women were ineligible) and were deemed to be the Aryan ideal, those in the middle range with a total score below 100 were designated 'mixed breeds' and those falling below zero were condemned as 'apelings'.

One can only imagine what Hitler must have thought of Liebenfels' assertion that: 'The most important and decisive erotic force for people of the higher race is the eye.'

THE MAN WHO EDUCATED THE GERMAN PEOPLE IN HATRED

'The charge that I have something to do with having stirred up the populace by propaganda or by my speeches to commit such atrocities is false. . . . My conscience is as clear as a baby's.'

Julius Streicher – editor and publisher of the rabidly anti-Semitic journal *Der Stürmer* – was described as 'one of the two genuine nutcases' by a US army psychologist, and by US army intelligence officer Lieutenant Dolibois as one of the 'real Nazi trash', a group that also included labour minister Dr Robert Ley and Hans Frank, the 'Butcher of Poland'.

SEXUAL SADIST

Leon Goldensohn, a Jewish US army psychiatrist who interviewed all of the Nuremberg defendants repeatedly over a course of six months, was prepared to study Julius Streicher face to face and remained admirably frank in his appraisal: 'Streicher is a short, almost bald, hook-nosed figure of sixty-one years. . . . He smiles constantly, the smile something between a grimace and a leer, twisting his large, thin-lipped mouth, screwing up his froggy eyes, a caricature of a lecher posing as a man of wisdom. . . . He seems to me to be a man of probably limited normal intelligence, generally ignorant, obsessed with maniacal anti-Semitism, which serves as an outlet for his sexual conflicts, as evidenced by his preoccupation with pornography. Circumcision is a diabolical Jewish plot, and a clever one, he said, to preserve the purity of the Jewish stock. Christ, a Jew, was born of a mother who was a Jewish whore. . . . (But) he denies any personal animosity toward the Jews.'

Dr Goldensohn concluded that Streicher was a sexual sadist whose pathological obsession with Jews and the lurid acts he imagined they perpetrated upon innocent Aryan girls was most likely a projection of his own inner conflicts, inadequacy and perverse impulses.

Streicher had been jailed at Nuremberg many years before on charges of indecency after assaulting a young boy with a bullwhip and boasting that it had given him sexual gratification. Now, as he awaited the verdict of the Allied judges, he taunted his guards with details of his lurid dreams and offered to show them physical evidence of his sexual potency.

UNPOPULAR

When he was served with the indictment by Major Airey Neave, a British judicial aide who had made a daring escape from Colditz, Streicher was pacing his cell 'like an ape exposing himself in a cage' with his shirt open and his hands on his hips in a gesture of defiance. He struck Major Neave as 'stupid, cunning and cruel', someone who would have made an Inquisitor. 'I am without friends,' he told the major, who didn't express any surprise.

The other defendants objected to sitting in the same dock as the 'obscene dwarf' and 'degenerate', who was known to possess the largest private collection of pornography in Germany. Goering was particularly eager to distance himself from Streicher, who had published slanderous lies about his family and hoarded stolen property from deported Jews that Goering had once had his eye on. Stealing from the Reichsmarschall was considered a cardinal sin.

STRIPPED OF HIS TITLES

As a reward for playing a central role in the Munich Putsch, Streicher was given the post of *gauleiter* of Franconia, where his home city, Nuremberg, was located. At first token appointees, *gauleiters* acquired enormous authority when the Nazis came to power in 1933, and Streicher used this to tighten his grip on Nuremberg. In particular, he ordered a one-day boycott of Jewish businesses. All of this was taken away from him in 1940, when his feud with Goering and aggressive use of his *gauleiter* post resulted in his being stripped of his party functions. He was allowed to go on publishing *Der Stürmer*, however. If it had not been for Hitler's enthusiastic support, its publisher would have been considered an embarrassment to the educated Nazis long before that time.

SENTENCED FOR HIS PRE-WAR ACTIVITIES

If Streicher thought that his lack of participation in the war might earn him a lighter sentence, he was rudely mistaken. His years of inciting racial hatred put paid to that. Despite his vehement protestations of innocence, the judges at Nuremberg found him guilty and sentenced him to death.

Aryans and Atlantis

Both List and Liebenfels declared that the accepted view of history was wrong and that the Teutonic people were the descendants of a superior race known as the Aryans, who had survived the destruction of their homeland of Atlantis at the time of the Flood. According to the revisionist vision of the two 'mystics', the Aryans had lost their intellectual and physical powers through interbreeding with primitive inferior beings over several millennia. It was therefore their duty to restore themselves to their rightful place as the Master Race by driving the *Untermenschen* (subhumans) from Europe – thereby preserving the purity of their bloodline. List and Liebenfels predicted that this New Order would be ushered in with the arrival of a Messiah who would lead the German people in a final apocalyptic battle with the inferior races – specifically

ein Starke von ober

hao

A portrait of the influential mystic and writer Guido von List

the Slavs, the negroes and the Jews, whom Liebenfels referred to as the 'Dark Ones'. List prophesied that 'the Aryo-German demands a self-chosen Führer to whom he willingly submits'. If that is true, the German people got the leader they wished for and deserved. Amazingly, this preposterous juvenile fantasy circulated as fact in Germany and Austria in the years preceding the First World War.

By embracing the mythology of the *völkisch* 'mystics', Hitler wrapped himself in a mantle of pseudo-philosophy and respectability and finally found a focus for his neurosis. He also acquired a potent symbol which was to become the emblem of the Nazi party and its brutality – the swastika. Both List and Liebenfels advocated the adoption of the *Hakenkreuz* (hooked cross) as the emblem of Aryan might (an ancient Nordic symbol of the primal fire from which the universe evolved), while List promoted the double sig rune of the Nordic alphabet as the symbol of racial purity – a symbol that was to be adopted as the insignia of the hated SS.

Another pernicious influence on the young Hitler was racist 'philosopher' Theodor Fritsch (1852–1934), whose *Handbook of the Jewish Question* he 'studied intensively'. Again, the text was not on the same intellectual level as Nietzsche or Hegel. It was merely a collection of short essays accusing Jews of the worst crimes in history, together with a section of anti-Semitic sound-bites attributed to famous authors, which the pocket-sized politician would have committed to memory to endorse his own views. Fritsch's rabid attack on Heinrich Heine, the 19th century poet and essayist, is indeed typical of his warped logic: 'In Heine two forces are noticeably fighting each other. It is as though a piece of Teutonic spirit within him is attempting to ascend to more ideal heights, until the Jew suddenly pulls him down again by the legs into the morass where he then wallows with delight and jeers at all ideals.'

What is particularly noteworthy about Fritsch is his frenzied attack on Sigmund Freud, whom he accuses of setting out to 'destroy the German soul . . . and the German family'. Hitler would have seized on that idea in particular, as it undermined the authority and insights of the emerging science of psychoanalysis, which would have made a man with his catalogue of complexes decidedly uncomfortable.

Wagner

A major influence on the nihilistic ideology of Adolf Hitler and his Nazi party was that of the composer Richard Wagner (1813–83). Wagner was undoubtedly a musical genius but many of his views were, by all accounts, as abhorrent as Hitler's. Both men appeared to share many of the same characteristics, so much so that one is bound to ask if Hitler's

> 'Wagner's music produced in him [Hitler] that escape into a mystical dream world which he needed in order to endure the tensions of his turbulent nature.'
>
> August Kubizek

admiration was intensified by his personal identification with his idol. As Hitler himself admitted, 'I have the most intimate familiarity with Wagner's mental processes.'

Both men were intolerably opinionated, self-obsessed and enamoured with the sound of their own voices. They considered themselves experts on a wide variety of subjects, but their writings and recorded conversations reveal that they only had a superficial understanding of what they were discussing and could offer no insights of value. As Robert Waite, author of *The Psychopathic God*, has noted, if their reputations and influence had depended on their written works alone they would have been dismissed as racist cranks. Waite also notes that both men wrote 'execrable prose', which was so convoluted and grammatically poor that their translators were often forced to capitulate and fall back on the original German.

The fault testified to their irrational mode of thinking rather than their lack of education – though in Hitler's case his grammar and spelling remained remarkably poor for a modern political leader.

Waite suggests that both men might have affected an exaggerated macho image in order to disguise their latent homosexuality. Wagner dressed up in pink silk gowns and composed amid clouds of perfume, while Hitler wielded a riding crop – he once beat his dog with it in an effort to impress a female admirer. Both men also displayed childlike abandon when they were pleased and attention-seeking temper tantrums when they couldn't get their own way. But perhaps the most significant obsession they shared was their suspicion that their real fathers were Jews. In order to exorcise that fear they denounced the Jews more vehemently than any other anti-Semites. In neither case was their Jewish parentage ever proven, but the possibility tormented them to the end of their days.

A turbulent nature

Beneath all the nationalistic pomp and pageantry of Wagner's operas, which extolled German virtues and heroism, were the composer's obsessions with incest and mother-love. Such themes and undertones, which bordered on the Oedipal, would not have been lost on Hitler, for whom Wagner's music was both quasi-religious and emotionally therapeutic.

The racist pamphleteers had politicized the young Hitler, but Wagner's talk of the advent of a German hero had inflamed him with a missionary zeal. There would be a new Barbarossa, Wagner said, who would restore German honour and sweep aside parliamentary democracy, which he dismissed as a Franco-Judaic deceit. Man was a beast of prey, Wagner wrote, and great civilizations were founded on conquest and the subjugation of weaker races.

Although Wagner apologists maintain that his ravings should not deter us from enjoying his music, it has to be remembered that it was Wagner who first proposed the idea of a 'final solution' to the 'Jewish Question'. There can be little doubt about what he was proposing because he talked about a time when there would be no more Jews, whom he called 'the enemy of mankind'.

Such was the self-indulgent rant of the artist who could afford to live in a fantasy world of his own making, but Hitler took his idol at his word and swore to lead this struggle between Teutonic supermen and subhumans, or perish in the process.

The deserter

The immediate result of Hitler's exposure to racist pamphlets was to enrol himself and his friend Kubizek in the Austrian Anti-Semitic League. To Hitler, Vienna was no longer the cultural capital of his homeland but a 'racist Babylon' seething with Jews.

But before he could begin preaching his new faith he learned that he was to be arrested by the Austro-Hungarian army for evading conscription. In May 1913, he fled to Munich where he found comfortable, well-furnished rooms above a tailor's shop in Schwabing, the artistic district, for just 20 marks a month. His average income at the time was 100 marks a month, which more than catered for his daily needs. He obtained it by selling his paintings for between 10 and 20 marks each. It was, by his own admission, 'the happiest and most contented' period of his life. But on 18 January of the following year the Austrian authorities finally caught up with him. He was arrested as a deserter and taken to the Austro-Hungarian consulate to explain his failure to report for duty.

Hitler must have presented a pathetic spectacle, and played the part of the nebbish (sincere but harmless fool) to the hilt, because he succeeded in persuading the consul general that he was 'deserving of considerate treatment'. He was freed on condition that he report to the military commission in Salzburg for assessment. On 5 February 1914, the commission declared him unfit for military service because of an unspecified complaint and he was dismissed.

He returned to his easy life and his rooms above the tailor's shop until August, when the old world of empires came to a sudden and violent end.

CHAPTER 4
Turbulent Times

There is a famous photograph taken of the crowd in Munich's Odeonplatz on the day that the First World War was declared in August 1914. Among the thousands of cheering people is the 25-year-old Adolf Hitler, captured in a moment of euphoria. His fellow citizens doubtless shared his patriotism and the belief that the coming war was just and could well be over by Christmas. But, for Hitler, the approaching conflict was not solely about avenging the assassination of the Austrian archduke or standing by an ally: it was a 'deliverance' from his monotonous, aimless life and, as such, it empowered him with a sense of purpose. The war also gave him a sense of identity and the opportunity to avenge the violation of his motherland.

> *To me those hours came as a deliverance from the distress that had weighed upon me during the days of my youth. I am not ashamed to say that, carried away by the enthusiasm of the moment, I sank down on my knees and thanked heaven out of the fullness of my heart for granting me the good fortune of being permitted to live in such a time.'*
>
> Adolf Hitler, Mein Kampf

Hitler had a 'good' war by all accounts. He earned a promotion to corporal in the List Regiment and his bravery earned him an Iron Cross Second Class in 1914 and an Iron Cross First Class in 1918. But his comrades disliked him; he was not promoted to a higher rank because the officers suspected that the men would not follow his orders.

The White Crow

There was something odd in Hitler's demeanour that led his comrades to shun him. One recalled that he looked at his rifle 'with delight, as a woman looks at her jewellery'. They called him the 'White Crow' because he never laughed or joked unless it was in response to the misfortunes of others. Hitler despised his comrades for their lack of patriotism and their disrespect for their officers and they in turn distrusted him because he kept himself aloof and didn't make an effort to join in.

There was something unsettling in his compulsive cleanliness, which amounted to a mania, and his almost religious aversion to smoking, drinking and women. He was known in the battalion as 'the woman hater' and would habitually lecture other soldiers about the dangers of

The jubilant Hitler is photographed as a face in the crowd as the First World War is declared in 1914

interracial intercourse. At every opportunity, he would hold forth on the evils of Marxism, Freemasonry and the International Jewish Conspiracy to the amusement of his comrades, who would deliberately provoke him in order to relieve the tedium of trench life.

'We all cursed him and found him intolerable,' recalled one comrade, who was disconcerted by Hitler's uncanny knack for evading certain death. Time and again he would escape unscathed from a heavy bombardment or emerge unharmed from a skirmish in which others had been killed or wounded.

The letters and postcards he wrote from the front are stiff and formal, revealing nothing of the writer's character – only his obsessions. In his correspondence to his landlord, and the baker who offended his sensibilities by sending a food parcel, Hitler warns of 'a world of enemies' and repeats his unwavering belief that he had been miraculously spared in order to fulfil a special mission. There is no hint of humanity, only of his neurosis.

Even after being wounded in the shoulder by shrapnel in October 1916, Hitler begged to be able to return to the front so that he could spend Christmas alone there at headquarters, where he served as a runner. Ever since the death of his mother he had ensured that he was alone at Christmas, a practice he continued even after his rise to power. Alone on the most festive day of the year, he could play the martyr to the hilt.

Stabbed in the back

When the armistice was announced in November 1918, Hitler was in Pasewalk hospital, Pomerania, recovering from the effects of chlorine gas inhaled during the battle of Ypres the previous month. Defeat was something he simply could not comprehend, despite the fact that the Allies now had the Americans on their side. He found it intolerable to think Germany had capitulated after all the privation and sacrifice it had endured: 'Everything began to go black again before my eyes. Stumbling, I groped my way back to the ward, threw myself on my bed and buried my burning head in the covers and pillows. I had not cried since the day I had stood at the grave of my mother.'

It was then that the myth of the 'November criminals' was born. Some of the German soldiers who could not bring themselves to believe that their almighty armed forces had been defeated began to talk of being 'stabbed in the back' by defeatists at home.

> 'We could have brought the struggle to a favourable conclusion if . . . co-operation had existed between the army and those at home. But while the enemy showed an even greater will for victory, divergent party interests began to show themselves with us. . . . No blame is to be attached to the sound core of the army. . . . It is plain enough with whom the blame lies.'
>
> General Hindenburg, November 1919

Versailles

The excessively harsh terms of the Versailles Treaty, which imposed punitive reparations on Germany in June 1919, prepared the ground in which extreme nationalism and the bitter fruit of fanaticism were to take root. They included the loss of all overseas colonies, the surrender of Alsace-Lorraine to France, and termination of Germany's occupation of the strategically vital Saar region and the Rhineland. The treaty was clearly intended to punish and humiliate Germany, which was required to accept all the blame for the hostilities.

In total, 13 per cent of German territory was taken by the victors, which meant that, overnight, six million Germans lost their citizenship. On top of that, 20 per cent of the German coal, iron and steel industry was apppropriated by the victors and the German army was reduced to 100,000 men – a force insufficient to defend Berlin. The greater part of the German navy was seized by the British, and Germany was prohibited from possessing submarines, tanks and heavy artillery and from developing an air force. In effect, Germany was stripped of her assets, denied the means of defending herself and billed for the damage and suffering she had caused during the war – valued at £6,600 million in 1921.

The terms of the treaty were not negotiable. To add insult to the perceived injury, Germany was also denied membership of the newly formed League of Nations, which implied that the nation as a whole was not to be trusted even in such a co-operative venture.

Birth of a republic

'Extreme times call for extreme measures.' Such was the sentiment with which millions of German citizens rationalized their decision to vote for the Nazi party in the 1920s – and with some justification. In the aftermath of the First World War, Germany was tearing itself to pieces. During the last weeks of the war, the generals had persuaded Kaiser Wilhelm II to transfer power to the Reichstag (the German parliament) so that they could blame the politicians for their defeat. On 3 October 1918, Prince Max von Baden formed a new government and that same day asked the Allies for an armistice. The German people were stunned by the sudden capitulation, having believed the press reports which stated that just 'one more push' was needed to ensure final victory.

The immediate reaction of the troops was to mutiny. Sailors took over the port at Wilhelmshaven and the navy base at Kiel, as well as other key installations around the country, while hastily elected councils comprising soldiers and workers seized control of the major cities. In

Bavaria, left-wing radicals declared a socialist republic and a series of strikes and demonstrations brought Berlin to a standstill. Then, in an effort to restore order, the Kaiser abdicated and a new government under Friedrich Ebert was formed. In January 1919, elections were held for a new National Assembly and in the following month the members met in the town of Weimar, after which Ebert declared that Imperialist Germany was no more. The country was now a republic and he was its president.

An epidemic of extremism

The birth of the republic was difficult, to say the least. For the first five years it witnessed a succession of armed revolutions and attempted coups, as extremists on all sides of the political spectrum struggled violently for control. The government's answer was to form the Freikorps – armed volunteers acting under orders from former army officers. They were allowed to run riot and shoot anyone they suspected of supporting the insurgents. It was anarchy on the streets, with the army on one side and the workers on the other. Transport and communications were brought to a standstill in an effort to force the Freikorps to stand down. This intolerable situation culminated in the so-called Kapp Putsch of March 1920, which only ended when millions of German workers downed tools. That was enough to force the leaders of the uprising, Wolfgang Kapp and General von Luttwitz, to flee to Sweden.

Ebert then demanded that the Freikorps be disbanded, which only inflamed the right-wing radicals. They vowed to fight on, to which end they formed underground organizations and assassination squads, which led to 354 murders by the end of 1923. It is not true to say that Hitler and the Nazis were solely responsible for inciting right-wing extremism in Germany at that time, for extreme nationalism had already reached epidemic proportions in the Weimar Republic. One wit described it as 'a republic with few republicans'.

The army as a whole was sympathetic to the right so could not be relied upon to support the government, while the judges treated right-wing extremists with extraordinary leniency, undermining the rule of law.

The situation was made even more intolerable by the fact that after 1920, the republic was ruled by coalition governments which were constantly in disagreement and struggled to keep the Communists and Nationalists from exerting any influence on policy. It is not surprising that in such a volatile and unstable situation the cry went out for a 'strong man' to bring order from chaos.

In 1925, in an effort to restore confidence in the administration, the ageing Field Marshal Paul von Hindenburg was elected president of the republic. It was no secret that Hindenburg did not support a republic but instead favoured the restoration of the monarchy and the return of the Kaiser. In this he was supported by the Nationalists, who were then the second-largest party in parliament; he was also backed by the civil service, industrialists, the judiciary and, most significantly, the army.

An absurd little organization

Many men who survived the horrors of trench warfare returned bitter and disillusioned from the so-called 'war to end wars', but Hitler returned to Munich more embittered than most. Not only was his belief in German supremacy shattered; he subscribed to the myth that the true reason for defeat lay not on the battlefield, nor even back at headquarters, but with the anonymous cabal of conspirators who had no backbone for continuing the war of attrition. Being a paranoiac, Hitler took this betrayal personally and vowed revenge. He did not have long to wait, for in September 1919 his army superiors assigned him to report on a small political party. The idea was that he would attend meetings in the capacity of *Vertrauensmann* (the army's 'trusted representative').

The Deutsche Arbeiterpartei (DAP) was a ragged collective of backstreet radicals with a racist agenda. Its membership numbered fewer than 60 and it had little prospect of making an impression on local politics. It had been founded by Anton Drexler, a railway engineer, and Karl Harrer, a journalist, with the intention of creating a national movement that would improve the lot of the workers. However, neither of them had a talent for public speaking or organization.

Hitler had chosen to attend a meeting in the Sterneckerbräu beerkeller in Munich's Tal district, where the DAP had invited a self-appointed expert in economics to talk on the subject of 'interest slavery'. When he had finished speaking, a member of the audience rose to argue the case for Bavarian sovereignty, which was a thorny but topical issue at the time. This incensed Hitler, who emerged from the shadows to shout him down. It was his unassailable conviction rather than the force of his argument that impressed Drexler, Harrer and the small audience. All agreed that Hitler was an impressive, emotive speaker with an intimidating manner which permitted no disagreement.

THE NAZI PARTY'S UNLIKELY BEGINNINGS

'This absurd little organization with its few members seemed to me to possess the one advantage that it had not frozen into an "organization", but left the individual opportunity for real personal activity.'

Adolf Hitler

Hitler was unimpressed by his first sight of the Deutsche Arbeiterpartei. It was an assemblage of disgruntled ex-soldiers, small shopkeepers and manual labourers who gathered in a back room of a Munich beer hall in the months following Germany's defeat in the Great War to bemoan their lot and argue about who was to blame for it.

The Deutsche Arbeiterpartei had been formed nine months earlier, on 5 January 1919, from the merger of two groups – the Committee of Independent Workmen and the Political Workers' Circle – after Germany's humiliating defeat in the First World War and the abdication of the Kaiser. Its leaders Anton Drexler, a locksmith, Karl Harrer, a journalist, Gottfried Feder, an economist and Dietrich Eckart, a failed playwright, feared that the new Weimar Republic was too weak to prevent their enemies, the Communists, from seizing power. The DAP opposed capitalism and also communism, which its members referred to as 'the plague

Anton Drexler (with moustache and swastika armband) at a meeting of the DAP in Munich

from the east', claiming it had been whipped up by a 'Jewish–Masonic conspiracy' led by Karl Marx.

Of the four founders, only one – Eckart – made a lasting impression on the future Führer that first night at the Sterneckerbräu beerkeller. The others were quickly discarded after Hitler had manoeuvred himself into a position to seize the leadership and use it as a platform for his virulent brand of extreme nationalism and anti-Semitism.

MUTUAL CONTEMPT

Hitler regarded Drexler with contempt because he had declared himself unfit to serve in the army during the war. He thought he was a poor leader – weak, uncertain and 'not fanatical enough'. The feeling was mutual. Drexler despised the 'Bohemian corporal' from the first, describing Hitler as 'an absurd little man'.

When Hitler took over as party leader in late 1921, Drexler was compensated with the title of honorary chairman, but he had no say in policy-making and left the party after the Munich Putsch, dying in obscurity in 1942.

Hitler thought more of Gottfried Feder, a former construction company owner who had taken up economics with the zeal of an evangelist. It was Feder's speech on 'interest slavery' at that first meeting which persuaded Hitler there was potential in the party.

But after Hitler was appointed chancellor in 1933, Feder's ideas were considered 'old-fashioned' and naive. His plan to break up large estates into smaller plots to serve the nearby cities, making them autonomous and self-sufficient, was opposed by rich landowners and industrialists, who persuaded Hitler and his new economic adviser Hjalmar Schacht that it was impractical. Feder was given the nominal position of undersecretary in the Reich Ministry of Economics and resigned as soon as he realized he had lost all influence with the party. He continued to preach his doctrine of rurbanization, or rural–urban fusion, as a lecturer until his death in September 1941.

HITLER GAINS LEADERSHIP

Harrer and Drexler had been members of the Thule Society, a group primarily concerned with proving the superiority of the Aryan race and its antediluvian origins in Atlantis. Harrer had formed the DAP as a radical discussion group limited to seven members, which is why Hitler's membership number was altered from 55 to 7 to give the impression that he had been a founding member of the original inner circle. Even Drexler scornfully referred to the DAP in its first incarnation as the 'Harrer Society', while Hitler criticized it for being 'the worst kind of club'. Desperate to build it into a real political force, Hitler used his gift for propaganda and organization to inundate the party with new members loyal to himself, so that when the crucial vote came he could wrest the leadership from its founders. By early 1920 he had generated sufficient support and Harrer was forced to concede the leadership. Harrer continued to edit the Nazi newspaper, the *Münchener Beobachter*, but died six years later, apparently of 'natural causes'.

Hitler then surrounded himself with ardent admirers who were not drawn from the working and lower middle class and did not share the values of the original members. Chief among these was Dietrich Eckart.

When the meeting ended, Drexler pressed a pamphlet into Hitler's hand entitled 'My Political Awakening'. The next morning Hitler read it with interest as he lay on his cot back at the barracks. Later that same day he received a written invitation to join the party, but at that time he didn't have any intention of doing so. He subsequently claimed he had been thinking seriously about forming his own political party and had only attended a second meeting in order to tell the committee he had no intention of joining their 'absurd little organization'.

At that second meeting, in the Alte Rosenbad in the Herrenstrasse, the pitiful state of the party's funds was discussed amid the odour of strong beer and stale cigarette smoke. As Hitler later recalled in *Mein Kampf*: 'In the grim light of a tiny gas lamp four people were sitting at a table. . . . The minutes of the last meeting were read and the secretary gave a vote of confidence. Next came the treasury report – all in all the party possessed seven marks and fifty pfennigs – for which the treasurer received a vote of confidence. This too was entered into the minutes. . . . Terrible, terrible! This was club life of the worst sort. Was I to join such an organization?'

In his highly embellished account of that fateful meeting, Hitler described how he struggled with his conscience for days before deciding to join, but finally submitted to fate. In fact, he was ordered to join the party by his superior, Lieutenant Mayr, who realized that the right-wing organization had the potential to attract ex-soldiers and workers away from the Communists, who were seen as a threat to the army and the stability of the German state.

> *'Do not mourn me, for I shall have influenced history more than any other German.'*
>
> Dietrich Eckart's dying words

Seizing the moment

During the first few months of his membership Hitler busied himself with typing invitations to meetings which took place in a gloomy back room at the Sterneckerbräu, only to watch as the same seven members took their places in the empty hall. Frustrated, he placed an advert in a local newspaper and was thrilled when more than a hundred people turned up. He was so delighted that he ignored Harrer's objections and gave an impromptu speech, which was greeted enthusiastically.

The next month, to the horror of his fellow committee members,

Programme of the National Socialist German Workers' Party

1. We demand on the basis of the right of national self-determination the union of all Germans in a Greater Germany.

2. We demand equality for the German nation among other nations and the revocation of the peace treaty of Versailles and Saint Germain.

3. We demand land (colonies) to feed our people and to settle our excess population.

4. Only a racial comrade can be a citizen. Only a person of German blood irrespective of religious denomination can be a racial comrade. No Jew therefore can be a racial comrade.

5. Non-citizens shall be able to live in Germany as guests only and must be placed under alien legislation.

6. We therefore demand that every public office no matter what kind and no matter whether it be national, state or local office be held by none but citizens.

7. We demand that the state make it its primary duty to provide a livelihood for its citizens. If it should prove impossible to feed the entire population, the members of foreign nations (non-citizens) are to be expelled from Germany.

8. Any further immigration of non-Germans is to be prevented.

9. All citizens are to possess equal rights and obligations.

10. It must be the first duty of every citizen to perform mental or physical work. Individual activity must not violate the general interest and must be exercised within the frame of the community and for the general good.

Hitler organized a meeting at the Hofbrauhaus, which seated 2,000. Harrer was so infuriated that he resigned, later claiming it was Hitler's anti-Semitism that had forced his hand. But to everyone's surprise, the meeting was a huge success. The guest speaker was yet another eccentric economic 'expert' and his theories were greeted with a stony silence by the increasingly restless audience. Seizing the moment, Hitler rose to his feet and began a tirade against the 'November criminals' and the Jews.

> *There was a hail of shouts, there were violent clashes in the hall. . . . After half an hour the applause began to drown out the screaming and shouting. . . . When, after nearly four hours, the hall began to empty I knew that now the principles of the movement which could no longer be forgotten were moving out among the German people.'*
>
> Adolf Hitler

The party was renamed Nationalsozialistische Deutsche Arbeiterpartei (the National Socialist German Workers' Party or NSDAP, which was later revised to 'Nazi'). Its manifesto, part of which can be seen on page 62, was drawn largely from Hitler's speech on that day, 24 February 1920. The manifesto ended with a demand for a 'strong central power' with 'unconditional authority over the entire Reich'.

> *'We agreed to meet on January 5th in a little eating-house in Munich . . . to found the Deutsche Arbeiterpartei.'*
>
> Anton Drexler

In the summer of 1920, Hitler adopted the swastika as the symbol of the NSDAP. What had once been an emblem of unity in the esoteric tradition now became the insignia of fanaticism. It is thought that Hitler must have seen it used as the emblem of the Austrian anti-Semitic parties, or possibly emblazoned on the helmets of the Freikorps who marched into Munich to put down the Kapp Putsch. Whatever its source, Hitler was shrewd enough to wrap his new symbol in the trappings of tradition by placing the black-hooked cross in a white circle bordered by red – the colours of old Imperial Prussia. But few people were fooled, for soon afterwards the Nazis revealed their true colours by staging the disastrous Munich Putsch.

Money, Money, Money . . .

If any single factor can be said to have tipped the scales in favour of the Nazis during the Weimar years it was rampant inflation, which saw ordinary Germans paying for a loaf of bread with what had once been a month's wages. People pushing wheelbarrows piled high with almost worthless Reichsmarks became a common sight in German towns and cities. This brought home to ordinary citizens the precarious nature of their economy and the ineffectiveness of their government. Wages were devalued overnight and savings were wiped out. Employers were forced to pay their workers twice a day so that they could buy food and drink for their families before the Reichsmark lost more of its value.

The problem was created by the Kaiser, who had borrowed heavily to fund the war, but it was exacerbated by the Republican government which printed more money than the economy could handle in order to balance the books. By spring 1923, the government was spending seven times more than it received in revenue, and was forced to buy coal from abroad. When the German government admitted it could not afford to make further reparation payments, France occupied the Ruhr.

In July 1914, four Reichsmarks were roughly equivalent to one US dollar. By the end of the war, twice as many marks were needed to buy one dollar. By January 1923, 18,000 marks were equivalent to around one dollar, but by the end of that year, one dollar was worth 4.2 billion marks. In December 1918, one mark would buy two loaves of bread. By December 1922, a loaf cost 165 marks and within a year the price had risen to 1,500,000 marks. German people lost patience with their elected representatives and, in their panic, believed anything was better than this. They were prepared to set aside any criticisms they might have had of Nazi 'excess' and willing to give these extreme nationalists a chance.

HITLER'S SOULMATE

*'Follow Hitler! He will dance, but
it is I who have called the tune.'*

Dietrich Eckart fancied himself as the
rustic poet in Ibsen's *Peer Gynt*. Fellow
party members recalled a stocky, short-
necked playwright looking like 'an
old walrus', with his small beady eyes
framed in shell-rimmed glasses.

Hitler revered Eckart, who he
referred to as his 'fatherly friend' and
honoured his memory with a bust in the
Reichschancellery. He also named an

*The young Eckart; but in his later
years he looked more like a balding
bank clerk than a revolutionary*

arena near the Olympic stadium in Berlin after him. It was Eckart who brought
together the diverse elements of the party's core followers – small businessmen,
paramilitary members of the Freikorps, and unskilled workers – under one
banner. They had one aim: to expose the 'Jewish Bolshevik conspiracy' which
they blamed for all their ills.

HITLER'S COACH

Eckart coached Hitler in the art of public speaking, correcting his grammar
and spelling and toning down his polemical discourses for publication. He
persuaded Hitler to contain his loathing for the ruling classes and make
himself more presentable in order to court the industrialists, financiers and
upper classes whose support would prove crucial to the party's fortunes. He
also used his contacts in theatre and publishing to introduce the uneducated
provincial rabble-rouser to influential members of Munich society, whose
financial contributions enabled the party to fund its political campaigns.

Eckart persuaded Hitler that the only sure road to power was via the ballot
box. He fed the flames of his anti-Semitism with fake documentary 'evidence'
such as the notorious *Protocols of the Elders of Zion*, a fabricated text describing
a plan for Jewish global domination, and other fantasies orchestrated by a
fictitious and supposedly omnipotent secret society, the Illuminati.

Eckart shared several significant character traits with Hitler which bound
them together and led the Nazi leader to dedicate *Mein Kampf* to the man he
called his 'North Star'. It appears both men had what can only be described
as a neurotic disposition. When Eckart was separated from a girl he wanted
to marry, he suffered a nervous breakdown triggered by feelings of rejection

and intense anxiety. Hitler suffered a similar psychosomatic crisis which his doctors identified as 'hysterical blindness', after he was gassed at the end of the war.

Both men were volatile, dogmatic and apt to turn on anyone who dared to criticize or disagree with them. They felt alienated and victimized and believed themselves to be superior to their own teachers and academics, who they despised for demonstrating the self-discipline and intelligence needed to acquire formal qualifications, qualities which neither man possessed. When Hitler was told that Eckart had dropped out of law school, he tellingly remarked that his friend had done so 'so as not to become the perfect imbecile'. Instead the pair put their faith in eccentric *völkisch* visionaries such as Lanz von Liebenfels and Guido von List and in crank 'philosophers' who fostered the myth of Aryan superiority. The latter declared that Germans were a master race descended from giants who had survived the destruction of Atlantis.

Both Hitler and Eckart had left their poor rural villages in the hope of finding artistic success and recognition in the big city (Hitler as an architect and artist, Eckart as a poet and playwright) and both were crushed when those ambitions were dashed. Neither could accept they lacked the talent required to be successful and they blamed others for denying them what they believed was their birthright, their destiny.

DRIVEN BY MORPHINE

While still in his twenties, Eckart became addicted to morphine, possibly to ease bouts of manic depression, and remained dependent on it until his death. According to Alfred Rosenberg, 'Without his sweet poison he could not live and applied the whole cunning of a possessor of this craving to get dose after dose.' His addiction affected his judgement and he began to read the writings of erratic philosophers and pseudo-intellectuals such as Ernst Haeckel, Otto Weininger and Gougenot des Mousseaux. Mousseaux had argued that Jews were the progeny of demons and predicted they would wreak havoc in Germany before being 'put in their place'.

Failing to be accepted by intellectuals and high society, Eckart turned on them, publishing virulent anti-Semitic diatribes in his tabloid scandal-sheet *Auf gut deutsch*. His initial fascination with the Jews, whom he had seen as 'exotic', now became an unhealthy obsession. Like Hitler, he used the Jews as a scapegoat for his own personal failure and for the nation's troubles. 'They stand apart with their superior cleverness and ambition,' he wrote. 'We must always brandish the hammer if we don't want to become the anvil.'

Just three years after welcoming Hitler to the party, Eckart was dead, burned out by alcoholism and morphine addiction.

The Hitler gang

Rudolf Hess was the first of Hitler's acolytes to join the Nazi party. He served with Hitler in the Great War, but failed to make an impression on his future leader. But after hearing Hitler speak at a rally in 1921, and presenting him with an essay extolling the qualities of the ideal German leader, he was welcomed into the fold. Hess wrote, 'Only a man of the people can establish authority. . . . He himself has nothing in common with the mass; like every great man he is all personality. . . . When necessity commands, he does not shrink before bloodshed. . . . In order to reach his goal he is prepared to trample on his closest friends.'

Hitler was flattered by Hess' portrayal and immediately offered the 26-year-old former economics student the role of secretary. Hess was beside himself with joy, like a man 'overcome by a vision'. He returned home to his wife repeating over and over, 'The man! The man!' He had found the master he was born to serve.

It is tempting to compare beetle-browed Hess' relationship with Hitler, the master mesmerist, to that of the cataleptic Cesare with Caligari in the classic German silent expressionist movie, *The Cabinet of Dr Caligari*. The film is set in a fairground where Cesare, a somnambulist, is exhibited by Dr Caligari. At night, while asleep, Cesare silently murders the nearby town's inhabitants under the orders of his master.

One of Hess' professors at Munich university described his pupil's disconcerting stare as 'somnambulistic' and recalled that Hess was uncommonly 'slow' and 'dull'. Hitler valued Hess' unquestioning obedience and his deference, but admitted he found him a tedious companion. 'Every conversation with Hess becomes an unbearably tormenting strain,' Hitler said.

Hitler used Hess as he used everyone else who came into his sphere of influence, but he despised his lack of interest in art and culture. He also thought that Hess' obsession with eccentric alternative therapies, biodynamic diets and esoteric ideas such as astrology, was symptomatic of a confused and disordered mind.

Hermann Goering was a formidable figure. A former fighter pilot in Baron von Richthofen's famous squadron, he saw himself as a war hero, an aristocrat and big game hunter. But he was more interested in acquiring medals and new uniforms than winning the war. His avuncular image hid a vindictive nature, which led him to carry a small black book in which he recorded the names of anyone who offended him. It was Goering who established the first concentration camps and created the Gestapo. After joining the party in 1921, his first position was deputy of the SA (*Sturmabteilung* or 'brown-shirts'), but he soon rose to the position of deputy leader. The only man he feared was Hitler, who promised him an active and prominent role in the coming fight.

At barely five feet (1.5 metres) tall and disabled by a distinct limp, Dr Paul Josef Goebbels was not the most imposing figure in the party, but he was a formidable personality. A caustic, sharp-tongued master of manipulation, his enemies nicknamed him 'the poison dwarf'. He had studied at

> *'I joined the party because I was a revolutionary, not because of some ideological nonsense.'*
>
> Hermann Goering

eight universities before finally receiving his doctorate, after which he had tried and failed to establish himself as a playwright and journalist. But he found his calling when he heard Hitler speak at the Circus Krone in Munich in June 1922. 'At that moment, I was reborn!' he exclaimed.

When Hitler was imprisoned in Landsberg after the Beer Hall Putsch, Goebbels wrote him a gushing letter intended to make the leader

A figure feared by many: Hermann Goering at Berlin's Sportpalast in 1935

remember his name. 'Like a rising star you appeared before our wondering eyes, you performed miracles to clear our minds and, in a world of scepticism and desperation, gave us faith. . . . You named the need of a whole generation. . . . One day, Germany will thank you.'

Goebbels followed his Führer's career with interest from that day on, but always from the sidelines because his socialist views were at odds with Hitler's own. In particular, Goebbels believed that the state had a right to the land and wealth left behind by the royal family. It was an issue he was prepared to defend in a public debate with his idol. At Bamberg on 14 February 1926 he got his wish, but Hitler's personal magnetism and powers of persuasion, rather than the logic of his argument, appear to have finally converted Goebbels. His diary entry for 13 April reveals the depth of his devotion: '[Hitler] can make you doubt your own views. . . . I am now at ease about him . . . I bow to the greater man, to the political genius.'

In October 1926 Hitler rewarded his 'faithful, unshakeable shield bearer' by appointing the 29-year-old Goebbels to the position of *gauleiter* for Berlin, with orders to rein in the rabid brutes of the SA and rout the Communists from the capital. Goebbels gave Hitler his assurance that he would not disappoint him.

Himmler

Without doubt, the most sinister figure in the Nazi inner circle was Heinrich Himmler, former secretary to Gregor Strasser, who became head of the SS, Hitler's praetorian guard, in 1929. Himmler was just 28 years old. At that time, the bespectacled bureaucrat commanded just 200 men, but within four years he would increase that figure to 50,000. He also introduced a tough selection programme to ensure the black-uniformed troops were seen as the elite. Ironically, the wiry hypochondriac would not have fulfilled his own entry criteria because he suffered from poor eyesight and chronic stomach complaints and was said to become sick at the sight of blood. But like Hitler, Himmler intended others to do his killing for him.

Himmler developed a mystical side to compensate for his physical shortcomings, believing himself to be the reincarnation of King Henry the Fowler, founder of the First Reich. Thus he could claim his strength came from the spirit – something that no one could test and find wanting.

Other leading lights in the party in the early days included the crackpot 'philosopher' Alfred Rosenberg, who replaced the ailing

Eckart as editor of the party newspaper. 'Hitler values me a great deal, but he does not like me,' he freely admitted. Rosenberg's reputation rested on his celebrity as author of the anti-Semitic tome *The Myth of the Twentieth Century*, which rivals *Mein Kampf* for the distinction of bestselling unread book in history.

Back-room radicals

From the moment Hitler took the floor at party meetings, no one was allowed to upstage him. Dissent was not tolerated, but drowned in the torrent of words that burst forth from him as if a dam had been breached. Hitler had found his voice and his platform, the party had its new spokesman and its fortunes were assured.

Kurt Ludecke, an early supporter of the party, described the hold Hitler exercised over his audience in those days. 'When he spoke of the disgrace of Germany I felt ready to spring on any enemy . . . I experienced an exultation that could be likened only to religious conversion.' But Hitler's increasing influence in the party was not entirely down to the power of his personality. Party members were impressed by the infusion of almost unlimited funds that his army paymasters put at his disposal, provided he took control of the organization.

While Hitler's rabble-rousing speeches began to attract large numbers of right-wing sympathizers to the monthly meetings in the Munich beerkeller, supporters of the Communist opposition also crowded into the back of the smoke-filled hall. They were intent on disrupting proceedings, and fist fights and barracking became a regular feature. Hitler determined to stamp these out by recruiting what was euphemistically described as a security detail.

The SA were recruited by Ernst Roehm, a bull-necked ex-army thug. Roehm promised his men free beer and uniforms and as much action as they could handle. But Hitler had another reason for wanting to surround himself with muscle. When he felt the time was right to make his play for leadership of the party, the SA would serve to intimidate the opposition. The ranks of the brown-shirted storm troopers swelled almost as rapidly as Hitler's audience, which was now treated to his speeches uninterrupted. All opposition was ruthlessly silenced in the alley at the back of the beer hall as Hitler's words rang out: 'The SA is intended to bind our young party members together to form an organization of iron, so that it may put its strength at the disposal of the whole movement to act as a battering ram.'

THE NAZIS' SELF-STYLED PHILOSOPHER

'I didn't say that the Jews are inferior. I didn't even maintain they are a race. I merely saw that the mixture of different cultures didn't work.'

Alfred Rosenberg – Nazi philosopher

Alfred Rosenberg instructed Leon Goldensohn, his psychiatrist at Nuremberg prison, to make accurate notes to reflect his patient's 'rather complex theories and reasoning'. Goldensohn interpreted this demand as an indication of the Nazi philosopher's arrogance and his assumption that everyone was his intellectual inferior. However, Goldensohn concluded that Rosenberg possessed a second-rate mind and mistook pomposity for profundity. He described him as suffering from acute envy, bitterness and a persecution mania. Rosenberg had slavishly recorded every minor compliment he thought Hitler had bestowed on him, but like a petulant child was deeply wounded by every perceived slight: 'In the evenings the Führer often used to invite this man or that for a long fireside discussion. Apart from the usual guests at his table, Goebbels, Ley and some others were favoured in this respect. I can say nothing on this subject as I was not once invited.'

DESPISED BY HIS COLLEAGUES

When Major Airey Neave entered Rosenberg's cell at Nuremberg to serve the indictment, he found a dejected and pathetic figure whose appearance was somewhere between 'an off-duty undertaker and a sick spaniel'.

Hitler, too, had the measure of Rosenberg. In 1924, when he was sentenced to four years in prison for leading the Munich Putsch, Hitler appointed Rosenberg temporary head of the Nazi party, not because Rosenberg possessed leadership qualities but because he lacked them. Hitler reasoned that if he appointed a strong personality he might lose the leadership by the time he was released from prison.

Rosenberg was flattered by the appointment and became an even more devoted servant, but would have been aware that Hitler's closest aides, particularly Goering and Goebbels, despised him. When Hitler assumed power as chancellor in January 1933, he continued to lavish pretentious titles on the party's self-proclaimed 'philosopher', none of which carried real power. He would compliment Rosenberg on writing an 'intelligent book', but in private he told his inner circle that *The Myth of the Twentieth Century* was 'derivative' and 'illogical rubbish'. Goebbels agreed, condemning it as an 'ideological belch' and nicknaming Rosenberg 'Almost' because he 'almost managed to become a scholar, a journalist, a politician – but only almost'.

> 'He had the greatest capacity for making the simplest proposition complicated and obscure.'
>
> Airey Neave on Rosenberg

RACIST THEORIES

Alfred Rosenberg was the son of a wealthy Estonian merchant and looked set for a career as an architect or engineer, until the Russian Revolution forced him to flee to Germany in 1918. A year later he joined the Deutsche Arbeiterpartei, after reading Houston Stewart Chamberlain's irrational racist tract *The Foundations of the Nineteenth Century* which fed his fanatical hatred for the Bolsheviks whom he saw as the manifestation of a worldwide Jewish conspiracy. Rosenberg then became the editor of the party's newspaper, the *Völkischer Beobachter*, which gave him the platform to discharge his bizarre racist theories.

These promoted the myth of the Aryan 'master race' and the inferiority of the Slavs, Jews and Gypsies. Rosenberg was also violently homophobic, which didn't win him any friends in the SA but ensured that he was a seminal influence on Nazi ideology. Despite his extreme prejudices, he was the only virulent anti-Semite in the Nazi hierarchy who made no secret of having a Jewish mistress.

His Estonian origins meant that Rosenberg always remained an outsider and was rarely taken seriously by those who knew him well. This made him all the more desperate for acceptance in his adopted country. Consequently, his racist theories became increasingly fanciful and irrational, and he grew intolerant of other people's opinions. A party colleague observed: 'In conversation one had the impression that he was not listening properly at all. Every now and then he would purse his lips when critical remarks were made or attempt a supercilious smile, which naturally gained him the reputation of arrogant unamiability. . . . He had entirely lost his . . . underdeveloped capacity for making contact and entering into conversation with other people.' Journalist Max Amann was less diplomatic, describing his former editor as 'a buffoon'.

By late 1944, Rosenberg finally realized he had lost his Führer's attention and that his memos and reports were also being gleefully ignored by other departments. It was a crushing blow to his ego and prestige, made all the more damning when he learned that while his bestselling book may have been widely distributed, it remained largely unread.

He was not the respected figure he imagined himself to be. The final humiliation came when he tendered his resignation from his ministerial post only to have it disregarded. There was no impassioned plea for him to remain, no acknowledgement of his faithful service. Evidently, no one cared whether he remained or resigned.

Perhaps that is why, when he was asked if he had any last words before he died, he simply replied: 'No.'

Hitler was more explicit when he described the part the SA was to play in the coming struggle. 'The National Socialist movement will in the future ruthlessly prevent – if necessary by force – all meetings or lectures that are likely to distract the minds of our fellow countrymen.'

Roehm's contribution to the rise of the party was not limited to providing protection and persuasion. As an army officer, he had influence with the Bavarian authorities who turned a blind eye to the Nazis' violence and intimidation of their political rivals. The authorities believed that the Nazis would crush the Marxist menace in the region. But within ten years the gangster tactics of Roehm's brown-shirts were seen as tarnishing the image of the party, and his homosexual affairs were an embarrassment the leadership was not prepared to tolerate. In 1934, Hitler would order the execution of Roehm and hundreds of the SA leadership in the Night of the Long Knives. This was Nazi 'politics' in practice.

Infighting

Within months of joining the party, Hitler had pressured Drexler into appointing him head of propaganda. Then, as he had planned, he forced the founders to elect him leader in the summer of 1921, after threatening to leave if they didn't. In a bid to popularize the party beyond Bavaria, he travelled to Berlin to negotiate with the north German Nationalists. Meanwhile Drexler was considering an alliance with the German Socialist party which was based in Nuremberg and led by the sadistic Jew-baiter and pornographer Julius Streicher, editor of *Der Stürmer*. It looked as though the party would split before it had had a chance to make an impression. And it seems that Hiter had become too autocratic for the party's liking, and much too ambitious. He returned to Munich to learn that his party was plotting against him and issuing libellous leaflets attacking his leadership and loyalties: 'A lust for power and personal ambition have caused Herr Adolf Hitler to return to his post after his six weeks' stay in Berlin, of which the purpose has not yet been disclosed. He regards the time as ripe for bringing disunion and schism in our ranks by means of shadowy people behind him and thus further the interests of the Jews and their friends. It grows more and more clear that his purpose is simply to use the National Socialist party as a springboard for his own immoral purposes and to seize the leadership in order to force the party on to a different track at the psychological moment. . . . Make no mistake. Hitler is a demagogue.'

This damning indictment was one that Hitler seized upon to strengthen his influence in the party. Under threat of legal action, the dissenters were forced to climb down and Drexler was effectively sidelined when he accepted the role of honorary president. Hitler was now acknowledged as absolute leader of the party.

Spreading the word

As the party's popularity increased, it began to hold meetings in larger halls and outdoor venues. The massed banner-wielding ranks of the SA, with their military discipline and sense of order, made a memorable impression on the press and visiting dignitaries.

One of the first outsiders to report on the growing movement was Captain Truman Smith, an assistant military attaché at the American Embassy in Berlin. He had been ordered to Munich to evaluate the importance of the party and its new leader. His report, dated 25 November 1922, makes it clear that Hitler was becoming a force to be reckoned with: 'The most active political force in Bavaria at the present time is the National Socialist Labour Party. Less a political party than a popular movement, it must be considered as the Bavarian counterpart to the Italian *fascisti*. . . . It has recently acquired a political influence quite disproportionate to its actual numerical strength. . . .

'Adolf Hitler, from the very first, has been the dominating force in the movement, and the personality of this man has undoubtedly been one of the most important factors contributing to its success. . . . His ability to influence a popular assembly is uncanny.'

Before returning to Berlin, Captain Smith managed to obtain a private interview with Hitler at his lodgings, which Smith described in his diary as a 'little bare bedroom on the second floor of a run-down house' at 41 Thierschstrasse, a lower-middle-class district. Afterwards he recorded his impressions of the man he considered to be 'a marvellous demagogue'. Smith wrote, 'Have rarely listened to such a logical and fanatical man.'

Within a year, Hitler would attempt to fulfil his promise by seizing power in the city by force.

The Beer Hall Putsch

By November 1923, Hitler was impatient for power. He was no longer a soapbox agitator, but a prominent figure in the radical nationalist movement. He had watched the newsreels of Mussolini's march on Rome in the previous year with awe and was inspired to attempt a similar coup d'état in Germany. His initial idea was to mobilize the disparate anti-republican Nationalist forces in Bavaria and, with these groups behind him, enlist the support of the armed patriotic leagues and the army under Roehm. All would then march on Berlin with Hitler at the head of the column. It was an audacious and absurdly ambitious plan, and it was fated to fail.

Part of the problem was that the public now supported the Weimar government, which was in open defiance of the French occupation of the Ruhr and would not look favourably on armed rebellion. The authorities were threatening to close down the SA party newspaper and arrest leaders of the armed groups which Hitler was counting on to join him. The SA leadership was restless to act.

'The day is coming,' Hitler was told by SA commander Lieutenant Wilhelm Brueckner, 'when I won't be able to hold the men back. If nothing happens now, they'll run away from us.'

Fearful of being abandoned by his 'troops', Hitler panicked and gave orders for the takeover of the city.

The original plan was to disrupt a military parade on 4 November, Memorial Day, and take the visiting dignitaries hostage. They would include Crown Prince Rupprecht and three regional leaders – State Commissioner von Kahr, General Otto von Lossow and Colonel Hans von Seisser, head of the state police. But the plan had to be abandoned when news reached the plotters that armed police had sealed off the route of their attack as a precaution.

An alternative plan was hastily drawn up for the morning of 11 November, Armistice Day. The SA was to storm strategic points in the city while a detachment attempted to force Kahr, Lossow and Seisser to join the revolution. A date was set, but it had to be brought forward when Hitler learned that the three regional leaders were to hold a public meeting at the Bürgerbräukeller in the suburbs of Munich on 8 November. He feared that the purpose of the meeting was to proclaim Bavarian independence, along with the restoration of the monarchy. It was now or never – he would have to act.

> 'I give you my word of honour, never as long as I live will I make a Putsch!'
>
> Hitler's assurance to the Bavarian Minister of the Interior, summer 1923

Bluff and blunder

At 8.45 on the evening of 8 November, Hitler led a large detachment of the SA to the Bürgerbräukeller and ordered them to surround it. A machine gun was set up at the entrance and the rear exits were sealed. Hitler burst in, disrupting Kahr's address, while the bewildered crowd sat in silence, unsure of what was happening. They did not have to wait long to find out. Brandishing a pistol, Hitler clambered on to a table and fired one shot at the ceiling. Then he jumped down and strode on to the stage. Waving the smoking firearm at a senior police officer, he ordered him to step aside – which the officer did, along with Kahr. This left the stage free for Hitler to address the crowd:

'The National Revolution has begun! This building is occupied by 600 heavily armed men. No one may leave the hall. Unless there is immediate quiet I shall have a machine gun posted in the gallery. The Bavarian and Reich governments have been removed and a provisional national government formed. The barracks of the Reichswehr and the police are occupied. The army and the police are marching on the city under the swastika banner.'

The last part of Hitler's statement was a lie. However, the crowd was intimidated by the presence of the armed SA men, though not by Hitler – one witness described him as looking 'ridiculous' in his ill-fitting morning coat. He went on to say, 'When I saw him jump on the table in that ridiculous costume I thought, "The poor little waiter!"'

Some called for the police to fight back. But their appeal fell on deaf ears for the police had secretly been ordered not to resist. A Nazi infiltrator on the force had telephoned their commanding officer earlier that evening and warned him of what was about to take place. Then Hitler herded the three leaders into a back room at gunpoint and threatened to shoot them there and then if they did not join his new government. Meanwhile Goering was attempting to quell the grumbling crowd in the hall by reminding them they had nothing to fear and that there was plenty of free beer.

Kahr took a chance and tried to call Hitler's bluff. Cornered, Hitler played his trump card. He announced that he had the support of General von Ludendorff, hero of the First World War, and that the general was on his way to ask them to reconsider the offer to join the rebels. In reality, von Ludendorff had been kept in the dark regarding the coup and when he arrived at the hall was livid to discover his name had been used to endorse such a chaotic enterprise. He was also furious to learn that Hitler intended to declare himself leader of the new regime while he, Ludendorff, would be relegated to commander of the army. But in the old soldier's mind the sword had been unsheathed and could not be returned to its scabbard without dishonour. He believed he had little choice but to tell the three hostages that it would be in Germany's interest if they joined the cause. Meanwhile, Hitler returned to the hall where the audience was getting restless and informed them that their leaders had agreed to form a new government.

This declaration was greeted with ecstatic cheers which persuaded the men in the back room that it might be better to go along with the mob for the moment. It was then that Hitler made a crucial blunder. He left the Bürgerbräukeller to sort out a clash between an SA battalion and a regular army unit at the Engineer's Barracks, leaving General von Ludendorff in charge. The general then released the opposition leaders on the understanding that they would organize their forces in support of the coup. Instead they immediately mobilized the army and the police, who stationed themselves in the centre of the city to await the rebels.

No one had thought to cut communications with the outside world, so as soon as word reached Berlin that an armed uprising was underway, orders were sent to the Bavarian army to suppress it before it could spread. State Commissioner Gustav von Kahr even had time to print up and distribute posters around the city, which refuted rumours that he had acceded to the demands of the rebels:

'The deception and perfidy of ambitious comrades have converted a demonstration into a scene of disgusting violence. The declarations extorted from myself, General von Lossow and Colonel Seisser at the point of the revolver are null and void. The National Socialist German Workers' Party as well as the fighting leagues Oberland and Reichskriegsflagge are dissolved.'

The final bluff

On returning to the beer hall and discovering his revolution was unravelling, Hitler was in a panic about what to do next. He couldn't call it off, but without his hostages he had little chance of success. It was Ludendorff who whipped the demoralized demagogue into action, shaming Hitler into acting by accusing him of being a defeatist and an armchair revolutionary. The only course open to them, the general assured him, was to attempt another bluff.

Towards noon, Ludendorff and Hitler marshalled their forces in the garden of the beerkeller and marched them down the narrow Residenzstrasse leading to the Odeonsplatz, with Ludendorff at the head. Although there may have been as many as 3,000 armed men marching behind Hitler and the general that morning, they did not look as intimidating as they hoped. 'If you saw one of our squads from 1923 marching by, you would ask, "What workhouse did they escape from?"' Hitler later confessed.

But their presence was sufficiently alarming to draw a detachment of 100 armed police, who awaited them at the end of the narrow street. The police were supported by an army unit at the rear. As the rebel force entered the square, Hitler pulled his pistol from his pocket and demanded that the police surrender. A moment later a shot rang out – no one knows who fired first – and the police emptied a volley into the advancing column. Sixteen Nazis were killed, while their leaders scattered at the sound of the first shots.

Hitler had linked arms with the man marching next to him and was pulled down when his companion was hit. According to several eyewitnesses, including one of the would-be rebels, Dr Walther Schulz, Hitler 'was the first to get up and turn back'. He escaped in a waiting car, only to be arrested some days later while hiding in the attic of a supporter. It was reported that he was 'almost incoherent' with rage.

> *Tomorrow will find either a National Government in Germany or us dead!'*
>
> Adolf Hitler at the Beer Hall Putsch

Hermann Goering, whose wide girth and bulldog ferocity meant that he cut a formidable figure in the party, was seriously wounded but managed to get treated by a local Jewish doctor. He was then smuggled to safety into Austria where his pain was eased with morphine, a drug to which he subsequently became addicted.

Hess also abandoned his fallen comrades and ran. He eventually found temporary shelter across the border in Austria, but was later arrested. Only Himmler escaped unnoticed. He had not been recognized by the authorities when they were rounding up the stragglers, so he was able to slip through the side streets and make his way to the railway station, where he boarded a train for home.

General Ludendorff, the nominal figurehead of the abortive coup, was given safe passage through the police lines.

Hitler on trial

The Beer Hall Putsch was a humiliating disaster for the Nazis and a personal blow to Hitler, whose political career appeared to be in tatters. But the trial was to prove a triumph. Hitler had been assured that the judges were sympathetic to the right-wing cause. He would be safe to argue that it was wrong to prosecute him for treason when he was only trying to bring down those who had wrested power from the Kaiser. Taking the stage in the dock before the world's press, he gave one of the most impassioned speeches of his life. For four hours he argued that he was not a traitor but a counter-revolutionary intent on restoring the nation's honour.

Stunning those who had expected him to deny complicity in the plot, as the Kapp Putsch conspirators had done years before, he freely admitted his involvement. Here was Adolf Hitler the actor, relishing his moment in the spotlight, knowing his every word would be recorded by the assembled reporters: 'I alone bear the responsibility. But I am not a criminal because of that. If today I stand here as a revolutionary, it is as a revolutionary against the revolution. There is no such thing as treason against the traitors of 1918.'

Nor would he deny that his part in the putsch was motivated by personal ambition: 'The man who is born to be a dictator is not compelled. He wills it. He is not driven forward, but drives himself. . . . The man who feels called upon to govern a people has no right to say, "If you want me, summon me, I will co-operate." No! It is his duty to step forward.'

In closing, he turned on the judges: 'It is not you, gentlemen, who will pass judgement on us. You may pronounce us as guilty a thousand times over, but the Goddess of the eternal court of history will smile and tear to tatters the brief of the state prosecutor and the sentence of this court. For she acquits us.'

Under Article 81 of the German Penal Code, the judges were obliged to find Hitler guilty for inciting armed rebellion, but they showed where their true sympathies lay by imposing a minimal five-year sentence, knowing that he would serve only a fraction of that. Hitler had lost the case, but won the admiration of the German Nationalists. And the storm of publicity surrounding the event had made him a prominent figure on the political scene.

The nine months Hitler was to spend in Landsberg prison would prove the most productive of his life.

Mein Kampf

Life in Landsberg was the closest thing to luxury Hitler had experienced. He was given a comfortable furnished private room with a view of the River Lech and was waited on both by prisoners and guards who considered it an honour to act as his servants. He slept until noon every day and was allowed to abstain from exercise, which he disdained. He reasoned that political leaders could not afford to take part in sport and other frivolous activities in case they were beaten and lost face. A steady stream of visitors brought him gifts and provided a much-needed audience; on his 35th birthday, admirers sent fruit, flowers and wine from all over Germany. By the end of the day the 'cell' resembled a 'delicatessen store'.

When the party's business manager, Max Amann, offered to publish his memoirs, Hitler welcomed the opportunity to relieve the tedium. He began to dictate to his faithful servant and secretary Rudolf Hess, who corrected the leader's schoolboy grammar and attempted to shape his rambling, random monologues into something cohesive and concise. It was not easy. Hitler was fired up by the chance to discourse on any topic he chose and once he had found his voice, the words would gush forth in a torrent. It was difficult and exhausting to keep him focused on one subject. But Hess had help from two anti-Semitic journalists, Father Bernhard Staempfle and Josef Czerny of the *Völkischer Beobachter*, both of whom toned down and even edited out some of the more inflammatory passages.

When it was finished, the manuscript was delivered to Amann who was horrified to discover that the inside story of the abortive putsch had been relegated to a few sentences. The remaining 782 pages were devoted to discourses on any subject about which its author believed himself to be an expert. These ranged from comic books to venereal disease (on which Hitler rambled for ten pages). Even the title invited derision. With a stroke of the pen, Amann reduced the unwieldy *Four-and-a-Half Years of Struggle Against Lies, Stupidity and Cowardice* to *Mein Kampf* (*My Struggle*). He then insisted on publishing the ponderous tome in two volumes of 400 pages each, but even that did not ensure reasonable sales. In 1925, the first year of publication, the book sold fewer than 10,000 copies and thereafter sales declined.

In 1933, the tide turned. Hitler became chancellor and every loyal German was required to own a copy of his book. By 1940, six million copies had been sold in Germany alone, and many more thousands were

Hitler in his surprisingly luxurious cell at Landsberg prison

sold abroad, making its author a millionaire. Even so, it is difficult to believe that more than a few thousand people managed to finish it. This is unfortunate for, as William L. Shirer, author of *The Rise and Fall of the Third Reich*, observed: 'the blueprint of the Third Reich, and what is more, of the barbaric New Order which Hitler inflicted on conquered Europe . . . is set down in all its appalling crudity at great length and in detail between the covers of this revealing book.'

Those who managed to read to the end of *Mein Kampf* learnt of Hitler's fanatical devotion to the concept of *Lebensraum* (living space), which permitted strong nations to take territory by force from their weaker neighbours. This theory tied in with its author's *Weltanschauung* (worldview) which stated that life was a struggle for survival and the strongest need have no compassion or concern for the weak.

They would also have discovered that the failure of the Munich Putsch convinced Hitler that armed rebellion might succeed in the short term, but would not win the hearts and minds of the people. Persuasion and propaganda were needed to convert the nation to the Nazi worldview: 'We shall have to hold our noses and enter the Reichstag. . . . If outvoting them takes longer than out-shooting them, at least the results will be guaranteed by their own constitution! . . . Sooner or later we shall have a majority and after that we shall have Germany.'

Reinventing Hitler

The reversal in the party's fortunes coincided with a drastic change of image for their leader. The man largely responsible for reinventing Hitler and making him presentable as a politician was Professor Karl Haushofer (1869–1946). The academic was a regular visitor to Landsberg prison, where he had introduced Hitler to the theories of geopolitics and the concept of *Lebensraum*. These two ideas were crucial to the formation of Hitler's foreign policy, but equally important were the changes the professor made to Hitler's personal image.

Haushofer persuaded Hitler to change his Bavarian lederhosen for a tailored suit and to discard the riding crop that had become his trademark. He convinced Hitler he should drink herbal tea after a long speech in order to quench his thirst, instead of his customary flagon of strong Bavarian beer which might have an adverse effect on his powers. The professor offered to train Hitler in the art of public speaking, and help him practise a range of gestures that would serve to emphasize his arguments and increase his self-confidence.

In the wilderness

Hitler would need all the self-confidence he could muster when he emerged from prison on 20 December 1924. His party had been declared illegal, its newspaper closed down by order of the state and Hitler had been banned from public speaking. There was even talk of deporting him to his native Austria. But little was done to enforce the bans on the Nazis and their newspaper or to prevent Hitler from speaking to private groups of followers who had remained loyal, despite the setbacks.

At that time, Hitler was no longer considered a threat. The runaway inflation of the early 1920s had been cured by a newcomer to the republican government, Dr Hjalmar Schacht, and other measures had been implemented to ease the burden on the German economy. For instance, the Dawes Plan had been introduced, which reduced Germany's reparation payments and brought investment from the United States. Security issues had been addressed by the Locarno Treaty and an acceptable compromise reached between the Weimar administration and the Allies which promised to bring Germany into the League of Nations in due course. Taken together, these measures helped to ease public anxiety and bolstered the vote for the ruling Social Democrats in the elections that were held that December. The Nazi vote was halved.

While his acolytes hovered around their demoralized leader, urging him to rekindle the faltering flame of the party, Hitler's interest in politics appeared to wane. A new obsession had taken hold of him. Her name was Geli Raubal, of whom more later.

CHAPTER 5

Storming to Power

Between 1924 and 1928 the Nazis made a serious tactical blunder in trying to appeal to the industrial workers, who remained loyal to the Communists and the Social Democrats. This strategy also isolated the party from the middle classes, who thought that the Nazis were now only interested in speaking for the working classes. As a consequence, the Nazi share of the vote declined. In the 1924 national elections they won 32 seats in the Reichstag, half as many as the Communist party and about a third of the number of seats won by the Nationalists and the Social Democrats, who won 95 and 100 seats respectively. At the end of that year, a second election was held after which the two leading parties gained more seats at the expense of the Communists, who dropped from 62 to 45, while the Nazi party lost 18 seats. Four years later, in May 1928, their share of seats fell to an all-time low of just 12.

Thirty-one million Germans had exercised their democratic right at the ballot box, but fewer than one million had cast their vote for the Nazis. Political commentators dismissed them as a spent force. The American correspondent William L. Shirer observed, 'One scarcely heard of Hitler or the Nazis except as butts of jokes.' But the Great Depression altered all that. In just over a year, unemployment tripled to almost four-and-a-half million. It was *Schadenfreude* writ large. The nation's misfortune was the Nazis' miraculous stroke of luck.

Hitler ordered the activists to target the rural communities, where farmers had been badly hit by falling prices and craftsmen were threatened with extinction by the growth of mass production. The Nazis also canvassed the smaller towns. Here shopkeepers were struggling for survival against the chain stores, and middle-class workers had seen the value of their savings wiped out.

As the party's newspaper reported in May 1928: 'The election results from the rural areas in particular have proved that with a smaller expenditure of energy, money and time, better results can be achieved there than in the big cities. In smaller towns, mass meetings with good speakers are events and are often talked about for weeks, while in the big cities the effects of meetings with even three or four thousand people soon disappear.'

Goebbels proved to be a master of manipulation and was not averse to fighting dirty if it earned extra votes. His philosophy was simple – if you repeat a lie often enough, people will begin to believe it. Hitler, too, believed that to indoctrinate the masses it was necessary to hammer home the same message again and again until all resistance crumbled and even the most intransigent citizens had been converted.

A typical Nazi leaflet from April 1932 read:

'Middle-class citizens! Retailers! Craftsmen! Tradesmen!

'A new blow aimed at your ruin is being prepared and carried out in Hanover!

'The present system enables the giant concern WOOLWORTH (America) to build a new vampire business in the centre of the city. Put an end to this system. Defend yourself middle-class citizen! Join the mighty organization that alone is in a position to conquer your arch-enemies. Fight with us in the Section for Craftsmen and Retail Traders within the great freedom movement of Adolf Hitler.'

It is clear from the above example that the Nazis drew much support by appealing directly to the voters' self-interest (despite their claim to the contrary) and that they exploited middle-class fears and prejudices regarding big business and Jewish-owned corporations. But it is generally overlooked that the core of Hitler's supporters in the 1920s and early 1930s was not politically motivated but made up of ordinary citizens who desperately wanted to believe in his promise to provide them with their basic needs – work and bread. Those who were aware of the activities of the SA reassured themselves that once in power, Hitler would bring the extremists into line. They did not realize that the Nazi party was extremist by definition.

Hitler seized the opportunity to spread his message by radio, which guaranteed an audience of millions, and he made exhausting tours of the country in the belief that a personal appearance by the leader would leave a more lasting impression. In the 1932 presidential elections, he crossed the country by plane and spoke in several cities each day. Posters were designed to appeal to particular groups of voters such as mothers, workers, farmers and shopkeepers. Even the timing of the poster campaign was calculated for maximum impact.

> 'Whoever conquers the streets, conquers the masses and whoever conquers the masses, conquers the state.'
>
> Nazi maxim

As organizer of the 1932 elections, Goebbels wrote to local activists: 'The Hitler poster depicts a fascinating Hitler head on a completely black background. In accordance with the Führer's wish, this poster is to be put up only during the final days [of the campaign]. Since experience shows that during the final days there is a variety of coloured posters, this poster with its completely black background will contrast with all the others and will produce a tremendous effect on the masses.'

A year later, the Nazi party merged with the German Nationalist party; this swelled its membership and fighting fund considerably and gave the Nazis a veneer of respectability. The leader of the GNP, Alfred Hugenberg, was a wealthy and influential newspaper owner who had also acquired the UFA film studios and cinema chain. He immediately put his newspapers and newsreels at Hitler's disposal.

Chancellor Hitler

Contrary to popular myth, the Nazis did not seize power by force, nor were they elected. In the last national elections, before Hitler became chancellor of Germany, the Nazi share of the vote had actually fallen from 37 per cent to 33 per cent, giving them fewer than 200 seats in the Reichstag, only a third of the total. The Nazis gained power because Hitler was handed the chancellorship by Hindenburg in the hope that it would end the political in-fighting that had brought the Weimar government to its knees.

For Germany, the repercussions of the Wall Street Crash of October 1929 were more than financial. The fissures in Germany's already precarious coalition were widened, until it finally crumbled when the Nazis and the Communists refused to prop up the tottering structure. President Hindenburg was then forced to take personal charge.

From 1930 onwards, Germany was governed by the almost senile Hindenburg, who took advice from an ambitious army officer, Kurt von Schleicher. Von Schleicher manoeuvred Hindenburg into appointing chancellors who would rubber-stamp measures benefiting the army. The first of these was Heinrich Brüning and the second was Franz von Papen, who succeeded Brüning in May 1932. In December of that year, von Papen was replaced by von Schleicher. This angered von Papen, who offered Hitler a place in his government should Hitler agree to help him unseat von Schleicher. But first von Papen would have to get the support of Hindenburg, who was known to distrust Hitler whom he called 'the upstart Austrian corporal'.

Earlier that year, Hitler had demanded the chancellorship only to be briskly rebuffed by Hindenburg. The minutes of that first meeting between Hindenburg and Hitler on 13 August reveal that the old soldier was not so senile as to be unaware of the threat that Hitler and his party posed to the democracy and to personal freedom:

'Considering the importance of the National Socialist movement

[Hitler] would have to demand the full and complete leadership of government for himself and his party. President Hindenburg thereupon stated emphatically that he had to respond to this demand with a clear and determined "No". He could not, before God, his conscience and the fatherland bear all responsibility of entrusting all Governmental authority to a single party, a party moreover, which held to such a one-sided attitude toward people with convictions different to theirs.'

However, von Papen persisted and finally managed to persuade the ailing president that he could restrain Hitler in two ways. First of all by limiting the number of Nazi ministers in the government and secondly by insisting that Hitler be forced to work with his political rivals in the cabinet.

Hindenburg relented and sacked von Schleicher. On 30 January 1933, Adolf Hitler was appointed chancellor of Germany.

Nazi Party Appeal to Voters, Presidential Election 1932

LEAD GERMANY TO FREEDOM

Hitler is the password of all who believe in Germany's resurrection.

Hitler is the last hope of those who were deprived of everything; of farm and home, of savings, of employment, survival and who have but one possession left: their faith in a just Germany which will once again grant to its citizens honour, freedom and bread.

Hitler is the word of deliverance for millions for they are in despair and see only in this name a path to new life and creativity.

Hitler was bequeathed the legacy of the two million dead comrades of the World War who died not for the present system of the gradual destruction of our nation, but for Germany's future.

Hitler is the man of the people hated by the enemy because he understands the people and fights for the people.

Hitler is the furious will of Germany's youth, which, in the midst of a tired generation is fighting for new forms and neither can, nor will, abandon its faith in a better German future. Hence

> Hitler is the password and the flaming signal of all who wish for a German future.
>
> All of them on March 13 will call out to the men of the old system who promised them freedom and dignity and delivered stones and words instead: We have known enough of you, now you are to know us!
>
> Hitler will win because the people want his victory!

Democracy into dictatorship

The Nazis celebrated their success with a mass torchlight parade of brown-shirted storm troopers through the streets of Berlin. Now no one could be in any doubt that Germany was under the heel of a fascist military dictatorship. But even as Hitler waved to the adoring crowds from the balcony of the chancellery, he was acutely aware that millions of Germans were still out of step with the movement. The dead wood of the democratic institutions would have to be cut away, leaving only the sturdy stock of the party. So the new government's first proclamation was aimed at reassuring the people of its conservative credentials:

'The new national government will consider its first and supreme duty to restore our nation's unity of will and spirit. It will safeguard and defend the foundation on which the strength of our nation rests. It will firmly protect Christianity, the basis of our entire morality, it will safeguard the family. . . . It wants to base the education of Germany's youth on a reverence for our great past, on pride in our old traditions. It will thus declare war on spiritual, political and cultural nihilism . . . the government will once again make national discipline our guide.'

The Reichstag Fire

Even as the echo of the jackbooted storm troopers died away down the Unter den Linden, Hitler knew that his hold on power could still be challenged by the Communists, who shared his contempt for democracy. At the last election, 63 per cent of the voters had rejected the Nazi call to arms and no one in the leadership could afford to rule out the possibility of a counter-revolution financed by the Soviets.

The burning of the Reichstag gave Hitler the perfect pretext for seizing power

The Nazis were in a minority in parliament and President Hindenburg had the power to dismiss Hitler at any time if he chose to do so.

Hitler would not be pacified until his grip on government was secure. What he needed was a specific threat to the new regime. No one is certain who dreamt up the idea of setting fire to the Reichstag and blaming it on the Communists – some historians claim it was Goering – but it was a brilliant and despicable demonstration of Nazi politics in practice.

On 27 February, the Reichstag building in Berlin was gutted by fire and a lone Communist, Marinus van der Lubbe, was hastily tried and executed for the crime. Van der Lubbe was an obvious fall guy who had been chosen by the Nazis because he was feeble-minded and would not speak in his own defence. The imaginary plot gave the regime the excuse it needed to imprison 4,000 Communist party officials and call fresh elections to endorse government policies.

On 28 February, Hitler successfully demanded that Hindenburg pass an emergency decree banning freedom of speech and political meetings by the opposition, and authorizing the state to search private homes. But although this severely restricted the opposition parties' ability to campaign, the Nazis did not receive the overwhelming endorsement they had confidently predicted. They secured 288 seats – still well short of a majority. More draconian measures were needed. A series of laws was drawn up with the intention of tightening the government's stranglehold on democracy.

First was the Enabling Act, passed on 24 March. This allowed Hitler to make laws without the approval of parliament. Then, in May, further decrees were approved which banned the Communist party. The following month, the Social Democrats were banned. In July, the regime pressured the Vatican into closing down the Catholic Centre Party in Germany in exchange for a guarantee that the Church would be permitted to operate without state interference.

Also in July the second major law, the Law Against the Formation of Parties, was passed by the regime. It forbade anyone from forming a new political

> '*I am not a pacifist. That is not my attitude. But all my impressions of war are so bad that I could be for it only under the sternest necessity – the necessity of fighting Bolshevism or of defending one's country.*'
>
> President von Hindenburg

party, under the threat of imprisonment. The following year saw the abolition of the state parliaments that represented the regions. Party and state were now one and the same.

The third significant measure was the Law Concerning the Head of the German State, enacted after the death of President Hindenburg on 1 August 1934. This law combined the offices of president and chancellor so that Hitler became absolute ruler of Germany.

Before Hindenburg could be buried, Hitler abolished the office of president and assumed the role of head of state. His first act was to demand that all members of the armed forces swear a personal oath of loyalty to their Führer, a shrewd and cynical move which ensured that they could not disobey an order from Hitler without being disloyal to the Fatherland.

With Hindenburg's passing, the old Imperial Germany was laid to rest. Hitler was now Führer of a new empire. He boasted that it would rule for a thousand years. But, in fact, Hitler's Third Reich lasted for barely 12 years.

The Night of the Long Knives

If anyone had harboured hopes that the Nazis might be brought to heel once they were in government, they were cruelly disillusioned by the events of 30 June 1934. On that day, Hitler's henchmen slaughtered their own in a bloodbath which left no one in doubt as to what the regime stood for – nor the lengths to which it was prepared to go in order to crush opposition and cover up its past 'mistakes'.

For some time, Hitler and Roehm had been in disagreement over the future role of the SA. Hitler was indebted to his old comrade, who had been instrumental in his rise to power. But Roehm's increasingly angry exchanges in the Reichstag with General von Blomberg, Hitler's first minister of defence, had become both an embarrassment and a threat to the Führer's authority. Time and again, Roehm had demanded that the SA be officially acknowledged as the 'people's revolutionary army'. He had also urged that the regular army be purged of the Prussian officer elite and the rank and file be assimilated into the SA.

> 'Rearmament was too serious and difficult a business to permit the participation of speculators, drunkards and homosexuals.'
>
> General von Brauchitsch

ERNST ROEHM TOO POWERFUL TO LIVE

'Brutality is respected. The people need wholesome fear. They want to fear something. They want someone to frighten them and make them shudderingly submissive. . . . They need something that will give them a thrill of horror.'

Hitler takes the salute at Franzen Field, Brunswick; Ernst Roehm is behind him

Ernst Roehm had marched home from the trenches in 1918 at the head of a column of bellicose and brutish thugs, who were returning from a war they had not finished fighting and which they were determined to continue in the beer halls and streets of Bavaria, then a breeding ground for extreme nationalism. Captain Roehm, the third son of a railway worker, was not a revolutionary at the time. He organized the SA, a paramilitary organization, under the banner of patriotism but their purpose was to mete out brutal retribution for what Roehm and his men saw as the betrayal of the undefeated German army.

BURNING AMBITION

Roehm was sickened by the shame of losing a war he was certain could have been won, and disgusted at the cowardice shown by his superiors. Fearing a Bolshevik revolution like the one which had toppled the Czar of Russia and robbed the aristocracy of their lands and titles, the German High Command had persuaded the Kaiser to accept the humiliating terms of surrender and the dishonour of abdication. And Roehm bitterly resented them for it.

During the First World War, Roehm had been severely wounded twice and awarded an Iron Cross First Class for his courage. But he would sooner have fallen in battle than skulk home in defeat. He therefore decided to raise an army of his own, to win back his honour and recover the territories stolen under the terms of the hated Versailles Treaty. His brown-shirt militia would tear down the rotten edifice of the Weimar Republic and crush the Communists, who were waging civil war in the streets and making a laughing stock of the new government, which seemed powerless to control them. It was a burning ambition he shared with his former comrade, Corporal Hitler, whom he called Adolf and addressed with the informal 'du'. Roehm was the only Nazi to be permitted that privilege.

EMBARRASSMENT TO THE CAUSE

Both Hitler and Roehm were enraged to think that German blood had been shed in vain, but following the ignominious failure of the Munich Putsch in November 1923 Hitler was shrewd enough to realize that real and lasting power could not be seized by force alone. The hearts and minds of the people had to be won and those who couldn't be persuaded would have to be bought with empty promises. As a last resort some would need to be strong-armed into seeing sense – and that is where Roehm, co-founder and commander of the 500,000-strong SA, would prove useful.

Roehm was squat, coarse and uncomplicated. He didn't think too hard or too much about politics. And he didn't care who he offended. He publicly ridiculed the pseudo-mystical Aryan 'philosophy' of Alfred Rosenberg (to the discomfort of true believers such as Himmler) and flaunted his preference for the company of hard-drinking, handsome athletic men, to the embarrassment of the army High Command. The latter demanded that Hitler deal with Roehm before the Reichswehr (forerunner of the Wehrmacht) took an oath of allegiance to its new commander-in-chief.

Roehm had dreamt of a military career from childhood and didn't see why his sexuality should interfere with his progress through the ranks. He had no respect for anyone who had not been in uniform and openly despised German civilians, whom he condemned as 'swine'.

But rumours of his 'unnatural' inclinations and those of his men were becoming a concern to the General Staff. Breaking a few heads was to be tolerated in such turbulent times, but blatant displays of homosexuality were taboo and threatened to tarnish the image of the army, even though the SA were not officially part of the regular armed forces.

THE GROWING SA THREAT

By 1932, the SA had become a terrorist organization, bombing buildings and sowing anarchy throughout the state. Within a year it had grown so large that the army High Command considered the paramilitary divisions to be a serious threat to law and order.

Hitler's reassurances that the SA was merely the political education arm of the party were disregarded as Roehm called for the amalgamation of the SA and the Reichswehr. The combined force would then be strong enough to stage a new revolution to crush the Communists and wrest power from the Weimar government.

Roehm became increasingly frustrated when Hitler began courting the aristocracy, industrialists, financiers and landowners whose support would be crucial to the party's increasing fortunes. Roehm argued that the party should be true to its socialist origins and should support, by force if necessary, workers' strikes against unscrupulous bosses. He was critical of his former friend, whom he now called an artist, a dreamer and, worst of all, a civilian.

After these words, Roehm was destined to die a violent death. On 2 July 1934, two SS officers walked into his cell at Stadelheim prison and offered him the opportunity to commit suicide. He refused, so the SS men shot him.

It was not an unreasonable request from Roehm's point of view. With a total of three million men at his command he led one of the largest armed forces in Europe, one that outnumbered the regular army by four to one. But the Prussian officers were horrified at the prospect of a bunch of hoodlums and sexual deviants, as they thought, tainting the honourable tradition of their regiments. Rumours of Roehm's homosexual activities, and those of his inner circle, were circulating with increasing frequency and it was only a matter of time before they became public knowledge. It was something that would discredit the entire movement.

Hitler was also disturbed to learn that his financial backers shared the army's concerns. Gustav Krupp, who had personally pledged three million Reichsmarks to party funds, confirmed the Führer's fears that the SA were now seen as Roehm's private army and therefore as a threat to the state. As the owner of the largest iron and steel works, Krupp was crucial to Germany's rearmament programme.

Rumours that the SA were arming themselves with heavy-calibre machine guns in open defiance of the Versailles Treaty could not be allowed to go unchallenged. Hitler had no close personal friends and would turn on a trusted comrade or colleague for the smallest infraction. Nevertheless, he made repeated efforts to persuade Ernst Roehm that the time had come to disband the 'old fighters' and accept that the revolution was over.

But Roehm was stiff-necked and not a man to be reasoned with. The turning point came on 11 April 1934, during naval exercises in East Prussia attended by General von Blomberg and the commanders-in-chief of the armed forces, General von Fritsch and Admiral Raeder. Hitler knew that he had to secure their support if he was to cement his hold on power, especially once the ailing Hindenburg was out of the picture. So while they dined aboard a cruiser, the *Deutschland*, en route to Koenigsberg [now Kaliningrad], Hitler outlined his plans to build a fleet that would be the envy of the world. He also described his vision of a new Wehrmacht which would be equipped with tanks and heavy artillery in defiance of the hated treaty, regardless of the expense.

> 'Haven't I worked hard all my life for this land and given Hitler all I had? Where would he be without me? Hitler had better look out – the German revolution is only beginning.'
>
> Ernst Roehm to Kurt Ludecke, June 1933

In return, Hitler pressed von Blomberg, von Fritsch and Raeder for an assurance that when Hindenburg died they would name him as successor and order every member of the armed forces to swear an oath of allegiance to their Führer as the Supreme Commander. If the three men placed their faith in him, he would curb the SA and guarantee that the regular forces would be the sole bearers of arms in the new Reich. Had he not already implemented, at the cost of billions of marks, a massive public works programme to revitalize the economy and restore the nation's pride? How could they say no to such an offer? Having secured their support, Hitler was free to act against the enemy within.

Settling old scores

When word reached Hitler that Roehm was planning a putsch (a fantasy hatched by Himmler and Goering to spur their leader into action), Hitler gave orders for the immediate arrest and execution of the senior SA leadership. It was the order Himmler and Goering had been waiting for – a chance to settle old scores with the Führer's blessing and without having to account for their actions.

On the night of 30 June 1934, 150 members of the SA leadership in Berlin were rounded up and summarily shot by black-shirted members of Himmler's personal bodyguard, the SS, and by Goering's special police squads. Many died with a last 'Heil Hitler' on their lips, believing that Himmler and Goering had ordered their deaths, not the Führer.

That same night, a column of black limousines pulled up in front of the Hanslbauer Hotel in Wiessee, near Munich, where Roehm was on vacation. Hitler, his face set in grim determination, watched as dozens of bewildered SA men were dragged from their beds and immediately executed. Then Hitler entered Roehm's room and spewed forth a torrent of abuse and accusations. Following his departure, Roehm was removed to Stadelheim prison where he was presented with a loaded pistol and told to accept a soldier's death.

'If I am to be killed, let Adolf do it himself,' he replied, defiant to the end. Two SS guards then entered the cell and shot Roehm in the back of the head.

No one knows for certain exactly how many men met their deaths in what became known as the 'Night of the Long Knives'. In his speech to the Reichstag on 13 July, in which he sought to justify the executions, Hitler admitted to 77 deaths. But in a postwar trial some of the perpetrators admitted that 'more than 1,000' had been murdered, including Gustav von Kahr who had helped to foil the Beer Hall Putsch and Father Staempfle who had edited *Mein Kampf* and was said to be privy to the true circumstances of Geli Raubal's death. Kahr was hacked to death with pickaxes and dumped in a swamp near Dachau; Staempfle was found face down in a forest outside Munich, his neck broken and three bullets lodged in his chest.

Other victims included two army officers, General von Bredow and General von Schleicher (Hitler's predecessor as chancellor), together with Gregor Strasser, who had openly defied Hitler's authority in the early days of the party. Dozens more were shot at random as the SS and SA assassination squads ransacked the offices and homes of party officials whom they suspected of disloyalty or other indiscretions. The former Prussian premier Franz von Papen escaped with his life, but his secretary was killed and other associates died later in prison. Erich Klausener, head of Catholic Action, was gunned down in his office and his entire staff were bundled off to a concentration camp.

Germany was now in a permanent state of emergency where civil liberties had been suspended indefinitely. Under such circumstances, few took comfort in Hitler's assurance that there would be no other revolution in Germany for a thousand years.

The next morning, Germans read the news with grim resignation and realized that the New Order meant justice would now be dispensed without even the pretence of a trial. Imprisonment and death were to be meted out at the whim of Reichsführer Himmler, Goering and the rest of Hitler's inner circle, all of whom acted as though they were the new feudal lords. In that respect they were right – Germany had descended into an unprecedented Dark Age.

Aftermath

The implications of the army's complicity in the Night of the Long Knives were profound. They had not only supplied transportation for the prisoners, they had also provided weapons for their executioners. In praising Hitler for his swift and decisive action against the 'traitors' in the days following the killings, General von Blomberg aligned the army with the dictatorship. Any thoughts the generals might have entertained regarding the enforced removal of Adolf Hitler were now out of the question. From this moment on, the credibility of the officer corps was fatally compromised.

ERNST ROEHM DOSSIER

- Roehm's homosexual activities and those of his men were an open secret. It has been alleged that the Nazi movement grew out of the homosexual underground in Munich and that the Bratwurst Gloeckl beerkeller where the early party meetings were held was a notorious gay meeting place.

- In 1919, Roehm ordered Hitler to spy on the fledgling German Workers' Party to see if it was worth funding as a front for the political wing of the army.

- Roehm was one of the earliest members of the German Workers' Party, and his support was crucial in helping Hitler become its president in 1921.

- In 1928, Roehm served as military adviser in Bolivia, but was summoned back to Munich when Hitler sent him a telegram saying, 'I need you'. Shortly after Roehm's return, membership of the SA increased to over one million.

- Roehm's private letters were published in a Munich newspaper in 1931. In them, he detailed his homosexual affairs. This was a great embarrassment to Hitler, whose political enemies accused his party of harbouring homosexuals, drug addicts and sexual deviants. 'The disgusting hypocrisy that the Party demonstrates,' said the newspaper editorial, 'outward moral indignation while inside its own ranks the most shameless practices prevail . . . every knowledgeable person knows that inside the Hitler party the most flagrant whorishness contemplated by paragraph 175 (defining homosexuality as a criminal offence) is widespread.

- Himmler complained to Roehm that SA commanders were chosen because of their sexual orientation and not for their abilities, and cited the case of 35-year-old Obergruppenführer Karl Ernst, who was promoted from hotel doorman to commander of a quarter of a million men. 'Does it not constitute a danger to the Nazi movement if it can be said that Nazi leaders are chosen for sexual reasons?'

- Hitler was finally persuaded to act decisively against Roehm after Himmler and Reynard Heydrich fabricated evidence implicating the SA leader in a planned coup funded by 'the old enemy', France.

CHAPTER 6
The Thousand-Year Reich

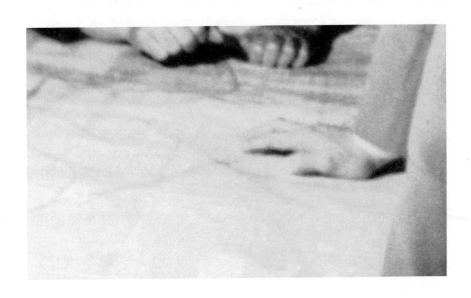

Six weeks after Hitler's appointment as chancellor, an obscure but promising young architect received a telephone call summoning him to Berlin. Albert Speer, then just 27 years old, accepted the invitation without hesitation and drove through the night from his home in Mannheim, arriving weary but eager at party headquarters. He was met by district organization leader Hanke, the official who had called him to the capital, and was told to report to the 'Herr Doctor', who wished to inspect an imposing 19th century building he had chosen for his new ministry.

Dr Goebbels greeted Speer with uncharacteristic cordiality and wasted no time in ushering him into an official car. Together they drove to the Wilhelmsplatz where a large crowd had gathered hoping for a sight of the Führer, whose chancellery was directly opposite. Speer surveyed the expectant faces of the strangers who now shared a common bond – hope for the future and faith in their Führer. As his car turned into the spacious courtyard of the ministry Speer sensed that a new epoch was beginning and he was taking his place at the centre of it all.

Speer joined the party in 1931, at a comparatively late stage, and was dismayed to discover that the local party members were petty bureaucrats of a 'low personal and intellectual level'. He could not imagine them governing the nation. But over the following weeks it would become clear to him that such nonentities were energized by the force of Hitler's personality. It was their desire to please him that oiled the wheels of the regime.

As they toured the building, Goebbels made it clear that no expense was to be spared in renovating the offices and great halls in the grand imperial style. In common with all of the regime's building projects, no budget had been agreed and no plans had been approved, so Speer had a totally free hand. Even so, when he prepared his sketches he opted for modest classical lines in keeping with the original architect's intentions. To his dismay, Goebbels found these 'insufficiently impressive' and commissioned a Munich firm to remodel the building in what Speer later referred to as an 'ocean-liner style'.

Speer was given a second chance shortly afterwards when Goebbels asked him to refurbish his private residence, a commission the young architect rashly promised to complete in just two months. Using three teams of labourers working round the clock, Speer managed to complete the job before the deadline, a feat which brought him to the attention of Hitler, as he had hoped. The other members of the Führer's inner circle were initially suspicious of the newcomer and resented having to share their leader's attention and favours.

Albert Speer's 'Cathedral of Light', at the 1937 Nuremberg rally

Whatever they all thought, it was perhaps inevitable that Hitler, himself a failed architect, would take to Speer and entrust him with the realization of his imperialist fantasies. It gave the Führer great pleasure to have someone with whom he could discuss his plans for the rebuilding of Berlin and the refashioning of Linz as the new capital of Austria.

Germania

Hitler's dream for Berlin was as a city of impressive monuments and public buildings. Everything was to be built on a scale which would dwarf the structures of the ancient world. Running through the centre of the capital would be a broad avenue 400 feet (122 metres) wide and 3 miles (5 kilometres) long. There would be a 400-foot-high (122-metre-high) triumphal arch at one end of the avenue, on which would be inscribed the names of the German war dead; a domed conference hall would grace the other end. Detailed plans were drawn up and models constructed to scale, but the war intervened and 'Germania', as Berlin was to be renamed, was never built.

Instead, Speer was asked to redesign the residences of top party officials. This gave him the opportunity to observe the leadership at close hand and understand how suspicious they were of one another. Goebbels was known to loathe Goering, Ribbentrop and Bormann, while Ribbentrop despised everyone in the administration – and the feeling was reciprocated. Goering mistrusted Ribbentrop, Goebbels, Bormann and Speer, though he commissioned Speer to redesign his home only months after it had been refurbished at considerable expense. (And all because Hitler had complained that it resembled a mausoleum.) It would appear that the leading Nazis adhered to the belief that one should keep one's friends close, but one's enemies closer.

A cathedral of light

With each commission Speer's reputation increased, but his most significant contribution to the regime was designing the setting for the annual Nuremberg rallies. When he first arrived in Berlin he noticed a sketch for the staging of a party meeting at Berlin's Tempelhof airfield and immediately claimed he could do better. Taking inspiration from the theatre and Ancient Rome he designed a large stage, at the back of which rose three huge swastika banners, each one taller than a ten-storey building. The banners were illuminated by powerful searchlights.

Later on he commandeered 130 anti-aircraft searchlights, placed at 40-foot (12-metre) intervals, each pointing upwards to create the illusion of gigantic pillars rising into the vaulting sky. In this 'cathedral of light', Hitler would assume a messianic stature in the eyes of his fanatical followers. The event became a ritual celebration of military might and the power of the collective will.

Centre of empire

Hitler frequently boasted that his empire would last for a thousand years, so he required buildings that would reflect the regime's historic significance and longevity. In 1938 he entrusted Speer with the design of a new chancellery in Berlin. It was to be erected on the site of the old Imperial chancellery and would extend along an entire city block on Voss Strasse. It was conceived on a scale that would invite comparison with the monuments of the ancient world and designed to intimidate visiting dignitaries. Hitler hoped they would be left in awe of the 'power and grandeur of the German Reich'. The entrance was certainly impressive. The courtyard, which was over 200 feet (61 metres) long, led to a short flight of steps. These were flanked by 42-foot-high (13-metre-high) neoclassical columns and by two bronze statues designed by Hitler's favourite sculptor, Arno Brecker.

Inside the chancellery, the floor and walls of the 150-foot-long (46-metre-long) Mosaic Hall were constructed from red marble. They were inlaid with eagles of grey marble and ornamented with gold decorations that recalled the palaces of the Roman emperors. Hitler had even adopted the Imperial eagle as an emblem. Golden eagle sculptures, grasping wreathed swastikas in their claws, adorned the entrances to the rooms.

In order to reach the Führer's office, visitors would have to pass through the Great Marble Gallery, which at 480-feet (146-metres) long was twice the length of the Hall of Mirrors at Versailles. It was lined with priceless tapestries on permanent loan from the capital's museum. Hitler's office was suitably imposing and tastefully furnished; the surface of his desk was inlaid with the motif of a sword being unsheathed.

> 'Both were bedevilled from childhood by thwarted, imagined and withheld love.'
>
> Psychologist and writer Gitta Sereny on Hitler and Speer

105

ALBERT SPEER

ARCHITECT OF THE NAZI DREAM

'Albert Speer was a war criminal. He did commit crimes against humanity and if the prosecutors at the Nuremberg tribunal had known everything about his activities during the Third Reich he would have hung.'

Professor David Cesarani

Speer, left, outlines his plans for a new style of classic German architecture

The 20 years Albert Speer spent in Berlin's Spandau prison gave him ample time to reflect on the part he had played in Hitler's regime. It was said his organizational skills had increased armaments production to such a degree that the Nazis were able to extend the war by at least another year, during which the conflict claimed hundreds of thousands more lives. But, for the former architect, incarceration and isolation also gave him invaluable time to write the memoirs which would make him an international celebrity and a very wealthy man. Just six weeks after his release from Spandau he was paid 50,000 marks for an exclusive interview by the German weekly news magazine *Der Spiegel*, the first of many lucrative deals. But there was one thing Speer secretly yearned for – and it would be denied him to the day he died – the recognition of his talent as an architect and the respect of his fellow professionals.

UNBUILT DESIGNS

Speer only saw one of his many grand designs built in his lifetime – the palatial new Reichschancellery in Berlin, beneath which Hitler would commit suicide in his concrete bunker in April 1945. The building stood in what would have been the new capital of the Third Reich, a city of imperial grandeur to be renamed Welthauptstadt Germania. In this planned city, long broad avenues flanked by massive classical edifices would converge on the Volkshalle, a domed conference hall three times the height of St Paul's cathedral in London. The dome was to have space for 180,000 people, who would gather to hear the proclamations of the emperor of the New Order. But Hitler's great modern metropolis was to remain a tabletop model and fantasy, which would be scrutinized by the dictator and his young alter ego even as the bombs and artillery shells shook the plaster from the ceiling of the chancellery.

PLAYING THE INNOCENT

If Speer failed to realize his dreams as an architect, he proved to have a formidable talent for self-promotion and as an actor on the public stage. At his trial at Nuremberg, he shrewdly accepted a degree of responsibility for his role in the regime, and his performance as the young artist who had fallen under Hitler's spell was so effective that the judges spared him the death sentence.

EVIDENCE OF GUILT

What the prosecution didn't know was that in the last days of the war Speer had driven through the night, braving Allied bombs, to recover his treasured art collection from the Brandenburg home of his friend Robert Frank. The next day he had deposited the 30 paintings in the vaults of the Commerzbank in Hamburg under his friend's name. It wasn't just their value he was safeguarding, but the part they could play in undermining his defence in a future trial. The paintings had been bought from a dealer who had a dubious reputation for acquiring artworks from Jews at a fraction of their true value. If Speer was linked to them it would undermine his testimony. He told his interrogators that the paintings had all been lost or destroyed; without them there was little to tie him directly to the crimes.

But there was further evidence of Speer's guilt. His former assistant, Rudolf Wolters, had kept detailed records of the 23,765 Jewish apartments that had been seized on his orders, causing 75,000 Jews to be 'resettled'. The buildings had been scheduled for demolition in preparation for the rebuilding of Berlin. Later Speer wrote to Wolters asking him to delete the passages that implicated him in the operation saying, 'I suggest that the relevant pages no longer exist.' But Wolters was apparently so disgusted by Speer's continual denials that he published the documents.

According to Professor David Cesarani, Speer used his imprisonment to perfect his alibi. 'He found the perfect formula for taking a degree of responsibility for the atrocities perpetrated by the Third Reich while not accepting personal culpability for them.'

REFORMED NAZI ROLE

On his release from prison in 1965, Speer was ready to admit that he had been swept up in the euphoria of the era and now felt foolish and partly responsible for its 'excesses'. He admitted responsibility but assumed no personal guilt. There were those who were not persuaded that his remorse was genuine and they poured scorn on his claim to have planned to assassinate Hitler in January 1945, a plan he kept entirely to himself until he needed to appear at Nuremberg. As one sceptic observed, 'Are we to believe the second most powerful figure in the Third Reich was prevented from pouring poison gas into the bunker's ventilation system for the want of a ladder?!'

> 'Hitler quite often told me:
> "You are fulfilling my dream.
> I would like to have been an
> architect. Fate made me the
> . . . sculptor of Germany.
> I would have liked to be
> Germany's architect. But I
> can't: you are. Even when I
> am dead you will go on, and
> I give you all my authority
> so that even after I am dead
> you will continue."'
>
> Albert Speer

SHUNNED BY HIS PROFESSION

Speer returned to the Zeppelinfeld at Nuremberg many years after his release, to visit the site of his greatest triumph once more. But all he could see were the weeds growing through cracks in the limestone steps leading to the podium where Hitler had given his rabble-rousing speeches. 'The Führer,' he sighed, 'would have been very mad at me for this poor stone quality.'

In the end, Speer betrayed Hitler by selling his mentor's original sketches to finance an affair he was said to be having with a married English woman. She was the same woman who allegedly was with him the morning he died in a plush London hotel in September 1981, aged 76.

Three years before his death, Speer consented to be interviewed by the BBC for a programme on the subject closest to his heart. At the end, he asked the interviewer if he wouldn't mind taking a gift to American architect Philip Johnson, who had designed the AT&T building in New York and whom he greatly admired. When the interviewer presented Johnson with the autographed copy of Speer's portfolio, a look of revulsion crossed the recipient's face. He thrust the book under the bench they were sitting on and refused to take it with him when he left the restaurant where they were having lunch. Had he known of it, Speer would possibly have felt that rebuff more keenly than the clanging of the cell door at Spandau.

'When diplomats see that, they'll learn to shiver and shake,' he said.

Beyond Hitler's private office lay the cabinet room, along the centre of which ran a long conference table ringed with two dozen Empire chairs. All were decorated with the eagle and the swastika. Ironically Hitler never held a cabinet meeting there, so ministers had to content themselves with a brief visit in order to see their names embossed in gold on the writing pad at their place of honour.

More than 4,500 labourers were hired to construct the new chancellery and thousands more were employed across the country to manufacture the luxurious fixtures and fittings. These included huge mahogany doors that were 5 metres (17 feet) high, gold wall lights, and gold plaques depicting Plato's four virtues: Wisdom, Fortitude, Temperance and Justice. Hitler boasted: 'You would hardly believe what a power a small mind acquires over the people around him when he is able to show himself in such imposing circumstances.'

Bormann, 'the Brown Eminence'

Hitler's indolence and his disdain for paperwork meant that no one in the new administration knew what their duties were and staff were continually being undermined by their colleagues. Hitler, whose orders were invariably vague and contradictory, summed up his attitude to the chaos he created by comparing himself to a gardener who looks over the fence from time to time to watch his plants struggling for the light. Matters were not helped by the structure of his administration, a Kafkaesque labyrinth of bureaucrats, with each district ruled by a *gauleiter*. These officials could block or delay orders if they did not like the office that had issued them.

Fortunately for the Führer, he was surrounded by sycophants ever eager to carry out his directives and record his every thought for posterity. The most faithful of these underlings was Martin Bormann, whose unquestioning subservience exceeded even that of his superior, Rudolf Hess.

Bormann was a short, stocky man with pronouncedly arched shoulders and a thin reedy voice which precluded him from public speaking. Instead he remained in the shadows, an anonymous but constant presence. He guarded his access to the Führer so zealously that he refused to take a holiday for fear that someone else would wheedle their way into Hitler's confidence. As a consequence he was reviled by the entire Nazi hierarchy, who named him 'the Brown Eminence' because of the colour of his uniform and his ever-lurking presence. His official duty was to manage the Führer's personal finances, which he performed with an obsessive enthusiasm. Bormann came up with the idea of demanding a royalty from the German postal service for every stamp that bore Hitler's portrait. This raised millions of marks within a few years. He also administered a secret slush fund from contributions made by the rich industrialists who had grown fat on lucrative rearmament contracts. The fund amounted to over 100 million marks in the first year alone.

Instead of lining his own pockets, as many officials might have been tempted to do in such a lax and self-serving regime, Bormann curried favour with his Führer by lavishing millions of marks on renovating the Berghof, Hitler's alpine retreat at Berchtesgaden. The modestly sized lodge was extended into a multi-storey chalet, the lower floors of which were hewn out of the mountainside to accommodate living quarters, kitchens and store rooms. But the most spectacular feature was the immense picture window, which offered a spectacular view of the Austrian Alps. Even though the mountain-top residence was practically inaccessible it was surrounded by barbed wire and heavily guarded at all times. In the mid-1930s, Bormann found the funds to construct a tea house on the summit; this became known as the Eagle's Nest, and was connected by a private lift shaft which had to be dug out of the granite. This feature alone was said to have cost up to 30 million marks, giving rise to the jibe that Bormann was the only person who had created a reverse gold rush by ploughing money into a mountain!

After joining the party in 1927 at the age of 26, Bormann became involved with a Nazi murder squad and was sent to prison for a year for his participation in the killing of his former elementary school teacher. But after marrying the daughter of a high-ranking Nazi official, he was able to persuade Hess to appoint him

> *'Hitler created in the political leadership of Germany the greatest confusion that has ever existed in a civilized state.'*
>
> Otto Dietrich, Hitler's press secretary

as his deputy. Bormann then shrewdly made himself available for the tedious paperwork which he knew Hess abhorred.

A born bureaucrat, Bormann knew that the real power of an administration was to be found in restricting access to the decision-maker. So from the moment Hitler woke up at midday until the early hours of the next morning, Bormann would trail after him with a pad and pencil recording every order, every passing remark. By this means he ingratiated himself with Hitler, who came to rely on him to draft his casual remarks into official orders and summarize the issues requiring his attention.

In Bormann's view, Hitler paid him the highest compliment he could imagine when he remarked, 'With him I deal in ten minutes with a pile of documents for which with another man I should need hours.'

MARTIN BORMANN
THE MAN THEY LOVED TO HATE

'In my dictionary, DUTY is written in capitals.'

Martin Bormann was referred to contemptuously by his jealous rivals in the Nazi hierarchy as 'the Brown Eminence', an allusion to his shadowy presence and insidious influence over their leader. Goering, Goebbels, Himmler and the rest of the Hitler gang despised him for the sycophantic fawning with which he had ingratiated himself with their beloved Führer, restricting their access to him. This was an act for which he would never be forgiven. In the words of an insider, he 'erected a positive Chinese wall through which people were admitted only after showing their empty hands and explaining in detail to Bormann the purpose of their visit.' By this means, he had absolute control over the whole machinery of the Reich.

RIGHT-HAND MAN
A former personal secretary to Rudolf Hess, Bormann became the power behind the throne by making himself indispensable to Hitler and proving to be an able manager of the Führer's financial affairs. While other Nazi leaders flattered their Führer's ego by complimenting him on his strategic genius and political shrewdness, Bormann worked quietly to increase Hitler's personal wealth and build his alpine retreat, the Berghof at Berchtesgaden, in a style and manner befitting the father of the Third Reich. In the construction of the Berghof, Hitler's every whim was indulged and no expense was spared. Bormann also found favour by purchasing Hitler's birthplace at Braunau

and his parents' house at Leonding and giving them as presents to Hitler. It was a shrewd and cynical move, and one for which the inner circle resented him even more. Hans Frank, governor-general of Poland, remarked that hatred was too weak a word to describe what they felt for Bormann, who always seemed to be hovering at Hitler's side in an ill-fitting suit, briefcase under his arm, poised to intercede on his leader's behalf if anyone spoke out of turn.

A short, squat figure with a moon face, he was described by those who knew him as 'coarse', 'banal' and 'a boot licker', but he was also dependable and uncommonly diligent. He didn't smoke or drink and ate sparingly in Hitler's presence, often sharing his Führer's preference for a vegetarian diet, but it was merely a ploy to appear modest and

unpretentious. In secret, he gorged on pork chops and any other meat left over after the guests had left.

It has been said that he didn't have an original idea in his head, that his wife Gerda was the ideologist in the family and that he simply repeated whatever she told him or overheard her saying in order to impress their guests. Observers reported that he was incapable of uttering a coherent sentence at a social gathering or of making small talk, yet he would word his official communications and reports as succinctly as a clinician reporting on the result of an experiment.

IDEAL OFFICE MANAGER

Bormann's lack of imagination and personality made him the perfect assistant for a tyrant who tolerated no dissent and demanded blind obedience. In other words, he was a 'yes' man who would dutifully record his leader's every utterance and observation, no matter how banal, as if it were the profound insight of an Einstein or an eminent philosopher.

A smiling Martin Bormann, sitting in the centre, between Goebbels (left) and Hitler (right) in a beerkeller

Bormann's official title gave the impression that he had no authority, but he was by Hitler's side whenever the Führer launched into one of his hysterical tirades against those he suspected of betrayal and was always ready with the names of those who were to blame. His advancement to the inner sanctum of the Reichschancellery baffled those who assumed that Hitler would promote those who had demonstrated bravery in the field. But the 'Bohemian corporal', as the Führer was disparagingly known, seemed unimpressed by acts of self-sacrifice and courage, which he considered obligatory when under fire. It appears he was more impressed by fastidious attention to detail, order, thoroughness and industry, the importance of which had been beaten into him by his father.

Hitler was documented as saying, 'I know that Bormann is brutal. But there is sense in everything he does and I can absolutely rely on my orders being carried out by Bormann immediately and in spite of all obstacles. Bormann's proposals are so precisely worked out that I have only to say yes or no . . . If I say to him, remind me about such and such a matter in half a year's time, I can be sure that he will really do so.'

Quiet rise to power

Bormann knew that real power and influence did not lie in titles and symbols but with having the ear and confidence of the leader. In this respect, he was the antithesis of Goering. While Goering strutted the world stage in gaudy uniforms and boasted of the titles bestowed upon him by an indulgent Führer, Bormann bided his time, manoeuvring himself into a position from which he was able to marginalize those officials he feared or distrusted. Then he could assimilate their responsibilities for himself.

Rosenberg, Ley and Reich Minister Lammers all found themselves excluded from the decision-making process and unable to bring their concerns to Hitler because they assumed that the Führer was displeased with them. They didn't dare risk incurring further displeasure by appealing to him to reconsider.

'Hess had obviously got on the Führer's nerves, and so Bormann took care of the queries and orders. Here is where he began to make himself indispensable. If, during our dinner conversation, some incident was mentioned, Bormann would pull out his notebook and make an entry. Or else, if the Führer expressed displeasure over some remark, some measure, some film, Bormann would make a note. If something seemed unclear, Bormann would get up and leave the room, but return almost immediately after having given orders to his office staff to investigate forthwith, and to telephone, wire or teletype.'

Alfred Rosenberg

The Führer always heard Bormann's version of events before any of the other leaders had their chance to present the facts. In this way he shielded his leader from the harsh reality of imminent defeat during the final days in the Führerbunker. On one occasion Bormann returned a dossier of photographs sent by Goebbels, which depicted the destruction of German cities, with a desultory note to the effect that the Führer didn't want to be troubled with 'trivial matters'. And when Goebbels submitted a detailed assessment of the desperate military situation, Bormann filed it at the back of his safe where it lay unread until after Hitler's death.

But he was much more than a self-serving, ruthlessly ambitious assistant. As Hitler became increasingly incapacitated and delusional, Bormann interpreted his offhand remarks as edicts, initiating orders which led to the murder of hundreds of thousands of Slavs. Their lives were of no value, he declared. Their women should abort, the more the better, to speed the extinction of the race. They would be allowed to keep their religion because it served as a 'diversion', but their towns and villages were to be destroyed. They existed only to serve their German masters.

Where did he go?

Ironically, for a man for whom anonymity was prized as much as influence, Bormann became better known after the war than during his lifetime. As the Nazis rose to power, he was rarely seen in public and throughout the war he deliberately kept a low profile. But after he had been condemned to death *in absentia* at the Nuremberg Trials, his part in the regime became common knowledge. The belated interest in Bormann was partly because his fate was to remain a mystery for more than 50 years. Had he escaped along the 'rat line' to South America? Had he fallen into the hands of the advancing Russians when they stormed the Führerbunker? Or had he been killed in the breakout and buried in the rubble of Berlin? There were even rumours that Churchill had ordered for him to be smuggled out of Germany so that he could help the Allies recover Nazi gold from Swiss bank accounts.

> 'Silence is usually the wisest course. And one should by no means always tell the truth.'
>
> Martin Bormann

In 1972, the discovery of what were thought to be Bormann's remains near the Lehrter railway station in Berlin did not silence the speculation. It was only in 1998 that his corpse was positively identified, after it had become possible to compare its DNA with that of one of his surviving family members.

MARTIN BORMANN DOSSIER

- Bormann enlisted as an artillery man in the Second World War, but he didn't see active service.

- On 17 June 1941, Bormann issued a secret directive to all regional *gauleiters* to destroy the power of the Church. He believed that Nazi ideology would not replace Christianity until the influence of the Church had been completely eradicated.

- He was instrumental in persuading Hitler to order the extermination of the Jews. On 19 August 1942, Bormann drafted a memo stating that 'the permanent elimination of the Jews from the territories of Greater Germany can no longer be carried out by emigration but by the use of ruthless force in the special camps of the East'.

- In July 1943, Bormann suggested that Eichmann be given responsibility for organizing the transportation of the Jews to extermination camps.

- He kept a card index file on party members and officials he distrusted and another on those he could coerce into serving as informers.

- His wife Gerda agreed to share her home with his mistress and encouraged him to father more children with the woman known only as 'M'. Gerda had given birth to ten children of her own, nine of whom survived.

- After Hitler had ordered the arrest of Hermann Goering for attempting to negotiate a surrender with the Allies, Bormann altered it to a death warrant. But Goering surrendered before the SS could kill him.

- Bormann was the official witness to Hitler's marriage to Eva Braun in the Berlin bunker at midnight on 29 April 1945, the night before they killed themselves to avoid capture by the Russians.

CHAPTER 7

Hitler – Behind Closed Doors

Between the wars, foreign dignitaries flocked to Berchtesgaden to take tea with the leader who had worked an 'economic miracle' by regenerating Germany. They were invariably shocked to find an indolent, ungracious host who slept in until midday, indulged in aimless monologues and ate copious quantities of cream cakes and chocolates. Moreover, he whiled away his evenings watching movies as if he were a retired gentleman who had no pressing matters of state with which to concern himself.

When Hitler did consent to meet with ministers and his inner circle, many important decisions were decided intuitively or without the consideration his visitors would have afforded them. He acted like a Ruritanian prince who was preoccupied with pomp and pageantry rather than the realities of modern diplomacy. Although he was often credited with astute political insight and shrewd statesmanship, his early successes were the result of a combination of bullying and bluff.

What he demonstrated was little more than pure animal cunning. He was able to sense the weakness of his prey and his enemies' lack of resolve to protect an ailing ally.

But for a time he deceived the great and the good. King Edward VII and his new American bride Wallace Simpson were among the guests at the Eagle's Nest on the Obersalzburg. The former British prime minister, David Lloyd George, was another visitor. He was so enthusiastic in his praise that his comments had to be toned down before they were published in the *Daily Express* newspaper: 'I have now seen the famous German leader and also the great change he has effected. . . . There is for the first time since the war a general sense of security. The people are more cheerful. . . . It is a happier Germany. One man has accomplished this miracle. He is a born leader of men. A magnetic, dynamic personality with a single-minded purpose, a resolute will and a dauntless heart. . . .

On top of the world: Adolf Hitler and guests share the mountain sunshine on the Berghof terrace

The old trust him. The young idolize him. It is not the admiration accorded to a popular Leader. It is the worship of a national hero who has saved his country from utter despondency and degradation . . . not a word of criticism or of disapproval have I heard of Hitler. . . . What Hitler said at Nuremberg is true. The Germans will resist to the death every invader of their own country, but they have no longer the desire themselves to invade any other land.'

Hitler in private

For all the talk of his personal magnetism and powers of oratory, the abiding impression of Hitler, derived from those who knew and attended upon him on a daily basis, was that of a shallow, gauche and insufferable bourgeois. He delighted in shocking his guests and companions. For example, he was in the habit of telling women that their make-up had been manufactured from human fat, sewage or kitchen waste. When meat was served, the avowed vegetarian would point out its resemblance to a roast baby, or describe the scene inside the slaughterhouse in graphic detail. Yet he fretted over his tea parties like a middle-class *Hausfrau*.

Hitler deliberately surrounded himself with those he considered his inferiors to avoid being reminded of his own intellectual shortcomings. If they were physically deformed, all the better. His personal adjutants, Bruckner and Burgdorf, were of low intellectual ability, as were his three SS aides, Fegelein, Günsche and Rattenhuber. Rudolf Hess was another example. He must surely have been the most intellectually challenged deputy leader of a modern European country. His ill-fated flight to Scotland in May 1940, in pursuit of peace, was naive in the extreme and quite possibly suggestive of insanity. Physically, too, they were an odd assortment. Hitler's chauffeur was so short he had to have blocks placed under his seat so that he could see over the steering wheel. This perverse policy could also be seen in the appointment of the club-footed Goebbels, the one-armed party business manager, Max Amann, and a stone-deaf assistant press secretary.

After the assassination of Ernst Roehm, Hitler appointed the one-eyed Victor Lutze as his successor,

> '*I shall become the greatest man in history. I have to gain immortality even if the whole German nation perishes in the process.*'
>
> *Adolf Hitler*

while Robert Ley, head of the Labour Front, was burdened with a speech defect which amused Hitler. He took a perverse delight in giving him as many public-speaking engagements as possible.

But not all of Hitler's appointments were intended to amuse. Many of the Nazi elite were sadists, sexual degenerates, drug addicts, alcoholics, pornographers and petty criminals, all of whom would have been jailed had they not scrambled to the top of the heap in Hitler's criminal administration. Hermann Goering, for example, was considered by his Führer to be 'the greatest genius in aviation history', but it is said that he spent most of the Second World War in a narcotic haze. Meanwhile, his foreign minister, Joachim von Ribbentrop, had as lamentable a grasp of world affairs as a fourth-form schoolboy. Hitler's childlike glee at causing confusion and his cavalier attitude to state affairs led him to duplicate various duties so that his ministers and officials would be too busy arguing among themselves to pose a threat to his leadership. It was also said that Hitler considered anyone who had recently had a holiday abroad as an expert in foreign affairs.

As with all tyrants and dictators, Hitler sowed the seeds of his own destruction by surrounding himself with sycophants and insisting on his own infallibility. Had he been willing to delegate authority to more able men and listen to the advice of the more capable officers in the armed forces, the Third Reich might have lasted far longer. But as his press secretary remarked, 'Instead of drawing to himself men of high character, rich experience and breadth of vision, he gave such persons a wide berth and made sure they had no chance to influence him. . . . [He] permitted no other gods beside himself.'

The Mad Messiah

In his exhaustive and penetrating study of Hitler's personality, *The Psychopathic God*, the historian Robert G. L. Waite argues that the Nazi state can be seen as the creation of a 'perverse child's fantasies'. He goes on to draw parallels between Hitler's New Order and the savage society created by the shipwrecked schoolboys in William Golding's novel, *Lord of the Flies*. Both Hitler and the central character in Golding's book are textbook psychopathic personalities who will typically begin their criminal career as the neighbourhood bully. They will dominate the vulnerable and 'dare' their followers to commit minor offences in order to tighten their hold over them. Tiring of this, they may seek notoriety in adulthood as the leader of a cult or sect because they seek adoration, self-aggrandisement and the vindication of their anger against the world.

Such people are contemptuous of the vulnerable. They celebrate mindless destruction and enjoy gratuitous cruelty. One of their ploys is to stage elaborate rituals with music, marching and the veneration of ancient symbols to create the illusion that their subordinates belong to a community with a respected tradition. As a result of this indoctrination, their followers will be less likely to question their leader's orders when asked to humiliate, intimidate or even murder those who don't conform. Devoid of conscience, the leader will blame his victims for having brought their fate upon themselves, while his collaborators will absolve themselves of responsibility, feeling neither compassion nor remorse. If called to account, they will say that they had been conditioned to follow orders.

Behind the mask

It is revealing that Hitler styled himself 'the greatest actor in Europe' – and with some justification, for he was a master of manipulation and deceit. He used his innate gift for mimicry to deceive his enemies into believing he was sincere and that his promises could be relied on. This he achieved by a combination of calculation and conviction, as he was not merely playing a role but living it to the full.

He was also capable of resorting to melodrama or faking one of his infamous rages if he thought it would achieve the desired effect. During a confrontation with Hjalmar Schacht, the German minister of finance in the Weimar administration, Hitler managed to bring tears to his eyes as he successfully pleaded with Schacht to remain in office. But the moment the minister had left the room Hitler turned on his associates and gave vent to his true feelings. The German secretary for foreign affairs witnessed another persuasive performance on 23 August 1939, when Hitler impressed the British ambassador Sir Neville Henderson. 'Only after Henderson had left the room did I realize that Hitler's performance was premeditated and acted.'

Hitler would also rehearse a conversation at length in private with his deputy, Rudolf Hess. Before meeting a foreign dignitary or diplomat, he would try out various voices until he found the appropriate tone.

He was a consummate actor, fulfilling the role expected of him so that everyone was taken in, but once he had departed the world stage not even his closest companions could convey the qualities which had captivated them. His architect and armaments minister, Albert Speer, who considered himself the only friend Hitler ever had, if indeed he was capable of friendship, confessed, 'In retrospect, I am completely uncertain when and where he was ever really himself, his image not distorted by play-acting.'

Father of the nation: Hitler embraces a suitably chosen little girl for the camera

Hitler's personal pilot, Hans Baur, recalled that it was only in the company of children, who he did not have to impress, that he showed anything resembling genuine human feeling. And yet he ordered the murder and enslavement of hundreds of thousands of children from afar and was responsible for many more becoming homeless orphans.

As the historian Robert Waite remarked, 'Hitler did not possess the qualities and attributes that he desired or that others wanted to see in him, he only gave the illusion of possessing them.'

The belief that Hitler suffered from a borderline personality disorder seems borne out by his capacity to be all things to all men and yet remain indefinable. Peter Kleist, who served as assistant to Nazi foreign minister Joachim von Ribbentrop, notes in his memoirs that Hitler's face always fascinated him because of the 'multiplicity of expressions it contained. It was as though it were composed of a whole series of individual elements without adding up to a single total. . . . A photographer, by selecting only a single moment out of context, could show only one aspect, thereby giving a false impression of the duplicity or multiplicity of being which lay behind it.'

Infallibility

Examples of Hitler's inability to deal with disagreement and disappointment are revealing. He was once described by a British diplomat as acting 'like a spoiled sulky child' when anyone dared to disagree with him, or if the topic of conversation was not to his liking. And his rages were legendary, invariably triggered by an insignificant or perceived slight. Military defeats would sober him, but if a servant dared to bring him the wrong kind of mineral water or it was suggested that he was whistling a tune incorrectly he would have a tantrum on the spot regardless of who might be watching. He would beat his fists, scream incoherently and even spread himself martyr-like against a wall as if crucified – strategies no doubt originally developed to obtain his mother's attention. On one occasion, he responded to a secretary's criticism of his whistling by assuring her that he had not deviated from the melody – it was the composer who was at fault!

A childhood acquaintance recalled that he was incapable of passing over something with a smile, while an official at the foreign office remembered, 'Concerning people, Hitler's judgements were usually bitter and derogatory. Qualities such as forbearance, humour and self-irony were completely foreign to him.'

It seemed that the only time he laughed was at the expense of others. According to his architect and armaments minister Albert Speer, 'He seemed to enjoy destroying the reputation and self-respect of even his close associates and faithful comrades.'

It might have been because his overbearing arrogance and contempt for others was tempered by a tendency to self-pity, which led him to seek reassurance and sympathy for all he imagined he had suffered and sacrificed on behalf of the German people. Hitler constantly whined about his fear of being forgotten until his acolytes were stung into reassuring him that he was a great man and destined to be remembered for centuries to come.

It was his morbid obsession with death and the obsessive fear of his own mortality that drove him to commission the building of an inordinate number of monuments to martyrs of the movement. He also planned monumental imperialist buildings with a view to what they would look like as ruins after a thousand years had elapsed, when the Reich had passed into history.

The death motif was as dominant a theme in the Third Reich as in many of Richard Wagner's operas. Nazi rallies were staged as if they were scenes from the opera *Götterdämmerung*, with theatrical lighting and massed uniformed ranks of SS troops in the role of the Teutonic knights, all to a score of Wagner's music. The object was to set the scene and stir the German soul. Significantly, the Nazis staged commemorations to fallen heroes more effectively than any other events in their busy calendar.

Inflexibility

Hitler was also rigid in his routines and habits. As his press chief noted with exasperation, 'He remained perpetually in the same company, among the same faces in the same atmosphere and, I may also say, in the same state of monotony and boredom, producing eternally the same speeches and declarations.'

Speer, too, remarked on how shallow Hitler appeared in private – a mere shadow of his fiery public persona. Recalling the long repetitious monologues with which Hitler entertained his guests and cronies, Speer said: 'The repertory remained the same. He neither extended nor deepened it, scarcely ever enriched it by new approaches. He did not even try to cover up the frequent repetitions. I cannot say I found his remarks very impressive.'

Hitler spoke incessantly on his favourite subjects: the early struggle of the party, his knowledge of history, his taste in architecture, his favourite film actresses and the private indiscretions of party officials who were not, of course, present. Contributions from guests were not required, only muted agreement with everything their host had said. Meal times were not a social event but an opportunity for a collective audience with the Führer.

However, this was a side ordinary citizens did not see. As the absolute ruler of Germany, Hitler was effectively deified in the eyes of millions of his adoring followers. He assumed a mystique comparable to that of the Roman emperors or the Egyptian pharaohs.

Goering summed up the German people's fascination with their Führer in a rare article published in 1934:

'There is probably nobody else right now who attracts the general interest as much as the Führer. And yet there is nobody whose qualities are as difficult to describe as are those of Adolf Hitler . . . there is no single quality or characteristic of his which, to our eyes, he does not possess to the highest perfection . . . the Führer is infallible. . . . What now is the secret of his powerful influence over his followers? . . . there is something mystical, unsayable, almost incomprehensible about this man. And the person who does not intuitively sense that will never comprehend it, for we love Adolf Hitler, because we believe, with a faith that is deep and unshakeable, that he was sent to us by God to save Germany.'

CHAPTER 8
Inside the Reich

Gradually, the conscience of a nation was being lulled into submission as if an anaesthetic were being administered. But few complained, at least not in public. Life was good: in the first year of Hitler's chancellorship unemployment was reduced by a third from six million to just under four million. Under Dr Robert Ley, a massive public works programme costing 18 billion marks guaranteed work for the hundreds of thousands of members of the German Labour Front. Private firms received massive subsidies if they contributed to the construction of the new motorway system, which saw 7,000 kilometres (4,350 miles) of concrete criss-crossing the country. There were also massive new municipal buildings to be erected in Berlin and other administrative centres, including a new Reichschancellery for the Führer and a complex of ministries on an imposing scale. Several were personally sketched by Hitler, who was finally realizing his adolescent ambitions.

In the following year, a further million people found work and the reduction increased year on year until, by 1939, only 302,000 able-bodied Germans were officially unemployed, just 0.5 per cent of the total workforce. For this reason, few grumbled at the loss of the unions, although workers were now banned from demanding higher wages, shorter hours or improved conditions. Strike action could not be taken under any circumstances. Workers were even prohibited from changing their jobs without permission. Performance-related pay was introduced, which benefited younger employees, but proved detrimental to the working lives of older, less able men and women. Enforced longer hours led to a marked increase in absenteeism. Progress had its price.

> 'We have put a stop to the idea that it is a part of everybody's civil rights to say whatever he pleases.'
>
> Adolf Hitler, 22 February 1942

The unemployment figures were also deceptive. Conscription was introduced in 1935, which meant that hundreds of thousands of young men were forced into the army, and this figure did not appear in the employment statistics. By 1939, one-and-a-half million men were in uniform and therefore no longer unemployed.

In rural areas, farmers received huge subsidies to produce less food. To keep prices artificially high, they were actively discouraged from being productive. Meanwhile, in the industrial regions, factories were working at full capacity to meet the targets of the rearmament programme. By 1938, the cost of this to the nation was 26 billion marks.

Although Hitler took the credit for this prosperity, the German economy had in fact improved as a consequence of the global recovery. By the end of the 1930s, the Great Depression had ended and confidence in the major financial institutions had been restored. Even the great road construction programme with which Hitler is credited was instigated by the government at the end of the 1920s. It is a little-known fact that in 1927, the Weimar Republic was spending more on new roads than the Nazis did in 1934.

Meanwhile the nation's youth was kept busy with healthy outdoor activities which combined physical training with Nazi indoctrination.

Hitler Youth

In 1939, a law was passed which made it compulsory for boys from the age of six and girls from the age of ten to join the Hitler Youth. The law stated: 'It is on youth that the future of the German nation depends. Hence it is necessary to prepare the entire German youth for its coming duties . . . all of Germany's youth is to be educated physically, mentally and morally in the spirit of National Socialism, to serve the nation and the racial community.'

The Hitler Youth was founded in 1926 and other youth groups were banned in 1933. Church youth groups were abolished three years later. Parents had little choice but to comply; those who resisted could be dismissed from their jobs, fined or even imprisoned.

Boys were required to join the *Pimpfen* (Little Fellows) between the ages of six and ten, at which point they would enrol in the *Jungvolk* (Young Folk) until they were 14. Then they would move up into the *Hitlerjugend* (Hitler Youth), which would train them for military service at the age of 18.

Girls joined the *Jungmädel* (Young Girls) organization at age ten. At 14, they moved on to the *Bund Deutscher Mädchen* or *Mädel* (the German Girls' League) until the age of 18.

In 1932, when the youth movement was in its infancy, there were 108,000 members. That number increased to nearly five-and-a-half million by 1936 and reached its peak in 1939, when the total membership of all youth organizations reached eight million. This ensured that every young person under conscription age was duly indoctrinated with the Nazi programme.

Any concerned parent who was not infected with the fever of National Socialism must have realized that the nation's children were being conditioned to be obedient servants of the state and then infused with Nazi propaganda and cynically prepared for war.

'Himmler is training young men who will make the world tremble,' Hitler remarked. It was Grimm's fairy tale of the Pied Piper brought to life.

The majority of German boys were happy to be part of the national youth movement and wore their uniforms with pride. They responded eagerly to its ideals of comradeship, loyalty and honour and the promise of sporting contests and camping in the countryside, where they would learn map reading, shooting, signalling and the mystical significance of the runic symbols. For many it was an adventure, a chance to belong. Merit badges were earned for newly acquired skills and individuals could test their capacity for self-discipline and physical endurance.

> 'The mission of women is to be beautiful and to bring children into the world.'
>
> Josef Goebbels, 1929

But not everyone was so enthusiastic. A few complained that the military-style discipline was oppressive. Every activity was preceded by repetitive drilling overseen by 12-year-old boys who clearly enjoyed shouting orders at their ten-year-old subordinates. Some relished the authority and unquestioning obedience they were able to command and enjoyed punishing those who didn't do as they were told. Offenders were given extra drill and latrine cleaning duties.

The youth movement motto was 'Youth must be led by Youth', but in practice it meant that bullies could torment those they disliked. Once indoctrinated with Aryan ideology, they would be taught it was their duty to 'monitor' their parents, teachers and other adults. They were also instructed to report any incidents or remarks which could be considered acts of disloyalty to the state. The idea was that they were little Hitlers in the making.

The regime's policy was made explicit by Dr Robert Ley, leader of the Nazi Labour Front:

'Our state . . . does not let a man go free from the cradle to the grave. We start our work when the child is three. As soon as it begins to think, a little flag is put into its hand. Then comes school, the Hitler Youth, the Storm Troopers and military training. We don't let a single soul go, and when all that is done, there is the Labour Front which takes possession of them when they are grown up and does not let them go until they die, whether they like it or not.'

Germany's children were indoctrinated from an early age

Strength through joy

The German Labour Front promoted a programme of leisure activities and social events for workers known as *Kraft durch Freude* (Strength Through Joy) which was intended to keep them happy and productive. Concerts, theatre visits, holidays and educational courses were provided at affordable prices for those who otherwise could not have afforded them. But in practice it was still the better-paid workers and the management who secured places on the more desirable outings, such as cruises to Scandinavia and Spain. One branch of the organization, known as the 'Beauty of Work' department, sponsored the building of leisure facilities and canteens in factories and other places of employment. However, workers resented the fact that they were expected to construct the facilities in their leisure time and at their own expense.

Ley incurred more resentment by promising every worker a car of their own, provided they paid for it in instalments. The beetle-shaped Volkswagen (People's Car) was said to have been designed by the Führer himself. He laid the foundation stone for the factory in 1938, amid much publicity. But a year later the factory had been turned over to the production of munitions and the cars were never delivered to the workers who had paid for them.

Euthanasia

In 1933, the Law for the Prevention of Hereditarily Diseased Offspring made sterilization compulsory for the physically disabled, the blind, the deaf and anyone suffering from epilepsy or depression. Even chronic alcoholics were included.

Then, in 1935, the Law for the Protection of the Hereditary Health of the German People was passed, which forbade people with hereditary or infectious diseases from marrying and producing 'sick and asocial offspring' who would become a 'burden on the community'.

Within four years, 200,000 compulsory sterilizations had been performed and a parallel programme for euthanasia was being planned with chilling efficiency. Gerda Bernhardt's mentally disabled brother, Manfred, was one of 5,000 children whose lives were taken by Nazi physicians in the early years of the regime.

Gerda remembers: 'Manfred was a lovely boy, but he could only say "Mama" and "Papa". . . . He only learnt to walk very late too. He always liked to be busy. If my mother said, "Bring some coal up from the cellar," he wanted to do it over and over again.

'My father was in favour of putting him in some sort of children's hospital and then Aplerbeck came up as they had a big farm there and the boy might be kept occupied.'

Aplerbeck had been designated a 'Special Children's Unit', where the staff decided which patients should live and which put to death by lethal injection because they were too much trouble to care for.

Gerda recalls the last time she saw her brother alive: 'They brought the boy into the waiting room. There was an orderly there when I was leaving. The boy stood at the window and I waved and waved and he waved too. That was the last time I saw him.'

At the time there was no official policy of euthanasia and no law authorizing it, only a *Führerstaat* (directive). Doctors were simply acting on instructions from their superiors, who knew Hitler had casually sanctioned the practice in a letter to his personal physician. That was enough to seal the fate of thousands deemed 'undesirable' or unworthy of life. Patients such as Manfred Bernhardt were given overdoses of luminal or morphine and their deaths were ascribed to common ailments to avoid raising the suspicions of their families. Prior to this, the method had been starvation. The records of the institution at Aplerbeck show that Manfred Bernhardt died of measles. In the same week, 11 other healthy children passed away prematurely.

Suspicions

Not everyone accepted the official explanation. One family was informed that their loved one had died from an infected appendix; however, unknown to the institution, the patient's appendix had been removed ten years earlier. Similar errors aroused the suspicions of dozens of other families who took their concerns to their priests, knowing they would not be listened to by the police.

In September 1940, a Protestant clergyman, Pastor Braune, wrote to the Ministry of Justice to voice his concerns about the systematic starvation of patients in the church-funded mental homes that were under his supervision:

'Visits to the institutions in Saxony plainly show that the mortality rate is being increased by withholding food. . . . Since the patients cannot possibly survive on that, they are made to take a drug (paraldehyde) which renders them apathetic. Oral and written reports make it movingly clear how the patients time and again call out, "Hunger, hunger". Employees and nurses who cannot endure this occasionally use their private means to still some of the hunger. But the result is beyond question. Hundreds have died a quick death in the last few months as a result of these measures.

'Nor are just those patients involved here who are absolutely beyond feeling. On the contrary, these are patients who know quite well what is happening and are watching how many funerals are taking place each day. One report describes the mortal fear of a patient who had an exact presentiment of the fate that is to meet him and his fellow sufferers.'

It was not until August 1941 that Hitler ordered an end to the programme of euthanasia in answer to a well-publicized and public protest by a leading cleric, Bishop Galen of Münster. The bishop had lodged an official protest with the district attorney and the police: 'lists are being made up in the hospitals and nursing homes of Westphalia of those patients who, as so-called "unproductive citizens", are to be moved and soon thereafter killed.

'It probably is to protect the men, who with premeditation kill those poor, sick people, members of our families, that the patients selected for death are moved from near their homes to a distant institution. Some illness is then given as the cause of death. Since the body is cremated immediately, neither the family nor the criminal investigation department can discover whether there really was such an illness and what the cause of death was.

'I have been assured, however, that neither in the Ministry of the Interior nor in the Office of the Reich Leader of Physicians, Dr Conti, is there much effort to hide the fact that premeditated killings of large numbers of the mentally ill have already taken place and that more are planned for the future.'

A dissenting voice

Few dared to speak out publicly against the regime, but certain members of the clergy, both Protestant and Catholic, criticized the Nazis from the pulpit when it became clear that they intended to supplant Christianity with a new pagan religion. The Christian cross was to be replaced with the swastika and pictures of saints were to be removed from all chapels, churches and cathedrals. Finally, the Bible was to be replaced by *Mein Kampf* and a sword was to be placed to the left of the altar in church.

In March 1935, Pastor Martin Niemöller of Berlin published an appeal to the congregations of Prussia warning against this new idolatory: 'We see our people threatened with a mortal danger. The danger is that of a new religion.'

Niemöller, a former submarine commander in the First World War, had initially welcomed the advent of the Nazis. But he had become swiftly disillusioned by their plans for a state-controlled Reich Church and by the rabidly anti-Christian sentiments expressed by Alfred Rosenberg and other members of Hitler's inner circle. In his bitter condemnation of the regime, Niemöller reminded his fellow Christians that the new religion would be a rebellion against the first commandment, which stated that believers were to worship only one God. The worship of blood and race, nationality, honour and freedom constituted idolatory, not idealism.

Faith in an 'eternal Germany', he argued, was threatening to replace faith in the eternal heavenly kingdom of Christ. This 'false faith' was an expression of the Antichrist.

It was therefore the duty of the Church to resist the secularization of its customs and the de-Christianization of its holy days. The mission of the Church was to protect its members from indoctrination that was at odds with Christian beliefs.

Niemöller's clerical status did not save him from the wrath of the regime. After ignoring repeated threats and warnings, he was arrested in July 1937 and sent to Sachsenhausen concentration camp and then to Dachau, where he remained for seven years until he was liberated by the Allies. More than 1,000 priests and laymen were arrested in the wake of Niemöller's protest, including 800 members of the Confessional Church which he had founded in response to the pro-Nazi German Christian movement.

With the more principled and vocal pastors removed from the pulpit, the remainder reluctantly gave their blessing to the regime. The Nazis did not pursue their plan for a 'National Reich Church', but ensured that every aspect of religious life was draped in the swastika and given a distinctive military cast. There were Nazi weddings, Nazi baptisms and, of course, Nazi funerals.

Genocide and the Jews

German Jews did not disappear overnight. They were robbed of their rights and deprived of their livelihoods through a steady and systematic programme of laws. These laws were made public in radio news bulletins, in the weekly cinema newsreels and in the newspapers, so the German people were well aware of what was taking place.

The random harassment of Jews by the SA in the early years of the Nazi regime became explicit party policy in April 1933, when Hitler ordered the boycott of Jewish shops and businesses. Even the ageing von Hindenburg knew what was going on. He voiced his disapproval in a letter dated 4 April 1933:

'Dear Mr Chancellor,

'In recent days a whole number of cases were reported to me in which judges, lawyers and justice officials who are wounded war veterans and whose conduct of office has been flawless, were forcibly retired and are to be dismissed because of their Jewish descent.

'For me personally . . . this sort of treatment of Jewish officials wounded in the war is quite intolerable. . . .

'If they were worthy of fighting and bleeding for Germany, they must be considered worthy of continuing to serve the Fatherland in their professions.'

With characteristic deviousness, Hitler replied that these measures were merely part of a 'cleansing process' that was intended to 'restore the healthy and natural balance' between Germans and Jews in certain professions. He went on to say that it was necessary to purge the system of an 'alien body' which was corrupting it from within. But the Nazis' secret intention was to isolate the Jews from German society until the 'Final Solution' was ready to be implemented.

> 'National Socialist and Christian concepts are irreconcilable.'
>
> Martin Bormann, July 1941

Legalized persecution

On 7 April 1933, the Law for the Restoration of the Professional Civil Service legalized the dismissal of all Jews from the civil service and public office. In the following month, books by Jewish authors were publicly burned in Berlin. More than one reporter was prompted to remind his readers that a hundred years earlier the German romantic poet Heine had warned, 'Where one burns books, there one eventually burns people.'

In September 1933, Jews were banned from all cultural activities and, in October, all Jewish journalists were dismissed from their jobs without compensation. In 1934, Jewish students were forbidden to sit examinations for professional qualifications and in May 1935 all Jews were expelled from the armed forces. That September, the infamous Nuremberg Laws deprived German Jews of their citizenship and the Law for the Protection of German Blood and German Honour prohibited both marriage and sexual relations between Jews and Gentiles.

A series of laws that drove Jews out of the medical, teaching and legal professions followed in 1936. Jewish doctors were only permitted to treat other Jews, Jewish lawyers were restricted to advising and acting for Jewish clients and Jewish teachers could only have private pupils who were also Jews. Jewish teachers and Jewish children were excluded from German schools.

Jews were also banned from public places such as parks, restaurants, cinemas and shops. However, during the 1936 Olympic Games, all street signs banning Jews from the centre of Berlin were removed for fear of drawing international criticism. But it was only a matter of time before the legalized persecution of the Jews erupted into open violence and attracted the attention of the world's press.

Kristallnacht

On 9 November 1938, a nationwide pogrom known as Kristallnacht (Night of Broken Glass) saw nearly 200 synagogues burned to the ground; 7,000 Jewish-owned businesses were destroyed and numerous Jewish cemeteries desecrated. Thirty thousand Jews were arrested and imprisoned in concentration camps. During the next week, 2,000 of them were murdered. The violence had been instigated by the Nazi leadership, who later stated that it had been a spontaneous reaction by outraged German citizens. The Nazis claimed that the assassination of a German diplomat by a Jewish extremist had provoked the populace to exact its revenge.

Kristallnacht – the morning after

Heine warned: 'Where one burns books, there one eventually burns people'

Berlin housewife, Emmi Bonhoeffer, has no patience with those who denied that they knew what was occurring. 'Of course in '38, when the synagogues were burning, everybody knew what was going on. I remember my brother-in-law told me that he went to his office by train the morning after Kristallnacht and between the stations of Zarienplatz and Zoological Gardens there was a Jewish synagogue on fire and he murmured, "That's a shame on our culture." Right away a gentleman sitting opposite him turned his lapel and showed his party badge and produced his papers showing he was Gestapo. My brother-in-law had to show his papers and give his address and was ordered to come to the party office next morning at 9 o'clock. He was questioned and had to explain what he had meant by that remark. He tried to talk himself out of it but his punishment was that he had to arrange and distribute the ration cards for the area at the beginning of every month. And he did this for seven years until the end of the war . . . he was not permitted to have a helper. He had to go alone. That was how they broke the back of the people.'

> *"The Jewish people will be exterminated," says every party member. Of course. It's in our programme. Exclusion of the Jews, extermination.'*
>
> Heinrich Himmler, 1943

When Emmi learned of what was taking place in the concentration camps she told her neighbours, who said they didn't want to hear such horror stories. It was too much to believe. Such things were created by foreign radio. When Emmi's husband heard what she had been saying he warned her that she was putting her family in the gravest danger. He reminded her that a dictatorship is like a snake – if you attack the tail it will simply turn and bite you.

At the end of 1938, further measures were introduced that legalized the theft of Jewish property and businesses. These could now be bought by the state at a fraction of their value; their former owners were thrown on to the street or into a concentration camp. In 1939, Jews were required to hand over all their assets, including jewellery, before being forcibly evicted from their homes and rehoused in ghettos.

Jews were to be physically removed from all aspects of German life and all memory of their existence was to be eradicated. The names of Jewish soldiers who had fallen in the First World War were chiselled from monuments and the military records of a further 100,000 Jews who had fought for the Fatherland were destroyed.

Hear no evil, see no evil

Despite what was happening to the Jews, most people turned a blind eye or chose to believe the rumour that they were being rounded up to be deported. Many harboured such delusions until the Allies liberated the death camps in 1945 and the awful truth was revealed for all to see. But some individuals witnessed the persecution of the Jews at first hand in the early years of the Nazi regime, and began to suspect the awful truth regarding the fate of the millions who had gone missing.

German housewife Christabel Bielenberg, whose husband was later executed for his part in the July plot to assassinate Hitler, is still haunted by the memory of the night she was asked to shelter a Jewish couple. She took them in against the advice of a neighbour, who was also a co-conspirator. Her neighbour reminded her that by taking the couple in she risked not only her own life and that of her husband but also those of their children, who would undoubtedly be sent to a concentration camp if the Gestapo found out. Nevertheless, she made the Jewish couple as comfortable as she could in her cellar. 'I simply could not say "no",' she remembers.

The couple stayed for two days. On the morning of the third day Christabel went down into the cellar to find they had gone. But not before they had cleaned and tidied up so that no trace of their stay would give their host away.

Some days later, she learned that they had been caught buying a ticket at a railway station and had subsequently been transported to Auschwitz. 'I realized then that Hitler had turned me into a murderer,' she said.

Half-a-million Jews possessed German citizenship in 1933. Many of them would have been assimilated into German society through intermarriage if the Nazis had not systematically murdered them. Some European Jews had the foresight to realize the fate that awaited them at the hands of the regime and were fortunate enough to be allowed to emigrate to Britain or America. They included the scientists Albert Einstein and Max Bergmann, film-makers Alexander Korda and Fritz Lang, and the actors Peter Lorre and Conrad Veidt. In total 280,000 Jews managed to flee to safety.

Many ordinary citizens remained, however, either because they didn't want to leave their families or because they had been denied visas to emigrate. Most countries limited the number of refugees they would take and not everyone who wanted to flee was allowed to do so. A few even clung to the belief that the Nazis would not harm them but would resettle them in the east. There were even some who were at first blind to Hitler's true intentions.

In his diary for March 1933, the playwright Erich Ebermayer recorded a meeting with the young widow of his former teacher. He expressed surprise at her naivety regarding the Nazis: 'the young widow is not at all opposed to the Nazis. On the contrary, she lectures us on the outstanding qualities of Adolf Hitler, on the greatness of the age which we are allowed to witness, on the national rebirth and is firmly convinced that no harm whatever will come to educated Jews in Germany. I am hardly capable of comprehending this degree of delusion. . . . Nor does this seem to be an isolated case. Not long ago I was witness to a scene in Leipzig, in which the wife of Supreme Court Councillor Simonson, baptized and fully and obviously Jewish, told my father apropos of Hitler's latest Reichstag speech, "Isn't he like a saviour?" My stomach did a turn.'

> *The Jew is a devil in human form. It is fitting that he be exterminated root and branch.'*
>
> Anti-Semitic rabble-rouser
> Julius Streicher

The Jews are our destruction

In 1941 the regime's Jewish strategy moved from discrimination to extermination. In November of that year, the leadership's policy was made explicit in an article penned by Goebbels. He affirmed that he shared his Führer's views and made it clear that anyone who assisted the Jews would be treated as a traitor to the state.

'Let me say once more.

1. The Jews are our destruction. They provoked and brought about this war. What they mean to achieve by it is to destroy the German state and nation. This plan must be frustrated.

2. There is no difference between Jew and Jew. Every Jew is a sworn enemy of the German people. If he fails to display his hostility against us it is merely out of cowardice and slyness, but not because his heart is free of it.

3. Every soldier's death in this war is the Jews' responsibility. They have it on their conscience; hence they must pay for it.

4. Anyone wearing the Jew's star has been marked as an enemy of the nation. Any person who still maintains social relations with them is one of them and must be considered as a Jew himself and treated as such. He deserves the contempt of the entire nation which he has deserted in its gravest hour to join the side of those who hate it.

5. The Jews enjoy the protection of the enemy nations. No further proof is needed of their destructive role among our people.

6. The Jews are the messengers of the enemy in our midst. Anyone joining them is going over to the enemy in time of war.

7. The Jews have no claim to pretend to have rights equal to ours. Wherever they want to open their mouths in the streets, in the lines in front of the stores, or in public transportation they are to be silenced. They are to be silenced not only because they are wrong on principle, but because they are Jews and have no voice in the community.

8. If Jews pull a sentimental act for you bear in mind that they are speculating on your forgetfulness. Show them immediately that you see right through them and punish them with contempt.

9. A decent enemy after his defeat deserves our generosity. But the Jew is no decent enemy. He only pretends to be one.

10. The Jews are to blame for this war. The treatment we give them does them no wrong. They have more than deserved it.'

But perhaps the most revealing example of the Nazi mentality at work is to be found in a speech made by Himmler to a group of SS leaders in Posen in 1943. The Reichsführer was attempting to justify the cold-blooded murder of millions:

'Let me, in all frankness, mention a terribly hard chapter to you. Among ourselves we can openly talk about it, though we will never speak a word of it in public. . . . I am speaking about the evacuation of the Jews, the extermination of the Jewish people. That is one of those things where the words come so easily.

'"The Jewish people will be exterminated," says every party member. Of course. It's in our programme. Exclusion of the Jews, extermination. We'll take care of it. . . . Most of you will know what it means to see 100 corpses together, or 500, or 1,000. To have made one's way through that and – some instances of human weakness aside – to have remained a decent person throughout, that is what has made us hard. That is a page of glory in our history that never has been and never will be written.'

> 'We had the moral right and the duty toward our nation to kill this . . . bacillus . . . we can say that we fulfilled this heaviest of tasks in love to our people. And we suffered no harm in our essence, in our soul, in our character.'
>
> Heinrich Himmler

After the invasion of Poland in 1939, Jews were required to wear a Star of David. This was reinforced in September 1941 by a decree signed by Reinhard Heydrich, Hitler's handsome executioner

143

HEINRICH HIMMLER

PUNY EXPONENT OF THE MASTER RACE

'We have only one task, to stand firm and carry on the racial struggle without mercy.'

Appearances can be deceptive. This was certainly true in the case of Heinrich Himmler, leader of the SS and head of the Gestapo, whose puny physique, poor eyesight and weak constitution would have prohibited him from being accepted into the ranks of the elite military units he commanded. With his round, rimless spectacles, dogmatic manner and obsession with herbal remedies and astrology, he gave the impression of being what Albert Speer called 'half schoolmaster, half crank'.

HIS NAME INSTILLED TERROR

Himmler was an unlikely addition to the rogues' gallery of Nazi war criminals. However, as Reichsführer-SS and head of the state secret police, he was indirectly responsible for authorizing an estimated 14 million civilian deaths in forced labour and extermination camps. And this does not include the countless thousands of unarmed POWs and resistance members murdered by the SS and the Gestapo, the hundreds of thousands liquidated by the *Einsatzgruppen* death squads in the conquered countries and the unknown number of civilians executed in reprisals for alleged acts of sabotage or harbouring enemy soldiers.

> 'One principle must be absolute for the SS man: we must be honest, decent, loyal and comradely to members of our own blood and to no one else. What happens to the Russians, what happens to the Czechs, is a matter of utter indifference to me.'
>
> Heinrich Himmler

HARSH CHILDHOOD

The second of three sons born to a Munich high school teacher, Himmler was hampered by an inability to make friends and form relationships, which left him isolated and distrustful. A classmate recalled him as having a 'half-malicious, half-embarrassed smile on his face', which didn't endear him to the other pupils, while those who met him in later life also spoke of his fixed, contemptuous or faintly mocking smile. Himmler's steely grey-blue eyes would fix on anyone he considered his inferior, as if probing for signs that betrayed their true intentions. His suspicious nature was fostered by his authoritarian father, Gebhard, who had been described by a former pupil as the kind of man who 'grovels to his superiors while oppressing his inferiors' and was not above publicly humiliating a pupil to whom he took a dislike.

His father's unrelenting schooling demanded that young Heinrich keep a diary of his activities, which was checked and corrected on a daily basis. It was this strict, inflexible adherence to regulations and the relentless drilling that promoted industry for its own sake, which instilled in Himmler an unquestioning obedience to authority and the craving to dominate others.

UNDER HITLER'S SPELL

There was only one person to whom Himmler deferred – Adolf Hitler. When he attended a political meeting in a Munich beerkeller in 1923, Himmler knew he had found a cause and was soon extolling the virtues of a man he believed to be the future saviour of Germany, proclaiming: 'A figure of the greatest brilliance has become incarnate in his [Hitler's] person.'

None of the party leaders gave the wiry, bespectacled youth a second look, but Hitler had an instinct for knowing who might be useful to him and by 1929 had made Himmler the head of his private bodyguard, the SS.

ABSOLUTE POWER

After Himmler assumed command in 1929, he enlarged the SS to a force of more than 50,000 men. Under the leadership of Ernst Roehm, the brown-shirted storm troopers of the SA had become all but unmanageable and the party's power threatened the German army itself.

Himmler, on the other hand, could be relied upon to enforce the Führer's will and his men were trained to obey without question. Therefore, on the Night of the Long Knives, Hitler entrusted the SS with rounding up and executing hundreds of high-ranking leaders of the SA and other 'dissident' elements, including any individuals who were in his way. Himmler and other Nazi leaders also took the opportunity to settle personal scores. For their loyalty, the SS were rewarded with unparalleled powers, which gave them absolute authority over every branch of the German armed forces and the civil authorities.

CONCENTRATION CAMP ROLE

If Hitler had failed to amass public support in the critical federal election of 1930 – which saw the NSDAP become the second-largest party in the Reichstag – Himmler might have become a chicken farmer. His marriage three years earlier to Margarete Boden, the 34-year-old owner of a private nursing home, had furnished him with the means to buy a small poultry farm; he simply needed to persuade his wife to sell her business and invest in the joint venture. But the unpopularity of the

> 'We have only one task, to stand firm and carry on the racial struggle without mercy.'
>
> Heinrich Himmler

Weimar government and the threat of a communist revolution persuaded many voters to put their faith in the extreme nationalists.

Once Hitler was established in the German parliament, he found a post worthy of his 'loyal Heinrich'. Having promoted Himmler to Reichsführer-SS the year before, Hitler now entrusted him with organizing the internment of the party's political enemies, undesirables and *Untermenschen* – 'subhumans'.

Given full authority to treat the internees as he saw fit, Himmler was free to work them to death after selecting the fitter specimens for the slave worker programmes at Peenemünde and other research establishments. Or he could sign them over to the medical division at Dachau to become subjects in sadistic experiments. Himmler saw himself as a patron of science – a barbaric and perverted science which deliberately subjected prisoners to spurious tests and unnecessary surgical operations that were really no more than acts of torture.

ELITE BROTHERHOOD

In Himmler's mind, the SS were a black-uniformed brotherhood upon whom he could project his distorted romantic ideals, but to whom he could never belong. Instead he exercised a strict paternal interest in the moral welfare of his men, testing their loyalty and fanaticism as rigorously as he evaluated their physical strength and courage under fire. He saw himself primarily as an educator, but according to one biographer exhibited an 'obsession with interfering in other people's private affairs and [an] almost voyeuristic interest in collecting details about their lives'. Under Himmler's patronage, the SS came to see themselves as an elite to whom the normal rules and regulations of warfare did not apply, a belief enforced by the fact that they were exempt from prosecution in the civil and military courts.

CREATING A MASTER RACE

On 12 December 1935, Himmler established the *Lebensborn* programme, which paired his men with 'racially pure' partners to produce perfect Aryan babies. The aim was to counter Germany's declining birth rate and swell the ranks of the SS and later to offset the casualties at the front. The 21 *Lebensborn* homes were decorated with furniture and fittings stolen from the homes of wealthy Jews, a process presided over personally by the Reichsführer, who also took it upon himself to screen suitable female partners. He took a personal interest in children born on his own birthday, sending them gifts and keeping a keen eye on their progress.

But the programme didn't produce enough children to meet Himmler's target, so in 1939 he gave orders for the SS to kidnap 'racially good' children from the eastern occupied territories. Many were orphans, but thousands were taken forcibly from their parents and subjected to Germanization, conditioning and indoctrination. It is estimated that 100,000 children were stolen from Poland alone. Those who resisted were beaten or transported to the death camps.

KNIGHTS OF THE ROUND TABLE
In a kind of Wagnerian fantasy, Himmler imagined himself presiding over a kingdom of contented peasants who tilled the land while slave workers laboured at heavy industry under the lash of their new masters. He would be enthroned in his lavishly refurbished medieval fortress at Wewelsburg, Westphalia. The castle had been chosen by the Reichsführer-SS for its mystical location. It was believed to have been built on a site where natural power lines of earth energy converged, making it an impenetrable outpost for the final apocalyptic battle with the barbarians from the east, which had been predicted by his personal astrologer and occult advisers. At Wewelsburg, the remains of fallen SS heroes were interred in the stone vault beneath the Great Hall while their comrades communed with their spirits, seated in eerie silence around a magnificent oak table like the knights of Arthurian legend.

FINAL BETRAYAL
An indication of how removed from reality Himmler had become by the end of the war can be determined by the greeting he gave to a representative of the World Jewish Congress, who came to discuss surrender terms on 21 April 1945: 'Welcome to Germany, Herr Masur. It is time you Jews and we National Socialists buried the hatchet.' On 1 May, Himmler met with Admiral Doenitz, who had been appointed Führer after Hitler's death, and spoke of his own 'widespread reputation' abroad, as if it was a reputation to be proud of.

Shortly afterwards, when SS officers learned of his attempts to make a separate peace with the Allies and of Hitler's anger at his betrayal, many committed suicide, feeling that they too had been betrayed by the man who had sworn them to an oath of loyalty.

In the end, Himmler's arrogance proved to be his undoing. He attempted to escape capture by disguising himself as a sergeant-major in the secret military police, a branch of the Gestapo, which qualified him for certain arrest. After being captured by the British at Lüneburg on 23 May 1945, he foolishly ordered his fellow POWs to do his chores for him, which prompted one of them to inform the guards. His identity discovered, Himmler swallowed cyanide and was dead within seconds. There was no alternative for a man who knew he would be forced to face the enormity of his crimes in the glare of a public courtroom, and even worse, forced to confront himself.

CHAPTER 9
Nazification

Nazification of the German nation was not achieved by intimidation alone. Conversion was a major factor. When cultural groups and academic institutions were encouraged to 'align' themselves with the party (a process known as *Gleichshaltung*), Nazi ideology was assimilated with enthusiasm. Every professional association, amateur club and society was expected to promote the party's *völkisch* values and work together for the greater good.

The main aim of the programme was the creation of a classless society. Until the Nazis initiated their Volks community programme, Germany was strictly hierarchical. Only sons and daughters of the titled and wealthy were permitted to enrol at universities, for example, and the majority of officers in the armed forces were drawn from aristocratic families. Under the Nazis, employers were encouraged to take their meals with their workers. In organizations such as the Labour Front, professional people mixed with the working classes as equals.

In this way, the nation was distracted from the government's more extreme measures: the banning of opposition newspapers; the abolition of the trade unions; the boycotting of Jewish businesses; and the imprisonment of political opponents in the new concentration camps at Oranienburg near Berlin and Dachau in Bavaria.

After the war, former Nazis denied any knowledge of what had taken place in the camps or in the euthanasia and sterilization centres. But their letters and diaries tell a different story. As early as 1934, activist Johann Schnur spoke in defence of his party's reputation: 'People reproached me with accusations that the Hitler movement was the destroyer of both Christian churches, that it removes all crippled and useless people, that it would dissolve the unions and thus threaten labour's rights, that social insurance would come to an end and that what the Nazis wanted was another war, and many other such things. When I heard these lies and slanders I tried to enlighten people.'

Propaganda

The Third Reich was the first totalitarian regime to recognize and exploit the power of radio. As soon as the Nazis were in office, Goebbels ordered the manufacture of millions of cheap wireless sets so that by 1939, 70 per cent of German homes had a radio. Speer remarked that, 'Through technical devices like the radio . . . 80 million people were deprived of independent thought. It was thereby possible to subject them to the will of one man.'

From 1934 onwards, all broadcasts had to be approved by the Ministry of Propaganda. Nazi foreign language broadcasts – 'grotesquely unconvincing', according to one writer – were aimed at converting listeners abroad, but it was forbidden for Germans to listen to foreign broadcasts, particularly the BBC.

Newspaper and magazine journalists were also vetted by the state. News items and features had to be approved by the state-controlled press agency, the DNB, and any story that put the regime in a negative light or did not meet with its approval was dropped.

Criticism of the regime was forbidden. In a speech to journalists on 10 November 1938, Hitler made their obligations clear: 'What is necessary is that the press blindly follow the basic principle: The leadership is always right!'

Goebbels kept tight editorial control over all publications within the Reich and evidently felt it necessary to issue a daily memo to ensure that journalists and editors kept to the party line. His instructions for 22 October 1936 betrayed his characteristic brand of sarcasm: 'It turns out time and again that news and background stories still appear in the German press which drip with an almost suicidal objectivity and which are simply irresponsible. What is not desired is newspapers edited in the old Liberalistic spirit. What is desired is that newspapers be brought in line with the basic tenets of building the National Socialist state.'

Under the Nazis, newspapers became little more than party broadsheets. Editors were told what to print and even where to place a story so that items showing the regime in a favourable light were given prominence. The views of foreign politicians, or news that reflected unfavourably on the regime, were relegated to the back pages.

General Instruction No 674, dated 1 September 1939, was typical: 'In the next issue there must be a lead article, featured as prominently as possible, in which the decision of the Führer, no matter what it will be, will be discussed as the only correct one for Germany.'

Aryan art and Nazi science

Nazification had its ludicrous side too. In their eagerness to purge the world of Jewish culture, the Nazis attempted to make a distinction between Aryan and non-Aryan art and science. Aryan art extolled the Nordic virtues of heroism, physical strength, comradeship, community, motherhood, patriotism and sacrifice. Degenerate art, as the Nazis called it, was that which distorted the symmetrical perfection of the human physique or explored the seamier aspects of life.

The fact that Hitler's favourite paintings often depicted scenes of putrefaction (one of them was *The Plague in Florence*, a fevered depiction of writhing humans by the Austrian artist Hans Makart) and morbid erotica (specifically the paintings of Franz von Stuck, which depicted naked women entwined with serpents or pursued by centaurs) was not public knowledge at the time. Neither was the fact that Goering had acquired a vast collection of 'degenerate art' for his private collection. 'Degenerate art' included modern movements such as Cubism, Dadaism and the Expressionists, while contemporary representational art (that is, realistic portraits and landscapes and sentimental portraits of rural life) was sure to obtain the state's seal of approval.

> *The basic principle with which we brought the whole German people to follow us was a very simple one. It was "The Common Interest Before Self-Interest"'*
>
> Josef Goebbels, 'Der Krieg als Weltanschauungskampf' speech, 1944

Jazz music was banned outright because it was considered to be the culture of the negro. Groups of rebellious youths known as 'swing kids' defied the ban. They gathered in secret and danced to the latest American records by the likes of Count Basie and Duke Ellington.

Film-makers such as the director Fritz Lang also came under scrutiny and discovered that their creative freedom was being stifled by the rigid controls demanded by the regime. Lang was called to the Ministry of Propaganda to meet Goebbels, who described the themes he expected the director to emphasize in his next film. Despite this it is rumoured that Goebbels also offered Lang the position of head of film production in Germany. Lang could only nod in agreement and thank the Reichsminister for his compliments. By the next morning, however, he had booked a passage to Paris and from there travelled to the USA.

Curiously, only about 200 of the 1,300 films approved by Goebbels were blatant propaganda. Goebbels knew people had little appetite for political films, but were more likely to accept his message if it was delivered in the guise of entertainment. As millions went to the movies every week at this time, the last thing the minister of propaganda wanted was to risk a fall in cinema attendance.

Eminent émigrés

All literature, music, film, theatre and art came under the control of the Ministry of Propaganda; it decided which artists, writers, musicians and film-makers were eligible for membership of the Reich Chamber of Culture. Those deemed unsuitable were denied membership and therefore unable to obtain work.

When Bonn university withdrew an honorary degree from novelist Thomas Mann in 1937, he countered with a written response. Although his letter contained a stinging indictment of the regime, his warning was dismissed as alarmist: 'The sole possible aim and purpose of the National Socialist system can only be this, to prepare the German public for the "coming war" by the ruthless elimination, suppression and extermination of any sort of sentiment opposing such a war, to make the German people into an utterly obedient, uncritical instrument of war, blind and fanatic in its ignorance.'

By 1939, nearly 600 authors had been blacklisted and had their books burned by the thousand. Some of these seem innocuous in retrospect. For instance, Karl Wachtelborn's *What Is Life? What Is Nutrition?* was considered 'harmful and undesirable' because it criticized the German diet. Then there was Dr Eugen Steinemann's *Basic Economics*, which accused the regime of promoting state-directed capitalism at the workers' expense.

Novels, too, were banned if they portrayed a negative aspect of German life, such as the criminal underworld described in Erich von Voss' *See Berlin, Then Go on Probation*. Emil Otto's *The Devil's Kitchen* was 'offensive' because it had an Italian criminal as a protagonist and was published at a time when Mussolini and Hitler were allies. Goebbels' bureaucrats were also offended by the erotic adventures of teenage girls in Margarete von Sass' *Game of Love*, but did not raise an eyebrow at the sadistic anti-Semitic pornography which passed for political satire in their own publications.

Aryan science was harder to define, but the regime found an expert willing to do it. Nobel prize-winning physicist Philipp Lenard (1862–1947), at that time a professor of physics at Heidelberg university, took on the job. In the introduction to his four-volume reference work *German Physics*, Lenard damned the discoveries of Albert Einstein (a Jew), while upholding the laws of Aryan science: 'In reality Science – like everything else created by man – is conditioned by blood and race. . . . People of different racial mixtures have different ways of pursuing science. [Einstein's] "relativity theories" were meant to reshape and dominate the whole science of physics, but when faced with reality, they lost all shred of validity. . . . It is a matter of course that the present work will nowhere need to deal with this mistaken intellectual structure. . . . The fact that they will not be missed will be the best proof of their unimportance.'

Such doublethink did not of course survive the regime or the light of reason. Nazi art is now seen as crude and unimaginative – the very antithesis of creativity – while Nazi science is considered a contradiction in terms.

Growing up under Hitler

History is shaped by kings and conquerors, but experienced by ordinary people. Only those who lived in Germany during the Nazi era can know what it meant to exist in those turbulent times.

Horst Krueger was the 14-year-old son of a Berlin civil servant when Hitler became chancellor in 1933. He recalled that memorable night in his bestselling autobiography, A Crack in the Wall: 'My earliest memory of Hitler is jubilation. I'm sorry about that, because today's historians know better – but I, at first, heard only jubilation. . . . It was a cold night in January and there was a torchlight parade. The radio announcer, whose resonant tones were closer to singing and sobbing than reporting, was experiencing ineffable events . . . something about Germany's reawakening, and always adding as a refrain that now everything, everything would be different and better.'

Krueger remembered that his mother and father were initially astonished by the euphoria sweeping the country and were puzzled and somewhat sceptical. But shortly afterwards the belief in a better future arrived in their quiet suburb as subtly as a new season: 'The time was ripe . . . a surge of greatness seemed to course through our country.'

The first evidence of this renewal was a cluster of flags flying from the windows of the houses in the quiet Berlin suburb of Eichkamp where Krueger lived and went to school. Many flags were handmade, some so hastily that the swastika was sewn on back to front. Horst's mother gave him a swastika pennant one day, simply because all the boys in the district were flying them from their bikes. It was not a political gesture, rather one which expressed the sense of community that people then needed so badly. His mother had bought the pennant from a Jewish vendor who was equally ignorant of its significance.

There were parades, processions and new holidays celebrating aspects of German life and culture. People seemed full of hope and had a sense of purpose. Members of the Labour Service marched through the streets with spades slung over their shoulders on their way to lay the new autobahns or build art galleries and opera houses. The old decayed heart of Imperial Germany was being ripped out and a vital new infrastructure was being installed.

In the meantime, street violence and the persecution of Jewish people raised concerns that the unruly element within the party might cause trouble for the new administration. In the narrow gaslit streets of Eichkamp, and behind the green shutters of their neat suburban homes, the 'good Germans' asked themselves, 'Does the Führer know about this?'

The Roehm purge of 1934 answered this question and many German citizens shook their heads in disbelief as they read their newspapers. It was clear that sexual deviants and bull-necked street brawlers had betrayed the party and nearly toppled the regime before it could prove itself. People agreed it was necessary to 'discipline' the unruly element and bring them into line.

As Krueger recalls, his neighbours were left 'disarmed, willing and docile' by the thought of being part of a greater Germany. They were on the bottom rung of society and only too willing to be swept along with the rising tide of productivity and prosperity. Men stood at street corners and talked of claiming their colonies back, of having faster mail deliveries because of the new highways. All agreed it was about time that Germany

> 'Suddenly one was a somebody, part of a better class of people, on a higher level – a German. Consecration permeated the German nation.'
>
> Horst Krueger, A Crack in the Wall

had its turn on the stage of world history. Their wives waited in queues at the post office and told neighbours it was their maternal duty to adopt children now that so many German mothers were having babies for the Fatherland.

After Hitler annexed Austria, many Germans were convinced that the Führer had been sent to them by God. Some dutifully cut his sayings out of the newspaper so they could discuss them with their family and friends. Hitler's territorial acquisitions, won against all expectations, had given the people faith in Providence and divine justice.

Myth of the persecuted people

According to Krueger, many Germans of his generation did not want to admit to their involvement with the Nazis. Straight after the Second World War, they claimed to have been a persecuted people who had been intimidated by the 'brown terror' of the SA and frightened into compliance by the 'night and fog' decrees which had given the Gestapo the right to drag suspects off in the middle of the night, never to be seen again. Twenty years later, those who had enthusiastically waved their swastika banners at the processions of Nazi storm troopers claimed to have been resistance fighters – secret agents who had gone into 'inner emigration'; sly foxes who had 'only pretended to go along in order to prevent worse'.

Some historians endorsed this revisionist view to relieve the nation of its burden of collective responsibility. Said Krueger: 'They make everything so intelligible . . . all except one point: why the Germans loved this man, why they honestly rejoiced at his coming, why they died for him by the millions.'

Krueger remembers that his neighbours were 'honest believers, enthusiasts, inebriates', but they were never Nazis. The real Nazis were, at most, five per cent of the population. They were largely made up of unskilled workers and the unemployed, who would have returned to obscurity had not the decent Germans in Eichkamp and throughout Germany not put at their disposal 'all the native energy, industriousness, faith and skills they possessed'. These honest citizens were proud of what Hitler had made of them, but they did not seem to realize that it was they who had created him. There would have been no need for the Gestapo or storm troopers if someone had tried to assassinate Hitler in 1938. The common people would have executed the potential assassin on the spot.

Over a few short years, Krueger witnessed the gradual transformation of his friends and neighbours from law-abiding citizens to enthusiastic supporters of the regime. None of them was likely to have been swept up in the euphoria of a mass rally or carried along in the wake of a torchlight procession. They had simply convinced themselves that life was better under Hitler and they hoped the rumours of war were no more than malicious gossip.

As Krueger admitted, 'I am the typical child of those innocuous Germans who were never Nazis, and without whom the Nazis would never have been able to do their work. That's how it is.'

His parents 'lived on illusions', for his mother saw Hitler as the artist who had made good. As a devout Catholic, she could not imagine that a leader who had been born into her faith would not put the interests of his people first. Hitler did not tell lies, he did not want war. But when war came and Krueger was sent to the Russian front, his parents became changed people. As they waved him goodbye at the train station they looked hungry, exhausted and fearful, 'like addicts suffering abrupt withdrawal'. They had been believers, but by October 1944 Krueger's father, who had never joined the party and had never understood his neighbour's enthusiasm for Hitler, was openly blaming the Nazis for betraying them: 'The bastards, the criminals, what have they done to us? After the war, we'll all be carted off to Russia.'

However, in 1945, when Krueger became a prisoner of war, the relentless resolve that had kept him sane and alive through five years of conflict deserted him. Krueger and his comrades had been born in Hitler's Germany. They grew up under the Nazis and were indoctrinated all their lives. Hitler not only conquered Europe, he also conquered the spirit of the German people. Although one day Hitler would surely be defeated, Krueger felt certain his generation would not be there to see it. They wouldn't have the strength to survive the coming struggle with the Allies. The war would go on and on – maybe for 30 years or more – and they would all die for Hitler, never having had the chance to know any other kind of life.

> 'Suddenly one was a somebody, part of a better class of people, on a higher level – a German. Consecration permeated the German nation.'
>
> Horst Krueger

Even the German language had been stolen by the Nazis. Nothing in the newspapers could be accepted as the truth. It was only when Krueger read of the news of Hitler's death in a POW paper in May 1945 that he realized he was free. 'I could not believe that there was such a thing . . . a whole newspaper that wasn't made by the Nazis. A real German newspaper without hatred and oaths of allegiance and the reaffirmation of eventual German victory. It was like a miracle . . . German sentences against Hitler.'

From an American prison camp, Krueger wrote: 'For the first time I felt what the future actually is; hope that tomorrow will be better than today. A future – there never could have been such a thing under Hitler.'

JOSEF GOEBBELS

SPIN DOCTOR TO THE THIRD REICH

'We shall go down in history as the greatest statesmen of all time, or as the greatest criminals.'

Josef Goebbels, for whom National Socialism was a religion

According to Magda Goebbels' biographer Hans-Otto Meissner, Josef Goebbels had no particular hatred for the Jews – in fact, he hated almost everyone. And the feeling was reciprocated: as a child, he was shunned by other children partly because of his physical deformity, but also because he abhorred company.

GETTING HIS OWN BACK

At the age of seven he had been diagnosed with osteomyelitis (inflammation of the bone marrow) and had to have an operation which left him with a club foot and a permanent limp. It also meant he had to wear a brace. He made no effort to befriend other boys and actively deterred any efforts to include himself in social or family activities. He became withdrawn and sarcastic, using his sharp tongue instead of his fists to fend off abuse. Consequently, other children (and adults, too) kept their distance, leaving the boy more isolated than ever.

As his mother remarked, 'Since he was physically inferior he had to prove to others, as well as to himself, that he was more intelligent. He jumped at the chance to make sport of them, to criticize them, to scorn them.'

It was his nature to blame others for his misfortune – first God, to whom he had prayed for a miracle cure but who had abandoned him, and then his own mother, whose blind faith in Catholicism and the curative power of the saints had proven inadequate when her son needed it.

Having lost his faith in religion, the young Goebbels retreated inwards, finding strength in his own not inconsiderable intellect and then in the Fatherland. 'I always hoped he would believe in my Catholic God,' his mother said, 'but he simply believed in Germany.'

PUBLIC SPEAKER

Goebbels dreamed of tapping into the sacred spirit of the German people, like finding the Holy Grail of Arthurian myth. He thought he sensed that spirit in *völkisch* nationalism and the power of public speaking, which he discovered while studying literature and philosophy at Heidelberg university. As he said: 'Success is the important thing . . . I do not care if I give wonderful, aesthetically elegant speeches, or speak so that women cry. The point of a political speech is to persuade people of what we think right, to . . . conquer the broad masses. Propaganda should be popular, not intellectually pleasing.'

When war was declared in 1914, Goebbels volunteered, encouraged by his teachers and classmates who were inflamed with patriotic fever, but he knew his disability would preclude him from recruitment. Instead, he ploughed his energies and gift for public speaking into politics, ranting against the wealthy but not, it appears, the Jews. Until he came under Hitler's spell, anti-Semitism was not an obsession with Goebbels, who held his Jewish teachers in high regard. He freely admitted that he had learned much from Jewish authors and scientists, although he later allowed his own writings in praise of these men to be added to the pyres of burning books.

He came to believe in only two things – his own greatness and his devout cynicism. Success was not attained through talent or hard work, he believed, but through sheer willpower and a complete lack of scruples which saw the strongest and most self-centred survive.

Despite Goebbels' deformity, he was a notorious serial seducer who detailed his numerous affairs with young actresses in his voluminous diaries – which totalled 30,000 pages. As the Reich minister for public enlightenment and propaganda, he commanded the biggest 'casting couch' in Germany, determining which young women would be awarded parts in film, theatre and radio, a pursuit which earned him the nickname 'The Ram'. He cynically said, 'Man is and remains an animal. Here a beast of prey, there a house pet, but always an animal.'

FINDS HIS RELIGION

The day he witnessed Hitler speak, in June 1922, Goebbels found his new religion and from that moment onwards devoted his life to converting others to the cause. 'National Socialism is a religion,' he said. 'All we lack is a religious genius capable of uprooting outmoded religious practices and putting new ones in their place. We lack traditions and ritual. One day soon, National Socialism will be the religion of all Germans. My party is my church, and I believe I serve the Lord best if I do his will, and liberate my oppressed people from the fetters of slavery. That is my gospel.'

Dissenters from the Nazi belief system were treated without mercy, in a manner not dissimilar to that of the Spanish Inquisition 500 years earlier. The New Order threatened to be a new Dark Age, but this time it would be on a far greater, mechanized scale. Ideas that were not consistent with National Socialist ideology were held to be as dangerous as armed resistance. Goebbels believed that he who proclaimed his beliefs loudest and for longest would prevail, whether he spoke the truth or not. That was the principle behind propaganda and Goebbels was, for a time, the master: 'The most brilliant propagandist technique will yield no success unless one fundamental principle is borne in mind constantly – it must confine itself to a few points and repeat them over and over. . . . It is not propaganda's task to be intelligent, its task is to lead to success.'

CHAPTER 10

Springtime for Hitler

In the pre-war years, Hitler commanded the admiration of many foreign dignitaries and the grudging respect of his neighbours. While the USA and the rest of Europe languished in the Great Depression, Germany enjoyed unprecedented growth.

In 1933, the first year of Hitler's chancellorship, unemployment had been reduced by a third to just under four million. The following year, a further one million unemployed found jobs as part of a massive public works programme guaranteeing positions for hundreds of thousands of men who were drafted into the building of the first autobahns. Meanwhile, the construction programme of new government buildings in Berlin was ramped up as Hitler realized his ambition for a capital to rival Paris and New York.

Germanophilia

By the time the Olympic torch was ignited in Berlin in 1936, Germany was the envy of the world. Politicians, celebrities and members of the aristocracy posed for the newsreel cameras with broad smiles on their faces and voiced their enthusiasm for the new Germany. Charles Lindbergh, the Duke and Duchess of Windsor and even the young John Kennedy praised Herr Hitler, unaware of, or in some cases unconcerned with, the price that had been paid for such rapid progress.

The young JFK, no doubt influenced by his father, US ambassador Joe Kennedy (known to the Nazis as 'Germany's best friend in London'), wrote, 'I have come to the conclusion that fascism is right for Germany and Italy. What are the evils of fascism compared to communism?'

There was work, bread and hope. Confidence and self-assurance had replaced despondency and resentment about the punitive reparations and restrictions imposed by the Versailles Treaty. Some might have seen it as arrogance, but there was no denying that Germany was strong again. So strong, in fact, that the Western democracies adopted a policy of appeasement to placate the dictator in the hope that each concession would be their last. Those who knew never to trust a tyrant warned of the dangers of acquiescing to each successive demand and of forestalling their own preparations for a war that was inevitable.

However, in the second half of the decade Hitler exercised a fatal attraction for many, particularly impressionable young women, who saw only the superficial glamour and gaiety of Berlin, the picture-postcard scenery and the new spirit of optimism that was evident everywhere in the Reich.

A German education

During the 1930s many wealthy English parents sent their daughters to private finishing schools in Germany and many of the girls came back after six months singing the praises of the National Socialist state. One of those wide-eyed adolescents was the paternal grandmother of Rachel Johnson, sister of the future London mayor Boris Johnson, and another, coincidentally, was Rachel's future mother-in-law. Both women were at school in Munich at roughly the same time (April 1938) and witnessed the euphoria after Hitler had annexed Austria without a shot being fired.

While researching her novel *Winter Games*, Rachel Johnson interviewed a dozen English women who had been in Germany in the late 1930s and they all spoke of having the time of their lives. She revealed her findings to the German magazine *Der Spiegel*:

'It was a rich experience, because England was very stuffy at that time – lots of unemployment, terrible food and nasty weather. In Bavaria they had the crisp mountain air, a healthy life, the opera, the mountains and handsome Germans in uniform. They couldn't believe their luck! No chaperones, no parents. They had everything, including sex.'

She went on: 'Sending your daughters to finishing school in Germany was the thing to do. Germany was probably our closest European partner at that time. And don't forget that George V changed the name of his family from "Saxe-Coburg and Gotha" to "Windsor" only in 1917, during the First World War. There were still aristocratic connections and friendships to Germany between the wars [. . .] Some moved to Berlin or Dresden, but Bavaria with its mountains, castles, museums and beer cellars was more attractive. . . . My maternal grandmother was in Bavaria in the 1930s, she was Jewish. She enjoyed the opera in Munich, skiing in the mountains and later fell in love with a ski instructor from Freiburg, a member of the National Socialist party. His family called her "die Jüdin", the Jewess. Their relationship went disastrously wrong and she came back to England.'

Although there were occasional items in the national newspapers and questions in the Houses of Parliament to raise public awareness of the plight of refugees, there was what Rachel called a 'wilful blindness' to the abuse of human rights in Germany, at least among those who wouldn't hear a word against Herr Hitler. One of the elderly women Johnson interviewed told her, 'Hitler was marvellous, the problem was, he went a little bit too far.' Another told her about a Jewish music professor who suddenly vanished. His pupils simply accepted it.

UNITY MITFORD

HITLER'S ARISTOCRATIC STALKER

'A perfect example of Aryan womanhood.'

Adolf Hitler

The obsessive Unity Mitford became a cheerleader for the Nazi cause

Hitler had ardent admirers among the British aristocracy, the most notorious of whom was the society hostess Unity Mitford, daughter of Lord Redesdale. Her father had given Unity the middle name 'Valkyrie' in homage to his favourite opera, Wagner's *Die Walküre*.

As a teenager, Unity decorated her bedroom wall with newspaper cuttings and swastikas. She later disrupted communist meetings dressed in the black shirt of the fascists, giving the Hitler salute and heckling the speakers. In 1936, Unity's sister Diana married Oswald Mosley, leader of the British Union of Fascists, in the house of Josef Goebbels with Hitler in attendance. But Mosley found Unity's provocative 'exhibitionism' an embarrassment.

Unity heard Hitler speak at the 1933 Nuremberg rally and was determined to meet him in the hope of becoming his mistress. She learned which Munich café he went to every day and stalked him until he finally invited her to his table. 'It was the most wonderful and beautiful [day] of my life,' she told her father. 'I am so happy that I wouldn't mind a bit, dying. I'd suppose I am the luckiest girl in the world.'

SPURNED AFFECTIONS

Unity would have been sorely disappointed to learn that Hitler thought her 'plain' and 'sexless'. Elmar Streicher, son of the infamous Julius Streicher, editor of *Der Stürmer*, recalled: 'As a woman she was so very tall, you had to laugh to see it. She simply wasn't sexy. She was a virgin to the day of her death, I'd put my hand in the fire to say that.'

Hitler indulged Unity's flattery because it pleased him to be pursued by a member of the British aristocracy and he would have been impressed by the fact that her grandfather had translated his favourite book, Houston Stewart Chamberlain's racist diatribe, *The Foundations of the Nineteenth Century*, and been a close friend of his favourite composer, Richard Wagner.

Hitler believed that Unity would prove useful in influencing pro-German sympathizers back in Britain and she could also be deployed writing Nazi propaganda for British newspapers. But the Nazi hierarchy regarded her as a harmless lunatic and laughed behind her back at her habitual heel-clicking and saluting every time Hitler entered the room. Her grasp on reality was certainly lacking if her reaction to the murder of SA leader Roehm and hundreds of former associates in the 'Night of the Long Knives' was indicative of her true feelings: 'Poor, sweet Führer, he's having such a dreadful time.'

Denied of Hitler's attention, his live-in mistress, Eva Braun, confided her views on the besotted British socialite to her diary: 'She [Unity] is known as the Valkyrie and looks the part, including her legs. I, the mistress of the greatest man in Germany and the whole world, I sit here waiting while the sun mocks me through the window panes.' But Braun knew how to win her man back. She attempted suicide in May 1935 by swallowing an overdose of sleeping pills. This appealed to Hitler's sense of melodrama; he responded by distancing himself from Unity and devoting himself to Eva, allowing her to stay overnight at his Munich apartment. Yet Unity persisted, unwilling to be deprived of the man she had set her heart on, even though her feelings were not reciprocated.

ATTEMPTED SUICIDE

Unity's passion for fascism remained undiminished, and Hitler rewarded her for this with a gold party badge and a private box at the 1936 Olympic Games. Her activities, however, were frowned on by British Intelligence, who categorized her as being 'more Nazi than the Nazis'. Guy Lidell, head of MI5, noted that her conduct 'had come perilously close to high treason'.

Unity's embarrassing behaviour was curtailed when she attempted suicide on the day war was declared between Britain and Germany. She shot herself in the head with a pearl-handled pistol Hitler had given her; incredibly, she survived and was brought back to Britain as an invalid. When she was reunited with her family, Unity confessed: 'I thought you all hated me, but I don't remember why.' She died eight years later, on 28 May 1948, apparently from an infection of the brain as a result of her self-inflicted wound.

Guy Lidell suspected that the story of her botched suicide was a convenient cover: 'We had no evidence to support the press allegations that she was in a serious state of health and it might well be that she was brought in [to England] on a stretcher in order to avoid publicity and unpleasantness to her family.'

Goebbels on the role of women

On 18 March 1933, six weeks after Hitler's appointment as chancellor, Josef Goebbels was invited to open an exhibition celebrating women's contribution to contemporary society. At this occasion, he took the opportunity to reassure the women of Germany that their faith in National Socialism was not misplaced. He began by acknowledging that the party had aroused fierce criticism for discouraging women from entering politics and then, in a characteristic example of Nazi doublespeak, he justified their exclusion by saying it was not from lack of respect. Quite the contrary, the party respected women too much to allow them to waste their talents in a field that did not suit the female character. Women were not inferior, they simply had a different purpose than men.

If the partnership of men and women was to benefit the state, women would have to accept that the female virtues of loyalty, selfless devotion and self-sacrifice would need to be applied to those areas of employment best suited to their sex and not to those, such as politics and the military, which were the preserve of men.

Germany's recent troubles, he said, were to be blamed on the 'feminization' of men and the 'masculinization' of women, as the men in power had been reluctant to enforce the measures needed for fear of becoming unpopular. In short, the previous administration had not been tough enough. Now it was time for firmness and resolve, characteristics which did not come naturally to women.

What was perceived to be progress was not, in the opinion of the National Socialists, an improvement but a dangerous diversion which had given women false hope and distracted them from their natural vocation and duty – the nurturing of the family and the raising of children. Modern society was merely a façade, concealing the decline of the family and its traditional values.

Mothers of the nation

Women were not to think they were missing new opportunities in the workplace. Instead they were ensuring the future of the nation by raising its new citizens with a shared belief and vision. This was not to say that those without children or who were employed had less of a role as 'mothers of the nation'. And the responsibility of the state was to support women so that they could fulfil their role. Goebbels assured the listening women that 'the national revolutionary government is anything but reactionary'. It was not opposed to progress; it assumed responsibility for its citizens by encouraging them to put their energies and abilities into their natural roles. More rights did not necessarily mean that women would be better off. The right to stand for public office would be a bad deal if it meant the quality of women's lives was diminished because they'd lost the opportunity to be mothers.

Goebbels had succeeded in appealing to women's emotions. Now he strove to appeal to their patriotic duty by reminding them that the German birth rate had declined. In the major cities he claimed it had fallen from two million to one million at the turn of the century, and for the past 14 years the birth rate in Berlin had been the lowest of any European city. It was not simply a matter of economics; it signified a dilution or weakening of the nation's strength. Where there had been seven children to one elderly person in 1900, there would be a ratio of one to one if the current trend was to continue. As a question of national necessity and survival, the new government would encourage larger families, though precisely how this was to be implemented would be revealed in the coming months.

Lebensborn – sins of the fathers

The popular perception of the *Lebensborn* ('Spring of Life') project is that it was a chain of Nazi stud farms where SS supermen mated with perfect specimens of Aryan womanhood. Although this was certainly one aspect of the programme which was implemented and closely monitored by Heinrich Himmler, its main purpose was to increase the birth rate in the greater Reich and reduce the high abortion rate, which had reached 800,000 per year in the early 1930s.

Because there was no financial state support for the unemployed in Germany in the interwar years, unwed mothers were likely to choose to abort rather than give their babies up for adoption or attempt to raise the child as a single parent on charity. To undermine the socialists and discourage emigration, Bismarck had introduced limited financial incentives for the working man, but single women were forced to find work or seek help from their families or charitable organizations.

In 1939, Himmler wrote to Field Marshal Keitel: 'According to statistics there are 600,000 abortions a year in Germany. The fact that these happen among the best German racial types has been worrying me for years. The way I see it we cannot afford to lose these young people, hundreds and thousands of them. The aim of protecting this German blood is of the highest priority. If we manage to stop these abortions we will be able to have 200 more German regiments every year on the march. Another 500,000 or 600,000 people could produce millions of marks for the economy. The strength of these soldiers and workers will build the greater Germany. This is why I founded *Lebensborn* in 1936. It fights abortions in a positive way. Every woman can have her child in peace and quiet and devote her life to the betterment of the race.'

When it was founded, in 1935, the stated aim of the *Lebensborn* organization was to support 'racially and genetically valuable families with many children'. Approximately 60 per cent of the women who were offered a bed in the new maternity wards were unwed mothers, who received the highest standard of care and the opportunity to give their babies up for adoption if they chose not to raise them themselves. The clinics even offered an SS christening with the children receiving a blessing under an SS dagger engraved with the motto 'My oath is loyalty', while the mother pledged allegiance to the party. The service was provided primarily for women who had become pregnant by married SS men. And there had been an increase in their numbers since high-ranking Nazis had been encouraged by Reichsführer Himmler to sire as many Aryan sons as they could. But the high standards of clinical care and privacy also made the *Lebensborn* clinics the first choice for expectant Nazi officers' wives.

Suffering the stigma

There was, however, a more sinister side to the *Lebensborn* 'adoption' programme.

In the occupied territories, local girls who became pregnant with the illegitimate child of a German soldier were left to raise the child alone after the war and endure the accusations and wrath of their neighbours, who damned them as Nazi whores and collaborators. The child would grow up not only with the stigma of illegitimacy, but also with the anxiety of not knowing the identity of their father, who they feared might have been a war criminal.

Some of these children endured abuse in institutions and in school if their teachers and classmates suspected they were 'Nazi bastards'. Many innocent children suffered a degree of mistreatment at the hands of their own countrymen similar to that meted out to non-Aryan children by the Nazis themselves.

There were 13 *Lebensborn* clinics in Germany and Austria, nine in Norway and others in France, Belgium, the Netherlands, Poland and Luxembourg. In Norway, German soldiers were urged to seduce women of 'Viking' blood, with the result that there were scores of *Lebensborn* children left to the mercy of the country's authorities once the war was over. Some of these children were confined in mental asylums, because Norwegians feared that they might contaminate Scandinavian blood through interracial relationships, and raise a new generation of Nazi sympathizers.

Abduction

In all, 8,000 babies were delivered in *Lebensborn* clinics in Germany and 12,000 in Norway. But this wasn't enough for Himmler, who ordered the SS to abduct blond, blue-eyed children from their parents in the occupied territories and send them for Aryanization by German foster families.

Folker Heinecke was a toddler when the advancing German army overran his parents' village in Crimea. He has no memories of his real parents and grew up with 'fanatical' Nazi foster parents whom he nevertheless learned to love. He eventually accepted that he was an orphan, but in his late sixties was desperate to find the grave of his birth parents so that he could finally feel he had come home. He managed to identify them and the name of their village through documents held by a Red Cross tracing centre.

> '*I don't want to end up as many of the other children like me have, driven bitter and mad over what befell them.*'
>
> Folker Heinecke, who was abducted as a toddler for the Lebensborn 'adoption' programme

Folker said: 'I stood there and tried to imagine the SS advancing down here, their tanks and their motorbikes and their armoured cars, and I tried to imagine them taking a little boy who was guilty of nothing . . . I just want to know who I was and what I might have been if things hadn't turned out the way they did. I have to keep searching to find something that might lead me to who my parents really were and where they are buried. Then I will have done my duty as a son. I will have honoured my real parents.'

Salon Kitty

Salon Kitty was a high-class Berlin brothel used by the Nazi intelligence service for spying purposes during the Second World War. While, on the one hand, the Nazis advocated marriage, motherhood and fidelity, on the other they thought nothing of forcing German women to have anonymous sex with Nazi officers and prominent party bosses.

Madame Kitty ran a first-class establishment on the third floor at number 11 Giesebrechtstrasse in Charlottenburg, a wealthy district of Berlin. The apartments had been refurbished to the highest standard, but what its clientele did not know was that there were new features behind the elegant façade. The walls had been fitted with concealed microphones which relayed every whisper and unguarded conversation to wax disc recording devices in the basement, which were manned by Gestapo agents.

In 1939, SS Gruppenführer Reinhard Heydrich was entrusted with tracing the source of high level leaks which threatened to give Germany's enemies warning of attacks on Belgium, France and the Netherlands, planned for the following spring. If the enemy had even the faintest suspicion of the *blitzkrieg* that was to be launched through the Ardennes, they might divert troops to thwart it. But how to identify which high-ranking army officers and diplomats couldn't be trusted to keep the secret? The problem was handed over to SS-Obersturmführer Walter Schellenberg, chief of the SD, the Reich Intelligence service.

By all accounts, Schellenberg was something of a prude, but he knew that the prospect of impressing an attractive woman was almost certain to loosen men's tongues. And there was no better place to eavesdrop than in the bedroom of a brothel, especially one closely monitored by the SD and operated by prostitutes trained to draw out significant details. Certainly, after hostilities had broken out it was important to monitor the political allegiances of prominent businessmen and military officers, to ensure that their loyalty could be relied upon.

The original plan was to install a few bugging devices in a brothel that was known to attract diplomats and military personnel, and then trust to luck. But shortly after Schellenberg had been given the task he was informed that the owner of the most prestigious brothel in Berlin was taking early retirement and might be persuaded to reopen her doors – in return for her freedom.

RECALLED FROM RETIREMENT

Kitty Schmidt had amassed a small fortune and managed to smuggle most of it abroad, where it was accruing interest in a British bank account. But she had been under surveillance by the Gestapo. On 28 June 1939, Kitty was arrested at the German/Dutch border and driven back to Gestapo headquarters in Berlin. There she was interrogated by Schellenberg and presented with damning evidence of her currency smuggling and use of false documents, all of which carried lengthy prison sentences. She could escape prosecution if she agreed to co-operate. She had no choice but to agree. The deal was that her Berlin apartments would be renovated to allow the installation of bugging devices and film cameras and 20 new girls would be employed, handpicked by Berlin's vice squad under the direction of Untersturmführer Karl Schwarz. While builders tore down the interior walls and bricked off the basement in Giesebrechtstrasse, the police raided night clubs and brothels throughout the city, bringing in more than a thousand girls to be questioned by a team of academics and psychiatrists, who helped eliminate those they considered 'emotionally unreliable'.

After seven days of intensive interviews, the 20 most suitable girls were selected. The successful candidates were taken to Ordensburg, the officers' academy at Sonthofen in the Bavarian Alps, where they spent almost two months learning foreign languages, along with current affairs, the use of codes, how to identify military insignia, and how to elicit information without arousing suspicion.

By March 1940, Salon Kitty was open for business. Madame Schmidt had been told to keep her regular girls for existing customers and to show a photo album of the new recruits only to clients who used the code, 'I come from Rothenburg'. These clients would then be provided with chilled champagne and other refreshments while they waited ten minutes for the girl to arrive.

In the first year of business, an estimated 10,000 men took advantage of Salon Kitty's services. Three thousand recordings were made, of which the most damning was by Mussolini's son-in-law, Count Galeazzo, in which he joked about how he and Il Duce ridiculed Hitler in private. More significantly, when Nazi Foreign Minister Joachim von Ribbentrop invited his Spanish counterpart Don Ramón Serrano Súñer to Giesebrechtstrasse, Súñer let slip his country's intentions to occupy Gibraltar. As the Rock was important for securing the German supply route to North Africa, this was strategically vital information which the Nazis were able to act upon just in time.

In July 1942, Allied bombing demolished the upper floors of Salon Kitty and the clients stopped coming. When Madame Kitty reopened on the ground floor, those who braved the Allied air raids were of little interest to the SD and they eventually handed the house back to Kitty with the warning that if she breathed a word of what had occurred there she would not live to see the end of the war. Kitty died in 1954, at the age of 71, without betraying the confidence of her clients. The 25,000 discs recorded in the basement at number 11 Giesebrechtstrasse were never found.

CHAPTER 11
Hitler's Women

From his formative years as the son of an authoritarian Austrian customs official and an over-indulgent mother, to his death in the besieged underground bunker beneath the Reichschancellery in Berlin in April 1945, Adolf Hitler sought unconditional devotion and emotional reassurance from women. At the same time he restricted the role of women in the Third Reich to almost medieval status, as embodied in the maxim '*Kinder, Küche und Kirche*' ('children, kitchen and church').

Under the Nazis, women were excluded from politics and discouraged from pursuing careers. The number of female students in further education was severely restricted and wages for employed women remained significantly lower than those of men. Yet the women of Germany voted for Hitler in huge numbers, reaching out to touch him during his stage-managed public appearances like the besotted fans of a glamorous movie star and weeping tears of joy if they were permitted into the presence of their beloved Führer.

'The weaker sex'

Hitler encouraged this adoration and demanded that women sacrifice their personal ambitions to serve their men, who would restore Germany's honour after the humiliating defeat of the First World War. In Hitler's mind, men were made for war and women were 'the weaker sex'. Their sole purpose was to tend the home, serve their husbands and produce blond, blue-eyed Aryan babies to fill the ranks of Germany's invincible military machine. Later, those young women selected for the SS *Lebensborn* breeding programme would not even be required to marry their state-selected Aryan mates.

Women not enticed into motherhood were viewed either as purely decorative specimens for men to flatter and fawn over, like the trophy wives and mistresses of the Nazi leaders, or playthings to be used by any man who desired them. There were only a few women who defied these Nazi stereotypes; one such was the film-maker Leni Riefenstahl (see page 306), who was fiercely independent but remained in thrall to Hitler until her death. Another was the test pilot Hanna Reitsch, who the Führer regarded as someone who had overcome the disadvantages of her sex to become the archetypal Wagnerian heroine.

Hitler's perception of women was that they were physically and intellectually inferior to men because they were impulsive, emotional creatures. The masses, male and female, could be seduced and manipulated by the power of Hitler's oratory because he believed that their collective will was feminine by nature and therefore susceptible to an appeal to their emotions.

Married to the Reich

Despite his views on female subservience, Hitler apparently refused all opportunities for intimacy throughout his turbulent life, claiming he was married to the Reich and would lose the adoration of his female followers if he married. Only in his final hours, when he had accepted defeat, did Hitler consent to marry his devoted mistress Eva Braun and allow her to die by his side. By then his health was failing and his mental faculties were impaired by a cocktail of drugs prescribed by his physician Dr Morell, known by Hitler's aides as 'the Reichsmaster of injections' and 'a quack'. A week earlier, Hitler had told Braun, dietician Constanze Manziarly and loyal secretaries Traudl Junge and Gerda Christian, that he wished his generals were as brave as they. These women had refused all offers to escape the capital while there was still a chance. But although he demonstrated a condescending respect for women, Hitler refused to entrust them with a significant role in the defence of the Reich.

Hitler's refusal to permit the deployment of women into the munitions factories and other essential services proved fatal to the Nazis, as it undermined Germany's ability to halt the Russian offensive. His promise to honour the mothers and daughters of the nation for their part in Germany's regeneration ended in betrayal and in the destruction of both the family and the Fatherland.

Thoughts of suicide

Hitler's volatile and turbulent nature had manifested itself after he became infatuated with a pretty young blonde he saw window-shopping in Linz with her mother in the winter of 1906. Her name was Stefanie Jansten (see page 35). The adolescent infatuation soon took a more morbid turn, with Adolf threatening to kidnap the girl and elope with her. When he realized he couldn't afford to keep his beloved in the manner to which she was accustomed, he contemplated a suicide pact in which they would jump hand in hand into the cold, dark waters of the Danube. 'Once more, a plan was thought up, in all its details,' Hitler's friend Kubizek confided in his autobiography. 'Every single phase of the horrifying tragedy was minutely described.'

To placate Hitler, Kubizek offered to find out all he could; where Stefanie lived, who she lived with and, most importantly of all, if she was involved with anyone else. When Kubizek asked why Hitler didn't simply talk to her himself, he was told that 'extraordinary human beings' like Stefanie and himself had no need of conventional forms of communication, but intuitively understood each other – they shared the same feelings and outlook without having to discuss it. When his friend expressed his doubts, Hitler flew into a rage. It wasn't the first or the last tirade Kubizek had to suffer during this fantasy affair.

Kubizek discovered that Stefanie's mother was a widow and they lived in nearby Urfahr. Her brother was a law student studying in Vienna and Stefanie loved to dance. It was the latter which sent Hitler off on another rant. How dare Kubizek suggest that he demean himself by engaging in public displays of dancing? He would never humiliate himself by engaging in such activities. 'Visualize a crowded ballroom and imagine you are deaf,' said Hitler. 'You can't hear the music to which these people are moving, and then take a look at their senseless progress, which leads nowhere. Aren't these people raving mad?' When he and Stefanie were married, she wouldn't have the desire to dance – Hitler was certain of that.

Kubizek had learned one more fact, which he shared with his volatile friend. Stefanie's real surname was Isak (or Rabatsch according to certain sources) and, though there is no evidence that she was Jewish, Hitler assumed she was. It didn't make the slightest difference to him at the time. He would find a way round it when the day came for them to announce their engagement. Of course, he never summoned up the courage to speak to her and some years later she married a young army officer and moved to Vienna.

Fear of intimacy

If Kubizek's account of their forays into Vienna's red light district is to be believed, sex held a morbid fascination for Hitler. One evening, after the pair had been to see Frank Wedekind's scandalous play *Spring Awakening*, with its scenes of rape and homosexuality, Hitler suggested they explore the back streets of the city. He described these as the 'cesspool of iniquity', where the prostitutes' shameless attempts to entice the two men to spend a few marks left him incensed and led to yet another lecture on syphilis and the dangers of consorting with such creatures.

One publication Hitler devoured advocated sexual abstinence for young men to preserve their strength in readiness for the coming conflict which would surely test their manhood to the extreme. *Unadulterated German Words* encouraged Austrian youth to stop eating meat because it reputedly stimulated the sex drive. Hitler consequently became a vegetarian and now had a patriotic excuse for shying away from the opposite sex, specifically women of loose morals, who were accused of corrupting and infecting Aryan males with racial and sexual disorders.

It is likely that Hitler's lifelong abhorrence of sex was psychological. As a child, he had witnessed his father forcing himself on his mother (an incident he described in *Mein Kampf*) and thereafter regarded sex as 'dirty' or something only animals indulge in. That long-repressed memory, together with the experience of being beaten then comforted, might have generated a sado-masochistic nature which, it has been alleged, characterized his later relationship with his niece Geli Raubal – who was apparently driven to take her own life because of her Uncle Adolf's 'unnatural demands'.

Beginnings of anti-Semitism

One of the last times Kubizek saw his friend was when Hitler arrived unexpectedly at the flat they shared in Vienna and found Kubizek with someone he assumed was his girlfriend. She was, in fact, his pupil, but Kubizek's reassurances did not mollify Hitler, who flew into another tirade in which he derided his friend's efforts to educate a woman.

Hitler never spoke to Kubizek again. He moved out soon afterwards and drifted aimlessly through the Austrian capital, selling watercolours to the tourists and living on a modest inheritance. He soon came under the influence of extreme nationalists such as Georg Ritter von Schönerer, leader of the German Nationalist party. Schönerer took the title 'Führer' and espoused a hatred for all foreigners in his virulently anti-Semitic and anti-Catholic pamphlets, which Hitler read with a growing interest. In a speech to the Vienna Parliament in 1887, Schönerer said: 'Our anti-Semitism is not directed against the Jews' religion. It is directed against their racial characteristics . . . everywhere they are in league with the forces of rebellion. . . . Therefore every loyal son of his nation must see in anti-Semitism the greatest national progress of this century.'

Such inflammatory sentiments were not confined to the lunatic fringe, but given widespread publicity in the pages of *Deutsches Volksblatt*, the rabidly anti-Semitic Viennese newspaper, and in a plethora of racist and semi-pornographic literature. This included *Ostara*, which featured the ramblings of the *völkisch* 'mystics' Guido von List and Lanz von Liebenfels. Their theories regarding the antediluvian origins of the Aryan master race were lapped up by the young Hitler. They also addressed his favourite fixations – syphilis and the dangers of women's rights – which he later expounded upon in considerable detail in *Mein Kampf*. *Ostara* was particularly reviled for its lurid stories of virtuous Aryan maidens seduced by malevolent Jews, but it enjoyed a wide circulation among those who wanted to satisfy both their violent sexual fantasies and their anti-Semitic prejudices.

It was in Hitler's nature to blame others for his troubles and Schönerer and his ilk had identified a convenient scapegoat for all of Austria's problems. Anti-Semitism had been endemic in Austrian society for decades, and now those so inclined saw Jews everywhere – the wealthy ones running the financial institutions and the poor orthodox Hasidim haggling in the streets, looking distinctly alien with their long black coats and traditional ringlets.

Hitler had finally found a focus for his resentment and a justification for his bigotry. However, it is curious that he was often mistaken for a Jew himself, and was teased by Reinhold Hanisch, a youthful acquaintance he lived with in a hostel for the destitute in Vienna: 'Hitler wore a long coat he had been given . . . and an increasingly greasy derby hat on the back of his head. His hair was long and tangled and he grew a beard on his chin such as we Christians seldom have, though one is not uncommon on Leopoldstadt or the Jewish ghetto. . . . Hitler at that time looked very Jewish so that I often joked with him that he must be of Jewish blood.'

Female admirers

Hitler's notoriety following the failed Munich Putsch earned him a growing band of female followers. His imprisonment at Landsberg gave him the status, in the eyes of some, of a persecuted freedom fighter.

Following the putsch, Hitler had been arrested at the home of one of his new admirers, Frau Helene Hanfstaengl. Helene was the American wife of an early Nazi supporter, Ernst Hanfstaengl, who later became Hitler's foreign press officer (although he subsequently became a fierce critic of the Nazis in general). Shortly before the police arrived, Hitler picked up his revolver and, after brandishing it like a ham actor in a bad melodrama, declared his intention to shoot himself. Helene intervened and snatched the gun from his hand:

'Think of all your loyal followers who believe in you,' she chided. 'How can you forsake all those good people who share your ideal of saving your country while you take your own life?' Hitler then buried his face in his hands and sobbed while Helene hid the gun in a barrel of flour in the kitchen.

'Munich Muttis'

Helene's son Egon said that his mother felt sorry for Hitler, particularly after he fell on one knee and confessed that if she hadn't been married and he didn't have his destiny to fulfil he would have married her, as she was his ideal. When she told her husband of the incident she reassured him that Hitler was no threat to his manhood as he was 'a neuter'. Her husband was of the opinion that, 'What Hitler is looking for in a woman is half-mother and half-sweetheart.'

It was a logical assessment, for a string of matronly admirers visited Hitler during the nine months he spent in confinement, bringing him home-made cakes and other delicacies. These were the 'Munich Muttis', ladies who perceived loneliness and suffering in his large, piercing blue eyes, and who wanted to mother him. Helene Hanfstaengl's sister-in-law, Erna, was seduced by this apparent helplessness, but later realized that 'these trivialities in clothing and behaviour' were 'calculated for effect'.

Ernst Hanfstaengl compared the scene at Landsberg to 'a delicatessen. There was fruit and there were flowers, wine and other alcoholic beverages, ham, sausage, cake, boxes of chocolates and much more'.

> 'This is the end – I will never let those swine take me. I will shoot myself first.'
>
> Adolf Hitler on his arrest following the Munich Putsch

Remarking of Hitler, the prison warden Otto Leybold remembered: 'He was always reasonable, frugal, modest and polite to everyone, especially the officials at the facility' and 'submitted willingly to all restrictions', but he refused to rise before noon or to take exercise. The only activity he indulged in was to pace the room overlooking the River Lech while dictating his manifesto *Mein Kampf* to his personal secretary Rudolf Hess.

Hitler's benefactors

The prison records show that Hitler received more than 300 visitors during his incarceration, among whom were General von Ludendorff, the First World War veteran who had been acquitted of his involvement in the failed coup, various Munich politicians and members of Hitler's inner circle such as Nazi 'philosopher' Alfred Rosenberg and Captain Ernst Roehm, leader of the SA.

Also listed among the prisoner's many 'benefactors' were several wealthy middle-aged women.

Viktoria von Dirksen

Viktoria von Dirksen was a fashionable Berlin hostess, the widow of the man who had built the city's underground system, and stepmother of the German ambassador to Moscow. She and Hitler were close friends in the early years of the movement, although she later became a fearless critic of the party and disagreed with him over the role of Crown Prince Wilhelm. While Hitler was vehemently opposed to a man he considered an 'unprincipled opportunist', Viktoria wished to see the prince installed as monarch. She nevertheless donated a large portion of her late husband's fortune to fund the Nazi party's electoral campaigns.

Elsa Bruckmann

Equally generous was Elsa Bruckmann (born Princess Cantacuzene of Romania), who was married to the Munich publisher Hugo Bruckmann. She introduced Hitler to wealthy industrialists and influential members of the aristocracy at her sumptuous Munich salon. In 1926 the Nazi party was on the brink of bankruptcy, a desperate situation which impelled Hitler once more to contemplate taking his own life. At the last minute, Elsa intervened. She sent Hitler a note enclosing her wristwatch and inviting him to choose any furniture he might like to furnish his private apartment. When she learned he had been threatened with eviction for failing to pay his rent and that his party was in dire financial need, she persuaded her husband to settle Hitler's personal debts and put their villa at his disposal. She then arranged a four-hour meeting with industrialist Emil Kirdof, who agreed to pay off the party's creditors and guaranteed substantial campaign contributions for the coming year.

Frau Bruckmann was the first of many female admirers who offered their jewellery and other valuables to secure loans for the future Führer. A contemporary record notes that Herr Hitler had deposited 'an emerald pendant with platinum and diamonds . . . a diamond ring (solitaire) . . . a red silk Spanish cover for a grand piano . . . ' The latter was probably a gift from Helena Bechstein, wife of the piano manufacturer, who bought Hitler a new Mercedes for 26,000 marks.

Elsa bought Hitler clothes and the rhino whip that became his trademark in the 1920s, until he was persuaded it was not a fitting accessory for an aspiring politician to be seen brandishing in public. The Bruckmanns also brokered the purchase of the Nazi party Munich headquarters, the Brown House on Brienner Strasse, for 1.5 million marks. This sum was raised with the aid of wealthy industrialists who were attracted to the party because they saw in Hitler 'the strong man' the country needed to crush the Bolsheviks and dismantle the unions. In the course of a year, the party acquired the backing of industrial heavyweights including the mining and steel magnate Fritz Thyssen, the steel baron Emil Gansser, the industrialist Werner von Siemens, and the board of Daimler. These illustrious supporters ensured that Hitler found a sympathetic audience for his speeches in major German cities and was no longer confined to the back-street beer halls of Bavaria.

Helena Bechstein

Helena Bechstein did more than just buy Hitler a Mercedes. She and her husband, Edwin, introduced him to their high society friends in Berlin and Bavaria and invited him to their villa in the Obersalzberg. Hitler was so impressed with the villa that he asked if they could help him buy a property in the area. 'Haus Wachenfeld' became Hitler's mountain sanctuary. He renamed it 'The Berghof' and proceeded to undertake extensive renovations, including the installation of the famous 'picture window' which ran the entire length of one wall and provided a panoramic view of the mountains.

Frau Bechstein later offered her jewellery as surety against a loan of 60,000 Swiss francs when the Nazi party needed additional funds. She also went so far as to pose as Hitler's mother in order to visit her imprisoned 'Wolf'. She developed this pet name for Hitler when she was expecting him to marry her 'plain-looking' daughter, Lottie. However, as soon as Hitler made it clear he would not be proposing to Lottie, Frau Bechstein lost her enthusiasm for politics.

Carola Hoffman

Carola Hoffman, the 61-year-old widow of a schoolteacher, had no ulterior motive. She had been an early supporter of the party and was happy to offer Hitler a home in the quiet suburb of Solln, which he used as an unofficial party headquarters on his release. For a time he regarded her as a substitute for the mother he had lost, addressing postcards to her as *'mein wertvoll kleine Mutter'* ('my precious little mother').

Winifred Wagner

Another avid admirer was Winifred Wagner, the British-born wife of the composer's son, Siegfried, who was dissatisfied with her effete husband's lack of attention and longed to find fulfilment with someone else. She and Hitler met in 1923 and although her initial impression was that he was 'rather common' (he often wore traditional Bavarian lederhosen, which the upper class would have considered only suitable for peasants), she took it upon herself to bring him on. He had every reason to resent being patronized – being taught how to hold his knife and fork, how to choose the right wine and not sweeten it with sugar and how to dress for the occasion instead of wearing a clash of colours to make an impression – but instead she found him a willing pupil.

Hitler may have been unsophisticated and poorly educated, but he was astute enough to realize that ingratiating himself with powerful people would be extremely beneficial. Besides, he had a talent for playing the deferential servant, though many found his habitual heel-clicking and hand-kissing a bit much. Winifred bought him clothes, and instructed him in the correct way to behave in polite society, the rules of dinner table etiquette and the value of small talk.

Winifred's husband's disapproval gave her further reason to persist in her re-education of the awkward and rather coarse working class 'fraud and upstart' (as Siegfried described him). Within a few months it was said that Hitler was seriously contemplating marriage in the belief that the union of their two names would ensure the adulation of the masses. Unaware of Hitler's aversion to romance, Winifred sent him food parcels while he was in prison and visited him regularly in Munich.

After becoming a widow in 1930, she made sure she was seen in his company so that the press and the gossip-mongers would be kept speculating about when the wedding might be announced. But after his appointment as chancellor, Hitler thought better of it and they remained merely 'good friends'. She called him *'mein Wölfchen'* (my little wolf) and would scold him when he had done something she disapproved of, while, according to Ernst Hanfstaengl, he stood shamefaced 'like a naughty schoolboy' and said nothing.

'He was a frequent visitor at Wahnfried, the Wagner home,' remembered Hanfstaengl, 'and there were many rumours that he would marry Winifred after her husband died. She perhaps came closer to fulfilling his ideal of half-mother and half-sweetheart than any other woman of whom we have any knowledge.'

Sexual relations

Ernst Hanfstaengl was also the source of rumours concerning Hitler's relationship with Henriette Hoffmann, the wayward daughter of the party's official photographer, Heinrich Hoffmann. She subsequently married Baldur von Schirach, leader of the Hitler Youth. According to Hanfstaengl: 'Henny, too, was a blonde and one of very questionable reputation. . . . Many extraordinary stories have been circulated in party circles about Hitler's relations with Henny. According to one of the most popular stories, Hitler had once obliged Henny to have very abnormal sexual relations with him. The nature of these relations was not specified, but it was said that later Henny . . . had told her father the entire story. Thereupon her father . . . had used Henny's story in order to blackmail Hitler.'

Whatever this 'abnormal' practice was, it could not have been mere rumour as it was referred to by several of Hitler's closest confidants usually in connection with the apparent suicide of Hitler's niece Geli Raubal (see page 186) in 1931, the mystery of which was never satisfactorily explained.

Otto Strasser, whose account must be read with suspicion as he fell out with Hitler and was expelled from the party in 1930, wrote: 'Like all others in the know, I had heard all about the eccentric practices to which Fraulein Hoffmann was alleged to have lent herself, but I had genuinely believed that the photographer's daughter was a little hysteric who told lies for the sheer fun of it. But Gely, who was completely ignorant of this other affair of her uncle's, confirmed point by point a story scarcely credible to a healthy-minded man.'

Another account, which must be regarded with equal suspicion, is published in the lurid exposé *Inside Information* (1940) by Hansjürgen

Koehler (believed to be the pen name of Franz Heinrich Pfeiffer, a former SS officer who fled Germany in 1935 and wrote a series of sensationalist anti-Nazi books). Koehler states: 'As a young girl [Henny] lived with her father in close proximity to Hitler. She was extremely pretty and attractive, and it appears that Hitler was in love with her for a while. But Hitler's make-up . . . prevented him from making normal approaches to her. So Henny was very soon disgusted and turned her attentions elsewhere like his earlier flames. . . . I had occasion to live for some months under the same roof as Hitler, and I have repeatedly noticed how susceptible the Leader was to pretty women and how quickly and skilfully he withdrew after his first advances.'

Koehler goes on to claim that Hitler had been engaged to the sister of his first chauffeur in 1923. Her name was Jenny Haug: 'Hitler was already conscious of his perversion which excluded the possibility of consummation, so although he courted her and took her out frequently he politely took his leave at her door. Practical Jenny was by no means content with this merely superficial attachment, for she suspected that her swain must be intimate with some other woman and as a consequence shrank from making love to her more violently. Hitler was annoyed about this and soon broke off the engagement.'

Hitler is also said to have enjoyed a flirtation with Ada Klein, secretary for the Munich publisher Max Amann, in the late 1920s. She visited him alone at the Haus Wachenfeld and in Emil Maurice's rooms, where the chauffeur excused himself to give them privacy. Klein told Frau Schroeder that there had been no intimacy between them, but Hitler had told her that she made him light-headed and taught him 'how to kiss'.

Perversion

The perversion to which Koehler and the other former associates allude is thought to be of a sado-masochistic nature, but such topics were not considered fit to print in the national press at the time. Even homosexuality was alluded to with coy euphemisms, so Koehler had to expressly rule out the obvious assumption.

What that 'abnormality' might have been was made public knowledge in 1943. The Berlin columnist Bella Fromm wrote: 'I rather believe, and many people have felt the same way, that he is asexual, or perhaps impotent, finding a sexual sublimation through cruelty. They take private films of an especially gruesome nature in concentration camps. Films that only the Führer sees. These are rushed to him and shown, night after night. Occasionally Hitler's interest in a woman may be aroused; he may feel attracted by her charm, but that is all. His emotions culminate in a kind of jealousy caused by his sense of frustration, in the knowledge that he cannot respond normally.'

Hitler's close Jewish companion

Hitler's rabid anti-Semitism did not, apparently, prevent him from enjoying the company and attentions of operatic soprano Gretl Slezak, who was widely known to have a Jewish grandparent. Despite this, Gretl continued to star at the Deutsche Oper in Berlin, thanks to the Führer's patronage. Christa Schroeder recounts how Hitler looked forward to every meeting with her, when she would regale him with the latest theatrical scandals.

In March 1938, on the Sunday before the Anschluss, Gretl invited her infamous admirer to a private evening supper at her apartment on the Kurfürstendamm. She had furnished two large five-armed candelabras which she hoped would provide a suitably romantic setting. Sitting next to him on the sofa she stroked his hand, but he shrank away saying, 'Gretl, you know that I cannot allow that!'

> *'It must be stressed that the Leader is decidedly not a homosexual. All such rumours are based on the fact that it cannot be proved that he has had any normal relations with women. His sexual abnormality is of quite different a nature.'*
>
> Hansjürgen Koehler, Inside Information, 1940

Christa Schroeder was also present at this intimate dinner and although she left the room several times to give them privacy, she was certain that when Hitler left the apartment a couple of hours later, he had not given in to Gretl's advances. But Gretl would not give up hope and just before New Year 1939 gave Schroeder a letter to pass to her 'chief'.

The secretary didn't ask what it contained, but if Gretl was imploring Hitler to return her affections and trying to assure him of her discretion, it did not have the desired effect. As Schroeder noted, he could not have had a romantic relationship with a performer in the theatre because she would have used it to advance her career.

Did Hitler harbour unhealthy feelings towards his niece Geli?

GELI RAUBAL

FATAL ATTRACTION

'Geli was allowed to laugh at her Uncle Alf and adjust his tie when it had slipped.'

Baldur von Schirach

Hitler's one great love, other than his mother, was not his mistress Eva Braun, but his niece Geli Raubal. While Braun provided companionship, idle amusement and relief from boredom, Geli aroused a passion that was to have fatal consequences for her and threatened to end the career of the future Führer. Hitler's official photographer, Heinrich Hoffmann, believed that Geli's death affected him to the extent that from that day on he could never again feel affection for any human being.

Geli was the youngest daughter of Hitler's half-sister Angela, who had recently answered Hitler's summons to serve as his housekeeper in his new alpine retreat Haus Wachenfeld, on the Obersalzberg near Berchtesgaden. Hitler later bought the villa and had it extensively rebuilt, renaming it the Berghof. Angela believed Geli would benefit from the bracing alpine air and the company of a man who was expected to lead his party to victory in the regional elections.

At first 'Uncle Adolf' was merely attentive to the pretty girl with the peaches and cream complexion and the infectious smile. Geli was a cheerful, vivacious girl and she enjoyed flirting with Hitler's young Jewish driver, Emil Maurice. Emil recalled: 'He [Hitler] liked to show her off everywhere; he was proud of being seen in the company of such an attractive girl. He was convinced that in this way he impressed his comrades in the party, whose wives or girlfriends nearly all looked like washerwomen.' At 19, Geli was half Hitler's age. Geli's mother noticed that Hitler was spending more time with her daughter than with his party comrades and that he was intensely jealous whenever she showed interest in other men.

If Angela had any misgivings about the nature of their relationship – the furtive glances and unchaperoned long walks in the country – she kept it to herself. But soon the rows began, stemming from Adolf's refusal to allow Geli to live in Vienna and pursue a singing career.

Heinrich Hoffmann observed, 'He watched and gloated over her like some servant with a rare and lovely bloom, and to cherish and protect her was his one and only concern.' But it seemed his attentions were not welcome and his demands were driving her towards a nervous breakdown. Hitler's former friend Ernst Hanfstaengl may have been closer to the truth about their relationship when he blamed Geli's death on Hitler's 'twisted tenderness'.

Geli complained to her mother that she was under constant surveillance whenever her uncle was away and shadowed by his bodyguards on those rare occasions when he permitted her to visit the nearest town. His constant need to control her was suffocating and his insistence on choosing her clothes and the company she kept made her feel like a prisoner. Whenever they argued, his mask of doting docility fell away, revealing a ferocious jealousy which left Geli in tears. He demanded that she put such foolishness aside and assured her that he would furnish her with everything she needed after they moved to Munich. He had just purchased a luxury apartment for them there, using party funds. This seemed to mollify her for the time being and they resumed their walks in the country and trips to the town. She certainly enjoyed his loyalty and appreciated his many gifts.

A SHAMEFUL SECRET

Over time, Geli's happy-go-lucky nature wilted under Hitler's domineering personality. But Angela suspected that her daughter was tormented by a more shameful secret. According to Hitler biographer Konrad Heiden, a compromising letter written by Hitler to his niece fell into the hands of a potential blackmailer and had to be retrieved by a trusted priest, Father Bernard Staempfle. The contents of the letter were said to be so potentially damaging to Hitler's political career that the priest was murdered on the Night of the Long Knives in order to ensure his silence.

Heiden is of the opinion that in the letter Hitler admitted he needed Geli to satisfy his masochistic desires, but there is no actual proof of this. However, according to a book by Otto Strasser, there were rumours at the time that there was 'something very unusual' about their relationship and Hitler's demands proved 'unbearable' for Geli. She spoke of being desperately unhappy because she could not do 'what he wants me to'.

When confronted by Angela's anxieties about her daughter, Hitler assured her there was nothing for her to worry about, that Geli simply resented the fact he had forbidden her to pursue an operatic career.

ALLEGATIONS

One possible reason for Geli's fear was offered by Otto Strasser in an interview conducted by American psychiatrist Walter Langer of the OSS (Office of Strategic Services) in Montreal in 1943. Geli had apparently told Otto 'that Hitler made

> '. . . as they walked through the streets after the meal, Hitler emphasized some threat against his opponents by cracking the heavy dog whip he still affected. I happened to catch a glimpse of Geli's face as he did it, and there was on it such a look of fear and contempt that I almost caught my breath. Whips as well, I thought, and really felt sorry for the girl . . . I could not help feeling that her share in the relationship was under compulsion . . . there is no doubt that Hitler was deeply attached to her, although she acted very peculiarly towards him. She seemed to be rather cool towards him at times and manifested more fear towards him than fascination for him.'
>
> Ernst Hanfstaengl describing an incident between Hitler and Geli at the Schwarzwälder café

her undress and that he would lie down on the floor. Then she would have to squat down over his face where he could examine her at close range and this would make him very excited. . . . He demanded things from her that were simply disgusting. She had never dreamed that such things could happen. When I asked her to tell me, she described things I had previously encountered in my reading of Krafft-Ebing's *Psychopathia Sexualis* when I was a student.'

It is conceivable that Henny Hoffmann was pestered to do the same. Strasser made further allegations of a similar nature in relation to Hitler and Leni Riefenstahl, while film director Adolf Zeissler was told another story by actress Renate Müller. She described being invited for a private audience at the chancellery in 1933. While she was there, Hitler threw himself on the floor and pleaded with her to hit and kick him until he was aroused.

Some people will argue that these accusations are unfounded and no more than Allied propaganda, but it is unlikely that such strikingly similar stories would have been told by a number of individuals on different occasions. There is also the suspicious death of Müller herself, who became a morphine addict and was committed to a sanatorium after her career collapsed because it was discovered that she had a Jewish lover. When Müller saw four SS men stepping out of a car outside her room at the sanatorium she jumped from a window, falling 40 feet to her death, apparently to escape their questioning.

MYSTERIOUS DEATH

At 10 o'clock on the morning of 19 September 1931, Geli's lifeless body was found in her locked bedroom. She had died from a single gunshot which had narrowly missed her heart and entered her lung. Hitler's revolver lay on the floor and was swiftly disposed of by a loyal aide. An unfinished note was discovered nearby, addressed, it is assumed, to her lover, a music teacher in Vienna. It ended, 'When I come to Vienna – hopefully very soon – we'll drive together to Semmering an . . . ' This suggests that either she had been interrupted (she was heard arguing with Hitler as he left the house) or that she had been killed to avoid a scandal.

Hitler's housekeeper, Anni Winter, is believed to have overheard that final argument. She heard Hitler say: 'You say you have to go to Vienna? Is it to see that filthy Jew, the one who claims to be a singing teacher? Is that it? Have you been seeing him secretly again? Have you forgotten I forbade you to have anything to do with him? Tell me the truth now. Why do you want to go to Vienna?'

Geli then replied: 'I have to go to Vienna, Uncle Alf, because I'm going to have a baby.'

The *Münchener Post* reported that 'The dead woman's nose was broken, and there were other serious injuries on the body,' which does not suggest suicide, but murder.

SUICIDE DOUBTS

Geli was buried in a Catholic cemetery in Vienna, which would not have been permitted had she taken her own life. Furthermore, with the body interred in Austria, there was no risk of the German authorities requesting an autopsy. Shortly afterwards, Father Johann Pant, the priest who had conducted the funeral service, fled to France. In 1939 he wrote a letter to the *Courrier d'Autriche* newspaper, saying the following: 'They pretended that she committed suicide; I should never have allowed a suicide to be buried in consecrated ground. From the fact that I gave her a Christian burial you can draw conclusions which I cannot communicate to you.'

SHRINE TO GELI

Whether wracked by guilt or genuinely distraught, Hitler ordered Geli's room to remain as it had been that day. It was roped off and preserved as a shrine to the one woman, other than his mother, he said he had truly loved.

Hitler was visibly shaken by the death of his niece, but his supreme self-confidence could not be shattered. The day after her funeral, 24 September 1931, he addressed a meeting in Hamburg and showed no outward signs of grief. There were city elections to contest and a campaign for the presidency to plan. He was more concerned that the rumours of his role in Geli's death did not distract from the message the party was attempting to instil in the voters, or taint his image as the one man who could restore Germany to its rightful place in the world. He would never again allow a woman to get close to him or share his innermost thoughts and feelings.

Hanfstaengl later wrote: 'His long connection with Eva Braun never produced the moon-calf interludes he had enjoyed with Geli and which might in due course, perhaps, have made a normal man out of him. With her death the way was clear for his final development into a demon, with his sex life deteriorating again into a sort of bisexual narcissus-like vanity, with Eva Braun little more than a vague domestic adjunct.'

CHAPTER 12

Women in the Fatherland

Hitler gloried in the adoration he inspired among his female followers, extolling their virtues as dutiful daughters and self-sacrificing mothers of the Aryan nation, but he did not welcome their active participation in the movement he had initiated. He was vehemently opposed to the idea of uniformed women marching in formation behind his ranks of Aryan supermen.

At the 1932 Nuremberg rally, Hitler admonished Reich youth leader Baldur von Schirach for allowing girls to join the parade, seeing it as a mockery of his all-male movement. He only relented when von Schirach informed him that the girls were determined to demonstrate their commitment and their exclusion would discourage women from working for the party.

From the earliest days of the movement, the Nazis had encouraged women to take an active and productive role in promoting National Socialism and converting their neighbours to the cause, but after Hitler's succession to the chancellorship in January 1933, the party betrayed its most ardent followers. Their energies and abilities were squandered in fruitless mass meetings which had no purpose other than to demonstrate support for the leadership. In the worst instances, highly motivated female leaders were replaced with minor male officials and dozens of proactive women's associations were

> *The Nazi revolution will be an entirely male event.'*
>
> Adolf Hitler

amalgamated under one centralized organization which had no power to influence policy. When its members expressed their concerns, the regime made it clear that it would not tolerate dissent, invoking the Law of Malicious Gossip (1934) to stifle criticism, suppress free speech and make even the telling of jokes about the leadership a crime punishable by imprisonment.

As the leadership became intoxicated with power and increasingly arrogant, its most misogynist members saw no need to moderate their pronouncements on the subject of a woman's role in the Reich. Nazi 'philosopher' Alfred Rosenberg failed to see that he was being both offensive and inconsistent in advocating polygamy and encouraging childless husbands to commit adultery in order to increase the population. This was not party policy but a male fantasy, in which it was imagined that women would be willing to submit to men in uniform for purely patriotic reasons and that only by making themselves subservient to their male superiors would women find their true selves.

Housewives flock to the party

And yet, 34,000 housewives (mostly middle class and middle aged) had enrolled in the party before Hitler assumed power, despite the fact that no concerted effort had been made to recruit them or even to address their particular interests. Of these, the majority were highly motivated zealots who had seized the opportunity to convert their neighbours to the cause and to conduct their campaigns without interference from men. The lack of male intervention and supervision gave female activists the opportunity to create their own hierarchy within the party and to set their own agenda.

They might have been undervalued and unappreciated, but at least the party's indifference left them free to organize themselves as they saw fit.

These female followers were aware of the party's aversion towards women in academia, the professions and politics, and still they justified their support by telling themselves it was not necessary to agree with everything the Nazis stood for and that their more regressive policies would be modified once they found themselves in the rarefied atmosphere of the Reichstag. The rabble-rousing tactics had only been used to stimulate debate and attract support in the initial stages of the campaign. Better to have reactionaries than revolutionaries in the Reichstag; better an autocracy than anarchy. Once the Nazis were in power, it would be possible to influence policy and curtail the more rabid elements.

Feminist historian Claudia Koonz reasoned that German women, both Catholic and Protestant, who had been raised in a Christian household had already learned to filter out misogyny from a doctrine they otherwise regarded as sacred. In other words, they had learned how to differentiate between the teachings of their saviour and those of his disciples. Besides, had Hitler not spoken of his reverence for women in general, and for his own mother, in such affectionate terms and with such candour that no one could doubt the sincerity of his respect for them?

The irrational nature of fascism precluded the possibility of a leader appealing to the masses through intellect. Therefore Hitler had to arouse his followers' basest emotions by appealing to their pride and their vanity, their love of country and hatred for their enemies. It was a crude but effective courtship, to which even the most intelligent women were not immune.

'Why I became a Nazi'

The most revealing insight into the mind and motivation of female Nazi supporters can be gleaned from entries submitted to an essay contest organized by sociologist Theodore Abel of Columbia university in 1936. Abel solicited entries from early converts to the cause (applicants who joined the Nazis prior to 1933) by writing to district party offices in Germany offering a cash prize for the best essay on the subject – 'Why I Became A Nazi'. In the following months, Abel received more than 581 entries, 36 of which were from literate middle-class women aged between 17 and 73. Although these could not be said to represent a random sample, it is generally accepted that they were fairly representative of the personality types who were attracted to Nazism.

The dominant theme in 32 per cent of the essays was a desire to be part of an ethnic community spirit, together with the compulsion to conform and find like-minded individuals or risk being an outcast from a popular movement. In 18 per cent of the essays, Hitler was identified as the personification of this '*Volksgemeinschaft*' (community spirit), but only 14 per cent identified anti-Semitism as a significant factor in joining the movement, while 23 per cent highlighted patriotism and a distrust of foreigners as their prime motivation. The group insulated themselves from their imagined enemies, who they identified variously as foreigners, Jews, communists, capitalists, liberals and even Catholics. The few who thought racism 'un-Christian' and a 'religious issue' were persuaded to think otherwise by their fellow converts.

All the women, bar the youngest, spoke of being traumatized by their experiences in the Great War. Most had lost loved ones and several had witnessed brutality first hand, leading them to express the wish that they had been born as males so they could fight for the Fatherland. About a quarter of the women had suffered a significant personal loss, usually the death of their father while they were children, and they had subsequently endured long periods of poverty. This had led them to join a party that offered them security, a shared purpose and a sense of belonging, giving meaning to their otherwise mundane and empty lives. In effect, the party became their substitute family and the Führer their father figure.

Unlike the typical Nazi supporter of the 1920s, three-quarters of the women had grown up in urban areas and were reasonably well educated, though only five had pursued their education into adulthood. Significantly, 48 per cent of the total respondents (predominantly male) had engaged in violence themselves 'such as to imply sadism or masochism', according to Abel. It was the opportunity to engage in violence that offered them the chance to cleanse themselves of their trauma or neurosis. But perhaps the most revealing aspect was the proliferation of religious language in the essays written by both men and women, which suggests it was not politics, nor extreme nationalism that attracted these militants.

Words such as 'faith', 'righteous', 'convert', 'holy', 'heaven', 'blessed' and 'crusader' are sprinkled throughout the entries, with one woman confessing proudly to having made a shrine to Hitler – not an uncommon feature of Hitler worship in the early 1930s – and another rejoicing in the fact that she had sacrificed her eldest son for the cause. 'How wonderful those years of struggle were,' she wrote, 'I would not have missed them for anything.' Tellingly, one woman described her conversion by saying, 'You do not learn about National Socialism, you have to experience it.'

Hitler knew he had evoked a primal longing deep within the German psyche when he declared: 'We are not a movement, we are a religion.' It was this religious aspect of Nazism that appealed unconsciously but profoundly both to men and women and which accounted for such highly emotive responses from men who would normally not have given vent so freely to what they would have considered 'feminine' emotions. Hitler had permitted them to do so, and in public, and this ensured that their devotion and allegiance were deeper and stronger than normally expected by a political leader or monarch from his subjects. Neither Franco nor Mussolini commanded anything like such reverence from their followers.

Equality hopes

Belonging to the Nazi party absolved individuals of responsibility for determining their own fate and removed any fear of what the future might hold. They merely had to comply, and all their thinking would be done for them. It was a question of faith, rather than political conviction. As with a quasi-religious cult, Nazism required its followers to submit to a charismatic leader who would reward their unquestioning obedience by leading them to the Promised Land, only it would be the Egypt of the pharoahs, in which they would be the masters and the conquered peoples their slaves. All they needed to do was put their trust in him.

If there was ambiguity in the commandments of *Mein Kampf*, Hitler's followers assumed that this was because they lacked the intelligence to interpret them, so they called for guidance and clarification on the points of doctrine which confused them. It didn't occur to them that the doctrine itself was muddled, contradictory, illogical and deliberately ambiguous because it was the work of an irrational man who spoke in absolutes and empty platitudes.

In desperation, one rural activist wrote to her local leader asking for permission to translate *Mein Kampf* into a language women could understand. She recommended substituting the title 'Our Struggle' for the original 'My Struggle', because she believed the problem lay in the fact that it had been dictated from a male point of view. But the confusion and ambiguity worked in the party's favour. As with Hitler's speeches, followers read what they wanted into the writing. With little or no substance pertaining to women's issues, Hitler's female supporters simply adapted party rhetoric to endorse their own views. Their male counterparts let them do so, as they had no intention of fulfilling any of the promises or policy recommendations the women's organizations had made once they were in office.

As far as the leadership was concerned, the various women's organizations were little more than party fundraisers which managed grass-roots membership drives, sewing circles and public speaking engagements. The leadership had no intention of rewarding their female activists with anything other than profuse expressions of gratitude for their efforts when the campaigning was over.

Not a democracy

For their part, women's leaders expected the party to discard their absurd '*Kinder, Küche und Kirche*' doggerel and be receptive to their recommendations in acknowledgement of the debt they owed. The leadership was aware of the women's demands, having closely monitored their speeches and read their pamphlets to ensure that they adhered to party policy, but they had no intention of granting them. The New Order was to be a dictatorship, not a democracy.

Women were informed of what was expected of them and they would defer to their male masters. In return, they would be assured of

Opposite page: *In the 1930s and 1940s, Hitler received the kind of attention from women that is reserved for pop singers and film stars today*

the state's legal and financial protection and support. A strong woman radicalized by political activity was perceived as a threat to the party hierarchy. According to Nazi dogma, like children, women should be seen and not heard. When victory came, the party would have to dissolve the majority of women's groups, replace its more independently minded leaders and establish party-endorsed organizations under the leadership of women it could control.

Women are betrayed

After 1933, there were no more elections. The regime no longer required female activists to sing its praises and drum up support. The situation was summed up in a party propaganda poster which declared, 'The German woman is knitting once again', as if that was an achievement to be applauded. But women's interest groups were not content with vague promises and platitudes. They were impatient to be actively involved in government. Among them was a group of female academics who published a manifesto entitled *German Women to Adolf Hitler*, which comprised studious essays in support of Nazi racial theories as they applied to the sexes, in the hope of persuading the leader to reconsider his policy discouraging women from entering academia and the professions.

One contributor claimed that prehistoric skeletons which were unearthed in Scandinavia revealed men and women had once been of equal size and strength. But men had starved their mates in order to subjugate them. The argument ran that if allowed the same opportunities, Aryan women would be the physical and intellectual equals of men.

If Hitler was gratified to read about highly educated women accepting the more fanciful racial theories at face value and being prepared to suspend logic and compromise their credibility in order to endorse them, he wasn't sufficiently impressed with them to accede to their demands. He expected nothing less than total obedience and saw no need to reward those who complied.

The situation was exacerbated by the fact that women themselves showed a surprising lack of solidarity. Even after Hitler's succession, few female leaders raised objections to the purge of women from political and public life. None publicly condemned the dismissal of the 74 liberal and socialist female political appointees or the 19,000 female regional and local officials. Nor did they protest when it became known that all married women had been dismissed from their civil service posts and that women would be barred from serving on juries and practising law because they were not deemed intellectually capable of logical thought or objective reasoning.

Growing female support

On the contrary, support for the new administration increased so rapidly in the first 12 months that party leaders were unable to decide how best to employ the number of independent women's organizations who rushed to offer their services to the state. Membership of the Nazi Women's Organization (the NSF) increased by 800 per cent and other groups obediently fell into line, pledging their allegiance to the new administration. If their educated middle-class members had misgivings about Hitler's bombastic style and virulently racist rhetoric, they kept it to themselves. After all, had he not sworn to honour the role of mothers, preserve traditional family values, restore order and crush the socialists? And still the restrictions and exclusions continued without a word of complaint from those who were directly affected.

Married female physicians were prohibited from practising their profession and, soon afterwards, single women doctors had their state-sponsored financial support withdrawn. Before the year had drawn to a close, the number of female university students was restricted (to 10 per cent of total admissions) by a quota system, a move supported by Gertrud Baumer, a former Weimar government official, who agreed it was a necessary step because academic standards for women had fallen under the previous administration. Whether Baumer made the statement in the hope of securing a post in the new government is not known, but she subsequently applied for a position only to reject what was offered.

Divide and conquer

If there were murmurings of discontent among the various women's associations, they were not allowed to surface. Dissent in Hitler's totalitarian state was effectively suppressed by the time-honoured tradition of divide and conquer. Similar responsibilities were given to competing departments which then had to defer to the Führer for final approval. The Nazi dictatorship presented a unified front, but institutionalized confusion and interdepartmental rivalry ran riot behind the scenes.

A similar strategy was employed to postpone decisions on women's issues and keep women's leaders at a distance. The once idealistic members now realized that their vision of an Aryan paradise of equal opportunity had instead manifested as a Kafkaesque bureaucracy administered by petty functionaries, all of whom were men with no interest in women's affairs. What they had failed to understand was that Hitler may have envisaged a Thousand-Year Reich, but his immediate aim was conquest not culture.

At first, the euphoria of election victory blinded female supporters to the fact that their backing was no longer required. Their considerable energies were being squandered and their input ignored. Women's leaders were excluded from official functions where they might have had the opportunity of meeting the Führer and lobbying on behalf of their members. Instead they had to be content with dealing with his minions: men like Gottfried Krummacher, a municipal administrator whose first official act was to abolish rival organizations and declare himself leader of the 'Women's Front' and its sister association, while proclaiming that he had been sent to 'pacify all of organized German womanhood'. Empty gestures were followed by empty promises.

Women's leaders replaced

Mass meetings were organized by party officials. Thousands attended, but the gatherings served no real purpose other than to demonstrate public support and love for the Führer.

By the summer of 1933, it was evident to many women's leaders that their efforts had been wasted, their ideals betrayed and their leaders replaced by male administrators who were 'worse than communists' (according to Maria Jecker, leader of the Reich Association of Housewives). Dr Auguste Reber-Gruber, head of the Nazi Teachers' Association, was moved to remark, 'Oh, how our old rivals would rejoice if they could see how badly the party treats its women.'

At the annual Nazi party rally in Nuremberg, seven days were devoted to military parades, Hitler Youth activities and interminable speeches, but not one speech addressed the subject of women's rights or the opportunities the revolution had won for its female participants. Subsequently, Rudolf Hess announced the establishment of the Women's Bureau, which effectively rendered all other women's organizations redundant and brought its members under the supervision of the Ministry of the Interior.

THE FEMALE FÜHRER

'The mission of woman is to minister in the home and in her profession to the needs of life from the first to last moment of man's existence.'

Gertrud Scholtz-Klink: 'the German woman must work and work, physically and mentally she must renounce luxury and pleasure'

They say that behind every successful man there is a woman. And it is as true for dictators as it is for businessmen. In Hitler's case it was the formidable Gertrud Scholtz-Klink, leader of the Nazi Women's League, whose fanatical loyalty earned her the nickname 'the Female Führer'.

In 1941, at the height of her influence, it was estimated that she governed some 30 million German women and had command over 20 million more in the occupied territories. And yet there were those who described her as nothing more than a figurehead appointed by the male-dominated leadership to give the impression that they valued the contribution made by their womenfolk. But she fitted in with the rigid bureaucratic Nazi mindset, being described by feminist historian Professor Claudia Koonz as: 'Stubborn, simple-minded and self-righteous' and by American journalist and author William L. Shirer as 'particularly obnoxious and vapid'.

Born Gertrud Treusch on 9 February 1902 in Baden-Württemberg, there was nothing in her early life to suggest she possessed leadership capabilities or ambitions beyond marrying as well as her background would allow. The daughter of a lowly civil servant, she worked first as a schoolteacher and then as a newspaper reporter before marrying Friedrich Klink in 1920, when she was barely 18. Although he was a minor official in the nascent Nazi party and an active member of the SA, Gertrud did not exhibit any serious interest in his activities or in politics until nine years later, when she had raised their six children to school age and was restless to pursue a life and career outside the home. On hearing of his death from a heart attack during a street brawl in March 1930, she marched down to the local party offices and demanded to be enrolled so that she might 'honour his martyrdom'. She soon graduated to recruiting supporters and became leader of the women's branch in Berlin.

Two years later Gertrud remarried, but was dismayed to discover that her new husband, country doctor Guenther Scholtz, had little interest in National Socialism and that politics came a poor second to his patients. By this time, her organizational skills and oratorical powers had brought her to the attention of Adolf Hitler, who appointed her leader of the National Socialist Women's League in 1933. Her critics, such as exiled newspaper editor Peter Engelmann, attributed her rise to her manoeuvrings behind the scenes, claiming she was as ruthless and devious as any of her male counterparts, while others believed that she was simply a strong archetypical Aryan mother chosen to put a face to the programme.

PREACHING THE GOSPEL

Although she publicly ridiculed the idea of women pursuing a political career and denounced the female politicians of the Weimar Republic for making shrill street corner speeches, she threw herself body and soul into the maelstrom of party politics. With the fervour of the converted, she urged German women to surrender their personal interests and ambitions to the service of their male masters.

In a speech to German women ('To Be German Is To Be Strong', 1936) she made it clear where every woman's duty lay: 'The National Socialist movement sees the man and the woman as equal bearers of Germany's future. It asks, however, for more than in the past: that each should first completely accomplish the tasks that are appropriate to his or her nature.'

That year, in recognition of her unstinting efforts and initiative, she was appointed director of the National Socialist Welfare Organization and awarded the Gold Medal of the NSDAP, a singular honour reserved for those who embodied the ideals of the National Socialist state.

LIFE OF LUXURY

But while she advocated restraint and moderation for her members in her role as head of the Women's League, in private she enjoyed a luxurious lifestyle and all the privileges that went with her position. She justified each extravagance by claiming that she worked tirelessly for her Führer, exercising control over every aspect of the female population of the Reich from adolescent *Mädchen* to mothers. She could not bear to think of a single child lacking the 'protection' of the state and even set up a scheme to unburden French girls of the babies they had borne to German soldiers, with the promise that she would send these children to good German homes.

In 1938 she divorced her second husband and acquired a third in 1940. This man, SS Obergruppenführer August Heissmeyer, was the head of an SS training school and father of five offspring from a previous marriage. When the couple gave all eleven children a new home in Berlin and Gertrud bore her seventh child in 1944, the party praised her as a 'fertility model'.

Motherhood did not dampen Gertrud's ardour for the cause nor did it see her limit her schedule of inspections to institutions and concentration camps, where female political prisoners were being brutalized. At a camp near Berlin she found everything 'quite normal' and 'in good order'. Her members were there in the capacity of 'social workers', assisting in the 're-education' of 'asocial' female political prisoners.

STRENGTH IN DEFEAT

If Gertrud noticed the people developed an increased eagerness to snap to attention whenever she entered a room and a tendency to follow her orders without question, would she have attributed it to her husband's position as head of the Ubergestapo or Supreme SS tribunal? Or would she have imagined it was out of respect for her leadership of the Women's League? When put to the test, she proved stronger than her husband. She was wounded five times during their breakout from Berlin in 1945, and later initiated an escape from a Russian POW camp. From there they fled to Bebenhausen castle to be offered sanctuary in the village by Nazi sympathizer, Princess Pauline of Württemberg.

When they were finally arrested by a combined force of American and French troops in 1948, Gertrud proudly admitted to having been a member of the Nazi party. Meanwhile, her husband made an attempt to recover a phial of poison, but was prevented from taking his own life. He vigorously denied having ever been a member and insisted he had always been a farmer.

A French military court sentenced Gertrud to 18 months in prison for forging documents and, in May 1950, a German de-Nazification court increased her term of imprisonment by a further 30 months and banned her for life from engaging in political or trade union activity. She was also prohibited from working as a journalist or teacher for ten years.

On her release, she returned to Bebenhausen and lived in quiet seclusion for 30 years. She remained a believer in National Socialism until her death in March 1999, at the age of 97.

Brides for Hitler

The lakeside model villa on Schwanenwerder island in a leafy suburb of Berlin was an idyllic setting for a summer school, but the *Reichsbräuteschule* was not a typical establishment for the daughters of Germany's reigning elite. Deportment and elocution lessons were not on the curriculum. The school's stated aim was to 'mould housewives out of office girls' and to that end its all-female staff provided a comprehensive course in cooking, needlework and other mandatory domestic skills, with additional classes in racial theory and genetics.

The young girls who returned from the fields laden with baskets of freshly picked flowers looked as though they could have stepped straight out of a recruitment poster for the League of German Maidens. With their peaches and cream complexions and their braided yellow plaits, they personified the image of the perfect Jungfrau. But healthy minds and healthy bodies were not enough to make these daughters of the Reich eligible brides for their prospective husbands. They would first have to be indoctrinated in the cult of National Socialism if they were to serve their men as the Führer commanded, and they would need to pledge allegiance to the party and their leader unto death.

The villa, one of nine established in the capital in the late 1930s (with others in Oldenburg and Tübingen), was furnished as a model home with all modern amenities and the latest domestic appliances.

Surviving photographs from the era, published in the state-sponsored biweekly magazine for woman, *NS-Frauen Warte*, show a group of radiantly healthy young girls demonstrating the required skills: posing attentively around a sewing machine, tending farm animals, singing to an accordion and preparing a wholesome meal of meat and vegetables for their menfolk.

The Reich Bride Schools were the brainchild of Reichsführer-SS Heinrich Himmler and Gertrud Scholtz-Klink. Although Scholtz-Klink was excluded from policy-making decisions, her face became as familiar to the German public as that of her superior. Himmler had signed a decree in 1936 stipulating that any young woman who wished to marry a member of the SS had to prove her National Socialist zeal by undergoing training as a 'good wife' and the heart of the Nazi household. Only then would a marriage certificate be approved. But it has been said that Himmler's interest in the institution was not entirely political. He was known to time his visits to catch the dancing classes and was often seen observing the girls' athletic activities with a keen interest.

Rules for Reich brides

The Reich Bride Schools might have remained little more than a footnote in history had it not been for the chance discovery of a rule book and other material at the Federal Archive in Koblenz in 2013. The recovered items revealed that the six-week course cost 135 Reichsmarks – a week's wages for the average typist or shop worker – and that classes were limited to 20 students, who would be required to live in. The girls were urged to attend for two months prior to their wedding day, 'to recuperate spiritually and physically, to forget the daily worries associated with their previous professions, to find the way and to feel the joy for their new lives as wives'.

The subjects taught at the schools covered every aspect of domestic life, from basic household skills such as ironing, interior decorating and gardening, to handy tips for removing stains from your husband's uniform and making small talk at official party functions. Great emphasis was put on child care, as the aim was to turn out dutiful,

Der Bund Deutscher Mädel in der Hitler Jugend (the League of German Girls in the Hitler Youth): girls danced together as they were groomed for future roles as wives, mothers and homemakers

hardworking *Hausfraus* and productive mothers who would breed blond, blue-eyed Aryan babies for the state – a duty encouraged by a loan of 1,000 Reichsmarks to the newly-weds, with a quarter of the money to be retained by the families on the birth of each child. The payment was stipulated by the Law for the Encouragement of Marriage Act passed in July 1933. In the three years following the introduction of the law, payments were made to 695,000 couples.

The young women who passed through these schools were also required to teach the regime's 'racial values' to their offspring and to be the moral centre of the family, whose credo was to be adopted religiously from *Mein Kampf*, leaving no room for the Bible. This secular belief system was central to the New Order and was to replace religious observance in the Nazi household. It included a neo-pagan marriage ceremony, conducted by a party official before an altar decorated with SS runes and wreaths of oak leaves. The services of a priest would not be required.

The schools had initially been set up to attract women betrothed to SS officers, but by 1940 the establishments were widening their selection process and relaxing entry requirements to entice girls who would make perfect partners for party officials and the SS rank and file. Enrolment only declined when the war turned against Germany and women were expected to work in munitions and armaments factories in place of the men who had gone to the front.

Working women

The regime had trumpeted its firm resolve to honour women, but when German industry required more workers to replace enlisted men, the Nazis' policies proved to be as flexible as their principles. Prior to 1936, the state had discouraged mothers with young children from taking jobs if their husbands were earning a reasonable wage. It offered financial and other incentives for families to toe the party line, including state-sponsored leisure activities, household education programmes and ceremonial awards. It even applied a crude form of organized peer pressure, with the *Frauenwerk* organization under Gertrud Scholtz-Klink frowning upon 'double earners' who put material gain before motherhood and shaming women back into the kitchen.

After 1936, however, the needs of the German war machine took priority and women were urged to put their children into day care if necessary, so that they could fulfil their patriotic duty and contribute to the rearmament programme (although women were excluded from working in munitions factories at this point).

But even after the recruitment drive, only a third of German women were in paid employment, a pitiful increase on the peacetime figure, and 87 per cent of these women were employed in clerical posts, catering and retail. It was only now that Nazi women's groups realized what little power they wielded and leaders such as Scholtz-Klink were revealed to be mere party stooges – self-serving opportunists who were unable to defend their about-turn as anything other than political expediency.

There would be no opportunity for their members to protest. The nation was gearing up for war and dissent was considered an act of treason. Women's leaders saw no option but to comply and in doing so became complicit in the crimes of the regime they had actively and enthusiastically assisted to power.

As Claudia Koonz noted in *Mothers in the Fatherland*, far from honouring the family as the heart of the *Volk* community, women's leaders had aided the state's intrusion into the home in order to control its members' activities, conduct and even their thoughts. Mothers and fathers who dared voice criticism of the leadership lived in fear that their own children, other family members or their neighbours might denounce them to the Gestapo. But an even more insidious influence would undermine the traditional family in the run-up to war.

> 'I know that it is easier to make a quick trip to the department store. It requires thought to purchase domestic products, remembering with each purchase that German goods provide German people with wages and food.'
>
> Erna Guenter, 'Wir Frauen im Kampf um Deutschlands Erneuerung', NS-Frauen Warte, 25 February 1934

In October 1939, Reichsführer-SS Heinrich Himmler charged the three million men under his command to father as many children as they could out of wedlock as part of their sacred duty to the nation. He dressed this directive up in the florid language of the Nordic heroic saga: 'The greatest gift for the widow of a man killed in battle is always the child of the man she has loved.' But following condemnation by Protestant and Catholic women's groups, Himmler was forced to withdraw the order.

The Nazi elite

The role of German women in Nazi crimes was not seriously considered by historians until the late 1980s. Up to that point, it was generally accepted that the majority of German women were as much victims of the regime as their civilian counterparts in the occupied territories. It was believed that the cruelty they suffered at the hands of the advancing Soviet troops and the privations they endured in the years immediately after the capitulation were sufficient punishment for their initial support for Hitler. After all, the men had done the killing while the women, with a few monstrous exceptions, had merely kept the home until it was bombed and shelled to rubble. The loss of their houses and apartments, their sons and sweethearts, fathers and friends, together with the carefree lifestyle they had enjoyed at the expense of others in Warsaw, Paris and other cities in the conquered countries was deemed fitting retribution. There was even grudging respect for the 'rubble women' of Berlin who cleared their capital brick by brick, even if they did lay the blame for such wanton destruction entirely on the Allies.

There might have been reluctance on the part of male historians to probe into the role of 'ordinary' women on account of the brutality they had suffered at the hands of the Soviets. It was easier to categorize the majority of German women as mere 'fellow travellers', a group officially recognized by the de-Nazification courts as meriting condemnation rather than imprisonment.

It was only with the publication of Koonz's *Mothers in the Fatherland* that this deliberate 'oversight' was addressed and the role of women in the Third Reich reassessed. But in spite of her admirable and thorough research, Koonz limited her study to the secretaries and filing clerks who oiled the machinery of state and kept its meticulous records. She marginalized the concentration camp guards and female staff at the euthanasia institutes as freakish aberrations, and the wives of Nazi officers as frivolous socialites. This means she identified the majority of the most fervent female Nazis as predominantly middle class and held all equally accountable.

A class apart

It is now clear that the Nazis created a new elite who considered themselves a class apart from the working women of Germany and distinct from the aristocracy. They openly flaunted their privileges and indulged in the luxuries which their male benefactors declared to be decadent and unbecoming of the master race. Like the wives and mistresses of the Roman emperors, these 20th-century social climbers were privy to the crimes being perpetrated in their name and it was in their interest to preserve the impression of innocence.

But the worlds of high fashion and the classless national community (or the image of it) that the Nazis wished to create were mutually exclusive. Haute couture was for the upper class. It was an expensive, time-consuming habit to indulge in. Shop girls, school teachers, clerks and secretaries didn't have the time to browse at leisure through fashion magazines on a regular basis and invest in a wardrobe that would give them the choice of a dozen outfits and the shoes to match. They had no choice but to comply with the regime's edict to dress modestly, with functionality uppermost in their minds. The Nazi hierarchy became the new elite – they were the nouveau riche, who took it upon themselves to live a life of luxury and leisure under the pretence of setting the standards for their inferiors to follow.

Dress rules for the *Hausfrau*

At first, Nazi propaganda appealed to women's patriotic duty, urging the loyal *Hausfrau* to buy only what was essential and functional and to purchase these goods from German stores, avoiding department stores such as Tietz, a chain owned by Jews. When Hitler came to power, these particular shops were 'Aryanized' and renamed 'Hertie'.

On 1 April 1933, the Nazis organized a national boycott of Jewish businesses, during which brown-shirted SA thugs painted the Star of David on shop windows and intimidated customers. But it would be impossible to man the streets in such numbers every day, so the Nazis called on women to avoid Jewish stores, hoping they would eventually be driven out of business and the owners forced to leave. The National Socialist Women's Federation urged German women to boycott Jewish stores as a matter of principle and as proof of their patriotism. 'The German housewife in every situation of life alone can decide victory in this fight. There will not be a pfennig henceforth for a Jewish shop, for a Jewish physician or attorney from the German woman.' But busy women had no need to shop around for approved Aryan suppliers when their usual stores stocked all they needed.

Hitler controlled every aspect of women's private and personal lives. He told them what to do and what to think, what to read and what to believe. He could order them to leave their lovers, to refrain from smoking and wearing make-up in his presence, and to marry in a Nazi-approved ceremony, forsaking their religious beliefs and renouncing their God for their Führer. He could not, however, influence the one thing any self-respecting woman reserves the right to determine for herself – how she dresses. Typically Hitler did not expressly forbid what he did not approve of. He merely indicated what displeased him and described the qualities and mode of dress he felt embodied the ideal Aryan woman.

Unpatriotic French fashion

There was no shortage of little Hitlers, male and female, eager to implement their leader's edicts. Agnes Gerlach, chairwoman of the Association for German Woman's Culture, was one. She tried to 're-educate' women through a series of articles in popular magazines, attempting to wean them off inappropriate products by categorizing them as 'decadent' and 'un-German'. The 'little luxury woman' and the 'masculine woman' were unfeminine images which had been created by the French fashion industry and its Jewish designers. They were trying to corrupt the German feminine form by squeezing it into unnatural and unhealthy shapes, just as the Chinese had done to women in ancient times, binding their feet so that they would not grow beyond a certain size. Experts were drafted in to confirm such statements. Arthur Hess of the Orthopaedic Shoemakers' Trade Association provided a statement affirming that 60–70 per cent of the German population suffered from a deformity caused entirely by restrictive shoes that had been designed by Jews.

Similarly, the French obsession with boyish female shapes was detrimental to procreation and therefore unpatriotic. The 'blurring of the sexes' was indicative of the influence of a 'foreign race'. To disfigure the broad-hipped German woman would be to dishonour her.

In the *National Socialist Yearbook* for 1934, Gerlach contributed an essay intended to sell the idea to party loyalists. 'How Do I Dress Myself as a German, Tastefully and Appropriately?' informed the readers that the use of hair dye and cosmetics was an undignified, artificial way of slowing down ageing. Better surely to maintain a regular exercise routine and leave nature to take its course? Constricting clothes could only lead to physical and psychological damage and ultimately to 'racial deterioration'.

'Exhibitionism leads to deformation of the body,' Gerlach argued, as if presenting a scientific fact rather than an ideological fallacy. It was important to respect cultural differences; Germany respected each of its female citizens and treated them as 'free', not 'kept'. This implied that French women only dressed to please their men and that men financed and dictated women's choice of clothes and personal appearance. But in fact it was the German leader who was dictating what women should wear, what work they should be restricted to and whose authority they must obey. German women were anything but free, but the majority of them were too dazzled by their adoration of Hitler to see that they were enslaved.

Another contributor was equally adept at twisting the truth. She snorted, 'Fashion must be individualistic – one thing is not right for everybody, especially when one nation wants to create fashion for everyone – as the French try to do it.'

One rule for the rich . . .

However, Magda Goebbels, wife of the Reich minister of propaganda, had no intention of playing the Teutonic warrior queen in shapeless smocks. She opted for haute couture, employing Parisian milliners such as Caroline Reboux to make her stylish hats (that were the envy of Marlene Dietrich) and Ferragamo for handmade shoes. Magda once famously declared, 'I hold it as my duty to appear as beautifully as I possibly can.' And if that meant dressing her Aryan body in clothes designed and handled by Jewish designers such as Max Becker, Richard Goetz, Paul Kuhnen and Fritz Gruenfeld, then so be it. But it made her the oddest choice for president of the Reich Fashion Institute (the Deutsches Modeamt).

The institute had been established to control, or at least attempt to influence, what German women wore and where they bought their clothes and other accessories. French fashion houses were out of bounds because Hitler hated the French; he condemned designers such as Chanel for encouraging women to cultivate the 'international silhouette' and dress in 'shapeless' unfeminine clothes when the Aryan ideal was the fuller figure suggestive of child-bearing fertility. A slim waist was frowned upon because it was thought that thin women would be unable to bear children. In 1933 Hitler declared 'no more Paris models', which might have prompted Josef Goebbels to remove Magda from her official post at the Deutsches Modeamt.

Champagne socialist

Frau Annelies von Ribbentrop, heiress to a champagne fortune and wife of the Nazi foreign minister, preferred English fashion. She insisted on furnishing her lavish home with chintz curtains and country-house furniture imported from Britain. She even had English springer spaniels, which she treated more humanely than she did her husband. It may have been her considerable personal wealth which led her to be so condescending towards him even in company, or it may have been her nature. Whatever the reason, her behaviour earned her the epithet 'Lady Macbeth', though she was one of only three women who Hitler listened to seriously; the others were Helena Bechstein and Winifred Wagner.

Believing Hitler was a coarse and uncultured provincial agitator, Annelies was a late convert to National Socialism. She was suspicious of anyone who claimed to be a vegetarian and a teetotaller, but thought it might be advantageous to play hostess to a leader who needed someone respectable like her husband to infiltrate the upper echelons of German society and, perhaps, represent them abroad. However, after hearing Hitler speak, her reservations evaporated. His vision for a greater Germany stirred something inside her and gave her the feeling that anything was possible. If the von Ribbentrops could prove themselves indispensable to the Nazi party there was more than money to be made – they would become principal players in the new society. Besides, Annelies thought it might be delicious fun to provoke her husband's notoriously liberal relations by flaunting her National Socialist credentials in public.

Annelies had been seduced by her husband's old-fashioned manners, but after providing him with five children she realized he did not possess the qualities she had projected on to him. He was superficial and sly, not a man noted for his ambition and intelligence. And he wasn't popular with the 'old guard', Nazi party members who had bloodied their hands in the early days of 'the struggle'. Nor was he well regarded by the leadership, though Hitler found him useful if only because he had travelled abroad and presumably had extensive knowledge of the attitudes held by the leaders of other countries.

As part of his champagne business, von Ribbentrop had cultivated useful contacts with influential figures such as Joseph Kennedy. He was an old-fashioned charmer, not a man to initiate anything. Even his aristocratic title had been obtained by petitioning an aunt to adopt him. As Goebbels put it, 'von Ribbentrop bought his name, married his money and swindled his way into office.'

Hitler hoped that the Reich Fashion Institute would 'reflect the nature and character of the German woman' and that 'The Berlin women must become the best dressed women in Europe.' Yet he discouraged his mistress, Eva Braun, and the other Nazi wives from wearing make-up, using hair dye, plucking their eyebrows, painting their nails or wearing furs. Smoking was forbidden for women in public places, where signs reminded them that they risked having cigarettes snatched out of their mouths by SA brown-shirts.

Jewish tailors preferred

The Nazi hierarchy was so fearful of 'contamination' that they set up the Association of Aryan Clothing Manufacturers, which guaranteed that all materials would be unsoiled by Jewish hands. This perverse marketing strategy may have satisfied the middle and working class women who couldn't afford designer fashion, much of which was created and manufactured by Jews. It is estimated that during the 1930s, 70 per cent of the high fashion items on sale in Berlin stores were made by Jewish tailors.

Magda Goebbels and Emmy Goering continued to patronize Jewish tailor Fritz Grünfeld during the war and soon discovered that the ban on French fashion and cosmetics worked in their favour. Their elevated positions enabled them to ignore Nazi policy and flaunt the designer fashions and luxuries that other women were denied.

Only Gerda Bormann dressed in *Tracht* (heritage clothing), as the Reich Fashion Institute dictated. She wore her braided hair in a bun and refused to wear lipstick in the belief that it was made from animal fat, as Hitler had stated. Every spring she was evidently pregnant with another child. She bore ten in all. Traudl Junge described Gerda as pleasant but pale and inconspicuous, and as patient in the company of the other wives as a prisoner who knows they must endure captivity if they want to be allowed out before their sentence has been served.

> *'She didn't actually come from a Nazi background: on the contrary, she had a strict Catholic upbringing. In no way was she a "Nazi bitch", as we used to say. Absolutely not.'*
>
> Wilfred von Oven, adviser to Josef Goebbels, describing his wife, Magda

EVA BRAUN

HITLER'S DEVOTED AND UNDEMANDING COMPANION

'Better that ten thousand others die than he be lost to Germany.'

For Christmas 1929, Hitler thought he had the perfect present for Heinrich Hoffmann and his staff – a framed photograph of their Führer in his military uniform. Or perhaps Hitler was eager to impress Hoffmann's pretty young assistant, Eva Braun, whom he had met that October. Eva was 17 years old, the daughter of a Munich schoolmaster and the very image of healthy Aryan maidenhood. The job at Hoffmann's studio was her first after leaving a Catholic convent and she was still living at home with her strict parents. But when work was over she had little on her mind other than enjoying herself, which meant socializing, swimming and shopping. She was in no hurry to find a husband and certainly wouldn't have seriously considered a relationship with a man more than twice her age.

Eva told her sister that Hitler had been introduced to her as Herr Wolf, the name he used when he travelled incognito and that she had been aware that he was looking at her legs while she was perched at the top of a ladder searching for some files. She referred to him as an 'elderly gentleman' although he was only 40, and recalled that they talked about music and the theatre over beer and sausages while he was 'devouring' her with his eyes.

It was only after he had left that her employer told her his real name. Over the following weeks, Hitler would come into the shop and offer Eva complimentary tickets to the theatre or the opera. He was in the habit of offering these to anyone who worked for the party, so Eva thought little of it at first, but then he invited her to the opera alone and she began to see him differently. Her father was against the relationship. It wasn't just the age difference, nor the fact that rival party newspapers had insinuated that there was something unhealthy in Hitler's relationship with his niece. Herr Braun simply disapproved of the former 'Bavarian corporal' and refused to take him or his party seriously.

After Geli Raubal's death, Eva wrote to Hitler expressing her sympathy, slipping the note into his coat pocket while he was distracted. A few weeks later she accompanied him to a restaurant and thereafter was rarely seen out of his sight. Frau Winter had the impression she was pursuing him and that Eva was not as innocent or as naive as she liked to appear. Hitler was as erratic as she was intense. She never knew whether he would be delighted to see her or unresponsive. Finally, in November 1932, she appealed to his sense of melodrama by feigning a suicide attempt. He responded as she had planned, by promising never to neglect her again.

SECRET RELATIONSHIP

Eva was devoted, obedient and undemanding. All she asked for was Hitler's assurance that he would love no other woman. It was a promise he found easy to make and keep. She accepted that she would have to remain in the shadows for much of the time when they had company and retire to her room whenever he entertained official visitors. It was part of a politician's life, she told herself, and every girl in Germany would envy her, if only they knew. She understood the need to keep their relationship a secret from the German public for fear of disappointing Hitler's female admirers. She liked the idea of being his secret lover. It appealed to her schoolgirl fantasies. However, she was less keen on his strict paternal rules. He forbade her to use make-up, smoke in his presence, wear fashionable clothes or cavort in her swimwear when performing her daily exercises.

> 'She wasn't at all the kind of ideal German girl you saw on recruiting posters for the BdM (League of German Girls) or in the women's magazines. Her carefully done hair was bleached, and her pretty face was made up quite heavily. When I first saw her she was wearing a Nile-green dress of heavy woollen fabric. Its top fitted closely, and it had a bell-shaped skirt with a broad leopard skin edging at the hem. . . . The dress had close-fitting sleeves, with two gold-coloured clips at its sweet-heart neckline.'
>
> Traudl Junge, Hitler's personal secretary, describing her first encounter with Eva Braun

It was galling for Eva to be forbidden from socializing with the other Nazi wives. But she suffered Hitler's 'eccentricities', the frequent humiliations of being spoken about as if she wasn't present, and the gifts of cash given openly as if she was the housekeeper. She told herself that he didn't mean to be insensitive – he was preoccupied and was making sacrifices to rebuild Germany into an empire that would last a thousand years. But for a man who aspired to emulate Bismarck, Charlemagne and Napoleon, and to oversee the construction of a new capital designed on a grand scale, he thought little of the people who supported him. Hitler treated Eva, his most loyal devotee, worse than his pet dog, rewarding her fidelity with cheap jewellery.

Eva Braun (second left) at her parents' home in Munich in 1938

LOYAL TO THE END

Several of Braun's close associates confided to others that there was no physical element to her relationship with Hitler. Julius Schaub, Hitler's chief adjutant, told an Allied interrogator that Hitler did not love her but was merely fond of her. Eva may have been shallow and self-centred, but when Goering and Himmler deserted Hitler she remained by his side to the bitter end, loyal and subservient to the very last.

Hoffmann described her as 'just an attractive little thing, in whom, in spite of her inconsequential and feather-brained outlook, he [Hitler] found the type of relaxation and repose he sought', while Hitler's nurse Erna Flegel, who witnessed the final days in the bunker in Berlin, remembered her as 'a completely colourless personality', whose death affected the survivors less than that of Blondi, Hitler's dog. Albert Speer was only moderately more charitable when he wrote, 'For all writers of history, Eva Braun is going to be a disappointment.'

CHAPTER 13

The Road to War

Three years after completing *Mein Kampf*, Hitler wrote a second, untitled book which he withheld from publication. He realized he could not afford to make others aware of his unshakeable conviction that a second European war was not only inevitable, but necessary. It was the only way to secure *Lebensraum* for the German people: 'Every healthy, unspoiled nation . . . sees the acquisition of new territory not as something useful but as something natural. . . . He who would ban this sort of contention from earth or all eternity might possibly do away with the struggle of man against man, but he would also do away with earth's highest force for evolution.'

Hitler's thinking in 1928 remained the cornerstone of his foreign policy once he was in power. He was apparently willing to negotiate with the Poles and the Romanians, but knew that even if he could coerce them into relinquishing territory he could not expect the Russians to be so obliging. Eventually there would have to be a war with the Soviet Union. It was Germany's destiny to engage in a life and death struggle with the Russian bear to prove the superiority of the Aryan race. If Germany proved worthy, the reward would not only be a vast expanse of rich arable land and an almost limitless supply of slave labour, but also the natural resources of the Crimea and Ukraine. These regions included the vast oilfields vital for sustaining a modern empire and its war machine. It would be a war the Germans could not afford to lose. Their belief in their own superiority depended upon it.

But first, Germany's borders had to be secured and the territories taken from her under the terms of the Versailles Treaty needed to be recovered. Czechoslovakia had to be conquered and Poland persuaded to submit to the New Order or be consumed by it. Then Germany would occupy the territory of its old enemy, France, and forge an alliance with England and Italy so that the invasion of Eastern Europe could be undertaken without the risk of a second front opening in the west. Even with his limited military experience, Hitler knew that fighting a war simultaneously on two fronts was a gamble no commander could afford to take.

A need for war

According to an aide, Hitler had a 'pathological need for battle'. He had once confided to his commanders that the 'need to strike' had always been a part of his nature and that the war, when it came, would be the same struggle he had once fought out within himself. His inner conflicts evidently drove him to manipulate and dominate others, testing their resolve to resist him in a clash of wills. It is revealing that whenever he succeeded in bullying his opponents into making concessions, he always gave his 'solemn oath' that those demands would be the final ones he would make.

But when opposed by someone who was equally headstrong and determined, he would became silent and morose and play the role of the long-suffering martyr – as he had done as a child when beaten into submission by his domineering father. Unable to stand up to his parent when he was alive, Hitler repeatedly acted out his revenge on the politicians and bureaucrats who opposed him in adulthood. He talked of 'disciplining' and 'training' them and of 'driving out their indolence', almost as though he had taken his father's place.

Mixed feelings

It is significant that Hitler could tolerate criticism from Chancellor Dollfuss of Austria, who opposed the annexation of his country by Germany, but flew into one of his infamous rages when Dollfuss dared to contradict him. It is possible that Hitler unconsciously transferred his feelings towards his parents to the countries he wished to conquer or embrace (ageing Imperial Austria and the violated, dishonoured German Motherland are the two obvious examples).

Hitler repeatedly referred to Germany as the Motherland rather than the Fatherland, and frequently made disparaging remarks about the country of his birth, Austria, which he described as old, exhausted and decaying. Yet he professed respect and shock when the supposedly demoralized Britain openly defied him.

'The reason that for years I talked about nothing but peace was that I had to. The necessity now was to bring about a gradual psychological change in the German people and slowly to make it clear to them that there are things which, if peaceful means fail, must be achieved by force. To do that it was necessary, not to praise force as such, but to describe certain foreign events to the German people in such a manner that the people's inner voice slowly began to call for force.'

Adolf Hitler's address to the German press, 10 November 1938

On the offensive

There could never be 'peace in our time' so long as Hitler was in power. He put no value on treaties and agreements. As he once told his foreign minister, von Ribbentrop, 'If I am an ally of Russia today, I could attack her tomorrow. I just can't help myself.'

Hitler believed war was the final aim of politics, the natural way of things, and that invasion gave the aggressor the opportunity to 'cleanse' the conquered land of the 'unfit and unworthy'. In 1933, however, Hitler was in no position to prosecute a war in Europe. The German army numbered fewer than 100,000 men (the figure imposed by the Versailles Treaty). Even Poland had twice that number and France commanded a far superior force – but neither of these nations had the stomach for a fight.

Recalling the sacrifices they had made at Verdun in the First World War, the French favoured a defensive strategy. So they dug themselves in behind the Maginot Line and waited for the war clouds to blow over. (The Maginot Line was a network of forts and bunkers running between Belgium and Switzerland for 140 kilometres/87 miles, parallel with the German border.) However, the Poles were not so blasé. They were rumoured to have approached the French High Command with a plan for a joint invasion of Germany. But France was not willing to risk Hitler's wrath. Besides, it still occupied the Rhineland on Germany's western border, which left the Reich open to attack at any time they pleased.

Hitler knew he would give the French an excuse to march into Germany if he rearmed in open defiance of the Versailles Treaty. So, in October 1933, he demanded that the French and the British reduce their armaments to ensure parity with the Reich, knowing full well that they would refuse. When they did so, he withdrew his delegation from the Geneva disarmament conference and pulled out of the League of Nations. He cited discrimination and the right of the German nation to defend itself against aggression. It was a cynical ploy, but one that wrong-footed the Allies and seriously undermined their credibility as peacekeepers.

> 'War is the secret ruler of our century; peace signifies nothing more than an armistice between two wars.'
>
> Deutsche Wehr, official German army magazine, 1925

The 'mad dog' of Europe

Hitler's second strategy was to divide and conquer. By signing a ten-year, non-aggression pact with Poland in January 1934, he drove a wedge between the Allies and gave the Poles a reason to postpone the modernization of their armed forces. This was to prove a fatal mistake for Poland.

The following year brought more good news for the Führer. The coal-rich Saar region of Germany had been taken in part payment for reparations, but under the terms of the Versailles Treaty it was to be returned to Germany if its inhabitants voted in favour of reunification. They did so and Germany found itself with a rich source of fuel for its rearmament programme, which would now be undertaken in the open. In March 1935, Hitler announced the formation of the Luftwaffe, the new German air force, under the command of Field Marshal Goering. He also re-introduced conscription. Both measures were blatant violations of the Versailles Treaty, but again none of the Allies did more than voice their disapproval.

Embarrassed by their failure to read Hitler – they had hoped the return of the Saar would appease him – Britain, France and Italy agreed to act together to forestall any future violations. France also signed a pact of mutual assistance with the Soviet Union, which in turn signed a similar pact with the Czechs. But the idea that such a display of unity would dissuade Hitler from taking more liberties backfired – it only served to embolden him. Hitler then asked the British if he could build up the German navy to no more than a third of the size of the British fleet. Incredibly, they agreed in the belief that it was better to know what their potential enemy was up to. Ironically, the British were the first nation to sign a pact with the Nazis. Such a move served to offend the French, who felt they were being excluded from the negotiations, but political instability at home rendered them effectively impotent at a time when they could feasibly have curtailed Hitler's grand ambitions.

Not everyone was oblivious to the danger. The British military delegate to the Geneva disarmament conference, Brigadier Arthur Temperley, was quoted as saying, 'There is a mad dog abroad once more and we must resolutely combine to ensure its destruction or at least its confinement until the disease has run its course.'

But, already, the alliance of anti-German nations was coming apart at the seams. In October 1935, Mussolini invaded Ethiopia. The French condemned the action, but did nothing to prevent it, while the British voiced their dismay at reports of tribesmen being bombarded with poison gas and driven from their land by tanks.

The Four-Year Plan

The argument that Hitler was forced into an unavoidable and inevitable conflict with the West in 1939, or that he envisaged only a limited conflict over the strategically vital port of Danzig and the Polish corridor, simply doesn't stand up to scrutiny. Three years earlier he had instigated what he called the Four-Year Plan, which was to ensure that by 1940 all the elements would be in place for a full-scale war in Western Europe. The first step was to reduce Germany's dependence on imports of the oil, rubber and iron ore which were needed for the manufacture of tanks, armoured vehicles and aircraft. This was done by producing synthetic fuel and rubber and increasing Germany's stockpile of low-grade iron ore.

While German factories worked to capacity to rearm the Reich, the future pilots of Goering's Luftwaffe trained in secret. As Germany was prohibited from having an air force, the Luftwaffe pilots pretended to be part of the League of Air Sports and honed their skills using gliders. At the same time, the old cavalry regiments were disbanded and soldiers were being trained in the rapid mobility and firepower of small armoured vehicles. This was in anticipation of the tanks which would soon be rolling off the German production lines. While this was taking place, their commanders were being trained to take part in a new, fast-moving mechanized form of warfare. Developed by General Heinz Guderian, it was known as *blitzkrieg*, 'lightning war', a military tactic using mobile forces and locally concentrated firepower to create disorganization among enemy troops. This would allow the aggressor to break through enemy front lines, demolish their defences and sow panic in the rear, making it difficult to regroup and retaliate.

But before the might of the German military machine could be unleashed, Germany's south-eastern flank would have to be secured by the annexation of Austria and the subjugation of Czechoslovakia. The assimilation of Austria would fulfil Hitler's lifelong ambition to reunite his homeland with the Greater Reich and would also supply his armed forces with tens of thousands of rabidly nationalistic new recruits. The swift subjugation of the Czechs would presumably forestall any armed invasion by Poland or the Soviet Union. When Field Marshal von Blomberg, the minister of war, and Colonel-General von Fritsch, the army commander-in-chief, learned of these plans, they protested vehemently and were removed on Hitler's orders.

Reoccupying the Rhineland

The next logical step in Hitler's campaign was to take back the Rhineland, 24,475 square kilometres (9,450 square miles) of German territory bordering Holland, Belgium and France. The Allies had declared it a demilitarized zone to prevent Germany from launching an attack in the west. By signing the Locarno Pact in 1925, the Germans had promised to respect the buffer zone in return for which co-signatories Britain and Italy guaranteed that France would not invade Germany.

But Hitler knew that if he could recover the Rhineland, which included the strategically important city of Cologne, he would enhance his reputation at home and silence the critics who believed the Nazis were incapable of government. It was a gamble, but the odds were in his favour. He knew Italy would not condemn him because it was engaged in its own military adventures in Africa. Also, France was going through yet another political crisis (it had experienced 24 changes of government during the decade) and Britain would surely not act unilaterally. So, on the morning of 7 March 1936, 22,000 German troops marched into the demilitarized zone to the cheers of the inhabitants, who stood on the street corners and threw flowers at the men they believed to be their liberators.

A detachment of 2,000 troops continued across the bridges into Cologne, with secret orders to turn back if the French opposed the crossing. But not a single French soldier could be seen. It was another bloodless coup for the former Bavarian corporal.

Hitler's boldness was rewarded later that month. A plebiscite was called to legitimize the move and show the world that the German people endorsed their Führer's leadership. The result was a 99 per cent vote in favour of his actions. Hitler's popularity with the common people was now at an all-time high. Against the advice of his military commanders, he had acted on his instincts and been vindicated. From this point on, he would assume command of the German armed forces, giving orders he expected to be carried out without question.

The audacious reoccupation of the Rhineland brought Mussolini around. Hitler had long admired the Italian dictator, but the feeling had not been reciprocated. When they first met in Venice in 1934 Mussolini complained that the German leader was like a gramophone with only seven tunes. But the intervening years witnessed Hitler's gambles paying off handsomely while Italy became isolated. Il Duce desperately needed an ally and Hitler was only too willing to oblige. He arranged for coal and weapons to be sold to the Italians and joined with them in the fight against the communists in the Spanish Civil War (July 1936–March 1939), which was effectively a rehearsal for the next world war.

Austria

In the early 1930s, Vienna was a microcosm of the political situation that existed in neighbouring Germany. After the First World War, the Allies had carved up the Austro-Hungarian Empire; fascists and socialists vied for control of the former capital, a struggle which frequently erupted in violence. While the citizens of Hungary, Yugoslavia and Czechoslovakia appeared willing to accept their new status as independent nations, the majority of Austria's six-and-a-half million inhabitants felt they had lost their identity and yearned to be united with the Fatherland. Forty thousand of these were fanatical Nazi party members who were active in Vienna. They were opposed by the socialists, who were equally committed to the communist cause. Fearing an armed rebellion, Austrian Chancellor Engelbert Dollfuss banned the Nazi party in March 1933, but could not control the rival militias who took their struggle to the streets.

In July 1934, Hitler seized the opportunity to stage a coup. He authorized a plan calling for 150 SS troops to cross the border dressed in Austrian army and police uniforms, with orders to storm the Vienna parliament building. In the confusion, Dollfuss was mortally wounded, but other members of the cabinet managed to mobilize the Austrian army, who promptly arrested the SS men and restored order.

Dollfuss was succeeded by his deputy Kurt von Schuschnigg, who also distrusted Hitler, but shrewdly gave the German leader assurances that his country would not join an anti-German alliance. In a gesture of good faith, Schuschnigg released 17,000 Nazis from prison, only to see them initiate a reign of intimidation and violence. In the following years, their subversive activities succeeded in undermining Schuschnigg's authority, and intensified the call for Austria's union with the Reich.

With conditions in his favour, Hitler summoned Schuschnigg to Berchtesgaden on 12 February 1938. Hitler demanded that Schuschnigg lift the ban on the Austrian Nazi party and appoint leading Viennese Nazis to key ministries. Schuschnigg was also to announce his support

Hitler is driven through the streets of Vienna in his Mercedes-Benz

for Anschluss (union with Germany). If he did not, Germany would take his country by force. Fearing for his life, Schuschnigg agreed, but told the Austrian parliament he would never agree to Hitler's demand. He would, however, consent to a plebiscite in order to give the people a chance to choose between independence and Anschluss.

On 11 March 1938, the day before the vote, Schuschnigg learned that Hitler had issued orders to invade the next day. In desperation he called on the Allies to intervene, but neither France nor Britain would take sides in what they considered to be a domestic dispute.

Schuschnigg's only alternative was to mobilize the Austrian army, but he knew the Austrians would not fire on their German brothers. In any case, the German army was superior in terms of numbers and weapons. That evening, and with a heavy heart, he made his final radio broadcast as chancellor. After declaring that no German blood was to be spilled if German troops entered Austria, he then resigned, to be succeeded by the pro-Nazi Arthur Seyss-Inquart. Next morning, the German 8th Army streamed across the border and took Hitler's homeland without a shot.

They were welcomed so enthusiastically that Hitler decided to make a personal appearance in Linz later in the day. Driving through the city in an open-topped Mercedes, he appeared to the adoring crowds like a conquering hero. Speaking from the balcony of the city hall, he told them, 'I have believed in my task. I have lived for it and I have fought for it. And you are all my witnesses that I have now accomplished it.'

Although no blood had been spilled, old scores were being settled away from the public gaze. An estimated 70,000 socialists and other 'enemies of the Reich' were rounded up in Vienna and many were imprisoned. Even Schuschnigg was to spend seven years behind bars. He was lucky – others were thrown into Mauthausen concentration camp on the Danube.

Anyone who wondered what the new administration would do for Austria only had to look out of their window in the ensuing days. On every street, SA thugs dragged Jews from their homes and businesses and forced them to scrub pavements, to the amusement of jeering onlookers.

Czech mate

The annexation of Austria aroused the nationalistic yearnings of many of the three million German exiles living in the Sudetenland on Czechoslovakia's western border. The Nazi-sponsored Sudeten German party, led by Konrad Henlein, exploited their insecurity while Goebbels'

Ministry of Propaganda drummed up false stories describing their persecution by the Czechs. It was all part of a carefully planned strategy to provide a pretext for invasion. Hitler had tasted the thrill of conquest and was now greedy for more.

On 24 April 1938, goaded by Hitler, Henlein demanded complete autonomy for the Sudeten Germans, knowing full well that the Czech president Edvard Benes would refuse. On 19 May, German troops massed along the Czech border but were held in abeyance by 174,000 armed Czech reservists. On learning of the Czech response, Hitler called off the attack. However, he must have been encouraged by the complacency of the French foreign minister, George Bonnet, who commended him for his 'dignified and calm restraint', while condemning the Czechs for provoking the crisis.

The speed with which the Czechs mobilized their forces forced Hitler to reconsider his tactics. He now realized that the only way to ensure success was to make a lightning pre-emptive strike that would give them no time to retaliate. He was right in believing that the Czech reservists were the only force to overcome. Even as the soldiers were marching back to their barracks, the Allies were selling out the Czechs in the belief that peace was worth having at any price.

The British sent an elderly diplomat, Lord Runciman, to act as an 'honest broker' but he allowed himself to be persuaded that the Sudeten Germans had a legitimate grievance and came away praising Henlein as an 'absolutely honest fellow'.

Believing themselves betrayed by the Allies, the Czech cabinet agreed to Henlein's demands. He could not follow through with this, of course, because he knew Hitler would settle for nothing less than total capitulation. Henlein's response was to order his thugs to start riots throughout the region in the hope of provoking the police. The Sudetens could then claim they were being persecuted and would be justified in calling for German intervention.

While the Czech authorities were battling to suppress the violence, diplomatic envoys and intelligence sources were filing reports in London and Paris. There were massive German troop movements towards the Czech border, travel restrictions for all but military personnel within the Reich were imposed, and civilian labourers were despatched to sites of strategic importance. There could be no doubt about it: Germany was preparing for war.

But if Hitler thought he could rely on the unquestioning obedience of his military commanders merely because he had rearmed them, he was sorely mistaken. The Chief of the Army General Staff, General Ludwig Beck resigned when he realized that Hitler was committed to war. Then on 17 July his counterpart in the navy, Vice-Admiral Günther Guse, voiced his concerns in a memorandum to his commander-in-chief. It was clearly designed to appeal to reason. 'There can be no doubt,' Guse wrote, 'that in a conflict European in scope Germany would be the loser and that the Führer's whole work so far would be in jeopardy. So far, I have not spoken to any ranking officer in any of the three branches of the armed services who did not share this opinion.'

But Hitler was spoiling for a fight. His nature and his standing with the German people demanded it.

Peace at any price

Unknown to the Allies, Hitler had set a date for the invasion of Czechoslovakia – 30 September 1938. So when British Prime Minister Neville Chamberlain flew to Berchtesgaden on 15 September, in a last-ditch attempt to seek a compromise to the Czech crisis, he was working against Hitler's timetable.

> *'Armies do not exist for peace. They exist solely for triumphant exertion in war.'*
>
> Adolf Hitler

By the time Chamberlain arrived at the Eagle's Nest, the 69-year-old politician was exhausted. After a seven-hour drive from Munich airport, he was not in the best state to debate the issue with a man of Hitler's volatile temperament. Their initial meeting was brief and uncomfortable for both men, with Hitler treating his guest as brusquely as he might a travelling salesman pushing a product he had no interest in purchasing. Hitler browbeat Chamberlain with a tiresome monologue in which he detailed yet again the many injustices imposed on Germany by the Versailles Treaty. He concluded with his assertion that the Sudeten question was one of race and not of territory, and for that reason it was not up for negotiation. When he heard this, the mild-mannered Chamberlain lost his composure: 'If the Führer is determined to settle this by force, why did he let me come here?' he barked angrily.

This unexpected outburst took Hitler aback. He responded by saying that if the Allies could guarantee that the Czechs would hand the Sudetenland over to the Reich, he would order his army to stand down. He'd give his 'sacred oath' that he would respect the sovereignty of the Czech state.

Under the illusion that he had won a concession, Chamberlain returned to cheering crowds in London. But behind the scenes the Czechs were seething. In their eyes they had been betrayed by Chamberlain's 'senile ambition' to 'play the peacemaker'. Instead of coming to their aid, France and Britain had given the Czechs an ultimatum. Unless they accepted Hitler's terms, the Allies would not consider themselves bound by any past agreement to guarantee Czech sovereignty. An embittered Benes convened a cabinet meeting and informed his colleagues that they had 'no choice' but to agree to the cession of the Sudetenland to the Reich. He told them, 'We have been basely betrayed.'

Chamberlain flew to Germany again on 22 September, believing he had appeased the dictator and that the signing of the terms of the agreement was a mere formality. Instead, Hitler rejected the Anglo-French proposals for an orderly withdrawal of Czech troops and police and demanded they do so immediately. When Chamberlain began to explain the impracticalities of such a move and the benefits of the Allied timetable, Hitler flew into one of his infamous rages and the meeting had to be abandoned.

Rumours of war

Chamberlain returned to London with his plans for a peaceful resolution in tatters. The Allies realized they could no longer labour under the illusion that Hitler could be reasoned with. He was intent on war and was well prepared because the Four-Year Plan had been fulfilled to his satisfaction. The German army had swelled from seven divisions to 51, among them five heavy armoured divisions and four light ones. The German navy boasted a formidable fleet consisting of two battleships of 31,200 tons, two heavy cruisers, 17 destroyers and 47 submarines. The Luftwaffe had grown from nothing to 21 squadrons, all manned by pilots who had gained considerable experience and skill during the Spanish Civil War. The German armaments industry was operating at full capacity and already exceeding the production peak of the last war. Nazi Germany was a nation armed to the teeth and straining at the leash. It is understandable that Britain and France were prepared to do everything they could to avoid a conflict. They knew there was a good chance they would be defeated.

The British attitude was summed up by Chamberlain in a broadcast to the nation made on 28 September. He tactlessly expressed his indifference to the fate of the Czech people by referring to their predicament as a 'quarrel in a faraway country between peoples of whom we know nothing'. Having resigned themselves to abandonment by their former allies, the Czechs called up an extra million reservists. For their part, the British could do little but dig trenches in public parks and prepare the civilian population for an imminent attack from the air. A blackout was introduced which required the windows of all domestic and business premises to be covered after dusk, so that no lights could be seen by attacking bombers. Vehicle headlights were also partially covered, which led to an increase in fatal traffic accidents and crimes committed under the cloak of darkness.

The great fear was that the Germans would use poison gas as they had done in France during the First World War. It was also expected that they would drop gas bombs on Britain's cities. The newsreels showed plucky Londoners trying on their government-issue gas masks and giving the 'V for victory' sign in defiance of the Nazi menace, but off camera the public mood was close to panic. Images of death raining down from the sky filled ordinary citizens with horror. Experts predicted one million injured in the first two months of the war.

Plans were put in place to send London's children to the countryside for their own safety. They were to stay with strangers willing to offer them bed and board, but their parents would have to remain behind. The anguish and suffering had begun even before the first shot was fired.

As the news of German mobilization reached the French High Command behind the high walls of their châteaux, the men of the Maginot Line were put on alert and more reservists were sent to reinforce their defences in anticipation of an imminent attack.

Selling out the Czechs

Perhaps it was this demonstration of the belated Allied resolve that prompted Hitler to postpone his planned invasion. But it's more likely that Mussolini's offer to mediate persuaded him to reconsider hours before the attack was scheduled to take place. On 30 September, Hitler met with the British and French premiers in Munich, under the watchful eye of the Italian dictator and the world's press. Relishing his role as international statesman, Mussolini informed Chamberlain and Daladier of Germany's demands, which he presented as his own proposals for peace. The Czechs would have to withdraw from the Sudetenland by 1 October, giving up its main fortifications and heavy industry; in return, the Allies would guarantee the new frontier.

Although the Czechs would have no say in the matter, the Allies assuaged their own guilt by telling themselves they had no choice but to sign the Munich Agreement.

When the Czech prime minister, Jan Syrovy, learned of the terms, he said it was a choice between 'being murdered or committing suicide'. In a radio broadcast to the nation that same evening he told his people, 'We had the choice between a desperate and hopeless defence and acceptance of conditions unparalleled in history for ruthlessness.'

The commanders of the Czech armed forces were not as spineless as the Allied leaders had proved to be. They offered to fight, despite the overwhelming odds against them, hoping that if they could hold out for several weeks the Allies might finally be shamed into action. But President Benes had lost all faith in Britain and France. On 1 October, the first German divisions marched unopposed into the Sudetenland.

The Munich Agreement did not avert war, it only postponed it. It was a shameful act of cowardice on behalf of the Allies, who were to pay the price for their appeasement policy in the coming conflict. Whether France and Britain could have altered the course of history by coming to the aid of the Czechs is a moot point, but what is certain is that appeasement did nothing to deter a dictator.

Peace in our time

As a postscript to the Munich Agreement, Chamberlain pressed Hitler into signing a hastily drawn statement affirming Anglo–German co-operation in the event of a future dispute. The Nazi leader apparently gave little consideration to the document, but Chamberlain believed he had secured the future of Europe. On his return to London, he triumphantly waved the scrap of paper that bore his and the Führer's signatures, while the crowds cheered themselves hoarse. He announced that he had secured 'peace with honour' and 'peace in our time'.

But Conservative MP Winston Churchill, who had been warning of the dangers of German rearmament for years, but to no avail, declared it was only 'the beginning of the reckoning'. He was not alone in this view. The French premier Daladier was acutely aware of the awful error he had committed in giving in to Hitler. As his plane approached the runway in Paris, he saw the waiting crowds of well-wishers and assumed they had come to attack him. When he saw that they were waving and smiling he turned to his assistant, murmuring: 'Idiots! They do not know what they are applauding.'

Hitler's territorial ambitions were not, of course, satisfied by the acquisition of the Sudetenland. The Sudeten Germans meant nothing to Hitler. They were merely a symbol of his authority, a trophy with which to taunt his enemies. He would settle for nothing less than the surrender of the Czech nation and the humiliation of their new president, Emil Hácha (Benes had resigned in October 1938, the month after Munich). In the early hours of 14 March 1939, Hitler received Hácha at the chancellery in Berlin, in the presence of Goering and von Ribbentrop, and presented him with an ultimatum. He could either invite the German army to quell the alleged disturbances in his country, thereby making the Czech state a German protectorate, or he could watch Prague being bombed to rubble by German Stukas.

Faced with such a threat and the intimidating physical presence of Hermann Goering, the 66-year-old Hácha had what appeared to be a mild heart attack before losing consciousness. The Führer's quack physician Dr Morell was called. He managed to revive Hácha briefly but he passed out for a second time. A stimulant was again administered, after which Hácha was reminded how many innocent Czech lives lay in the balance if he did not sign the two declarations that had been prepared for him by the Nazis. The first declaration requested Germany's 'protection' and the second ordered the Czech army to lay down its arms. Hácha held out until 4 a.m., at which point his resistance and his health gave way, then he signed both documents. Six hours later, a column of several hundred German armoured vehicles rattled through the cobblestone streets and squares of Prague. The snow lent a Christmas card look to the picturesque city, but it wasn't the weather that kept the crowds away.

Too little, too late: the fate of Poland

History relates that the world went to war to defend beleaguered Poland, but not soon enough to save it. The truth, however, is not so simple. Since 1935, Poland had been ruled by a military junta. Three years later, the Polish government threatened Lithuania with invasion if it did not restore the road, rail and other communication links which had been cut following a dispute dating from the Polish occupation of Vilnius in 1919. Fearing that Germany might attack them if they mobilized in their own defence, the Lithuanians acceded to the junta's demands. Their belief was that Polish occupation would be the lesser of the two evils.

During the Czech crisis, the Polish pro-Nazi junta had been offered a share of the spoils provided that they aligned themselves with Germany in the event of war breaking out. The Poles declined as diplomatically as they could under the circumstances, which only infuriated Hitler and intensified his distrust of the junta. When that crisis passed, the Nazis pressed Poland to join the Anti-Comintern Pact against Russia. But, again, the Poles prevaricated in the hope that the Nazi eagle and the Soviet bear would eventually turn on each other, leaving Poland to watch the conflict in safety from the sidelines.

By January 1939, Hitler's patience with the Poles was wearing thin. He received the Polish foreign minister, Colonel Josef Beck, at Berchtesgaden and repeated the demands he had made some months earlier. They included the return of the Baltic port of Danzig and the right to build road and rail links through a strip of land running from the Vistula river to the Baltic Sea. Known as the Polish Corridor, it divided Germany from East Prussia. Although Colonel Beck was a Nazi sympathizer, he realized that making these concessions would signal the end of Polish independence – so he refused to agree to Hitler's ultimatum.

Just when it looked as though Poland would go the way of Czechoslovakia, the British belatedly declared their willingness to go to war to defend Polish sovereignty. It was an extraordinary turn of events. Britain and France had failed to come to the aid of democratic Czechoslovakia, but now they were declaring themselves ready to go to war to support a pro-Nazi junta. Even Hitler, the master of diplomatic duplicity, had not foreseen this turn of events. According to Admiral Canaris, Hitler reacted to the news by pounding his desk with his fists and promising to cook the British 'a stew they will choke on'.

> 'Now we are told that this seizure of territory has been necessitated by disturbances in Czechoslovakia. . . . If there were disorders, were they not fomented from without?. . . Is this the end of an old adventure, or is it the beginning of a new? Is this the last attack upon a small state or is it to be followed by others? Is this, in effect, a step in the direction of an attempt to dominate the world by force?'
>
> Neville Chamberlain,
> 17 March 1939

Hitler would not be denied his war a second time. On 15 March, German troops marched into Bohemia, Moravia and Slovakia. This meant that Poland was now fenced in by German troops on three sides, with the Russians to the east. It was an indefensible situation. Confident of a quick victory, Hitler issued a top secret directive to his armed forces on 3 April. Codenamed 'Case White', it detailed plans for the invasion of Poland, to be executed no later than 1 September. It was an imaginative and audacious plan – a decisive lightning strike spearheaded by massed divisions of tanks, supported by air strikes, with infantry bringing up the rear to mop up pockets of resistance. The attack was to be directed and co-ordinated by a network of modern communications.

The idea was the brainchild of Colonel Günther Blumentritt and generals Gerd von Rundstedt and Erich von Manstein. Hitler familiarized himself with the details of the attack and made suggestions, but the only constructive part he played, according to General Warlimont, was planning the assault on a bridge at Dirschau.

Attack at the first opportunity

On 23 May, Hitler convened a meeting of the German General Staff and laid out his strategy. No minutes were permitted to be recorded, but Lieutenant-Colonel Rudolf Schmundt made handwritten notes that documented Hitler's determination 'to attack Poland at the first opportunity'. He added, 'We cannot expect a repetition of the Czech affair. There will be war. Our task is to isolate Poland. Success in isolating her will be decisive. . . . The Führer doubts the possibility of a peaceful settlement with England . . . England is our enemy and the conflict with England is a matter of life and death. . . . The aim must be to deal the enemy a smashing or a finally decisive blow right at the start . . . . Preparations must be made for a long war as well as for a surprise attack and every possible intervention by England on the continent must be smashed. . . . If we succeed in occupying and securing Holland and Belgium, as well as defeating France, the basis for a successful war against England has been created. . . . There are no further successes to be achieved without bloodshed.'

Poland's Colonel Beck was equally belligerent. On 28 March he summoned the German ambassador and told him that any attempt by the Nazi Senate in Danzig to alter the status of the free city would be regarded as an act of war. The indignant ambassador protested that

Beck evidently wished to negotiate at the point of a bayonet. 'This is your own method,' Beck replied coolly.

By early May 1939, with war looking more likely than ever, Beck told the Polish parliament: 'We in Poland do not recognize the concept of peace at any price. There is only one thing in the life of men, nations and states that is without price and this is honour.'

This was not mere bravado. Poland could call up more than two million men, and France had also assured Poland that it would attack Germany by air and launch a full-scale invasion within 15 days of the first shot being fired. But unknown to the Poles, the French had no intention of honouring their guarantee. Their public support for Poland was merely intended to persuade the Russians to side with the Allies. French intelligence had overestimated the resilience of Germany's 'west wall' and advised the High Command that they were incapable of breaching the German defences.

The British were less forthcoming, offering vague promises of reinforcements and bombing offensives against the invader. Their reluctance was understandable, for at that time they only had one armoured brigade and five infantry divisions, a vastly inadequate number of fighter planes and no anti-aircraft guns or radar installations to mount an effective defence. The British armaments industry was still in mothballs following the First World War and it would take at least a year to produce sufficient munitions to supply its armed forces.

Eve of war

Hitler believed the next war would be a limited one and that it would be over swiftly. His commanders were in agreement, with the exception of General Georg Thomas who argued that Poland would be the spark to ignite a world war. But Keitel rebuffed such doubts by saying that Britain was too decadent, France too degenerate and the United States too uninterested to wage war. None of these countries would sacrifice its sons for Poland. But both Keitel and Hitler had overlooked the possibility that, as a democracy, Britain could elect a new and more capable leader to defy the Nazi tyrant and the United States could be roused to action if attacked. On the eve of war, Hitler doubted that the Allies would be able to back up their threat with action. In the event of hostilities, Britain would have to send troops from Egypt under the watchful eye of the German navy and the U-boat wolf packs which were prowling the Black Sea.

A memorandum written by Admiral Hermann Bohm on the eve of the planned invasion of Poland noted, 'In the Führer's view, the probability of the Western powers intervening in the conflict is not great. . . . France cannot afford a long and bloody war. Its manpower is too small, its supplies are insufficient. France has been pushed into this whole situation against its will; for France, the term war of nerves applies.'

Hitler correctly assumed that France had been exhausted by the Great War and would capitulate rather than become immersed in a second protracted conflict. But if any single event can be said to have convinced Hitler that the time had finally come to settle the Polish question, it was the signing of the non-aggression pact between Germany and Soviet Russia on 21 August 1939. The news of the accord came as a total surprise to the Allies and sent shock waves around the world. It seemed inconceivable that the communist state could come to an agreement with the fascist dictatorship – yet this should have been foreseen.

Russia sides with Hitler

Britain had been making advances to Russia for more than a year, but had bungled the situation badly by sending a minor foreign office official to negotiate with Molotov, the Russian minister for foreign affairs. Molotov had interpreted this as a slight and an indication that the British had no serious expectations of success. Either that, or they thought an agreement would be a mere formality. Furthermore, the British civil servant was dispatched by boat, so arrived a week later than he would have done had he flown to Moscow. By this time, the Nazis had persuaded the Soviets to seal their deal. Aside from the diplomatic gaffe, the Soviets distrusted and despised the Western democracies, who were in no position to offer any significant concessions or inducements. The Nazis, however, were prepared to sign a secret protocol promising the Russians not only half of Poland, but also all of Latvia and Estonia if they collaborated.

The Russians had another reason for siding with Hitler. They were simply not ready for war. Stalin's purges of the officer corps had decimated the Red Army leadership and left the rank and file demoralized and lacking discipline. They could not be relied upon to fight if there were no experienced officers to command them. In siding with Germany, Stalin secured his own position and furthered his own interests, but he also gave Hitler a free hand to do as he pleased in Western Europe. All Hitler needed now was a pretext to invade.

REINHARD HEYDRICH

HITLER'S HANGMAN

'I must admit that this gassing had a calming effect on me, I was always horrified at executions by firing squads.'

Heydrich (second from right) and Himmler (second from left) were both inspired by Germany's mythical past

With his blond hair, blue eyes and Nordic features, SS Obergruppenführer Reinhard Heydrich – Himmler's second-in-command – personified the cold-blooded, clinically efficient Nazi officer. He was a highly educated, cultured idealist who was caught up in the maelstrom of extreme nationalism and corrupted by a regime that rewarded blind obedience and ruthless efficiency. But an objective assessment of his personality reveals that the zeal with which he organized the most barbaric crimes of the Nazi era may have been inspired by revenge rather than a perverted idealism.

Heydrich was raised a Catholic in the predominantly Protestant town of Halle, where his father founded a musical conservatory and his mother enjoyed a career as a professional pianist. The family was prosperous, which made Reinhard the envy of his classmates who propagated unsubstantiated rumours that the family had inherited their wealth from Jewish relatives. Heydrich's arrogance and accomplishments, which included proficiency on the violin, only added to their antagonism.

REVILED IN HIS YOUTH

But life at home was not as ideal at it appeared to be. Heydrich's mother was a strict disciplinarian and beat the boy for any infraction of her rigid rules. School life was equally harsh as classmates ridiculed his thin falsetto voice, while the older boys physically attacked him and taunted him about his reputed Jewish ancestry. He grew up bitter, not with his tormentors – but with the Jews on whom he blamed his troubles. Had he not been ostracized because of his alleged racial origins, he believed he would have been popular and respected. Someone had to pay for his humiliation. He became quiet and withdrawn, putting his energy into athletics and winning several fencing competitions, but his achievements didn't impress his adversaries.

On leaving school Heydrich enlisted in the navy, believing it would bring him the status and respect to which he felt he was entitled, but his fellow cadets were equally unforgiving, goading him over his presumed Jewish origins and his love of classical music and taking every opportunity to embarrass and belittle him. They called him 'Billy Goat' because of his high bleating laugh and reviled him for his arrogance and stated ambition to become an admiral.

Despite his unpopularity, Heydrich seemed destined for an illustrious military career, but in 1931 he was court-martialled and dishonourably discharged for breaking off his engagement to his pregnant fiancée, an act 'unbecoming an officer and a gentleman'. He told the tribunal that he refused to marry a woman who had given herself to him so freely. By doing so, she had proved herself unsuitable to be the wife of an officer.

FAVOURED BY HIMMLER

Heydrich's next romantic entanglement was with a fanatical Nazi, Lina van Osten, who persuaded her future husband to apply to the small but rapidly expanding SS, where his ambition would be recognized and rewarded.

Himmler took an immediate liking to the tall, slender Heydrich who appeared to embody the qualities the Reichsführer valued so highly – namely, thoroughness and the ability to formulate a detailed plan of action from the vaguest idea. Himmler asked Heydrich to draw up a blueprint for a new security service, the SD (*Sicherheitsdienst*), and was so impressed by the proposal that he hired him immediately. The SD would be independent of the Gestapo and charged with investigating those citizens and officials suspected of disloyalty to the party. It would rely on a network of informers and electronic surveillance, including bugging premises, tapping telephones and using hidden cameras. The organization was to play a crucial role in the discrediting of two top German generals who expressed opposition to Hitler's war plans in 1937. Werner von Blomberg and Werner von Fritsch were framed for crimes they had not committed, giving Hitler reason to dismiss them and assume the role of commander-in-chief.

ALLEGATIONS OF JEWISHNESS

Heydrich had shown little interest in extreme nationalism or the Nazi party and was marginalized by his fellow naval officers for his lack of political zeal, but after his appointment he redoubled his efforts to convince his new employer of his commitment to the cause. Yet rumours of his Jewish ancestry persisted, forcing Himmler to accede to demands for an official investigation during which Hitler personally interviewed Heydrich in order to reassure himself that the rumours were false. Following the interview, Hitler told Himmler that Heydrich was: 'a highly gifted but also very dangerous man, whose gifts the movement had to retain. . . . [Heydrich could be] extremely useful; for he would eternally be grateful to us that we had kept him and not expelled him and would obey blindly.'

Heydrich proved to be both conscientious and committed and soon compiled thick files on those of questionable loyalty; this earned him rapid promotion. Within two years he had been promoted to brigadier general and earned the admiration and respect of Himmler.

In June 1934, just two months after Himmler was appointed head of the newly formed Gestapo with Heydrich as his second-in-command, the pair hatched a plot to purge the SA of its leadership and settle old scores with dozens of former enemies within the state.

As Himmler's power grew, so Heydrich's influence increased until he was the second most feared man in the SS.

WANNSEE MEETING

On 20 January 1942, Heydrich, now Obergruppenführer of the Reich Main Security Office (the RSHA) – which commanded the Gestapo, the SS Intelligence Service (SD) and the Criminal Police (KRIPO), as well as the Foreign Intelligence Service – convened a meeting of top Nazi officials in a suburb of Berlin. The setting was a villa overlooking the Grosser Wannsee, a favourite beauty spot for vacationing Berliners.

The stated purpose of the meeting was the planning and implementation of Goering's order of 31 July 1941 for the rounding-up, transportation and extermination of the 11 million Jews in Germany and the occupied territories of the East ('the total solution of the Jewish question'). However, Heydrich used it to establish his authority over the various departments that would be co-ordinating their combined resources in the forthcoming operation. He spoke for an hour, during which he outlined the progress that had been made on marginalizing the Jews from German society. Then he moved on to the difficult question of establishing the criteria for determining who would be considered suitable for 'resettlement' and who would be exempt, on the grounds of intermarriage, military service (many Jews had served in the Great War) and continuing usefulness to the state. Jews were not the only people deemed unworthy of life. The population of the conquered territories was to be reduced by 30 million through starvation, as food and other vital supplies were to be diverted to Germany.

The proceedings were conducted in a brisk and businesslike fashion, with Heydrich's deputy, Adolf Eichmann, recording the minutes as if it were a conventional board meeting of I.G. Farben, the company that would soon be bidding to supply the gas chambers with the lethal pesticide Zyklon B.

LANGUAGE OF DEATH

Heydrich was shrewd enough to realize that the discussion would have to be documented in coded language. This would render their true intentions unclear if the war turned against them and they were brought to account for their crimes. So he instructed Eichmann to use euphemistic 'office' language when compiling the report at the end of the day. It was decided that 'evacuation' should be used when what was really meant was 'extermination'.

Heydrich employed Jewish people to police the round-up and ensure the orderly transportation of neighbours, friends and even family members from the ghettos to the extermination camps. But accomplice or not, all would meet their deaths when their usefulness expired. In deceiving the victims into believing they were merely being resettled in the East, and making them pay for the privilege, Heydrich believed he had proved himself intellectually superior and was therefore finally free of the 'stigma' of racial inferiority to his Aryan comrades.

ASSASSINATION

Hitler rewarded Heydrich's initiative by appointing him deputy protector of Bohemia and Moravia (the Nazi-renamed former Czechoslovakia). Heydrich flaunted this position by riding in an open-topped Mercedes without an armed escort, showing his contempt for a population he believed had been terrorized into submission.

But his arrogance would prove fatal. He was mortally wounded by two Czech OSS agents on the morning of 27 May 1942. He might have recovered had he allowed Czech surgeons to operate on him, but he distrusted them.

By the time his chosen physicians arrived, the wound had become infected by fibres from his uniform and the horsehair upholstery of the car. He died from blood poisoning on 4 June.

Enraged, Hitler took retribution for Heydrich's murder by ordering the execution of every adult male in the villages of Lidice and Ležáky and the burning of both villages to the ground. Eighty-one of Lidice's children were deported to Chelmno extermination camp; the remainder were deported to Germany for adoption by Nazi families. Four pregnant women had their babies aborted at the hospital where Heydrich died and then were sent to Ravensbrück concentration camp to die with their families and neighbours. In total, more than 1,300 people were murdered and an estimated 13,000 imprisoned as punishment for Heydrich's death.

Heydrich's assassination had been sanctioned by exiled Czech president Benes in the hope that German reprisals would rouse the Czech people to open rebellion. But the uprising did not happen and many Czechs felt thousands had been needlessly sacrificed to eliminate one hated Nazi.

'The gentlemen were standing together, or sitting together and were discussing the subject quite bluntly, quite differently from the language which I had to use later in the record. During the conversation they minced no words about it at all . . . they spoke about methods of killing, about liquidation, about extermination. . . . After the conference, Heydrich, Müller [General Heinrich Müller, head of the Gestapo] and myself sat cozily around the fireplace. We had drinks. We had brandy. We sang songs. After a while, we got up on chairs and drank a toast. Then we got up on the tables and went round and round. On the chairs. On the tables. Then we sat around peacefully, giving ourselves a rest after so many exhausting hours.'

Adolf Eichmann describing his experience of the Wannsee Conference

REINHARD HEYDRICH DOSSIER

- Heydrich engineered a purge of top-ranking Soviet officers in 1937 by supplying Soviet agents with information that implicated the officers in a planned coup against Stalin.

- After the Anschluss in March 1938, Heydrich established the Central Office for Jewish Emigration to fleece Austrian Jews of their property and valuables in return for exit visas. When Goering saw the potential for enriching himself, he authorized a branch to be set up in Berlin.

- Heydrich orchestrated the 'spontaneous' protests of Kristallnacht in November 1938 as a reprisal for the assassination of a German diplomat in Paris by a Jewish youth whose deportation to France he had authorized.

- Heydrich conceived Operation Himmler (aka Operation Konserve) to give Germany an excuse to invade Poland. The SS planted the bodies of murdered concentration camp prisoners at a German radio station at Gleiwitz (see page 248).

- Following the invasion of Poland, Heydrich formed the SS *Einsatzgruppen* (Special Action Groups) whose task was to round up and execute leading politicians, the aristocracy, the professional elite and the clergy in the East, as well as members of any group which might pose a threat to the occupying forces and their puppet administration. Leaders of the *Einsatzgruppen* vied with one another to see how many Jews they could execute in a day. By the end of the war it was estimated that they had murdered a total of 1,300,000.

- Heydrich proposed that Jews in the occupied territories should be rounded up and herded into ghettos until their deportation or liquidation could be arranged. Meanwhile starvation and disease would reduce the numbers that had to be dealt with. By the middle of 1941, half-a-million people had died in Krakow, Warsaw and Lodz.

CHAPTER 14
Total War

The first shots of the Second World War were fired by men who were already dead. On 31 August 1939, a squad of SS men picked out a dozen male inmates from a concentration camp close to the Polish border and ordered them at gunpoint to dress in Polish army uniforms. They then shot all but one of them in cold blood. The dead bodies and the lone survivor were driven to the German radio station at Gleiwitz on the Polish border, where the SS staged a fake attack.

They burst into the studio, broadcast a brief message announcing the Polish invasion of Germany and then shot the remaining prisoner to make it look as though he and his dead comrades had been killed during an attack on the radio station. The raid was codenamed Operation Himmler. Now the Nazis were free to retaliate.

Contrary to popular belief, the German invasion of Poland did not begin with columns of Panzer tanks driving deep into Polish territory, but in a more conventional manner. At dawn on 1 September 1939, the German battleship SMS *Schleswig-Holstein* opened fire against a fortress 6.5 kilometres (4 miles) north of Danzig. The battleship had sneaked into port several days earlier under the guise of a ceremonial visit, and was in position to pound the fort the moment Hitler gave the order. It was 4.45 a.m. and the Second World War had begun.

The famed German *blitzkrieg*, when it finally came, had a less than auspicious start. While Stuka bombers strafed the enemy's airfields, railways and military installations, the spearhead of Hitler's mechanized columns became shrouded in fog and, in the confusion, was shelled by its own artillery. Only one in six divisions boasted tank support – the remainder were infantry divisions supplied in the main by horse-drawn wagons. But the massed mechanized columns made incredible progress despite the poor condition of the Polish roads, in some cases advancing 64 kilometres (40 miles) in a day. It was a textbook double-pincer operation, intended to encircle the main Polish forces and cut off their retreat to the Vistula river. However, on the second day, the XIX Panzer Corps led by Lieutenant-General Guderian came to a grinding halt, having run out of fuel and ammunition. Before the Polish divisions could mount an attack, German supply columns broke through the Polish lines and had the Panzers moving again. Elsewhere, the German 4th Army encircled two divisions of Polish troops in the Danzig Corridor and destroyed them in a matter of hours. It was during this battle that the Polish cavalry made their suicidal charge against the German armour.

Britain and France issued an ultimatum on the second day. They threatened to go to war if Hitler did not give an assurance that he would withdraw his troops by 3 September. No such assurance was forthcoming and from that day onwards Britain and France were officially at war with Germany. This time there was no patriotic rush to enlist, as there had been in 1914.

Poland

Seven days after the invasion started, the German 14th Army was encroaching on Krakow. Guderian reported to Hitler that he had suffered fewer than 1,000 casualties, thanks to the mobility and superior firepower of the Panzers. In the following weeks, obsolete Polish tanks and artillery proved to be no match for the fast-moving and heavily armed German Panzers which attacked en masse, while the Poles deployed their inferior tanks defensively in support of their infantry. The Polish air force ultimately fared no better. It was thought to be no match for the Luftwaffe. The majority of its 900 elderly aircraft were considered useful only for training; but the Polish pilots made up for the inadequacy of their machines with their skill and courage, downing or severely damaging 400 of Goering's fighters. Tragically, the effectiveness of Poland's fighting men was fatally undermined by their leaders, who could not co-ordinate an effective defence because they foolishly relied on civil communications, which were easily disrupted by the Germans.

Soon the Germans were advancing on Warsaw, but they did not take the capital as easily as expected. On 10 September, the bulk of the Polish army was reinforced by survivors from the battle in the Danzig Corridor and together they attacked the flank of the German 8th Army which was situated 112.5 kilometres (70 miles) west of the city. For two days they harassed the Germans until Rundstedt was forced to divert two divisions to counter-attack. By 17 September, Warsaw was encircled and the Polish army had virtually disintegrated. In all, 52,000 men had been captured and an estimated 750,000 killed. There were still pockets of resistance, which would cost the Germans dearly, but it was only a matter of time before the last defenders threw down their arms and surrendered.

If the remnants of the Polish army hoped to hold out until the Allies came to their aid, they would be sorely disappointed. The British were afraid to bomb German cities in case they killed civilians. So they contented themselves with dropping leaflets over the Rhineland, while the French sent nine divisions 11 kilometres (7 miles) into German territory. This was a token diversionary manoeuvre designed to send out a message of sympathy to the embattled Poles. Incredibly, the British Air Ministry decided against bombing German munitions factories or the newly acquired Skoda works in Czechoslovakia, which had been converted to aeroplane production. This was because the British considered these facilities to be private property and feared that the Germans might retaliate.

Warsaw surrenders

If the Poles had any heart left for the fight they must have lost it at this moment. The fatal blow was not delivered by the Germans, as expected, but by the Russians. Thirty-five divisions of the Soviet army were ordered to occupy the eastern border region in anticipation of the partition of Poland. The news of the Soviet incursion prompted the chief of the Polish armed forces, Marshal Rydz-Âmigly, to flee to Romania, closely followed by the other members of the government. After having been betrayed by the Allies, the Polish army and the people had now been abandoned by their own leaders. Nevertheless, they held out in the besieged capital for a further ten days, although they had no food or water and were continually under bombardment by the Luftwaffe and German artillery. On 27 September, the city of Warsaw finally surrendered and 140,000 exhausted and wounded Polish soldiers were taken into captivity.

> '*I do not ask my generals to understand my orders, but only to carry them out.*'
>
> Adolf Hitler, 1939

On the next day, the 24,000-strong garrison at Modlin fell into German hands, leaving the remnants of the Polish army surrounded on three sides, with their backs to the Romanian border. A few days later, 150,000 men were killed or captured, leaving 100,000 to escape into Romania – but not before they had fought their way through the Ukrainians, who had sided with the Russians. The last Polish troops held out at Kock, a garrison 121 kilometres (75 miles) southeast of Warsaw, until 6 October.

Hitler's conquest of Poland was complete, at the cost of 8,000 German dead, 5,000 missing in action and just over 27,000 wounded. But Poland's suffering was not over. In fact, it was just about to begin. When the Panzers and the Wehrmacht moved out, the Nazi administrators and the *Einsatzgruppen* (SS death squads) moved in.

War in the west

The conquest of Poland sowed the seeds of Hitler's defeat. It convinced him that he was a military genius guided by Providence, and he had no need of his generals' advice. He believed his lack of formal military training and his experience as a common soldier in the trenches gave him a greater understanding of tactics than his own commanders. He also convinced himself that he had conceived the plan for the invasion. But although he took credit for it at the earliest opportunity, he had merely approved the work done by his commanders.

Shortly after the fall of Poland, Hitler called a meeting of his senior staff at the new Reichschancellery in Berlin. His object was to inform them that he demanded their unconditional obedience. During the course of a three-hour speech he told them, 'Neither a military man nor a civilian could replace me. I am convinced of my powers of intellect and decision. No one has ever achieved what I have achieved. I have led the German people to a great height. I have to choose between victory and destruction. I choose victory. I shall stand or fall in this struggle. I shall shrink from nothing and shall destroy everyone who is opposed to me.'

The last remark was intended to intimidate anyone who might be contemplating deposing him, for Hitler distrusted his senior officers. He still blamed them for Germany's defeat in the previous war and despised those who had warned him against prosecuting another war they believed Germany could not win.

> 'We are not interested in the prosperity of the country . . . . What we are interested in is establishing German authority in this area. . . . We will judge it by how impossible it will become for Poland ever to rise again. . . . What we have here is a gigantic labour camp.'
>
> Hans Frank, governor-general of occupied Poland, November 1940

In the previous year, he had sacked Field Marshal von Blomberg, the commander-in-chief of the armed forces and replaced General von Fritsch, the commander-in-chief of the army, because they had dared to express the opinion that Germany could not win a major war in Western Europe. Then he had announced the formation of a new command structure to be known as *Oberkommando der Wehrmacht* (OKW), which would be manned by his

The Germans goose-stepped their way into Poland in 1939. The invasion began on 1 September and was over by 6 October, when the country was partitioned between Germany and the Soviet Union

personal military staff and run by General Keitel, whose unquestioning compliance had earned him the nickname the 'Nodding Ass'.

Hitler takes command

The German armed forces were now under Hitler's personal command. Where did he wish them to strike next? The answer came when Hitler convened a conference of the High Command to announce an autumn offensive against the neutral Low Countries of Luxembourg, Holland and Belgium. It was the next logical stage, and Hitler was confident of success. He would rely on the same tactics that had brought victory in Poland – a decisive thrust by massed armoured divisions across the countryside, bypassing the towns so that the Panzers did not become trapped in the narrow streets.

The German generals had expected that Britain and France would have negotiated a peace treaty by now, following their failure to act to save Poland. General von Brauchitsch reminded the Führer of his serious concerns: only five armoured divisions were available; munitions were seriously depleted after the Polish campaign; and an autumn offensive across open countryside was certain to become bogged down in mud. Hitler replied curtly that it would rain on the enemy too.

In the event, bad weather persuaded him to postpone the attack until the following spring. His decision was also influenced by Russia's ill-considered invasion of Finland in November 1939, which foundered when the Finns proved surprisingly resilient. Hitler felt obliged to go to the aid of the Soviets. His thinking was that if he did not act decisively the British might intervene, cutting off Germany's supplies of iron ore from Sweden and threatening the German fleet in the Baltic.

The Finnish ski troops put up formidable opposition, but they were eventually crushed by sheer weight of numbers. At this point the Norwegian government made it known that they would not put up a struggle. They had seen what the Luftwaffe had done to Warsaw and Belgrade and did not want the same fate to befall Oslo.

But they couldn't prevent the British from landing at the port of Narvik and mining Norwegian waters. The Norwegian campaign suited Neville Chamberlain, who wanted to keep the war at a safe distance. Even at this late hour he still hoped Hitler might be deposed if the clash of armies could be postponed long enough.

But Hitler was in it to the end. He insisted on planning the Norwegian campaign personally, stubbornly refusing any advice from Brauchitsch. This almost resulted in the first German defeat of the war. Although the British plan had been improvised at short notice, the Royal Navy managed to sink ten German destroyers and pin the German troops down in the hills above Narvik.

The British troops had landed without heavy weapons, maps or skis, which were essential in that terrain, even in early spring when the battle was at its height. Unable to pursue the Germans across the snow, the British kept to the main roads and were forced to retreat every time they encountered the enemy, who held positions in the surrounding hills. Meanwhile, Stukas dive-bombed the British destroyers, their presence proving decisive. The lesson of Norway was clear: air supremacy, not sea power, won battles.

After six weeks of bitter fighting, the Royal Navy limped home and Norway fell to the German forces. The bulk of the British Expeditionary Force was captured and immediately paraded before the Nazi newsreel cameras, while Hitler characteristically took the credit. Victory was achieved against a determined enemy, he told his inner circle, 'because there was a man like me who did not know the word impossible'.

General Warlimont's verdict was somewhat different. He believed the incident exposed Hitler's 'deficiencies of character and military knowledge'. General Jodl had intercepted the Führer's contradictory orders because he was creating 'chaos in the command system'. Earlier Jodl had reasoned with the Führer, urging him to have faith in his commanders and not to consider a battle lost until the last shot was fired.

The Norwegian adventure also reflected badly on Winston Churchill, who was then First Lord of the Admiralty and chiefly responsible for planning the campaign. But it was Chamberlain who was finally driven from office on 9 May 1940 by an outraged House of Commons who had lost patience with his appeasement policy. His successor would have to be a man with the courage to take the fight to the enemy in North Africa and the Mediterranean, a man with a gift for oratory who would inspire the nation in its darkest hour. That man was Churchill.

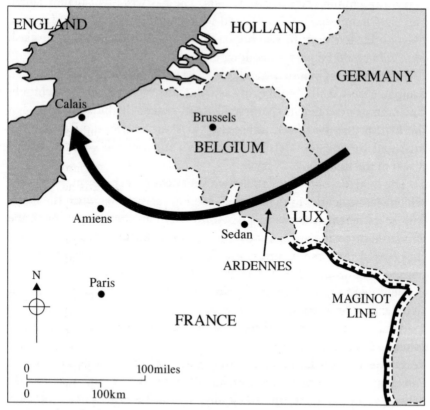

Blitzkreig in the west: Manstein's plan to attack through the Ardennes was originally considered too risky, but eventually proved decisive

Blitzkrieg

The spectre of near defeat in Norway haunted Hitler throughout the winter of 1940 and into the new year, prompting him to revise his original plan for the attack on Western Europe. He thought it likely that the Allies would anticipate his opening gambit because it was the same as the strategy employed by the German army in 1914. Besides, he had overlooked practical considerations such as the network of canals and rivers in the Low Countries, which could impede the progress of his armour. While he brooded on the problem, news arrived that one of his staff officers had been captured after his plane crashed in Belgium. He had been carrying with him the invasion plans. Assuming that the maps and documents had fallen into enemy hands, Hitler ordered his commanders to come up with a new plan, one that would catch the Allies off guard.

Coincidentally, a talented staff officer, Major-General von Manstein, had drawn up a detailed and audacious plan for an attack on France through the Low Countries, but it had been shelved by his superiors who considered it impractical. Now they were forced to dust it off and present it to the Führer as a viable alternative. Manstein proposed a decisive thrust by massed armour through the Forest of the Ardennes (see map opposite), which was considered virtually impenetrable and therefore would be lightly defended. This manoeuvre would avoid the problem of the Maginot Line, which would be circumvented as the mechanized columns raced toward the River Meuse near Sedan, held by a comparatively small French force. Then it was westwards across the plains of northern France to the channel ports of Calais and Le Havre. This would surprise the British Expeditionary Force, who were expecting an attack through Belgium. Speed was of the essence. The armour must strike hard and fast and on no account should the commanders be tempted to disperse their forces or risk losing the initiative.

German military intelligence confirmed that the narrow winding roads through the Ardennes were wide enough for tanks, but there was a chance that the Allies might learn of the plan before the offensive began. They would then be able to mount a decent defence. If they did so, the German armour could be brought to a grinding halt and the Panzers picked off one at a time. It was a desperate gamble, but Hitler thrived on taking risks and was willing to try it.

On the afternoon of 9 May 1940, Hitler boarded the Führer Special, an armoured train which had served as his headquarters during the Polish

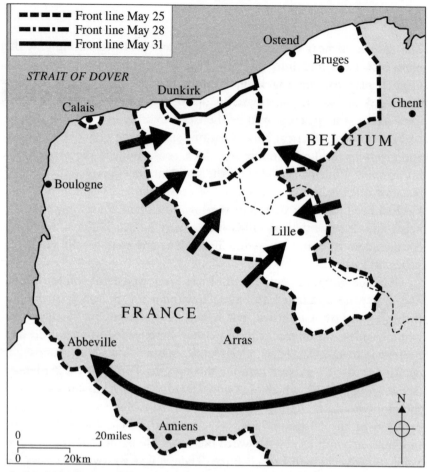

▬ ▬ ▬ ▬ ▬	Front line May 25
▬ ▪ ▬ ▪ ▬	Front line May 28
▬▬▬▬▬	Front line May 31

STRAIT OF DOVER

Ostend

Bruges

Dunkirk

Calais

Ghent

BELGIUM

Boulogne

Lille

FRANCE

Abbeville

Arras

0   20miles

0   20km

Amiens

N

At Dunkirk, the British found themselves with their backs to the sea as the German mechanized columns advanced towards them

campaign. From Berlin, the train travelled to the Belgian border where a car waited to take the dictator a short distance to the Felsennest, a complex of bunkers and spartan living quarters which had been blasted out of a hilltop. It was from here, at 5.35 the next morning, that Hitler watched as German bombers, fighters and transport planes filled the sky. At the same time, columns of tanks and armoured vehicles streamed through the forest towards the unsuspecting defenders.

In terms of men and machinery, the Germans and the Allies were well matched. Hitler could boast almost three million men marshalled along a 483-kilometre (300-mile) front, while the Allies had a similar number, but under separate commands and with no cohesive plan of defence. The Germans had 7,400 artillery pieces while the French had 10,700 and the French could field 900 more tanks than the Germans, who had 2,500 Panzers to France's 3,400. However, the Germans aimed to use their tanks en masse as they had done in Poland and they had superiority in the air, outnumbering the Allies two to one. The decisive factor would be surprise.

Plagued by doubt

The image of Hitler as a mad military genius is largely the creation of popular historians and is at stark odds with the facts. According to General Halder, Hitler's chief of staff, the Führer was extremely reluctant to take any risks during the spring campaign of 1940 and was continually trying to hold back the advance for fear that the extended supply lines would be cut and his armies encircled. He was consumed with doubt after the initial successes, which saw German tanks overrun the Dutch and Belgian defences and advance 161 kilometres (100 miles) on the first day of the offensive. Even the decimation of the French 2nd and 9th Armies beyond the Meuse on 13 May (which vindicated the decision to attack through the Ardennes) did not dispel his mood. 'He rages and shouts that we are doing our best to ruin the entire operation,' wrote Halder.

Then, on 17 May, Brussels fell. Still Hitler seemed intent on sabotaging his own success. On several occasions he ordered the Panzers to halt when they should have pushed onwards. His most critical error was in allowing the British to evacuate 338,226 men (including 139,000 French troops) from the beaches of Dunkirk. The Panzer commanders watched in frustration from a few miles away because they were forbidden to fire on the stranded soldiers. When questioned, the Führer refused to explain this extraordinary decision, though it was thought he was afraid that the tanks would become sitting targets in the sand. He trusted Goering to strafe soldiers on the beach, but the Luftwaffe was too busy fending off the RAF to harass the troops on the ground. It was the gravest tactical error Hitler made prior to the invasion of Russia, for those same Allied troops would return years later as part of an invasion force which would liberate Italy, North Africa and, finally, Western Europe.

Hitler's blunder was forgiven when France fell three weeks later. The French were afforded the final humiliation when required to sign the surrender at Compiègne, in the railway carriage where the armistice had been signed in 1918. 'My country has been defeated. This is the result of 30 years of Marxism,' Marshal Pétain exclaimed.

But the rout of the once formidable French army was inevitable. They were led by tired old men (General Gamelin was 68 years old and General Weygand, his successor, was 72) whose tactics dated back to 1914. And all were infected with the fatal affliction of defeatism. It weakened the head and swiftly worked its way through the entire system so that the soldiers threw down their weapons at the first sight of serious fighting and accepted the inevitable – occupation.

In just 46 days, the German army had conquered Western Europe and sent the British scurrying back across the English Channel to lick their wounds and mourn the loss of 100,000 Allied troops (with an additional two million interred in German POW camps for the duration). The Wehrmacht had lost just 27,000 men, with 18,000 more missing in action. Standing before the Eiffel Tower in Paris, Hitler proclaimed himself 'the greatest strategic genius of all time'.

The bulldog spirit

In June 1940, with Britain defiant but practically defenceless, Hitler sanctioned Operation Sealion, the seaborne invasion of the British Isles. After committing half-a-million men and several hundred tanks to the operation, he then postponed it in the mistaken belief that the Royal Navy and the RAF could repulse his mighty armada as it crossed the notoriously unpredictable English Channel. The invasion, he decided, was to be launched only as a 'last resort'.

Hitler feared that a single defeat would destroy the image of the Wehrmacht's invincibility. He preferred to play it safe, to have his bombers harass the depleted Royal Navy and pound the Channel ports before turning their attention to obliterating the British airfields. At the same time, his fighters would swat the celebrated Spitfires and Hurricanes from the skies. He told himself that the British had lost the war, but simply hadn't accepted the fact. He was bemused by the stubborn defiance of the new British Prime Minister Winston Churchill, who swore to fight on the beaches and vowed that the British people would never surrender.

Churchill, said Hitler, was fortified by liquid courage. It was only a matter of time before the British came to their senses and sued for peace. After all, according to Nazi genealogists, they were of the same racial stock as their German 'cousins'.

Eagle Day

On the afternoon of 13 August 1940, Goering launched *Adlertag* (Eagle Day), the start of his aerial offensive. It began with a Stuka attack on the RAF base at Detling in Kent, which destroyed 22 British aircraft on the ground. Hundreds of German bombers then made a massed raid on the British coastal defences and airfields, the first of 1,485 sorties flown that day. Bad weather gave the RAF a brief respite, but the raiders returned two days later. This time, radar gave the British prior warning of the attack so they were able to intercept it before the German bombers could do much damage. Goering lost 75 aircraft to Fighter Command's 34 (with another 16 destroyed in their hangars), but as Air Chief Marshal Hugh Dowding remarked at the time, Goering could afford to lose that many and still win. The RAF had lost half its strength in France and 100 planes in defending Dunkirk. But thanks to the efforts of Lord Beaverbrook, the British armaments minister, new Spitfires were now rolling off the production line at the rate of 100 a week. The problem was that the RAF did not have the pilots to fly them.

In the ensuing weeks, British pilots were scrambled several times a day and the stress of being continually on standby was beginning to fray their nerves. By the end of August the RAF had lost 231 of its original complement of 1,000 pilots and their replacements were woefully inexperienced. Even when Polish pilots and other nationalities were drafted in, the RAF was still vastly outnumbered in the air.

The bombing of London

The most crucial day of the aerial war was 7 September 1940, when Goering assembled the largest armada of aircraft ever seen – 1,000 planes were stacked 3 kilometres (2 miles) deep and blackened 2,072 square kilometres (800 square miles) of sky. This time their target was not the enemy airfields, but the docks, warehouses and factories of London.

Another of Hitler's biggest blunders, and one of the costliest of the war, was ordering the Luftwaffe to break off their daily attacks on the RAF airfields while they were still operational to target the capital instead. This gave the British time to regroup and mount co-ordinated attacks on the returning bombers. It was not a tactical miscalculation so much as an error of judgement, the significance of which can be gleaned from a comment made by Luftwaffe commander Theo Osterkamp. He complained, 'It was with tears of rage and dismay that, on the very point of victory, I saw the decisive battle against the British fighters stopped in favour of attacking London.'

Battle of Britain

The change of tactic was prompted by British raids on Berlin, which did little damage but so enraged the Führer that he allowed himself to became distracted from a legitimate strategic target. It marked the turning point in the Battle of Britain, for it gave the RAF more time to assemble their much vaunted Big Wing (a co-ordinated attack by several squadrons). At the same time, it presented them with a soft target – slow-moving Junkers and Heinkel bombers, often without fighter support.

For the rest of September 1940, the two sides waged a war of attrition in the air which the British won by the skin of their teeth. They started to wear down the Germans who began to lose morale faster than they lost their comrades.

On 12 October, after the Luftwaffe had suffered their severest losses to date and the bombing of London had been answered by repeated British raids on Berlin and other German cities, Hitler cancelled Operation Sealion. He immediately turned his attention to Russia and the Eastern Front. Unwilling to admit defeat, he told his pilots that the raids on London had simply been 'camouflage' for the forthcoming Russian campaign.

Hitler had seriously underestimated the will of the British to resist tyranny and been foolish to put his faith in Goering's Luftwaffe. It could boast superiority in numbers, but its fighters were out-manoeuvred by the superior Spitfires, which were able to return to their bases to refuel before rejoining the battle. The German fighters, on the other hand, could only engage in aerial combat for ten minutes before their fuel ran short. If the German flyers were shot down and survived they would be imprisoned for the duration, while the RAF pilots could rejoin their squadron that same day.

The Germans were at another disadvantage. They were unaware that their formations were being monitored by radar, Britain's top secret weapon, which gave the thinly-stretched RAF squadrons ample warning of an attack. They could then intercept the enemy before it struck its target. It has been said that radar won the Battle of Britain, but victory was still very much dependent on the pilots.

HERMANN GOERING

THE 'FAT MAN'S' TASTE FOR EXCESS

'I am what I have always been, the last Renaissance man, if I may be allowed to say so.'

When Hermann Goering handed himself over to the US 36th Infantry Division on a snow-blocked road near Radstadt, Austria, on 7 May 1945, he was travelling in style. His five-ton Mercedes-Benz 540K had bullet-proof glass, a steel-reinforced body and a set of plump suitcases strapped to the roof.

His entourage consisted of some 20 vehicles and his wife, sister-in-law, daughter, General von Epp (*gauleiter* of Austria), his chef, valet and butler, plus assorted aides and bodyguards – in total, about 75 people. But compared to the previous heady decade of licentious living, the Reichsmarschall was suddenly down to 'the bare necessities'.

HITLER'S SWASHBUCKLING DEPUTY

Hermann Goering was frequently depicted in Allied newspaper cartoons as a flamboyant, blustering buffoon, strutting the world stage in a series of ostentatious uniforms like a Ruritanian prince in a comic operetta. But although he was notorious for awarding himself medals and glorifying in the official titles Hitler bestowed upon him, the former First World War flying ace was no fool. Nor was he ever considered a figure of fun by those who feared his volatile temper and vindictive cruelty.

Born in Marienbad, Bavaria in 1893, Goering was the fourth of five children (three were from his father's first marriage). His father was a former cavalry officer and consul general and his mother a farmer's daughter. But Goering was raised as an aristocrat thanks to the generosity of his mother's lover, who allowed his mistress and her son to live in one of two castles he owned on the Austrian border.

During the early months of the First World War, Goering served in the infantry, but was transferred to the air force in 1915. He became an ace in Manfred von Richthofen's JG1 squadron, earning the Iron Cross and the Pour le Mérite. After von Richthofen's death, Goering became squadron leader and ended the war with 15 kills to his credit.

His marriage to Swedish Baroness Carin von Krantzow in February 1923 brought him into the social whirl of the German nobility, which was to prove invaluable when he later sought funding for the Nazi party and Hitler's endorsement by the ruling classes.

RUTHLESS RISE TO POWER

Restless and impatient for action, Goering joined the nascent Nazi party in 1922 not out of any revolutionary or political ideals, but because he wanted to combat communism. He did so in the beer halls and back streets, by breaking heads and strong-arming those who voiced dissent at party meetings. Within a year he had been appointed head of the SA and was in the front ranks on the march through Munich during the failed Beer Hall Putsch of 1923. Wounded in the leg and groin, Goering fled to Austria and soon became addicted to morphine.

Goering (in pale coat) at a military exhibition in Vienna in 1941

An amnesty allowed him to return to Germany in 1926, where he rose to power as Hitler's second-in-command. He was appointed president of the Reichstag in 1932, when the Nazis became the major party in the German parliament. Rudolf Hess held the official title of deputy Führer from 1933 until his ill-fated flight to Britain in May 1941, when Hitler stripped him of it, but Goering had already been appointed Hitler's successor.

It is believed Goering conceived the idea of setting fire to the Reichstag in February 1933 in order for the Nazis to seize power. Whether or not this is true, Goering was instrumental in rearming the German military, despite restrictions imposed by the Versailles Treaty. He was also responsible for founding the Gestapo, Germany's hated secret police force, and he conceived the idea of concentration camps, which he attempted to justify by comparing them to the internment camps the British had constructed during the Boer War.

His ruthless determination to settle scores, no matter how old they might be, was revealed by the thoroughness with which he implemented the purging of the German High Command and the massacre of dissident elements in the SA on the Night of the Long Knives in June 1934. These were acts for which he would remain stubbornly unrepentant to the end.

As he said, 'Each bullet which leaves the barrel of a police pistol now is my bullet. If one calls this murder, then I have murdered; I ordered all this, I back it up. I assume the responsibility, and I am not afraid to do so.'

But Goering lost both face and favour after his much-vaunted Luftwaffe failed to win the Battle of Britain in the summer of 1940. He retreated even further into the background after failing in his boast to be able to supply the besieged 6th Army at Stalingrad, which saw the tide of the war turn in favour of the Allies.

CHEATING THE HANGMAN

Ironically, it was only after the war, when he stood trial at Nuremberg, that Goering once again demonstrated a sharp intellect and magnetic presence (he scored 138 in an IQ test conducted by a prison psychiatrist). It was perhaps his most compelling public performance and one that earned him the grudging respect of many members of the prosecution and the press. Everyone knew he would be found guilty and sentenced to hang. This was the last time he would command the world stage.

But Goering refused to allow the victors satisfaction by executing him like a common criminal. On 15 October 1946, he committed suicide in his cell by biting into a capsule of cyanide that had allegedly been smuggled in by a sympathetic guard.

Goering's mother predicted that her son would either be 'a great man or a great criminal'. Her assessment proved prophetic. At the conclusion of the Nuremberg Trial in 1946, the Reichsmarschall was convicted on four counts: conspiracy to wage war, crimes against peace, war crimes and crimes against humanity, for which he was sentenced to death. The 'lesser' crime of looting was disregarded, despite Goering having ordered and organized the theft of some of the world's greatest art treasures.

PERSONAL TREASURE HOUSE

His own 'appropriations' unit catalogued more than 4,000 liberated works of art, including 1,800 paintings by such masters as Matisse, Degas, Vermeer and Van Gogh, a haul estimated to be in excess of 20 per cent of the great art treasures of Europe. He had the finest pieces crated up and shipped off to furnish his imposing hunting lodge in the Schorfheide forest, north of Berlin. Carinhall, named after his late first wife, also housed a private casino, an indoor swimming pool and two model train sets that took up the entire attic and basement space of approximately 400 square metres (478 square yards). Visiting VIPs were invited to watch Goering playing with his trains, which travelled through Bavarian-styled model villages inhabited by figures including an SS man who waved at the passengers. For the climax of the demonstration, Goering had fitted a model Stuka dive-bomber above one of his model railway layouts and liked to send it down a wire to drop wooden bombs on the moving trains.

Goering's art collection gave him particular pleasure. He told a prison psychiatrist at Nuremberg, 'I am so artistic in my temperament that masterpieces make me feel alive and glowing inside.' Yet he hung priceless masters haphazardly like cheap prints in a pawn shop. Some idea of the value of the collection can be gleaned from the fact that a single painting, Van Gogh's *Portrait of Dr. Gachet*, was auctioned in 1990 for $82.5 million. But it was a mere fraction of the treasure Hitler had amassed for his planned Führermuseum, which was to have been built in Linz to commemorate the Third Reich's final victory over the Allies.

EARLY ACQUISITIONS

Goering began purchasing art in 1928, as soon as he was assured of a regular income from his post in the Reichstag. When the Nazis increased their grip on power and he was appointed president of the German parliament, he was able to seize priceless treasures from private collectors – who were threatened with imprisonment if they refused to sign over their property. As soon as the Nuremberg Laws were passed, Goering used them to confiscate art treasures from Jewish art dealers and wealthy families under the pretext that all Jews were enemies of the Reich so their property was forfeit. In 1943 these bills of sale were declared null and void by the British government, but it was already too late for the rightful owners, many of whom had been transported to extermination camps. To give his appropriations a veneer of legitimacy, Goering would claim that certain paintings, statues or items of silverware were 'on loan', or he would ask the owner for an invoice that he had no intention of paying.

DAYLIGHT ROBBERY

The extent of the Nazis' rapacious plundering can be gleaned from the fact that Goebbels commissioned a 1,000-page inventory of the artworks to be taken from public galleries in France and that the ERR (*Einsatzstab Reichsleiter Rosenberg*) seized an estimated 22,000 objects of inestimable value from the conquered territories. The EER was set up to study the archaeological origins of the Aryan race, but became an agency of the German Foreign Office which was authorized to seize rare manuscripts and books that might substantiate these theories – and burn those which didn't. By October 1944, 1,418,000 railway wagons were needed to ship the contents plundered from national libraries and archives, ecclesiastical authorities, Masonic lodges and private collections.

Once war was declared, all pretence at legitimacy was unnecessary and the wholesale and open looting of art in the occupied territories was carried out by the Kunstschutz military corps under Goering's orders. Although national galleries and museums were stripped of their treasures on the pretext that they were being saved from Allied bombings, several curators in Italy and France risked their lives to make secret inventories of the stolen works, while members of the resistance followed the transports so that they could inform the Allies of the location of the stolen objects.

THE BITER BIT

Curiously, in the last days of the war, Goering exchanged many of the most valuable pieces by Impressionist painters for 'less degenerate' works which were of considerably lower value.

But a Dutch art dealer, Han van Meegeren, had the last laugh at the Fat Man's expense. In 1942 he persuaded Goering to part with 150 masterworks in exchange for a painting purported to be by Jan Vermeer. However, *Christ and the Adulteress* has since been revealed as a clever forgery. When Goering learned he had been fooled, a US official reported that 'he looked as if for the first time he had discovered there was evil in the world'.

Churchill neatly summed up the feelings of a grateful nation when he paid tribute to the courageous pilots who had repulsed the invader against overwhelming odds. 'Never in the field of human conflict was so much owed by so many to so few.'

Battle for the Balkans

In October 1940, Mussolini began an ill-advised invasion of Albania as a stepping stone for an assault on Greece. But the attack on Greece was poorly planned and executed and left the Italian troops struggling to secure a foothold on the mainland. The British occupied the islands of Crete and Lemnos in preparation for a counter-offensive. Their presence threatened the balance of power in the Balkans and put British planes within striking distance of Romanian oilfields, which Hitler had just acquired from his new axis ally, dictator Ion Antonescu.

Reluctantly, Hitler was forced to come to Mussolini's aid. In early 1941 he allocated ten divisions to Greece and dedicated a substantial force of 25,000 paratroopers to the taking of Crete, the largest airborne assault force ever assembled. He also decided to secure Yugoslavia by force, before the pro-British Serbs could wrest control of the country from the pro-German Croats. But before he could do so, Serbian officers of the Yugoslav armed forces staged a coup. Hitler was incandescent with rage and ordered the total destruction of Belgrade in an offensive codenamed 'Operation Punishment'. The new Yugoslavian government was practically defenceless. And when it despatched planes to intercept the first wave of German bombers, they were shot down by their own anti-aircraft batteries (the Yugoslavs were using Messerschmitt Me 109s bought from the Germans).

In the confusion, a tiny force of German soldiers, without tank support, was able to walk into the smouldering ruins of the capital and take it from the startled, shell-shocked defenders, who threw down their arms and surrendered. When the final reckoning was made, the German High Command was startled to discover that they had captured the entire country with minimum casualties – 151 men killed and 400 wounded.

The Desert Fox

In February 1941, Hitler despatched one of his most able and talented tacticians, General Erwin Rommel, to rescue his Italian ally who was struggling in the vast desert of North Africa. Mussolini had invaded Libya to gain credibility with Hitler – he felt that Hitler was winning too much, too quickly. Mussolini believed he needed 1,000 Italian dead to be able to sit at the conference table with the Führer. He exceeded his own expectations, however, when the comparatively small British 8th Army under General Wavell struck the string of Italian fortifications at Mersa Matruh, 129 kilometres (80 miles) east of Sidi Barrani. In the first three days of fighting, two British divisions and a few tanks managed to secure the surrender of 39,000 Italian soldiers. There were so many prisoners that the captors lost count and recorded their haul as 'five acres of officers and 200 acres of other ranks'.

More significantly, even though the British now dominated an area the size of England and France combined, they were woefully under strength and their tanks were prone to mechanical failure whenever the rough desert sand worked its way into the tracks. Fortunately, the Italian tanks were of even worse quality (to the extent that they were given the nickname 'rolling coffins'). While the Afrika Korps had no experience of desert warfare, Rommel had the foresight to ship over tank transporters which enabled the Germans to recover their tanks when they broke down or were damaged. The British simply abandoned theirs; they also made the tactical error of splitting their forces in order for several divisions to be diverted to Greece. Britain should have taken Tripoli first, thereby securing North Africa, and only then sent any remaining men and *matériel* to Greece.

Within four months of landing, the Afrika Korps had seized the initiative by advancing 1,609 kilometres (1,000 miles). They pushed the British 8th Army all the way back to Egypt. For this, a grateful Führer promoted the Desert Fox to field marshal.

Over the next 16 months, the Desert War raged back and forth as each side exploited a temporary advantage in men and *matériel*. At one point, Rommel's absence through illness swung the war in favour of the Allies; on another occasion, the sacking of a British commander demoralized the 8th Army so badly that the Germans gained the upper hand. In the space of a few months, the city of Bengazi changed hands no fewer than five times until finally, in July 1942, General Montgomery took command of the 8th Army and manoeuvred Rommel into a battle of attrition at El Alamein. It was to be the last significant British victory before the Americans entered the war. Churchill put it into perspective: 'This is not the end. It is not even the beginning of the end, but it is, perhaps, the end of the beginning.'

Crete

The Germans did not have it so easy on Crete. Hitler had made it known that the island was to be in German hands by the end of May 1941. This would enable him to devote his attention to the invasion of Russia, which was scheduled for June. His commanders complied, but at enormous cost and to little strategic advantage. Hitler did not use the island as a base for dominating the eastern Mediterranean, despite the sacrifice of 4,000 men and the loss of more than 300 aircraft, resources which might have been put to more effective use in Russia.

The Allies also lost 4,000 men in the Battle of Crete, with another 12,000 captured. The remainder had been spirited away under the noses of the Germans in an operation that cost the Royal Navy two destroyers and three cruisers. For the Germans it was a hollow victory – they had met with fierce resistance from Greek and Allied forces as well as Cretan civilians, and suffered heavy losses. Their parachute divisions had proven ineffective against ground troops who were dug in and well prepared. They only triumphed through sheer weight of numbers after landing reinforcements and overwhelming the Allied defensive positions in the north of the island.

Hitler declared himself 'most displeased' with the affair, a view echoed by General Ringel, commander of the 5th Division: 'This sacrifice would not have been too great if the Crete campaign had meant a beginning, not an end,' he asserted.

Barbarossa

Hitler's optimism on the eve of 'Operation Barbarossa', the invasion of Soviet Russia, struck his more pragmatic commanders as naive in the extreme. But his confidence was largely justified. Morale in the victorious Wehrmacht was at its height whereas the opposite was the case in the Red Army, which had lost 30,000 of its most experienced officers in Stalin's political purges of the 1930s. Hitler believed the ordinary Russian soldier had no stomach for fighting and would turn on his communist oppressors once he saw the Germans as his liberators. Furthermore, while Russia might appear to be a vast unconquerable continent, it was Hitler's intention to halt the advance 1,931 kilometres (1,200 miles) inside the border, on a line from Archangel to Astrakhan. He was going to ignore Soviet Central Asia, which was an inhospitable wasteland with no natural resources. Even so, he was asking the

Wehrmacht to achieve something just this side of the impossible. But in Hitler's mind the vast distances that needed to be covered were mere points on a map.

Intelligence reports had led the German High Command to believe that the majority of Russia's 12,000 aircraft and 22,700 tanks were unfit for combat. It was common knowledge that Russian pilots were forced to signal to each other by dipping their wings because few had serviceable radios. More significantly, the German front-line divisions totalled three million men with another 500,000 in reserve, while the Russians were thought to have only a third of that number. Something of the scale of the German forces can be gleaned from the fact that it took 17,000 trains to transport the troops to the staging areas in Prussia, Poland and Romania on the eve of the invasion.

Russian resilience

But Hitler and the *Oberkommando der Wehrmacht* had fatally underestimated the enemy's resilience and resources. Stalin was able to call on 17 million men and several million women of military age, who could be trained to fire a rifle even if they had never drilled in their lives. And there would be no shortage of weapons, tanks and ammunition. Munitions factories were being built deep in the Urals. These would deliver the new Soviet T34 tank and the terrifying Katyusha rocket launcher at an incredible rate, while the Germans would find it extremely difficult to replace lost tanks and artillery once they were deep inside enemy territory.

Moreover, the soldiers of the Red Army would not be fighting for an ideology or their country, but for their lives. They feared the commissars even more than the Nazis. There was a slim chance of survival if they were captured by the Germans, but it was certain that their own officers would not hesitate to shoot them if they dared to retreat. Stalin had even decreed that the families of deserters would be jailed for their treachery.

A war of extermination

The German plan of attack was disarmingly simple in theory; a three-pronged thrust would see Army Group North capture the Baltic ports of Riga and Tallinn and then advance on Leningrad. Meanwhile, Army Group Centre would race towards Moscow, leaving Army Group South to capture Ukraine. There was general agreement that the Germans had to destroy the main Soviet armies before they could retreat into the interior, but Hitler and the High Command disagreed on the strategic importance of Moscow. Hitler saw it as nothing more than a geographical location on the map. After the Russian front lines had been smashed, he intended to strip the spearhead of its armour and divert it to capture the oilfields of Ukraine.

The commanders argued that the Panzers should stay with the main thrust to ensure the capture of the Russian capital because, as the Soviet command and communications centre, it would be heavily defended. But Hitler overruled them. This critical disagreement would lead to confusion, which was compounded by the divisive nature of the two competing command groups – *Oberkommando der Wehrmacht* (OKW), Hitler's personal staff, and *Oberkommando des Heeres* (OKH), the Supreme High Command of the Army. OKW sided with its Führer and OKH advised caution.

If any of the German High Command imagined that the Russian war was going to be a conventional military campaign, they were in for a rude awakening. When Hitler addressed them shortly before the invasion, he made it clear that this was to be 'a war of extermination'. He reminded them that the Soviet Union had signed neither the Geneva Convention nor the Hague Convention governing the conduct of war and the treatment of prisoners. This meant that German soldiers would therefore not be bound by the customary rules of war. Nor would the Wehrmacht be accountable for crimes against the Russian civilian population. Armed civilians would be summarily executed. In 1940, Hitler proclaimed: 'This struggle is one of ideologies and racial differences and will have to be conducted with unprecedented, unmerciful and unrelenting harshness.'

CHAPTER 15
The Tide Turns

At 3 a.m. on 22 June 1941, several thousand guns lit up the night sky as the Germans poured wave after wave of men and machinery into Soviet Russia. In the central sector, infantry divisions crossed the Bug river in boats and amphibious tanks which had been intended for the invasion of Britain. Overhead, hundreds of bombers headed for Soviet airfields and key installations, some of which lay as far as 322 kilometres (200 miles) to the east.

Stalin's pathological mistrust of the Allies had led him to discount repeated warnings from the British and American intelligence services, which had even given him the precise date for the invasion. But he was aware that the last war had been started by Russian mobilization, so was reluctant to alert the army until he had received confirmation. On 22 June, Stalin received confirmation he could not deny. On that first day, a dozen Red Army divisions were destroyed, thousands of prisoners rounded up and 1,800 Soviet planes shot down or put out of action, thereby eradicating the world's largest air force at a stroke. By the end of the first week it was clear that Soviet armour was no match for the Panzers. Although the dreaded KV1 heavy tank had thick armour-plating, it was cumbersome and its crews were poorly trained. The Soviet tank could take as many as seven hits and still keep rolling, but it proved vulnerable to the German infantry who were able to sneak up on it and blow up its tracks.

Again, while the Russian infantry was a fearsome adversary, the troops appeared to have no sense of tactics. They made repeated suicidal charges into the German machine guns, as if fighting in the trenches of the last war. Half-a-million Soviet soldiers were killed in the first two weeks alone. It appeared that Hitler's assessment of the enemy might be accurate after all.

However, as the days passed, rapid progress created its own problems. In several sectors the Panzers forged ahead, leaving their supporting infantry units far behind and their own flanks exposed. Under the command of General von Kleist, five Panzer divisions overran the Russians in the south, near the so-called Stalin Line, but without infantry support they could not prevent entire divisions of Soviet troops escaping to launch counter-attacks on their rear and flanks. The terrain also generated its own difficulties for the invaders. German intelligence had failed to provide up-to-date topographical maps, so the advancing armour frequently came to a halt as its commanders struggled to orientate themselves in a vast, featureless landscape which appeared to have no horizon. To add to the confusion, the maps they had been given were misleading. Time and again the armoured columns would get bogged down in narrow dirt roads because the commanders had mistaken the red lines on the map for main highways.

The situation was not helped by Hitler's continual meddling as he followed the progress of his forces from the safety of the *Wolfsschanze* (Wolf's Lair), his new headquarters in the forests of Rastenburg in East Prussia, where he would remain until November 1944. After the invasion of Russia, Hitler made only rare visits to his other HQs – in Ukraine, Berchtesgaden and Berlin. His generals were driven to despair by his interference and obsession with irrelevant details. When they pressed him to clarify his often vague and contradictory orders, he would break into a tirade about the treatment of prisoners or the effects of shelling on front-line troops.

Such problems were exacerbated by personal enmity between the generals. On one occasion, Field Marshal von Kluge, an over-cautious traditionalist, threatened Guderian, the hero of *blitzkrieg*, with court martial for deliberately disobeying an order to slow his advance when there had been an obvious opportunity to push on. Again, it was Guderian who allowed 100,000 Soviet troops to escape encirclement at Smolensk in late July. His ambitions led him east to Yelnya (a key objective on the road to Moscow) instead of north, where he was to link up with General Hoth.

But the relentless advance on all fronts and reports of mass capitulation by the Soviets led the warring factions to overlook such infractions. Any serious criticism of Hitler's leadership was also forestalled. On 27 June 1941, Colonel-General Guderian's Panzer Group 2 and General Hoth's Panzer Group 3 formed a ring of steel around half-a-million Soviet troops besieged in the city of Minsk, while a smaller pocket was encircled at Bialystock. After days of savage fighting, thousands of Soviet troops lay dead or dying and 300,000 were taken prisoner. More than 2,000 Soviet tanks were captured or put out of action and 4,000 tanks were lost at Smolensk. Such disasters demanded retribution. Stalin summoned the regional commander, General Pavlov, and his senior officers to Moscow on 30 June and had them executed for treason.

The profligate squandering of human life continued. The siege of Leningrad, which began in September 1941 and lasted for two long years, cost the Russians more dead than the combined Allied casualties of the entire war. One Wehrmacht colonel compared the situation to an elephant that had kicked over an ant hill. The elephant, he said, might kill millions of ants, but there would always be more and in the end the ants would overwhelm him and eat him to the bone.

'The Russians have lost the war'

When news reached Hitler that his armies had extended 644 kilometres (400 miles) along a 1,609-kilometre (1,000-mile) front in just three weeks, he was overjoyed. A week later, these same armies would control an area double the size of Germany. 'The Russians have lost the war,' Hitler told his staff, and they were in no position to argue.

Against their advice, he diverted the armour from Army Group Centre, then within 322 kilometres (200 miles) of Moscow, to other objectives – many of which were hopelessly unattainable. 'We laughed aloud when we received these orders,' remembered von Rundstedt, who had been told to take a position 644 kilometres (400 miles) away.

With von Kleist's Panzers just 19 kilometres (12 miles) from Kiev, Hitler ordered him to break off the attack and turn south to trap the retreating Red Army.

The capture of 665,000 Soviet troops appeared to justify Hitler's decision, but there were millions more to replace them and the opportunity to take Kiev would not come again. Of more importance, the diversion used the one resource the Germans could not afford to waste – time. When Hitler finally gave his permission for the attack on Moscow, it was too late.

The German troops thought the first snowfall in October might slow their advance, but they had no idea how disastrous it would be. Hitler was so confident of early success that he had refused to provide winter clothing for his men. This oversight would prove to be his undoing. Soon the Russian winter bit so deep that oil froze in the engines of the armoured vehicles and weapons malfunctioned because they were not furnished with the right kind of lubricant. Ultimately, a greater number of German soldiers (113,000) would die of frostbite and disease than from combat wounds.

While the invaders endured the freezing temperatures, the Russians were secretly smuggling reinforcements and tanks across the frozen lakes in preparation for a spring offensive. They were getting ready to drive the Germans back over the Stalin Line and hoping to push them as far as the Fatherland. Among the Russian reserves were 40 divisions of the Siberian Front, who were among the best-trained troops in the world. They were also clothed and equipped for a winter campaign. Stalin had

Stalingrad after the first months of the German attack

kept them back in anticipation of an attack by Japan, but the assault on the US fleet at Pearl Harbor in December 1941 meant that the Japanese were now locked in battle with the Americans. Stalin's reserves were free for redeployment against the Germans.

Typically, Hitler blamed his generals for the reversal of German fortunes – particularly Brauchitsch, who he called a 'vain, cowardly wretch'. When the commanders witnessed the contempt with which the Führer spoke of his former chief of staff, they began to lose faith in his infallibility.

Stalingrad

With the spring thaw, the Germans renewed their offensive. Their principal targets were Stalingrad, a key industrial centre, and the oilfields in the Caucasus. Progress towards both objectives was initially encouraging, but soon the advance on the oilfields was halted by a Soviet counter-offensive, while the attack on Stalingrad stalled when the 6th Army encountered fierce resistance in the north and south of the city. When Halder, chief of the Army High Command dared to suggest a tactical withdrawal, he was replaced by Lieutenant-General Zeitzler.

'What we need now is not professional ability but National Socialist ardour,' Hitler told his staff.

Hitler dismissed news that the Soviets had marshalled a million men to break through and reinforce the defenders, and described reports of increased Soviet tank production as 'idiotic nonsense'. It was not only

Hitler but the entire Nazi leadership that was in denial. At Christmas 1940, the German people gathered round their radios to hear a broadcast from the staunch defenders of Stalingrad, unaware that it was being broadcast from a studio in Berlin. In the besieged city of Stalingrad, communication lines to the 6th Army had been cut weeks before. But even if the officials at the Ministry of Propaganda had told the truth, few would have believed them. They had told lies for so long that no one knew what to believe any more.

> *'Comrade, kill your German.'*
>
> Red Army slogan, 1943

Besides, it was inconceivable that the victorious army of 1940 could be freezing to death on the banks of the Volga, deprived of warm clothing, low on ammunition and cursing the regime which had abandoned them to their fate. They would get no help from Hitler, whose behaviour was becoming increasingly erratic. His unusual sleep routine had developed into insomnia and had taken its toll on his health and his temperament. When Friedrich von Paulus requested permission to break out from the besieged city in January 1943, the Führer replied with an ultimatum. 'The 6th Army will do its historic duty at Stalingrad to the last man,' he declared.

Germany in retreat

When von Paulus realized the hopelessness of his position – he was surrounded by three Soviet army groups – he saw no virtue in sacrificing his men for the Nazi ideal, so he surrendered. Of the 240,000 men killed or captured, only a few thousand saw the Fatherland again.

Hitler's reaction was predictable. He flew into another of his infamous rages and berated the man he had just promoted to field marshal, as a means of stiffening his resolve: 'I can't understand why a man like Paulus wouldn't rather die. The heroism of so many tens of thousands of men, officers and generals is cancelled out by a man like this who hasn't the character, when the moment comes, to do what a weakling of a woman would do,' he screamed.

It was evident to all who witnessed this outburst that Hitler was losing control. As news of further defeats on the Russian front and in North Africa (where Rommel had been out-foxed by Montgomery at El Alamein) filtered through to the Wolf's Lair, the Führer became increasingly isolated. He withdrew to his underground bunker, where night and day were indistinguishable, and there he paced his suite of three small rooms with their undecorated concrete walls and plain wooden furniture. Although he pored over maps and reports which made it plain that his empire was shrinking day by day, he could not accept the facts because they conflicted with his fantasy. His initial anger at von Paulus was supplanted by a belief that the blame lay with the Romanian and Hungarian conscripts, not the Wehrmacht. His allies had let him down. No one was to be trusted.

Hitler's withdrawal beneath the earth was not to protect himself from air raids (which were rare) but from reality. He stubbornly refused to see the devastation that had been inflicted on German cities by Allied bombing raids, which were penetrating further into the Reich and becoming more intensive. In his new capacity as armaments minister, Speer would have to travel to visit Hitler, as would the other Nazi leaders. They frequently regretted doing so because he was often brusque and unwilling to hear bad news. They had not seen their Führer for some time and it was a shock to find how he had aged in the intervening months. He was unsteady on his feet and had to grip his left arm to stop it trembling. Everything required great effort. When he spoke, it was with the effort of a recovering addict. Speer blamed the dramatic change in his leader on Dr Morell's diet of anti-depressant drugs and other homegrown narcotics.

Members of Hitler's 'Invincible Army' huddle together for warmth after being captured by the Red Army in 1942

Hitler now ate alone, emerging from the glare of the artificial light only once or twice a day to walk Blondi, his Alsatian, and confer with Goering, Himmler and Ribbentrop, who had established their own headquarters nearby. Goering, however, was out of favour. Hitler had never forgiven him for losing the Battle of Britain and for his empty boast that no bombs would ever fall on Berlin. Now the Führer openly criticized him for failing to supply the besieged survivors of Stalingrad.

However, the Reich would endure, Hitler insisted, saying that 1943 would be the year of 'clenched teeth'. He made only two more major public speeches before his death, neither of which expressed compassion for the plight of the German people. Their purpose was to assure his countrymen he was still in command and expected them to fight on. He left it to Goebbels to raise their morale and deflect blame for the disastrous defeat at Stalingrad. In a rousing speech before the party faithful and invited veterans at Berlin's Sportpalast, Goebbels declared that the Allies' demand for unconditional surrender meant victory or destruction for Germany. There would be no honourable surrender. He called for total war. He was greeted with tumultuous applause and hoarse cries of '*Sieg Heil!*' It was the last significant Nazi rally of the war.

Reversals

On the Eastern Front, it was no longer a question of how much territory had been taken, but how much could be held and for how long. There would be no more victories, only stabilizing actions, strategic withdrawals and (very seldom) counter-attacks such as Manstein's miraculous retaking of Kharkov in February 1943 – for which Hitler typically took all the credit.

But the celebrations were short-lived. By May, Tunis was in Allied hands and shortly afterwards the Axis forces surrendered in North Africa. In July 1943, the Allies landed in Sicily, the 'soft underbelly of Europe', and in September they began the march on Rome that was to end with Italy's surrender and the death of Mussolini in April 1945.

In summer 1943, the tide of the war in Europe turned against the Germans after Hitler defied the advice of his generals and launched a last major offensive in Russia. But even half-a-million of his most battle-hardened troops and 17 Panzer divisions could not break the Soviet line along the central front. The Russians, who by now outnumbered the enemy by as many as seven to one, fought back. They forced the exhausted Germans all the way back to the Polish frontier.

By the time the Allies landed in Normandy on D-Day (6 June 1944), Hitler was issuing orders for units that no longer existed. Even Rommel and Rundstedt were circumventing his instructions, he complained. They were forcing him to authorize retreats and plotting against him. In the bunker at Rastenburg, his staff dismissed these rantings as the delusions of a war leader under extreme stress. But, for once, Hitler's paranoia was well-founded.

Assassination attempts

As early as July 1944, it was clear to all but the most ardent Nazis that the war was lost. It was also obvious that Hitler would fight to the bitter end, destroying Germany in the process. Each day the Allies gained a firmer footing on the continent. In the east, the Red Army was regaining ground, but at a terrible cost. Their determination to rid their Motherland of the Nazi scourge was intensified with the discovery of each new atrocity committed by the SS against captured soldiers and innocent civilians. It was no longer a war of conquest but of retribution.

Some high-ranking members of Germany's officer corps believed that if Hitler could be replaced there would be a chance for a negotiated peace. This would hopefully stop the Soviets at the borders of the Reich. Otherwise the Red Army would forge ahead and take Berlin. The time had finally come for a coup, for the only certain way to topple a dictatorship is to decapitate it. Hitler was to be assassinated, but they would have to act swiftly.

There had been earlier attempts on Hitler's life. In September 1938 a conspiracy was hatched by senior military officers. They included Admiral Canaris and Lieutenant-General Beck, chief of the Army High Command, who were ready to take action in order to prevent an invasion of Czechoslovakia. Then Chamberlain gave in to the dictator's demands and Czechoslovakia was handed over without a shot being fired. Hitler was regarded by his people as a great statesman and the immediate risk of war had been averted. The conspirators were forced to abandon their plot.

A year later, on 8 November 1939, a lone assassin planted a time bomb behind the speaker's podium in the Bürgerbräukeller in Munich, but it exploded 13 minutes after Hitler had left the hall. He had cut short his annual address to the Alte Kämpfer (the 'Old Fighters', early Nazi party comrades) of the Beer Hall Putsch because he was overwhelmed by a feeling that he had to return to Berlin, even though nothing of importance awaited him there. Nine people were killed in the blast and 60 were wounded. Hitler attributed his lucky escape to the hand of fate, which had saved him once again.

In 1943, following the German surrender at Stalingrad, dissenters within the officer corps conspired to blow up the Führer's plane while it was in the air. They intended to use plastic explosives captured from the partisans. A package was taken on board disguised as a gift for an officer serving at the Führer's headquarters, to be discreetly retrieved when the plane landed safely at its destination. Although the detonators discharged, it seems that the cold air at high altitude prevented the explosives from igniting. Hitler had escaped death yet again. A week later, the conspirators had a second chance. Hitler was scheduled to tour an exhibition of captured Soviet weapons in Berlin; this would give the plotters the opportunity to explode a bomb in his vicinity. But, again, the Führer changed his plans and walked through the hall without stopping to view the exhibits. The plotters came under suspicion by the Gestapo, who failed to find evidence against them.

Operation Valkyrie

The conspirators were given new hope when Lieutenant Claus von Stauffenberg was recruited to their cause in autumn 1943. An aristocrat and distinguished army officer, he had been severely wounded in North Africa, losing an eye, his right hand and two fingers from his left hand. He was entrusted with planning Hitler's assassination. But his first idea, which involved setting off a bomb during a demonstration of new military equipment, was frustrated. The equipment was destroyed in an Allied air raid.

Another attempt was thwarted before it began. In March 1944 Stauffenberg found a willing assassin, Captain Breitenbuch, who was prepared to shoot Hitler at point-blank range. The attack was to take place during a staff meeting of Army Group Centre. But on the morning of the briefing, an SS guard stopped Breitenbuch as he attempted to follow Hitler into the conference room, telling him he did not have clearance to attend.

Then, in June, Stauffenberg was promoted. He became General Fromm's chief of staff, which gave him direct access to the Führer. Acutely aware of the urgency of the situation, Stauffenberg obtained two packets of plastic explosive and an acid fuse, which he placed inside a standard briefcase. This type of slow-burning fuse would make it possible for him to activate the device and still have ten minutes to escape before the explosion. On 11 July, he was invited to attend a briefing at the Berghof where Himmler and Goering were also to be present. It was the perfect opportunity to take out the Nazi leadership in one go. But neither Himmler nor Goering kept their appointments. Frustrated, Stauffenberg gave his report to the meeting and left.

The next attempt was made on 15 July at the Wolf's Lair, but again Himmler failed to appear and Stauffenberg left the compound with the explosives in his briefcase. All these delays placed an insufferable strain on the 35-year-old veteran, who was still recovering from his wounds. But news of the arrest of one of the key conspirators, Julius Leber, gave the plot new urgency. It was decided that the next time Stauffenberg had access to the Führer he would prime the bomb, even if there were no other members of the Nazi hierarchy present. Hitler's death alone would free the conspirators to negotiate an armistice with the British and Americans before the Russians could enter Germany. Operation Valkyrie, the assassination of the Führer and the takeover of the Nazi administration, was rescheduled for 20 July, at the next planned briefing at the Wolf's Lair.

The drama unfolds

At dawn on 20 July, Stauffenberg and his aide, Lieutenant von Haeften, boarded a plane at Berlin Tempelhof for the 483-kilometre (300-mile) flight to Rastenburg. Stauffenberg carried his regular briefcase containing his papers, while Haeften held an identical briefcase filled with explosives. At the airfield in East Prussia they were met by a driver who knew nothing of their plans; he drove them to the heavily guarded compound for the first in a series of meetings which were to culminate with the daily Führer briefing at 12.30 p.m.

At 12.20 p.m. Stauffenberg excused himself on the pretext of having to change into a fresh shirt. He and Haeften entered the briefing hut and hurriedly primed the bomb while the other officers waited impatiently outside. It was a hot and humid day, so hot in fact that the steel shutters of the briefing room were raised and the windows were wide open. Stauffenberg had to arm the detonators by breaking open an acid capsule using pliers specially made for his injured hand. He only had minutes in which to do it. But before he could arm the second packet, a staff sergeant entered the room and reminded them the Führer was waiting. They had their backs to the sergeant so he didn't see what they were doing, but the interruption forced them to abandon their plan to prime the second packet. Haeften took it with him and waited in the car while Stauffenberg joined the officers in the briefing room, carrying half the amount of explosive that the conspirators had intended to use.

The Führer was seated on a stool musing over maps spread before him on a large wooden table. As Stauffenberg entered, he looked up for a moment, then continued with the briefing which was being given by Lieutenant-General Heusinger. Stauffenberg had less than five minutes to plant the bomb and get a safe distance from the building, but he kept his composure. He asked an adjutant if he could stand next to Heusinger because he was hard of hearing. This placed him within inches of his target. Unnoticed, he slipped the briefcase under the table and leant it against a thick concrete support before finding an excuse to leave. As he did so, Colonel Brandt took his place. Seeing the briefcase poking out from under the table, Brandt idly pushed it further away with his foot.

In a few moments Stauffenberg was at a safe distance, waiting anxiously by the car with Heusinger. It was 12.45 p.m. The next instant a tremendous explosion shook the forest, and the briefing hut erupted in smoke and flame. Surely no one could have survived the blast? Without waiting to see if there were any survivors, the bombers leapt into the car and ordered the driver to head for the airfield. They tossed the second packet of explosive into the trees as they sped along and, after a heart-stopping moment at a checkpoint, managed to bluff their way through and board the plane back to Berlin.

But Hitler had survived. The concrete table support had deflected the force of the blast, which was further diffused by the open windows. If Stauffenberg had been able to arm the second packet of explosive, the assassination attempt might have been successful. In the event, Hitler walked unharmed from the wreckage. His face was blackened, his hair singed and his clothes were in tatters, but he was alive.

It seemed that the Führer did indeed lead a charmed life.

But those around him did not. Colonel Brandt and three other senior officers died of the wounds they received in the blast, while 20 others were injured.

Aftermath of the July Plot

It has been estimated that as many as 5,000 people lost their lives as a result of the failure of the July Plot. Some of these committed suicide in order to avoid interrogation at the hands of the Gestapo, while others, such as Field Marshal Rommel (who was accused of complicity in the plot despite lack of evidence), did so in an attempt to protect their families from reprisals.

The principal conspirators – Claus von Stauffenberg, Ludwig Beck and Carl Goerdeler – were shot by firing squad as soon as their part in the plot was discovered. When Himmler heard of their fate, he ordered their bodies to be exhumed and burned and the ashes scattered. Their co-conspirators were not so fortunate. Many were tortured to death or hung from meat hooks while being slowly throttled with piano wire. The spectacle was filmed in colour for Hitler's perverse enjoyment.

All the conspirators knew the risk they were taking, but as General von Tresckow wrote before taking his own life on the Eastern Front on 21 July 1944, 'The moral worth of a man only begins at the point where he is ready to sacrifice his life for his convictions.'

As an officer of the Wehrmacht, von Tresckow knew that at the end of the war he would be condemned by the world for his part in countless atrocities, but felt he had redeemed himself by this belated gesture of defiance: 'Now the whole world will assail and curse us. But I am as solidly convinced as ever I was that what we did was right. I believe that Hitler is the arch enemy not only of Germany, but of the whole world.'

Count Helmuth James von Moltke, who had hosted a gathering of anti-Nazis, was arrested in 1944 but not tried and executed until a year later. He, too, was convinced he had a duty to try to topple the regime.

He told his sons shortly before his death: 'All my life, even in school, I fought against a spirit of narrowness and force, of arrogance, intolerance and pitiless absolute logic which is a part of the German equipment, and which found its embodiment in the National Socialist state.'

Even if the conspirators had been successful in decapitating the leadership, they would have found it difficult to convince a Nazified nation that the removal of Hitler was in its best interests and morally justifiable as a means of averting further suffering. With that end in mind, Beck drafted an address which would have been delivered to the press and broadcast over the airwaves once the news of Hitler's death had been confirmed. It serves as a damning indictment of the dictator by his own generals and is a stinging rebuff to those historians who maintain Hitler was a strategic genius: 'Monstrous things have taken place under our eyes in the years past. Against the advice of his experts, Hitler has unscrupulously sacrificed whole armies for his desire for glory, his presumption of power, his blasphemous delusion of being the chosen and inspired instrument of what he calls "Providence".

'Not elected by the German people, but reaching supreme power by the worst of intrigues, he has created confusion by his demonical arts and lies, and by his incredible waste, which appeared to bring benefits to all, but which in reality has thrown the German people into tremendous debt. To maintain his power, he has established an unbridled reign of terror, destroying justice, banishing decency, mocking the divine commands of pure humanity and destroying the happiness of millions.

'With deadly certainty, his mad contempt for all mankind ultimately had to result in catastrophe for our people. His self-bestowed generalship had to lead our brave sons, fathers, husbands, brothers into disaster. His bloody terror against defenceless people had to bring disgrace to the German name.'

Battle for Berlin

Hitler escaped unscathed, but the scale of the conspiracy had shaken him. He now regarded even his most loyal generals with suspicion. When he was told that the Red Army was massed along a broad front from Warsaw to the Carpathian Mountains in preparation for the last push that would ultimately take it to Berlin, Hitler shrugged the warning off as 'the greatest bluff since Genghis Khan'. But the presence of 2.2 million Soviet soldiers, 6,400 tanks and 46,000 heavy guns was a cold, sobering fact. The combined forces of generals Zhukov and Konev heavily outnumbered the remnants of the German armed forces. They had eleven times more infantry, seven times more tanks and twenty times more artillery. This was the endgame.

The final reckoning

Germany was being bombed by the British by night and the Americans by day. The German Luftwaffe had evaporated months earlier during the ill-fated Ardennes offensive, known as the Battle of the Bulge. Hitler had squandered 100,000 men, 800 tanks, 1,000 aircraft and 50 trainloads of ammunition in that last desperate gesture in December 1944, wasting the entire German reserves which could instead have been used in defence of the Rhine. Even von Rundstedt condemned the offensive as 'a second Stalingrad'.

Now there were not enough men of combat experience to defend Germany's cities, just the old men of the *Volkssturm* (Germany's Home Guard) and the boys of the Hitler Youth.

These remnants of Germany's manhood fought on mainly through fear rather than fanaticism, for on every street corner deserters were hung from lampposts with placards around their necks – a warning to those who refused to do their duty.

Dresden, Cologne, Hamburg and dozens of Germany's other major centres were little more than charred, smouldering ruins, their citizens reduced to scavenging for scraps. Water, electricity and gas supplies had been disrupted months earlier and the sewage system was no longer functioning. All major roads were pockmarked with craters and strewn with rubble, and the rail network was a mangle of twisted rails and abandoned rolling stock. There was nowhere for the terrified civilians to go but down into underground stations and cellars of bombed-out buildings, just as the people of Warsaw, Belgrade and London had done only four years earlier.

And now their Führer shared their fate. In January 1945, as the Allies closed in, he retreated to the bunker beneath the chancellery in Berlin. Surrounded by his staff as the Russian shells shook the ground above them, he was now mentally and physically under siege.

Assault on the Reich

On 7 March 1945, the Allies crossed the Rhine at Remagen after German engineers failed to blow up the main railway bridge there. Soldiers of the US 9th Division removed the remaining demolition charges under fire in order to secure the route into Germany. Hitler responded by sacking von Rundstedt and ordering the execution of the five officers who had failed to destroy the bridge.

Despite this breakthrough, several Allied commanders believed the war could have ended six months earlier if the advance had not been halted prematurely. At that point, the Rhine was held by a Danish SS division and another unit consisting of elderly men, both of which would have been happy to surrender. But the opportunity was squandered by the Allied leadership, who wanted to conserve petrol. By the time the order was given to advance, Germany had reinforced the Rhine region.

But elsewhere the Germans were in retreat. The Reich was shrinking at an astonishing rate. Finland, Estonia, Latvia and Lithuania were soon cleared of the German invaders. In the south, Ukraine was in Russian hands, Romania was out of the war and Bulgaria was free. Elsewhere, Greece had been liberated and Josip Tito's partisans were in control of Yugoslavia.

On the evening of 23 March, the Allies launched their last major offensive of the war. The event was watched with grim satisfaction by the British Prime Minister Winston Churchill and Field Marshal Montgomery. After weeks of bombing along the Ruhr, more than 3,000 guns opened up the attack west of the Rhine at Wesel. Then a million men poured across the Rhine in order to engage General Model's Army Group B. At dawn, Churchill insisted on crossing with the troops, who were able to advance 9.5 kilometres (6 miles) into enemy territory before encountering serious resistance. When victory came, on 18 April, the Allies netted 317,000 prisoners, more than the Russians had captured at Stalingrad.

Finally, on 25 April, soldiers of the US 1st Army and Soviet soldiers of the 5th Guards Army shook hands at Torgau, 112.5 kilometres (70 miles) southwest of Berlin. On the same day, one million Russian soldiers paused before they made the final attack on the capital of the Third Reich.

The bunker

On 19 March 1945, Hitler ordered the destruction of Germany's infrastructure, including surviving factories and power plants, the communications network and transportation and other resources. His plan was that nothing of use would be left for the Allies or the Germans. This scorched earth policy, known as the Nero Decree, was Hitler's way of punishing the German people for their failure to fulfil the Aryan ideal.

When news reached Hitler that Goering and Himmler were attempting to negotiate a separate peace to save their own skins, he raged that he had been betrayed. At this point, he finally conceded that the war was lost. Just after midnight, on 29 April, he prepared his exit from the world. In a quiet civil ceremony he married his mistress Eva Braun, who had said she intended to die by his side whenever he was ready. While the inmates of the bunker celebrated the wedding with cake and champagne, in a surreal atmosphere of desperate gaiety, Hitler ordered his physician to test a cyanide capsule, given to him by Himmler, on his dog, Blondi. Hitler suspected that Himmler might have substituted the poison with a sedative so that the Soviets could capture his leader alive and put him on trial.

When the drug proved to be fatal, Hitler presented each of his secretaries with a small box containing a cynaide capsule as a parting gift. At this point he was a wizened shell of his former self, his penetrating gaze dulled with drugs, his face sallow and his hands shaking. As he moved, he shuffled like an old man. An SS guard was quoted as saying he looked closer to 70 than his actual age of 56.

Final words

At 2 a.m. on 29 April 1945, Hitler dictated his political testament to his secretary, Traudl Junge, while the thud of Russian artillery intensified above the bunker. Junge was expecting finally to learn the reason for the war and why it had come to such an inglorious end for her country.

> 'If the war is lost, the people will be lost also. It is not necessary to worry about what the people will need for elemental survival. On the contrary, it is better for us to destroy even these things. For this nation has proven itself to be the weaker.'
>
> Adolf Hitler, 18 March 1945

But to Junge's dismay, Hitler repeated the same old arguments. He cynically blamed the Jews for the war he had started by the brutal invasion of neighbouring lands, a war the Nazis had prosecuted with such brutality that the Allies had no option but to demand Germany's unconditional surrender.

'It is untrue that I or anyone else in Germany wanted war in 1939. It was desired and caused by none but those international statesmen who were of Jewish descent or who were working for Jewish interests. . . .

'After a six-year struggle which, in spite of all reverses, will one day be inscribed in the pages of history as the most glorious and courageous kind of evidence of a nation's will to live, I cannot leave this city which is the capital of the Reich. Since our forces are too small to withstand the enemy's attack on this particular spot, since our resistance has been slowly undermined by creatures whose lack of character is matched by their folly, I wish by remaining in this city to join my fate to that which millions of others too have taken upon themselves. Besides, I do not wish to fall into the hands of enemies who, for the amusement of their misguided masses, need another spectacle arranged by the Jews. I therefore reached the decision to stay in Berlin and to choose death voluntarily at the moment that I should feel that the residence of the Führer and chancellor can no longer be defended. . . .

'From the sacrifices of our soldiers, and from my own bond with them unto death, in one way or another the seed will rise in German history and there will be a radiant rebirth of the National Socialist movement.'

Hitler concluded by announcing a new cabinet and choosing his successor, Admiral Doenitz. It was a surreal moment, but one that was characteristic of Hitler's state of mind.

Suicides

Hitler rose at 6 a.m. on the last morning of his life, having slept fitfully. The atmosphere in the bunker was subdued. Amid empty bottles and dirty dishes, the partygoers slept off their drink. Some discussed the most painless and effective method of committing suicide, with the clinical detachment of people who knew the end would come and were now simply resigned to it.

At noon, as preparations were being made for a Wagnerian funeral, Hitler convened his last conference. But petrol was in short supply and the shelling made an elaborate ceremony impossible.

After a simple lunch of salad and spaghetti, Hitler said his farewells to Junge, Bormann, Goebbels and the last of the inner circle. He was now so frail that his final whispered words were lost in the low thud of the incoming shells.

Then Hitler and his new bride entered their private apartment and closed the door behind them. It was 3.30 p.m. Moments later, a hysterical Magda Goebbels pushed through the small group waiting outside in the corridor and tearfully begged the Führer to reconsider his decision to take his life. She was ushered from the room and the door was closed behind her. The suffocating silence was shattered by a pistol shot. One of the Goebbels' children was playing on the staircase: 'That was a bull's-eye,' he said.

No one cried. Instead, almost as one, the members of his staff lit cigarettes, something Hitler had forbidden in his presence. Hitler was dead and his death freed them, as it did everyone else, of his overpowering influence.

When his valet and two SS bodyguards entered the room, they found Hitler slumped on the left side of the blue-and-white velvet sofa with his hands clasped in his lap. His 7.65 mm pistol lay by his side and blood was trickling down from a hole in his right temple. He appeared to have taken poison, but his bride had then delivered the *coup de grâce*. Eva Braun lay dead beside him, her legs tucked underneath her. She, too, had taken cyanide.

The bodies were draped in a blanket and carried upstairs, where they were laid in a shell crater by the entrance to the bunker. The corpses were doused with petrol and ignited with a taper from the valet's notebook. There was no funeral oration and no solemn Wagnerian music, just the whining of shells and the dull thud of the explosions, which were now only yards away. But there was one final lie to be told. When Admiral Doenitz described Hitler's death to the German people in a radio broadcast the following day, he said their Führer had died fighting at the head of his troops.

That same day, 1 May 1945, Goebbels and his wife killed themselves after first poisoning their six children. They could not imagine living in a world without their Führer or leaving such a desecrated inheritance to their offspring.

The fate of the others

Martin Bormann broke out of the bunker that night and made his way towards what he hoped were the American lines. It was subsequently assumed that he was either dead or in hiding; reports in the 1960s suggested he had escaped to South America. But in the 1970s a skeleton was discovered when building contractors dug up a plot in West Berlin. Forensics experts claimed it was Bormann and, in 1998, DNA testing confirmed their findings.

On 23 May, Heinrich Himmler, disguised as an ordinary soldier, was captured at a Russian army checkpoint at Bremervorde in northern Germany and handed over to the British for questioning. While being examined by a doctor, he bit into a cyanide capsule hidden in the hollow of one of his teeth, and died within minutes.

Weeks later, Goering surrendered. He was eventually put on trial at Nuremberg with other leading Nazis, among them Dr Robert Ley, who hanged himself before the trial began. Goering also took his own life in his cell, but only after the trial at which he was sentenced to death. Of the 20 remaining defendants, Ribbentrop, Keitel, Kaltenbrunner, Rosenberg, Frank, Frick, Streicher, Seyss-Inquart, Sauckel and Jodl were hanged in the gymnasium behind the courthouse on 16 October 1946. Speer and the Hitler Youth leader, von Schirach, were sentenced to 20 years' imprisonment, while Neurath received a 15-year and Doenitz a ten-year sentence.

Propaganda official Hans Fritzsche, economist Hjalmar Schacht and former vice-chancellor Franz von Papen were acquitted of all charges. Rudolf Hess, who had been in Allied hands since his inexplicable flight to Scotland in 1941, was sent to Spandau prison for the remainder of his life. He died there in 1986. Admiral Raeder and Walther Funk, Schacht's successor, were also sentenced to life imprisonment.

Other trials followed, some presided over by German judges.

These were less well-publicized but no less shocking, not just for the enormity of the crimes that were uncovered but for the revelations about the characters of the men who had committed them. Many of these people were so unexceptional, so colourless, that it gave rise to a new phrase, 'the banality of evil'. But the public quickly tired of hearing of the horrors and court reports grew shorter, until they disappeared from the front pages altogether. It was, perhaps, too appalling to make comfortable reading in the aftermath of such a ferocious war.

Hitler's war

The Second World War was Hitler's war. With the invasion of Poland in September 1939, he instigated a conflict that raged for six long years through 27 countries and claimed the lives of an estimated 64 million people, 40 million of whom were civilians.

Six million victims of the Second World War were Jews, systematically exterminated with chillingly mechanized efficiency in concentration camps whose names are now synonymous with unimaginable suffering. Hundreds of thousands more were worked to death in slave labour camps or died of starvation and disease as a direct result of the Nazi policy of genocide.

To this toll must be added untold numbers of Nazi-determined 'undesirables' – homosexuals, ethnic minorities, political rivals, the disabled and people privy to potentially embarrassing secrets about the Führer's past. There were also the partisans and resistance fighters who were executed without trial, and hundreds of thousands of innocent men, women and children in the occupied countries who were arbitrarily murdered in reprisals for alleged acts of resistance.

In Eastern Europe, whole communities were obliterated in a day as Hitler's death squads swept through the countryside, committing acts of savagery not seen since the Dark Ages.

And, of course, millions of German civilians died as a result of the fighting on the Home Front and in the Allied bombing raids which left their country in ruins. In the aftermath, the two superpowers, the USA and the Soviet Union, faced each other across a Europe divided by barbed wire and minefields in a Cold War that threatened nuclear Armageddon for decades to come. This was Adolf Hitler's legacy.

HJALMAR SCHACHT
BANKING ON HITLER

'No one can find his future with us who is not behind Adolf Hitler, heart and soul.'

Hitler's minister of economics and former head of the Reichsbank, Hjalmar Schacht, received a copy of his indictment on the charge of crimes against peace in his cell at Nuremberg with the demeanour of a schoolmaster whose authority was being questioned. With barely suppressed contempt, he made it clear that he expected to be acquitted: 'I am, after all, a banker.' But if he imagined his choice of career would absolve him from his part in funding Hitler's war, he was mistaken.

In the opinion of the United States' consul general in Berlin, it was Schacht's 'resourcefulness, his complete financial ruthlessness, and his absolute cynicism' that enabled the Nazis to fund their rearmament programme. 'If it had not been for his efforts . . . the Nazi regime would have been unable to maintain itself in power and to establish its control over Germany, much less to create the enormous war machine which was necessary for its objectives in Europe and later throughout the world.'

BRINGING HITLER TO POWER
The son of a Danish baroness and a Prussian aristocrat, Schacht had a fluid interpretation of right and wrong when it came to money. During the First World War he had been dismissed from public service for siphoning 500 million francs' worth of Belgian bonds, set aside for reparations, into the Dresdner Bank – which, coincidentally, had been his previous employer. It was this proclivity for unconventional business practices that made him useful to Hitler, who described Schacht as someone with a 'consummate skill at swindling other people'. Once Hitler had assured himself that Schacht wouldn't do the same to him, he invited the banker to raise funds for his campaign. Though never a member of the Nazi party, Schacht was instrumental in bringing Hitler to power by raising considerable sums for the NSDAP between 1926 and 1932. He also played a part in petitioning President Hindenburg to appoint Hitler to the chancellorship in January 1933.

WAR FUNDING
It was said Schacht objected to the Führer's plans to wage war, but only on the grounds that it would be too expensive. When faced with the dictator's

determination to avenge himself on the victorious Allies who had imposed
punitive reparations after the First World War, Schacht devised a plan for
funnelling funds into the Reich that could not be disrupted by hostilities.

In 1930, he suggested the establishment of a new clearing house for
the world's major banks, which would facilitate payment of Germany's
reparations. The Bank for International Settlements (BIS) was to be based in
Basel, Switzerland and Schacht would be its first president. The appointment
was Chancellor Hitler's reward for Schacht's invaluable support during 'the
struggle', but once in place Schacht would use his influence to convince the
world's major banks to invest in the regeneration of Germany.

The honour tribune during the parade for Adolf Hitler's birthday, 20 April 1938, on Unter den Linden, Berlin. Schacht is on the far right, wearing a bowler hat

However, Hitler didn't trust the banker and was openly offensive towards him. He once said that Schacht couldn't resist 'cheating someone out of 100 marks' if he had the chance. But he added that as the other bankers were 'a bunch of crooks', Schacht was not obliged to be 'scrupulously honest' with any of them.

In the pre-war years, Schacht succeeded in channelling vast sums into Germany from foreign investors. Hitler used the money to fund rearmament; he also ploughed it into an ambitious programme of public works which earned the grudging admiration of other nations. Even after Hitler's succession to the chancellorship had staunched the flow of capital to Germany from Europe and the United States, an estimated 294 million Swiss francs continued to pour in from pre-existing agreements.

When Hitler annexed Austria in 1938 and demanded its gold reserves be transferred to the Reichsbank, the BIS obligingly deposited 22 tons of gold from the Austrian national bank into the regime's account. And as Hitler greedily swallowed up successive countries, he acquired their gold reserves, even when those accounts were held in trust abroad. This was because the BIS managed accounts for both the aggressor and the country that had capitulated.

When German troops entered Prague, the Bank of England transferred £6,000,000 in Czech gold reserves to the BIS. The British could have delayed this, but the governor of the Bank of England, Montague Norman, was said to be on very friendly terms with his fellow BIS member Hjalmar Schacht and didn't see any reason to withhold the funds, which eventually found their way into the coffers of the Reichsbank.

RELEASED ON APPEAL

After war was declared, Schacht was sidelined for the duration and spent the last year of the conflict in various concentration camps, having been accused of participation in the July Plot to kill Hitler. Those who had taken part in the plot denied his involvement. Schacht, they said, was incapable of acting on principles he didn't possess.

After his liberation by the Allies, he was indicted at Nuremberg for assisting the Nazi military machine, but was acquitted after turning state's evidence against his co-defendants.

He was subsequently convicted of war crimes by a German de-Nazification court and sentenced to eight years in prison. In 1948 he was released on appeal, went on to set up his own bank, and continued to prosper.

> *The most dangerous and reprehensible type of all opportunists, someone who would use a Hitler for his own ends, and then claim, after Hitler was defeated, to have been against him all the time. He was part of a movement that he knew was wrong, but was in it just because he saw it was winning.'*
>
> Robert H. Jackson, chief prosecutor at Nuremberg

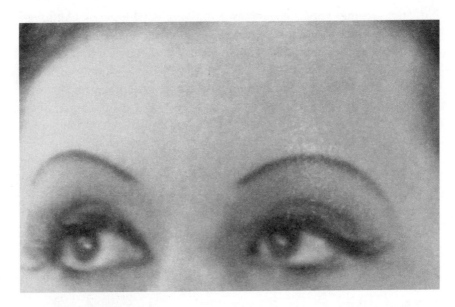

CHAPTER 16

Sex and the Big Screen

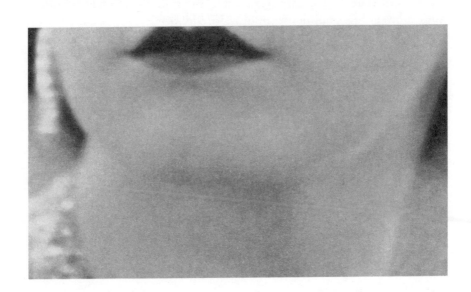

No other regime used imagery as effectively as the Nazis. Although Hitler possessed a remarkable gift for oratory, he understood that the most direct method of reaching the masses was through simple symbols and strong, iconic imagery.

Both Albert Speer, who stage-managed the Nuremberg rallies, and Josef Goebbels, who presided over the Ministry of Propaganda, knew that powerful images could make an indelible impression on the human subconscious, stirring primitive emotions and awakening archetypal aspects of the psyche. Goebbels became convinced of this after speaking with the German film-maker Fritz Hippler who acted as his assistant and later directed the notorious and inflammatory propaganda feature *The Eternal Jew* (1940). Hippler believed that visuals were always more powerful than a verbal argument, which depends so much for its impact on the personality of the speaker, and he compared the cinema screen to a mirror in which the masses would see Germany, especially the poorer classes for whom cinema-going was the one form of culture they could afford.

Goebbels agreed. Rational thought was for intellectuals and required patience, insight and a receptive mind. The masses were more easily won over by appealing directly to their emotions and basest instincts.

But while the theatrical pomp and pageantry of the annual rallies incited the faithful to get in step behind the leadership, and propaganda posters proclaimed National Socialist slogans to the general population, captive audiences in the dark, reverent hush of Germany's Kino theatres were subjected to a subtler form of indoctrination.

Visual appeal

In the 1920s, Goebbels had exploited the power of radio, broadcasting Nazi propaganda to great effect, but the potential of cinema to influence the civilian population had not yet been fully utilized. German films made a considerable impact at home and abroad during the silent era, when the expressionist classic *The Cabinet of Dr Caligari* (1920), the early science fiction epic *Metropolis* (1927) and G. W. Pabst's social realist drama *Pandora's Box* (1929) captivated audiences with their contrasting visual styles. But Goebbels was no patron of the arts. Although he was a doctor of literature and philosophy and the author of several unpublished novels, he saw art primarily as a medium for distributing a political message and communicating a shared vision, rather than as a form of self-expression.

Taking over Ufa

In January 1933, as soon as he had made himself comfortable behind his desk in the Ministry of Public Enlightenment and Propaganda and successfully fended off a rival bid for control of German cinema by Alfred Rosenberg's Front For German Culture, Goebbels embarked on a programme of indoctrination through print media, the fine arts, state-sponsored leisure activities, music, theatre and cinema. In late April he made an official visit to the Ufa (Universum Film AG) studios in Neubabelsburg, west of Berlin, to reassure management and production staff that German film was in good hands. However, he stressed that 'alignment' with Nazi policy was required if those employed in the industry wanted to continue in their present posts. Film would have to be 'a champion of German culture', not shallow entertainment copying the degenerate art of Hollywood. According to the Nazis, Hollywood cinema had a hidden agenda to corrupt Aryan society: the American studios were run by Jews and their films featured coloured actors and decadent Negro jazz music. In the new Germany, kitsch and inferior art would not be tolerated.

The principal German studio, Ufa, had just been hit by a substantial loss in revenue because of a blanket boycott of German films by Britain and America and could not afford to lose state sponsorship. So it accepted the inevitable and agreed to submit all films to the new Reich Film Board for approval. In return for Ufa's co-operation, the Nazis established a new source of funding, the Film Credit Bank, with the pledge of ten million marks towards new productions. Although the main shareholders were legitimate financial institutions (the Dresden Bank, the Deutsche Bank, the Commercial and Private Bank as well as the government's Reichs Kredit-Gesellschaft), the money was effectively under Goebbels' personal control as he decided which projects would receive state funding (typically this was between 50 and 70 per cent of their production costs).

Goebbels had become a despot in his own domain, but saw himself in the role of an orchestral conductor, co-ordinating the efforts of many talented individuals hired to perform a chosen piece under the guidance of his baton. He would choose the programme, audition the performers and dictate the tempo. But he would not be satisfied with issuing guidelines and directives. After the completion of each film he would have a private screening and invariably demand changes to comply with Nazi policy.

Film buff

But Goebbels had a genuine passion for movies; he watched at least one every day, even during the war. Although he steeled himself to view every type of film so that he could learn something from even the most mediocre potboiler, he disliked crime and American screwball comedy and considered rustic dramas to be 'vulgar'. According to director Arthur Rabenalt, Goebbels' favourite American movies were *Gone With the Wind* (1939), *Ben Hur* (1925) and Disney's *Snow White and the Seven Dwarfs* (1937). He derived great pleasure from two of the German musicals he had helped put into production – *Es leuchten die Sterne* ('The Stars Are Shining', 1937) and *Patrioten* ('The Patriots', 1936) – which were seen by between 15 and 25 million people and proved highly profitable.

Goebbels understood that audiences didn't go to the cinema to be educated, but to be entertained. Nazi cinema would out-glamorize Hollywood. Its stars would shine brighter than those of MGM, Warner Brothers and Fox. He, Josef Goebbels, would wield more power than the studio moguls in Hollywood. He would enjoy the company of the most beautiful women in the Reich, stars such as Olga Tschechowa, Marika Rökk, Zarah Leander and Kristina Söderbaum who, he imagined, would be grateful for the celebrity status his patronage guaranteed. How grateful they would actually be, only time would tell.

Zarah Leander

Before Hitler assumed power, the Nazis had prohibited Jews from working in the film industry and banned the screening of films made by Jewish directors. But after Marlene Dietrich left Germany for Hollywood in 1930 there were few female stars of a similar magnitude to take her place. Curiously, although she had publicly criticized the Nazi regime, Dietrich was repeatedly petitioned by Goebbels to return and star in German films. As late as November 1937, he noted that she would not be free from her Paramount contract until the following year, but that she 'remained committed to Germany'. Goebbels' belief in the pulling power of the film star obviously ran deep.

The four actresses who possessed even a glimmer of Dietrich's charisma were all foreigners and one, Zarah Leander (1907–81), was known to have Jewish grandparents. Goebbels was deeply suspicious of her for this reason, and her insistence on being paid two-thirds of her salary in Danish krone was a constant irritant to him, as was her repeated refusal to apply for German citizenship.

At a private party, Goebbels reputedly asked her outright if she was Jewish. 'Zarah – that's a Jewish name, isn't it?' he inquired; to which she replied, 'Well, what about Josef?'

Leander was a statuesque Swede with a smoky voice enhanced by cigarettes and a fondness for a Scandinavian liquor known as Aquavit. It was rumoured that the composer Franz Lehár was forced to transpose her arias down two octaves when she starred in his operetta *The Merry Widow* in Stockholm in 1931. Apparently she was bombarded with fan mail addressed to 'Herr Leander' from admirers who had only heard her recordings. But when she made the transition from stage to screen there could be no doubting her gender.

A 1938 issue of *Filmwelt* announced the arrival of a new screen goddess: 'This incredibly impeccable and sculptured face mirrors everything that moves a woman: wistfulness and pain, love and bliss, melancholy and resignation. In her attitude as an actress, Zarah Leander is the epitome of "spiritualized sensuality". As dark as her low, undefinable alto – which is able to represent so excitingly the expression of hidden female desires – is also her essence.'

Her luminous Nordic beauty and heavy accent drew comparisons with Greta Garbo. Although Goebbels confided to his diary that he thought her 'very overrated', she was popular with German audiences who flocked to see Leander in a series of erotically charged films, the first of them *Zu neuen Ufern* ('To New Shores', 1937), which made her the highest paid female actress in Nazi Germany. Leander's final Ufa contract guaranteed her half-a-million Reichsmarks for three pictures, which she invested in a fish cannery in her native country as if anticipating her return if the Nazis lost the war.

Leander was given roles that emphasized her smouldering sensuality and her rendition of suggestive songs such as 'Can Love Be a Sin?' added to her allure. The songs were specially written for her by her favourite songwriter Bruno Balz, who she defended when he was arrested by the Gestapo for 'immoral acts' with a Hitler Youth member in 1942. It was the only time that Goebbels came to Leander's aid, because he too wanted to spare Balz from public humiliation and a jail sentence. The songwriter was too valuable to morale.

Otherwise Leander declared herself neutral, admitting that she was a 'political idiot', although recently declassified documents from the Swedish secret service suggest that she might have been a Soviet spy.

Gay icon?

Zarah Leander's height proved a problem during the making of her most celebrated film *The Great Love* (1942). According to her co-star Wolfgang Preiss, the producers couldn't find women who were tall enough to form a chorus line during a dance number. Then someone had the bright idea of using men. But where would they find enough men of the right height and build who would be willing to be dressed in women's clothes?

In one of the most bizarre episodes in the history of the Third Reich, members of the SS were drafted in to don wigs, women's costumes and make-up and everyone on the set was sworn to secrecy on pain

Swedish-born actress and singer Zarah Leander became a star of the state-owned Ufa in the 1930s and 1940s

of death. But the deception is all too obvious if the scenes are viewed in close-up, where the men's stubble is clearly visible. Even if it had not been for this episode, Leander's androgynous, high camp act would have ensured she became a gay icon.

In 1943, when her Berlin home was bombed by the Allies, Leander returned to Sweden, to the consternation of her German fans and condemnation from Goebbels, who banned her films and accused her of being a traitor to the Reich.

Kristina Soederbaum

There was no mistaking Kristina Soederbaum (1912–2001) for a man in drag. The curvaceous Swedish blonde starred in ten box-office hits in Nazi Germany, all directed by her possessive husband Veit Harlan who became known for directing the most bombastic, expensive and colourful films of the period, as well as the most notorious, *Jud Süss*. But more remarkably she enjoyed stardom during the Third Reich without having to submit to Goebbels' obsequious charm. It might have been that the diminutive, club-footed Goebbels did not fancy having to face down Harlan, who was fearless when it came to defending his wife from overzealous admirers. Or perhaps the propaganda minister could not afford to make an enemy of one of the few loyal Nazi directors left in Germany at the time.

Harlan cast his new wife in brooding melodramas in which she frequently played the tragic heroine who sacrifices her honour and then herself to save her man. She was deflowered and drowned so often that she was dubbed *Reichswasserleiche* ('the Empire's water corpse'). Her corn-coloured hair and porcelain skin were lit to emphasize her fragility and from 1941 all her films were photographed in luxurious Agfacolor, which brought out the bloom in her china doll complexion.

Her most popular films were those which pandered to the Nazi creed, although she also made innocuous romantic movies such as *Verwehte Spuren* (1938), later remade as *So Long At The Fair* (1950) with Dirk Bogarde, and *Die Reise nach Tilsit* (1938), which was itself a remake of F. W. Murnau's *Sunrise* (1927). The latter became a cause célèbre after Magda Goebbels walked out of the premiere when she thought she recognized a veiled reference to her husband's affair with the Czech actress Lída Baarová.

But it was *Jud Süss* (1940) that brought Soederbaum and Harlan before a Nazi war crimes court after the war, on charges that the film had contributed to the Holocaust. In order to encourage the mute co-operation of the civilian population, it had been shown in almost every major city in occupied Europe shortly before the round-up and transportation of Jews to the death camps. The couple were cleared, but their careers were over. Soederbaum performed in the theatre in a play written by her husband and was vilified by former fans, some of whom threatened to murder them both. She made a few inferior German films in the 1950s, then earned a modest living as a professional photographer.

Olga Tschechowa

No less glamorous was Olga Tschechowa, who was born in Russia of German stock. A star of the Soviet stage and the former wife of Mikhail Chekhov, nephew of the famous playwright, she emigrated to Berlin in 1920. At Ufa she worked with F. W. Murnau and later featured in films directed by René Clair and Alfred Hitchcock. But her greatest performance came when she cast herself as a friend to Adolf Hitler, while acting, allegedly, as a Soviet spy.

Unknown to the Nazis, she had received her travel papers in exchange for future services. Little was required of her until Hitler came to power, but then her Soviet paymasters were impatient to learn what the German leader planned as his country stepped up its rearmament programme and demanded the return of territories in the east.

By the early 1930s, Olga had made the successful transition from silent movies to talkies and was one of the biggest box-office draws in Germany, starring in such films as *Der Choral von Leuthen* (1933), a historical pageant celebrating the life of Frederick the Great.

Hitler was an admirer and when he invited her to dine alone with him in Berlin she saw the opportunity to repay her debt.

When photographs of her cosying up to the dictator at a reception appeared in the Russian press, Tschechowa was accused of being a traitor to her country. However, behind closed doors she intervened to save the life of her brother, a Soviet assassin who had been sent to Germany to kill Hitler. After the plot had been uncovered, he was sent to a concentration camp and was certain to be executed, but Olga used all her feminine wiles to secure his release. Her intervention brought her to the attention of Heinrich Himmler, head of the SS and the Gestapo, who ordered an investigation into her off-screen activities. But the star had her spies in the regime and, on hearing the news of her imminent arrest, stage-managed a surprise for Himmler. The Reichsführer burst into her apartment and found Olga had company – Hitler was being entertained. He ordered Himmler to leave at once.

From that moment on, Olga Tschechowa was assured of Hitler's protection. She continued to star in German films and enjoyed her celebrity and the patronage of the Nazi elite. After the war she was summoned back to Moscow, where Stalin received her in private. What passed between them is not known, but she was then free to return to Germany and resume her career until the 1970s. She died in Munich in 1980, aged 95.

Marika Roekk

Musical comedy actress, singer and dancer Marika Roekk (1913–2004) was already an international star of musical revue when the Nazis stormed to power in 1933. But the Egyptian-born beauty of Hungarian parentage had yet to make a movie. Her first German feature set the pattern for a series of escapist entertainments in which she styled herself as the German Ginger Rogers, an ever-cheerful sprite who danced, sang and laughed her way across the screen all through the war years to the delight of cinema-goers. These upbeat morale-boosting movies were appreciated all the more when the bombs were falling and defeat seemed inevitable. Her German debut *Light Cavalry* in 1935 was quickly followed by several variations on the same formula and in 1940 she received lavish praise and a large bouquet of flowers for her dual role in *Kora Terry* from a grateful Führer, who appreciated the diversion from the serious business of subjugating Europe. She acknowledged the gesture in a gushing telegram: 'If I somewhat diverted you, mein Führer, for a few brief moments from the burden of your important responsibilities, I shall be forever proud and happy. With a German salute, your Marika Roekk.'

After the war, she was shocked to be banned from performing for three years. But she was soon back in favour with the Allied occupying forces, who were also in need of cheering up, and with the Austrians, who had not lost their taste for frothy, saccharine-sweet sentimental songs and girls with a permanent smile.

Lilian Harvey

Of the quartet of 1930s German starlets who shot to fame during the Third Reich, only Lilian Harvey (1906–68) satisfied the Nazis' racial requirements – and she was half English. Born Helene Pape in London, to a British mother and a German father, Lilian was sent to live with an aunt in Switzerland when the Great War broke out. From there she studied at the Berlin State Opera School of Dance and found her way into pictures in the early 1920s. Her singing and dancing abilities and facility with languages made her an asset in 'talkies', specifically in a series of 11 operettas she made at Ufa with screen partner Willy Fritsch. It was routine to film the same story in three languages, using the same sets but with a rotating cast. Harvey was able to demand three times her co-stars' salaries by virtue of her fluency in German, English and French.

Laurence Olivier made his screen debut starring opposite Lilian in the English version of *Hokuspokus*. Her most celebrated film *The Congress Dances* (1931) brought offers from Hollywood, but after four poorly performing films for 20th Century Fox she returned to Germany to be reunited with her lover, director Paul Martin. Had she stayed to star in *George White's Scandals* she might have become a major star in America, because it made a name for her replacement, Alice Faye.

Lilian's girlish, feather-brained personality was summed up by the anonymous reviewer of *My Lips Betray* (1933): 'A likeable and occasionally lyric comedienne, her efforts to enliven a heavy-handed and humourless script result in a performance stuffed with that particular form of girlish charm which drives strong men to dipsomania and homicide.'

Although she affected a girlish personality on screen, she appears to have been made of much sterner material in reality. After she found herself under contract to Josef Goebbels, who made it clear that he would not tolerate her friendships with several Jewish colleagues who had been deprived of their positions, she defied him and was subsequently warned off by the Gestapo. In 1937 she put up bail for Jewish choreographer and friend Jens Keith, who was being charged under Paragraph 175 of the German Criminal Code, which criminalized homosexuality. With her agreement, he fled to France and Lilian was arrested and threatened with imprisonment for having aided a fugitive.

Fearing for her life, she escaped first to France and then to England, abandoning a considerable fortune she had amassed through her earnings in the movies. Her property was confiscated and her bank accounts were seized, leaving her with nothing but the jewels she was wearing when she arrived in England. Fortunately they were emeralds and diamonds valued at almost £60,000.

Runaway director

When Goebbels visited the vast and rambling Ufa film studios in Babelsberg during his first year in office he must have felt the same as Orson Welles when given complete control of his first project, *Citizen Kane* (1941). The studio was indeed the 'biggest electric train set a boy ever had', and he also had casting-couch privileges and intended to use them. Goebbels, who favoured dark-eyed brunettes, naturally assumed that the leading German film-makers and their stars would consider it an honour to work for the Reich. He summoned them one by one to the chancellery for a personal interview, but they were not all as grateful as the Nazis expected.

Fritz Lang admitted he was flattered to hear that Hitler was a big admirer of *Metropolis* (1927) and of *Die Nibelungen* (1924), which had brought the Führer to tears. Hitler had said of Lang: 'Here is a man who will give us great Nazi films.' But the director wisely asked for time to consider such an important proposal as film-maker in chief to the Reich, and used it to arrange safe passage to America. His disappearance forced the Nazis to turn to their stock journeymen directors like Karl Ritter, although they were more than fortunate in having documentary film-maker Leni Riefenstahl (see page 306) to helm two of the most memorable and visually impressive records of the Nazi years: *Triumph of the Will* (1935) and *Olympia* (1938).

Goebbels lavished praise on *Triumph of the Will*, which he preferred to overtly political feature films such as *Hitlerjunge Quex* ('Hitler Youth Quest', 1933) and *Hans Westmar* (1934). He believed the latter paled in comparison to the grandeur and choreographed parade of military might on display in Riefenstahl's documentaries.

Hitler's last film appearance

Although Riefenstahl's *Triumph of the Will* was a great success in Germany and attracted critical acclaim for its aesthetic qualities (and condemnation for its political content), Goebbels advised Hitler not to make any further appearances on film. He did not want to risk over-exposing his 'star', so he ensured that the Führer only figured briefly in newsreels. Instead, dramas such as *The Great King* (1942), which depicted the life of Frederick the Great, substituted a historical figure for Hitler. Their depictions of benign leadership suggested a parallel with contemporary events.

Goebbels witnessed the impact Eisenstein's *Battleship Potemkin* made on audiences and wanted the Nazi heroes and heroines in German films to arouse equally strong reactions and feelings. But he knew that if he commissioned nothing but patriotic militarist pictures the audience would quickly tire of them and seek entertainment elsewhere, so he shrewdly balanced historical epics with frivolous musical comedies and emotive melodramas. These would appeal to all audiences and stave off their desire to see foreign movies, which had been banned in Germany. During the Third Reich, 90 per cent of the films produced and approved by the Ministry for Propaganda had no overt political content.

LENI RIEFENSTAHL

A WONDERFUL, TERRIBLE LIFE

'Reality doesn't interest me.'

Leni Riefenstahl (born Hélène Bertha Amalie), the high-spirited daughter of a wealthy Berlin businessman, was always determined to do what she wanted and damn the consequences. Barely out of her teens, she toured Europe as a 'free' dancer under the auspices of Max Reinhardt and seemed destined for a glittering career until a knee injury forced her to abandon the stage at the age of 22. Undeterred by this setback, she found fame as a movie actress after tracking down Arnold Fanck, the director of her favourite film, *Mountain of Destiny*, and persuading him that she could be his muse. She starred in a series of critically acclaimed and commercially successful 'mountain films' (*bergfilms*) during the late 1920s, which included *The White Hell of Pitz Palu* (1929). She did her own climbing (famously in bare feet, for one scene) and performed her own stunts, which included being swept away in an avalanche and emerging unscathed. Dubbed 'Hitler's pin-up girl', she was admired for her indomitable courage and chiselled Nordic features. But she became fascinated by the art of film-making and withdrew from acting to work behind the camera. It is possible that she abandoned acting after failing to secure the leading role in von Sternberg's *The Blue Angel* (1930), which went to her rival, Marlene Dietrich.Fanck taught Riefenstahl how to combine unusual camera angles, coloured filters, diffused lighting, lenses and different film stock to determine the look and emotional impact of a film and he showed her how editing could heighten tension and bring drama to a scene. Riefenstahl was inspired: 'The editing room became a magic workshop for me.'

However, once she had learned all Fanck could teach her and sensing that his career was threatened by his refusal to make propaganda films for the new Nazi regime, she seized her chance to star in and direct her own series of 'mountain' films. Her first feature, *The Blue Light* (1932), was awarded the Silver Medal at the Venice Film festival that year and brought her international recognition. Hitler honoured Riefenstahl with an invitation to the chancellery and an offer to document the 1933 party rally in Nuremberg.

VICTORY OF FAITH

As a devoted admirer of the man she believed would make Germany the envy of Europe, Riefenstahl felt privileged and more than capable of presenting the party in all its military glory. In 1937, she would tell the *Detroit News*: 'Hitler is

Leni Riefenstahl on location, filming Triumph of the Will *in Nuremberg in 1934*

the greatest man who ever lived. He truly is without fault, so simple and at the same time possessed of masculine strength.'

A year before her death in 2003 she told *Die Welt* that the first projects Hitler offered her were crude propaganda features, *SA-Mann Brand* and *Hitlerjunge Quex*, which were later given to other directors. She claimed to have turned them down, which made Hitler angry. But when he asked her to document the 1933 Nuremberg rally she agreed. She couldn't afford to miss out on the opportunity to align herself with the leader whose presence would guarantee the film worldwide distribution and earn her enormous publicity. Hitler ordered Goebbels to put the resources of the Reich Film Board at her disposal, but Goebbels did nothing, presumably in the hope that the Führer would forget about it.

> 'By that time Goebbels, for many reasons, already hated me and he did not follow Hitler's direction. As a result there was a big argument between Goebbels and Hitler. . . . he called Dr Goebbels and chewed him out in my presence. I almost sank into the floor, it was frightening. Because Hitler wanted me to come out on top against Goebbels, his aversion to me was increased.'
>
> Leni Riefenstahl

Even with Hitler's endorsement, Riefenstahl experienced resentment from the male-dominated film industry and the party simply because she was a woman. 'The party attempted to boycott the project. In Nuremberg I received neither film supplies nor money, simply nothing at all.'

Then Albert Speer provided Riefenstahl with a good cameraman, Walter Frentz, who brought two experienced assistants with him. According to Riefenstahl, though, they were Nazi hirelings who attempted to sabotage the film: 'Party people knocked over the cameras and a lot was destroyed.' She complained to Speer who advised her to inform Hitler. 'But then I'll have even more enemies,' she said, to which he replied, 'You must tell him everything.'

Soon afterwards, a low-level party employee rented a tiny room for her to edit the film in – it was an out-of-service elevator. It was a blatant attempt to show what he and his colleagues thought of her. An old cutting table was installed and a female assistant was ordered to help her.

The resulting film was *Victory of Faith* (1933), but after all her efforts Hitler refused to approve the film's release. Riefenstahl said that Goebbels had it destroyed because every shot of Hitler included Ernst Roehm, the SA leader who had been murdered on Hitler's orders by the time *Victory of Faith* was ready for release. In comparison with her subsequent films, the movie was flat and clumsy, so the claim it was shelved because it included shots of Roehm might have been a face-saving excuse.

TRIUMPH OF THE WILL

Uncharacteristically, Hitler gave the director a second chance the following year. When she was commissioned to make *Triumph of the Will*, she planned and orchestrated her shots meticulously months in advance, to avoid disappointing the Führer again: 'During the preparations I walked around Nuremberg with the camera people, especially with Sepp Allgeier who was the most important to me, and determined the camera positions with him and how we would cinematically dramatize the crowds.'

In order to divert the audience from the static nature of the speeches, she had the idea of setting up a track around the speaker, ensuring audience interest by keeping the camera moving even when the subject was still.

Riefenstahl's own assessment of *Triumph of the Will* (1935) was that it was 'primitive and simple'. But she thought it was helped immensely by the addition of Herbert Windt's music. Although several key sequences appear to have been restaged for the cameras, the result is a visually impressive example of film as propaganda, though repulsive in its veneration of the fascist military mindset and its deification of Hitler. At its premiere, Hitler presented the director with a bouquet of lilac and declared her to be the 'perfect German woman'.

After complaints of under-representation by the German military, she returned to Nuremberg in 1935 and directed the short film *Day of Freedom*, which included shots of the German forces. In the same year, the Nuremberg Laws were introduced, which legitimized the regime's racist ideology and paved the way for the mass murder of millions of enemies of the Reich.

> 'I didn't stage a single scene, but rather I simply picked up with the camera what there was to see in the arena. It's also been written that I had who knows how many cameramen for the film, when in reality I had only thirteen and of these only two or three that were very good, the best being Allgeier. The rest were students. The quality of the film was determined on the cutting table and by the background music.'
>
> Leni Riefenstahl

Riefenstahl insisted she had no choice but to put her talents to the service of the Nazi regime, but other film-makers such as Fritz Lang and Billy Wilder had emigrated to Europe and America rather than provide propaganda for a dictatorship. Riefenstahl's claim to have remained in Germany in order to fight anti-Semitism rang hollow when it was learned that not only had she never raised a finger to do so, nor spoken out against the Nazis, but had in fact denounced her Jewish co-writer Béla Balázs to the notorious Jew-baiter Julius Streicher. She had then removed both Balázs' name and that of her Jewish producer, Harry Sokal, from the credits of the 1938 reissue of *The Blue Light*.

Two years later she sold her talents to the regime again, documenting the 1936 Berlin Olympics with funding from Goebbels' Ministry for Propaganda.

OLYMPIA

The resulting documentary, *Olympia* (1936), which took two years to edit, established the template for future sports films with its innovative use of multiple camera set-ups, slow motion, cranes for overhead shots and rails to obtain fluid tracking shots. 'I had the desire to make the Olympic idea visible in the film – from its roots to the present.' Riefenstahl achieved this by filming the athletes as if they were living works of art – a theme introduced in the opening

sequence which showed the competitors as Classical statues coming to life through a series of dissolves – and by lighting them to heighten the muscle structure and the body beautiful in slow motion. 'Goebbels himself chose me for the Olympia film – even though he was against me as a woman – he had high regard for me as an artist,' recalled Riefenstahl.

But Goebbels was 'very annoyed' to see footage of the black runner Jesse Owens included and demanded that the French distributor cut him out of the film. It is said that the distributor would only agree to this if the sequences showing Hitler were excised too.

The film was premiered for Hitler's 49th birthday and rapturously received at international film festivals; but if Riefenstahl expected her consummate artistry to be sufficient to win her invitations to Hollywood, she was mistaken. During a promotional visit to New York in November 1938 she was incensed to learn that all but two of Hollywood's film-makers refused to receive her, with the exception of silent comedy producer Hal Roach and Walt Disney. When informed that none of the Jewish studio moguls would allow her on the lot because of the events of Kristallnacht earlier that week (when 30,000 Jews were sent to concentration camps and more than 1,000 synagogues burned to the ground), she vowed to remain in the USA until 'this damn Jewish thing is no longer in the headlines'.

The VIP rostrum on the opening day of the Berlin Olympics, 1936: Leni Riefenstahl can be seen recording proceedings (top right)

UNAPOLOGETIC

Riefenstahl, self-absorbed and contemptuous of her critics, would be smeared with the stigma of Nazism until her death at the age of 101, for no amount of vehement denials could absolve her of guilt by association. She remained stubbornly unapologetic to the end, declaring, 'Work and peace are the only messages of *Triumph of the Will.*'

In retrospect, she claimed to be 'appalled' to discover what atrocities the Nazis had committed and thereafter viewed her documentaries in a different light. 'As it later became known what terrible things happened in his name and his party, one was appalled, very deeply and rightfully appalled.' But she insisted that during the time that she was 'Hitler's favourite film-maker' she had 'never thought about politics'. And yet, when France fell she wrote to Hitler, expressing her unbounded admiration.

Riefenstahl remained a loyal and enthusiastic supporter of Hitler. In 1939 she served as a front-line correspondent in Poland, where she witnessed the massacre of civilians in Koñskie. Despite claiming to have been horrified at the executions, she filmed Hitler's triumphant entry into Warsaw just weeks later. She was subsequently accused of promising Romany labour camp prisoners their freedom in return for acting as extras in an unfinished film, *Tiefland*. All were later gassed at Auschwitz, according to fellow inmates, though Riefenstahl claimed: 'Nothing happened to any of them,' a statement she was subsequently forced to retract.

Riefenstahl demonstrated physical courage during her days as a star of Fanck's 'Alpine films', but she was morally spineless and complicit in glorifying a murderous regime. She admitted that in the beginning she was 'very impressed' by Hitler, particularly the way he had reversed unemployment, but in 1937 she was shocked to hear him condemn Goya and Van Gogh as 'degenerate' during the opening of an exhibition in Munich. If he could make such misjudgements on art, she thought, what might he be capable of with regard to politics?

Goebbels was in awe of Riefenstahl's talent, describing her in his diary as 'the only star who understands us' and commending her National Socialist zeal, but he harboured a personal animosity towards her because she commanded Hitler's rapt attention.

POST-WAR PARIAH

After the war she was treated as a pariah by the film community both in Germany and abroad. 'I was made out to be a monster, maybe because I was a woman, or perhaps because I had made more famous films, so that envious persons came on the scene. The newspapers wrote, 'Should we let her live?' or,

'Shouldn't she be on trial in Nuremberg too?' I was suddenly slandered as a super-Nazi, as a leader who, like Joan of Arc carrying the flag, marched the troops to victory at Orléans . . . it was simply jealousy and blind hatred. Others wanted to de-Nazify themselves by attacking me. By doing that they wanted to say, "I'm not like Riefenstahl, she really was a fanatical National Socialist."'

Boosting flagging morale

After the defeat at Stalingrad in 1943, Nazi cinema concentrated on morale-boosting subjects exemplified by *Münchausen* (1943), the beautifully shot escapist fantasy chronicling the far-fetched 18th-century adventures of Baron Hieronymus von Münchausen. Goebbels' pet project, the film was designed to rival Hollywood, celebrate the 25th anniversary of the Ufa studios and denigrate the inhabitants of the countries visited by the fictional Münchausen. The master spin doctor made the most of his ministerial authority through his amorous exploits on the casting couch. But by the following year, when the Allies invaded Fortress Europe, even he could see that his days of luxury and sexual conquest were numbered.

The last production Goebbels supervised was a thinly veiled allusion to Germany's impending doom. A metaphor for the critical situation, *Kolberg* (1945), a 19th-century costume drama, dramatized the courageous last stand made by the inhabitants of a German town besieged and eventually overrun by the armies of Napoleon. It featured 200,000 German troops drafted in from the Eastern Front and the film premiered just months before capitulation.

The strange affair of Dr Goebbels

The Nazi elite were as duplicitous and self-serving as any politicians, proving the old adage about absolute power corrupting those who possess it.

As minister of propaganda, Goebbels promoted race hatred, but carried on a secret affair with an 'inferior' Slav, Czech movie actress Lída Baarová. They met at a party the year before she found fame at the age of 20 with her first German starring role in the romantic drama *Barcarolle* (1935). According to Baarová: 'He told me he loved me time and again and I felt his eyes burning into my back every time we were in the same room together. . . . His voice seemed to go straight into me. I felt a light tingling in my back, as if his words were trying to stroke my body.'

She eagerly accepted invitations to share intimate evenings aboard Goebbels' yacht *Baldur*, but he seemed over-eager to impress her. He invited her to a Nazi party rally where he was due to deliver a speech and promised to give her a secret sign to demonstrate his devotion. It alarmed her to think that she might be getting involved with someone who was so intense and possessive, but as she prepared to make a quiet exit a messenger arrived with a bouquet of roses and a framed photograph of her tenacious suitor. 'He was a master of the hunt, whom nobody and nothing could escape,' she recalled.

But to her surprise he proved a patient lover, content to have her company during weekend trips to his lodge on the shore of Lake Lanke outside Berlin and taking her on drives to the country in his chauffeur-driven limousine. He would call her for long talks on the telephone, adopting the alias Herr Muller, and would hang up if it was answered by her live-in lover and co-star, Gustav Froehlich, who played Freder in Lang's *Metropolis*.

Eventually Goebbels couldn't contain his feelings any longer and after inviting her to the lodge he lit a log fire, drew her close and kissed her saying, 'Liduschka, I have never in my life been so inflamed with love for a woman.' He could be charming and amusing, she remembered, entertaining her with his accurate impressions of Hitler, but also cruel and vindictive, as when he rescinded Froehlich's exemption from military service and had him sent to the front, so he could be alone with Baarová. However, Goebbels still had Magda to contend with.

In the autumn of 1938, Goebbels called his mistress to inform her he had confessed all to his wife and that Magda had demanded a meeting to discuss the terms under which she might be prepared to allow the relationship to continue. According to Baarová, Magda told her, 'I am the mother of his children, I am only interested in this house in which we live. What happens outside does not concern me. But you must promise me one thing: you must not have a child by him.'

End of the romance

Goebbels bought both women expensive jewellery to seal the arrangement, but Magda later changed her mind and took her troubles to Hitler. Baarová claimed that Goebbels was sobbing when he called the next morning to tell her that Hitler had refused to grant Magda a divorce. Furthermore, he had threatened to remove Goebbels from his post and reassign him to Japan if he refused to break off the relationship. 'My wife is a devil,' he told her.

'Goebbels fell in love with me, but I didn't love him,' Baarová told the London *Times* many years later. 'I was afraid of him and what he would do because I kept turning down his offers, although he always behaved charmingly and was always very nice to me. I remember he once gave me a gold bracelet for Christmas. Hitler made a huge fuss about it. He called Goebbels in and told him to drop me and return to his wife and children. I couldn't take the pressure and I returned to Prague. Goebbels never tried to contact me again.'

At the 1942 Venice film festival Baarová found herself sitting uncomfortably close to her former lover, who publicly snubbed her. 'He must have recognized me, but he did not make a single movement. He was always the master of self-control.'

Desperate to win back Hitler's approval after being reconciled with his wife, Goebbels conceived *Kristallnacht* in November 1938, ostensibly as a 'spontaneous' reaction to the assassination of a German embassy official in Paris.

Alone and penniless

Hitler was also smitten with the Czech actress after spotting her during a visit to the film studios in 1934. Whenever he noticed her at official functions, he would stare at her unsmilingly while appearing to be listening to another guest. Hitler enjoyed the company of glamorous young film stars and, at the first opportunity, invited Baarová to tea at the chancellery. She arrived at the wheel of her own Mercedes, which Hitler found rather daring. Her high spirits and supreme self-confidence reminded him of his 'beautiful and tragic' niece, which she took as a compliment until he told her that Geli had shot herself out of love for her 'Uncle Adolf'. Baarová became a regular guest at the Führer's intimate parties, but after she declined an offer to apply for German citizenship, saying she had no desire to renounce her Czech nationality, she found herself frozen out of the Führer's inner circle.

When Hitler learned of her affair with his propaganda minister he ordered her expulsion from Berlin and banned her films from being screened. With his approval, the Gestapo organized hecklers to shout abuse when she attended the premiere of her new film, *Der Spieler* ('The

Player', 1938), and soon afterwards she left Germany, knowing her life would be intolerable if she stayed.

From Prague she travelled to Italy in search of work, later finding parts in films by de Sica and Fellini, and then to Austria where she secured a small role in Rainer Werner Fassbinder's *The Bitter Tears of Petra von Kant* (1972). But accusations that she had been a Gestapo spy plagued her to the end of her days and the work eventually dried up.

'There's no doubt that Goebbels was an interesting character,' she admitted in 1997, 'a charming and intelligent man and a very good storyteller. You could guarantee that he would keep a party going with his little asides and jokes.' But he was entirely without principles. 'Thanks to him I fell into the depths of Hell,' she said. But if she didn't regret the affair she certainly regretted her decision to remain in Germany when she could have accepted an offer to work in Hollywood. 'I could have been as famous as Marlene Dietrich,' she brooded, alone and penniless in her Salzburg apartment.

She kept no souvenirs of the affair, having torn up every photograph she possessed of herself and Goebbels together. Her last wish was to return to her native country, but she remained in Austria until her death in 2000, because she feared she would not have been welcome in the country she had betrayed.

CHAPTER 17

The Road to Nuremberg

At exactly 10 a.m. on 20 November 1945, Sir Geoffrey Lawrence banged his gavel on the desk in the Palace of Justice in Nuremberg. As presiding judge, he made an opening statement, saying: 'The trial which is now about to begin is unique in the history of the jurisprudence of the world.'

This was the first time that those defeated in a war had been put on trial by an international court of the victors. The proceedings were taking place under the auspices of the United Kingdom, the United States, the Republic of France and the Union of Soviet Socialist Republics.

The reason these nations took this step became clear on the second day of the trial when US Supreme Court judge Robert H. Jackson made the opening statement for the prosecution: 'The wrongs which we seek to condemn and punish have been so calculated, so malignant, and so devastating, that civilization cannot tolerate their being ignored, because it cannot survive their being repeated,' he said. 'That four great nations, flushed with victory and stung with injury stay the hand of vengeance and voluntarily submit their captive enemies to the judgment of the law is one of the most significant tributes that Power has ever paid to Reason.'

He conceded that the tribunal was both novel and experimental, but the four nations conducting it had the support of another 17 in their effort 'to utilize international law to meet the greatest menace of our times – aggressive war'.

Surveying the defendants, Jackson said: 'In the prisoners' dock sit twenty-odd broken men. Reproached by the humiliation of those they have led almost as bitterly as by the desolation of those they have attacked, their personal capacity for evil is forever past. . . .

'What makes this inquest significant is that these prisoners represent sinister influences that will lurk in the world long after their bodies have returned to dust. We will show them to be living symbols of racial hatreds, of terrorism and violence, and of the arrogance and cruelty of power. They are symbols of fierce nationalisms and of militarism, of intrigue and war-making which have embroiled Europe generation after generation, crushing its manhood, destroying its homes, and impoverishing its life. They have so identified themselves with the philosophies they conceived and with the forces they directed that any tenderness to them is a victory and an encouragement to all the evils which are attached to their names.'

The 21 Nazi leaders were charged with crimes against peace, war crimes, and crimes against humanity – and with having a common plan or conspiracy to commit those crimes. (In total, 24 Nazis were indicted at Nuremberg, but only 21 faced trial because one was considered too ill and senile, one was missing and one committed suicide in custody.)

This was the first of 12 trials involving more than a hundred defendants and several different courts which took place at Nuremberg from 1945 to 1949. The trial of 16 German judges and officials of the justice ministry considered the criminal responsibility of judges who enforce immoral laws. Doctors were tried for the hideous experiments they conducted on inmates of concentration camps and members of *Einsatzgruppen* were tried for the indiscriminate murder of civilians.

While the Nuremberg Trials had no precedent, they set one. The following year, 1946, Japanese war leaders were put on trial in Tokyo. The principles established at Nuremberg were written into international conventions. More recently, international criminal tribunals have been set up to try war criminals from Rwanda and the former Yugoslavia, and the International Criminal Court began sitting in The Hague in the Netherlands in 2002.

Errors of the past

Normally in war defeat was punishment enough: the losers would either be killed on the battlefield or find themselves in the hands of the victors, who could do what they liked with them. Before modern times there was no clear definition of what constituted a war crime and, largely, the victors found it expedient to be magnanimous.

However, after the wholesale slaughter of the First World War, the victorious allies sought to bring enemy war criminals to book. In the Versailles Treaty which concluded the war Kaiser Wilhelm II was publicly arraigned for 'a supreme offence against international morality and the sanctity of treaties'. He was to be brought before a special tribunal composed of five judges from the United States, the UK, France, Italy and Japan. Others who had violated the laws and customs of war were also to be brought before tribunals and punished, and the German government was obliged to hand them over, along with any evidence that might help to convict them.

When the treaty was signed on 28 June 1919, a note was sent to the Dutch government requesting the extradition of the former kaiser, who had been granted asylum in the Netherlands after abdicating in November 1918. However, the Dutch refused to comply, maintaining that to do so would violate Dutch neutrality.

In February 1920, the Allies submitted a list of 900 names to the German government, including that of the chief of the General Staff, Field Marshal Paul von Hindenburg, who would go on to become the president of Germany under whom Adolf Hitler became chancellor. The Germans refused to hand over those named, but asked instead to be allowed to try them in German courts. The Allies agreed. The list was then whittled down to 45, of whom only 12 came to court.

The trial took place before the Reichsgericht – or supreme court – in Leipzig, comprising seven judges. Just six of those named were convicted and they were sentenced to between six months and four years in prison. The highest-ranking was a captain. The Allies thought the big fish had got off the hook, while those who had been prosecuted were given a mere slap on the wrist. However, Germany felt it was unfair that only Germans were prosecuted when atrocities had been committed on both sides. The trials also seemed to flout established legal principles, causing great resentment in Germany, especially among former servicemen. They petered out in November 1922. Outrage at the humiliation inflicted by these trials fuelled Hitler's Beer Hall Putsch in 1923.

> *The punishment of these crimes should now be counted among the major goals of the war.'*
>
> British Prime Minister Winston Churchill

Meanwhile, the whole German nation was being punished by the 'war guilt' clause in the Versailles Treaty and the huge reparations that the country was being forced to pay. These grievances contributed to the rise of Nazism, resulting in the Second World War. Those gathered at Nuremberg decided that this must not be allowed to happen again.

War like no other

It was plain to those who lived through it that the Second World War was like no other war. Not only had more than 50 million people died during the fighting, millions more were wounded, some permanently disabled, and countless homes were destroyed and lives wrecked. This war had been waged in the service of an ideology that demanded the dispossession, subjugation and elimination of millions of innocent people. Death squads following the advancing German troops had ruthlessly murdered civilians. Millions more were used as forced labour and herded into concentration camps and death camps. Indeed, the indictment of the 24 Nazi leaders at Nuremberg brought a new word into the English language – genocide. Count 3 stated that the defendants 'conducted deliberate and systematic genocide – namely, the extermination of racial and national groups.' Clearly, such crimes could not go unpunished.

Hitler had made no secret of his intentions. He had written of his desire to rid Germany of its Jewish population and to subjugate the Slav people in the east, who he considered subhuman. As early as April 1940, the British and French governments and the Polish government-in-exile issued 'a formal and public protest to the conscience of the world against the action of the German government whom they must hold responsible for these crimes which cannot remain unpunished'.

Even before the United States entered the war, President Franklin D. Roosevelt warned Germany that 'one day a frightful retribution' would be exacted for the summary execution of hostages in France. The British Prime Minister Winston Churchill concurred. In November 1941, he said: 'The massacres of the French are an example of what Hitler's Nazis are doing in many other countries under their yoke. The atrocities committed in Poland, Yugoslavia, Norway, Holland, Belgium, and particularly behind the German front in Russia, exceed anything that has been known since the darkest and most bestial ages of humanity.'

Representatives of nine occupied countries in Europe met in the Palace of St James in London and declared 'among their principal war aims the punishment, through the channel of organized justice, of those guilty of or responsible for these crimes, whether they have ordered them, perpetrated them or participated in them'.

In July 1942, Churchill was contemplating what would happen if Hitler fell into British hands. 'We shall certainly put him to death,' he said. 'Instrument – electric chair, for gangsters, no doubt available on lend-lease.'

By July the following year, he had decided that other Nazi leaders should be summarily shot rather than put on trial. He suggested that a list of 50 or so be drawn up. Any caught by advancing troops could be executed on the spot without reference to higher authority. This could be made legal if Parliament passed an act of attainder, outlawing them. However, acts of attainder are specifically banned by the US Constitution.

Following the Red Army's victory at the Battle of Stalingrad, turning the tide on the Eastern Front, the Soviet premier Josef Stalin signed the 'Statement on Atrocities', largely written by Churchill, which was

Roll call at Buchenwald concentration camp – two prisoners in the foreground are supporting a comrade who looks in danger of collapsing. Fainting was an excuse for guards to 'liquidate' unproductive inmates

part of the Moscow Declarations in October 1943. It said that German soldiers and members of the Nazi party who had taken part in atrocities, massacres and executions would be sent back to the countries in which these abominable deeds had been done, for punishment, and 'German criminals whose offences have no particular geographical location . . . will be punished by joint decision of the governments of the Allies'.

> 'It is hard now to perceive in these men as captives the power by which as Nazi leaders they once dominated much of the world and terrified most of it. Merely as individuals, their fate is of little consequence to the world.'
>
> Robert H. Jackson, Chief Prosecutor at Nuremberg

The United Nations War Crimes Commission was set up in London to collect information on war crimes. But it had no Russian representative, as Stalin had insisted that each of the Soviet republics be represented separately, which would have proved too unwieldly.

When Churchill, Stalin and Roosevelt met in Tehran in November 1943, Stalin proposed executing 50,000–100,000 German staff officers. Churchill, who had served as an officer himself, was against the idea of executing soldiers who had fought for their country and said he would rather be 'taken out into the courtyard and shot' himself than sanction such a thing.

Still, when it came to killing committed Nazis, Churchill was not so pernickety and the British ambassador in Moscow reassured the Russians on this point, saying: 'I am sure that the political decision that Mr Churchill has in mind will be accompanied by all the necessary formalities.'

Stalin argued for show trials, having used them to purge opposition in the Soviet Union in the 1930s. But Churchill and Roosevelt were afraid that putting Hitler and his henchmen on trial would give them a forum in which they could justify their actions. The massacre of 84 US prisoners of war by *Schutzstaffel* (SS) troops at Malmedy, Belgium, during the Battle of the Bulge in December 1944 had strengthened America's thirst for vengeance.

The summary execution of major war criminals was advocated by the US Secretary of the Treasury, Henry Morgenthau, who had the ear of the president. However, the Secretary of War, Henry Stimson, argued that establishing the guilt of the Nazi regime before an international tribunal would play a vital part in rehabilitating the German people who had, after all, voted Hitler into power in the first place. What was needed was some legal and practical way of going about it.

Stimson assigned Lieutenant Colonel Murray Bernays, an attorney at the War Department, to the task. The US Constitution prohibited *ex post facto* laws – that is, laws made up after the event to criminalize actions that were not illegal when they were committed. Neither was it practical to try separately everyone who had committed a crime during the war. Nor was it right to punish the entire German people for something their leaders had done.

Bernays suggested that the laws of criminal conspiracy could be used. The allegation would be that the Third Reich was a premeditated criminal enterprise. Consequently members of the Nazi government, the Nazi party, certain state agencies, the *Sturmabteilung* (SA) paramilitaries, the SS elite troops and the Gestapo secret police could be convicted and condemned simply on the basis of their membership. The leaders would not be able to claim they were not responsible for atrocities because they hadn't personally taken part in them.

Roosevelt continued to sit on the fence. But when he died, on 12 April 1945, his successor, President Harry S. Truman, was won over. He appointed Supreme Court justice Robert H. Jackson 'chief of counsel for the prosecution of Axis criminals' – that is, war criminals from Germany, Italy, Japan and their allies. And, eventually, the British were persuaded that execution without trial was contrary to the principles of common law.

The London Charter

After appalling images of the Holocaust filled the newsreels, there was an increasing appetite for those responsible to be brought to justice. Lawyers from the four major powers – the US, UK, USSR and France – met in London in July to discuss the details of the trial.

They came up with the three categories of crime – crimes against peace, war crimes and crimes against humanity. When it was pointed out that formulating these new offences risked creating *ex post facto* laws, Jackson said: 'Aren't murder, torture and enslavement crimes recognized by all civilized people?'

Another potential pitfall was that after Nazi Germany had invaded the west of Poland on 1 September 1939, the Soviet Union had occupied the east of the country on 17 September. To avoid the defence of *tu quoque* – 'you also' – the Soviets decided attack was the best form of defence and insisted on adding to the indictment the massacre of a thousand Polish officers in the Katyn Forest, which they themselves had been responsible for.

There was also a problem with procedure. The British and Americans had an adversarial system very different from the French and Soviet systems in which witnesses were examined by a panel of investigating judges. So a hybrid was devised. There would be opposing lawyers for the prosecution and the defence, as in the Anglo-Saxon system, but there would be no jury; judgment would be passed by a panel of four judges, one from each of the four powers, with four alternates in reserve should any of them fall ill.

These principles were embodied in the London Charter of the International Military Tribunal, which was signed on 8 August 1945.

The venue

Next a venue had to be decided on. The Soviets favoured Berlin, but this was impractical because the city had been devastated by Allied bombing. The Palace of Justice in Nuremberg incorporated a large prison, about 80 courtrooms and some 530 offices – and was largely undamaged. The Nazi party had held its rallies in the city and the anti- Semitic laws that among other things stripped Jews of their German citizenship had been introduced at a rally there in 1935 and were known as the Nuremberg Laws. It seemed fitting that the Nazi party and its cohorts should meet their demise there.

A compromise was reached. According to the London Charter, Berlin was to be the permanent home of the International Military Tribunal; the first formal session took place there under Soviet Major-General Iona Timofeevich Nikitchenko on 18 October 1945. But the first trial was to take place in Nuremberg, starting on 20 November 1945.

CHAPTER 18
The Accused

The worst of the Nazis – Adolf Hitler; head of the SS and principle architect of the Holocaust Heinrich Himmler; and propaganda minister Josef Goebbels – had committed suicide. Others, such as Adolf Eichmann, the bureaucrat who organized the Holocaust, and Josef Mengele, the doctor who performed hideous experiments on the inmates of Auschwitz, had eluded capture. However, 24 top Nazis were indicted, along with seven organizations.

The highest-ranking was Reichsmarschall Hermann Goering. He had joined the Nazi party in 1922 and risen to become its second-highest-ranking member. When Hitler seized power, he established the Gestapo, the secret political police. As head of the Luftwaffe – the German air force – Goering became Hitler's designated successor in 1941. In April 1945, believing Hitler to be hopelessly surrounded in Berlin, he assumed command, only to be repudiated by the Führer. He surrendered to the Americans with his wife, daughter, valet and 16 pieces of matching luggage – along with 20,000 of the paracodeine tablets to which he was addicted – evidently expecting to be treated as a plenipotentiary.

He was initially wined and dined by the American 7th Army who had captured him and photographed with a glass of champagne in hand alongside the flag of the Texas division to whom he had surrendered. When this got bad press, he was taken to a prisoner of war camp at Augsburg, then to Camp Ashcan – formerly the Palace Hotel – in Mondorf-les-Bains, near Luxembourg, where senior Nazis were interrogated.

In the dock

Alongside Goering in the dock was Rudolf Hess, who had been Hitler's deputy until secretly flying to Britain in 1941 in what seems to have been an attempt to broker a peace deal. He complained of amnesia and appeared distracted, but medical personnel who examined Hess reported him sane and fit to stand trial.

Also on trial was Admiral Karl Doenitz, who was president of what was left of Germany for just a few days after Hitler's suicide. As leader of the Kriegsmarine, he had instigated a U-boat campaign against the merchant shipping that was bringing supplies from the United States and Canada to Britain. Hans Frank had been minister of justice and governor-general of occupied Poland. Wilhelm Frick was the author of the anti-Semitic Nuremberg Laws. Propagandist Julius Streicher had been the editor of the anti-Semitic weekly newspaper *Der Stürmer*. Alfred Rosenberg was the Nazi ideologist who promoted racial theory and the persecution of the Jews, later becoming Reichminister for the occupied eastern territories.

Ernst Kaltenbrunner had been the leader of the Austrian SS and Germany's Reich Security Main Office (RSHA), which administered the Holocaust. Foreign minister Joachim von Ribbentrop negotiated the German-Soviet Non-Aggression Pact (also known as the Molotov-Ribbentrop Pact) in August 1939; this allowed Hitler, then Stalin, to invade Poland. Ribbentrop also signed the Tripartite Pact with allies Italy and Japan in 1940, before the German-Soviet Pact was abrogated by the Nazis' attack on the USSR the following year. Ribbentrop's predecessor Konstantin von Neurath was also on trial. As Reichsprotektor for Bohemia and Moravia, he had imposed the Nuremberg Laws there.

Fritz Sauckel was responsible for slave labour, overseeing the deportation of some five million people. Alfred Jodl was the German general in charge of most of Hitler's military campaigns, while Field Marshal Wilhelm Keitel was head of the German High Command. Erich Raeder was commander-in-chief of the German navy.

Nazi leader Arthur Seyss-Inquart was chancellor of Austria during the Anschluss. After serving as governor of the new province of Austria, he was deputy governor of Poland, before becoming Reichskommissar of the occupied Netherlands.

Economist Walther Funk was the Third Reich's minister of economic affairs and president of the Reichsbank. His predecessor in the economics ministry, Hjalmar Schacht, was also on trial. Baldur von Schirach was head of the Hitler Youth. Albert Speer was minister for armaments and war production, which used slave labour.

Franz von Papen had stepped down as German chancellor to make way for Hitler and served briefly as his vice-chancellor. And Hans Fritzsche had worked under Goebbels at the Ministry of Propaganda.

In absentia

Head of the party chancellery and Hitler's right-hand man, Martin Bormann, had disappeared on 1 May 1945 and was tried *in absentia*. Head of German labour Robert Ley had been indicted, but committed suicide in prison, hanging himself with a towel in the lavatory while awaiting trial. The industrialist Gustav Krupp von Bohlen und Halbach, who had helped finance Hitler's rise to power and profited from armament production, was found to be too ill and senile to stand trial.

Seven organizations were also on trial: the leadership corps of the Nazi party; the Reich cabinet; the elite black-shirted *Schutzstaffel* (SS); their intelligence service the *Sicherheitsdienst* (SD); the Gestapo secret police; the brown-shirted *Sturmabteilung* (SA); and the general staff and High Command of the German armed forces.

Security

The defendants were kept in separate cells with a guard stationed outside each day and night. They were not allowed to talk to one another during their 20-minute exercise period or in the showers. They were brought up to the courtroom one by one in an elevator and passed through a series of checkpoints, each telephoning ahead on the prisoner's arrival. The war in Europe had been over barely six months and security was tight, and there was fear that a 'Werwolf' organization of dedicated Nazis was still operating.

In the dock, the defendants sat on two wooden benches with a line of white-helmeted US military policemen behind them. Defendants still on speaking terms were permitted to exchange opinions in the dock, during recesses. They were not allowed to wear any military insignia, nor could military men be addressed by rank – otherwise they would have had to be treated in accordance with the Geneva Convention, which prohibits solitary confinement.

As some of the defendants had been arrested in only the clothes they stood up in, a Nuremberg tailor was employed to run up suits for them. (According to the *New York Times*, Hans Frank had been captured wearing 'only lace panties'.) Court suits could only be worn during court appearances and had to be taken off directly the prisoner was returned to his cell.

The execution of a French boy by German soldiers

RUDOLF HESS

HITLER'S 'YES MAN'

'He knew and was capable of understanding Hitler's inner mind, his hatred of Soviet Russia, his lust to destroy Bolshevism, his admiration for Britain and earnest wish to be friends with the British Empire, his contempt for most other countries. No one knew Hitler better or saw him more often in his unguarded moments.'

Winston Churchill, *History of the Second World War*

When Rudolf Hess, Hitler's former deputy, appeared in the dock at Nuremberg, hesitant, uncertain and confused, he gave the impression that he was suffering from some form of mental disorder. He even denied knowing his fellow defendants. Whether he was feigning it or not, his condition didn't save him from being handed a life sentence and he ended his days as the sole inmate of Spandau prison.

During a psychological assessment to gauge if he was fit to stand trial, Hess admitted to simulating memory loss and was diagnosed by prison psychiatrist Dr Kelley as a 'self-perpetuated hysteric'. But it was Kelley's belief

Rudolf Hess descends the red carpet ahead of assorted dignitaries during a state visit

that Hess may well have been suffering from temporary memory loss, as his behaviour throughout the trial was odd, to say the least.

Hess suffered severe stomach pains whenever he was under stress which probably made it difficult for him to follow proceedings. But at times he would appear lucid and capable of understanding the charges levelled against him. 'It is just incomprehensible how those things came about,' he said when the indictment was handed to him. 'Every genius has the demon in him. You can't blame him [Hitler] – it is just in him . . . It is all very tragic.'

EARLY SIGNS OF INSANITY

Hess may have been unstable from the start. In Nazi newsreels he always appeared agitated, edgy or over-eager to be seen as the Führer's indispensable right-hand man. His public speeches verged on the hysterical as he attempted to whip up the same excitement that only Hitler could generate.

BIZARRE FLIGHT TO SCOTLAND

When Hess saw that Bormann was usurping his privileged position as Hitler's private secretary, he conceived a plan to win back the Führer's favour. He would fly to Scotland to broker a separate peace deal with the British so that Germany would be free to invade Russia without having to fight a war on two fronts. After parachuting into a farmer's field on 10 May 1941, he demanded to be taken to see the Duke of Hamilton, insisting that he was expecting him. Naturally, the farmer and the local constabulary assumed Hess was insane. After his injuries were treated and he had been interrogated by British intelligence he was turned over to psychiatrist Dr Henry Dicks of London's Tavistock Clinic.

ACUTE PARANOIA DIAGNOSIS

Dicks found the deputy Führer sullen but willing to answer questions, presumably hoping that if he was thought to be sincere he would get to meet the duke and make his case for an honourable British surrender. But when it became apparent that his captors had no intention of agreeing to his request, Hess became irritable and unco-operative. He evaded probing questions by claiming to have lost his memory. He picked at his food which he feared might be poisoned and popped homeopathic pills by the handful. Dicks diagnosed acute paranoia.

Hess' discomfort became acute once the psychiatrist raised the question of sexuality. Being a Freudian, Dr Dicks sought the answer to his patients' neuroses in the repression of their sexual desires and he would have been familiar with the rumour that Hess was a transsexual whose cross-dressing habit had earned him the nickname 'Black Bertha'.

Thereafter Hess attempted suicide twice, once by jumping from a height and the second time by stabbing himself with a bread knife, but he only succeeded in damaging a knee and inflicting a flesh wound on his chest.

During his imprisonment Hess was allowed to write to his wife and in one letter, dated 15 January 1944, explained why he had so little to tell her: 'I have been sitting here for literally several hours, wondering what I can write to you about. But I get no further; and that I regret to say is for a very special reason. . . . I have completely lost my memory.'

CHAPTER 19

Opening the Prosecution

At 9.30 a.m. on 20 November 1945, the doors of the courtroom opened. The defendants were already in place behind a low wooden partition. They included Goering (in one of his powder-blue uniforms), Hess, Ribbentrop, Keitel, Rosenberg, Frank, Frick, Streicher, Funk and Schacht. Kaltenbrunner would join them later as, at the time, he was suffering from the first of two subarachnoid haemorrhages. He subsequently recovered and, although his lawyer attempted to have him excused from the trial on health grounds, the tribunal refused and he was forced to attend. Doenitz, Raeder, von Papen, Seyss-Inquart, Speer, von Neurath and Fritzsche sat behind the others, in the second row.

At 10 a.m. the marshal announced the imminent entry of the members of the tribunal. The judges filed in. The marshal called the court to order and the room fell silent. Lord Justice Lawrence read a brief statement. Then the indictments were read. Goering sat through it all with an air of studied indifference. Ribbentrop sweated profusely and Funk sobbed. CBS correspondent William Shirer noted: 'Shorn of the power and the glory and the glittering trappings of Nazidom, how little and mean and mediocre they looked.'

Justices Lawrence and Parker also mopped their brows under the high-powered lights which had been installed for the movie cameras. Some of the accused fell asleep (they had been woken at 6 a.m.). Many of the journalists found the courtroom stifling and left, even though the regulations of the court required them to stay in their seats. The following day, the regulations were revised so that they could come and go as they pleased.

Pleas

The next morning, the defendants were asked to enter a plea. Goering, who was called first, tried to read a prepared statement. Lawrence cut him off immediately, saying he must only plead guilty or not guilty.

'I declare myself in the sense of the indictment not guilty,' he said.

His statement was quickly released to the press. In it, he said: 'As Reichsmarschall of the Greater German Reich I accept the political responsibility for all my own acts or for acts carried out on my orders. These acts were exclusively carried out for the welfare of the German people and because of my oath to the Führer. Although I am responsible for these acts only to the German people and can be tried only before a German court, I am at the same time prepared to give all the necessary information demanded of me by this court and to tell the whole truth

In the dock, from left to right: Goering, Hess, Ribbentrop and Keitel

without recognizing the jurisdiction of this court. I must, however, most strongly reject the acceptance by me of responsibility for acts of other persons which were not known to me; of which, had I known them, I would have disapproved and which could not have been prevented by me anyway.'

The rest pleaded not guilty, except for Hess who said simply: '*Nein.*'

Lawrence said that he interpreted this as 'not guilty', which brought a rare moment of laughter to the court.

Justice Jackson

Lead American prosecutor Jackson then spelt out the justification for bringing the trial. This was not a case of victor's justice.

'If these men are the first war leaders of a defeated nation to be prosecuted in the name of the law,' he said, 'they are also the first to be given a chance to plead for their lives in the name of the law.'

Hundreds of tons of German documents had been examined. These had been found in German army headquarters and government buildings, and in salt mines. They included articles, letters, diaries and memoranda written by the accused, along with orders issued by them. The defendants were to be condemned out of their own mouths.

Jackson quoted from Streicher, writing in *Der Stürmer* in 1942: 'Not only is Germany not safe in the face of the Jews as long as one Jew lives in Europe, but also the Jewish question is hardly solved in Europe so long as Jews live in the rest of the world.'

'Of the 9,600,000 Jews who lived in Nazi-dominated Europe, 60 per cent are authoritatively estimated to have perished,' Jackson pointed out. 'Five million, seven hundred thousand Jews are missing from the countries in which they formerly lived, and over 4,500,000 cannot be accounted for by the normal death rate nor by immigration; nor are they included among displaced persons. History does not record a crime ever perpetrated against so many victims or one ever carried out with such calculated cruelty.'

Not only had these men been out to kill all Jews worldwide, they were also in a criminal conspiracy to wage war. Reading from the minutes of a 1938 meeting attended by Goering, Raeder, Neurath and others, Jackson showed that Hitler had announced his decision to make a lightning attack on Czechoslovakia and Austria, and in May 1939 had advised his staff 'to attack Poland at the first suitable opportunity. We cannot expect a repetition of the Czech affair [where Britain and France backed down]. There will be war.'

> *The Jews are a race which has to be eliminated; whenever we catch one, it is his end.'*
>
> From Hans Frank's diary, quoted at Nuremberg

It was clear that Hitler did not care about the legality of these actions. In the files of the German navy staff was the 'Memorandum on Intensified Naval War', dated 15 October 1939, which said: 'If decisive successes are expected from any measure considered as a war necessity, it must be carried through even if it is not in agreement with international law.'

A directive written by Keitel showed German collusion with Japan before the attack on Pearl Harbor to 'establish and maintain a new order of things'. Ribbentrop's reports showed him urging Japan to join the war to 'hasten the victory'. And a captured memorandum from Hitler's headquarters, dated 29 October 1940, stated that: 'The Führer is at present occupied with the question of the occupation of the Atlantic islands with a view to the prosecution of war against America at a later date.'

In the Commando Order of 18 October 1942, Hitler had ordered that British commandos were 'to be slaughtered to the last man' after capture. Orders signed by Hess commanded the arrest or liquidation of enemy airmen and parachutists. Jackson also quoted from a letter about the fate of Soviet prisoners of war from Rosenberg to Keitel in February 1942: 'Of 3,600,000 prisoners of war, only several hundred thousand are still able to work fully. . . . The camp commanders have forbidden the civilian population to put food at the disposal of the prisoners, and they have rather let them starve to death . . . when prisoners of war could no longer keep up on the march because of hunger and exhaustion, they were shot before the eyes of the horrified population, and the corpses were left. In numerous camps, no shelter for the prisoners of war was provided at all. They lay under the open sky during rain or snow. Even tools were not made available to dig holes or caves . . . in various camps, all the "Asiatics" were shot.'

In a speech made on 25 January 1944, Frank, then governor-general of Poland, boasted: 'I have sent 1,300,000 Polish workers into the Reich.' Sauckel reported that 'out of the five million foreign workers who arrived in Germany, not even 200,000 came voluntarily.' This fact was reported to Hitler, Speer, Goering and Keitel. Rosenberg's ministry ordered the enslavement of children aged ten to 14.

From a report of SS General Jürgen Stoop on the destruction of the Warsaw ghetto, Jackson read: 'Jews usually left their hideouts, but frequently remained in the burning buildings and jumped out of the windows only when the heat became unbearable. They then tried to crawl with broken bones across the street.'

Jackson also referred to the inventories kept by Goering and Keitel of the artworks and other valuables they had looted. When justifying the legality of prosecuting the defendants, he even quoted the German

Military Code, which said: 'If the execution of a military order in the course of duty violates the criminal law, then the superior officer giving the order will bear the sole responsibility therefore. However, the obeying subordinate will share the punishment of the participant: (1) if he has exceeded the order given to him, or (2) if it was within his knowledge that the order of his superior officer concerned an act by which it was intended to commit a civil or military crime or transgression.'

The litany of iniquity continued all day. This time, Goering made no pretence of indifference. Even Hess gave up reading and listened to the speech. When the tribunal adjourned at 5.15 p.m., colleagues clustered around Jackson to congratulate him on his exposition, which the press called 'magnificent'.

Documentary evidence

Colonel Robert Storey, executive trial counsel for the United States, then explained how the evidence had been gathered and collated. Assistant US prosecutor Ralph Albrecht explained the complex structure of the Nazi party and its integration with the apparatus of the state, while Major Frank Wallis presented evidence of the defendants' involvement.

On the fifth day of the trial, another US assistant prosecutor, Sidney Alderman, began presenting evidence on the planning and waging of aggressive war. He displayed charts showing the Nazi invasion of Czechoslovakia, then read a paper written by General Jodl entitled 'Strategic Position in the Beginning of the Fifth Year of the War' and delivered to Nazi *gauleiters* in Munich on 7 November 1943, which detailed Germany's attacks on surrounding countries.

The film

On the afternoon of the eighth day, the lights were lowered and a film was shown of the liberation of the concentration camps. The images of men and women reduced to walking skeletons, the disfigured bodies of women who had survived medical experiments, the piles of bodies and the gas chambers and crematoria are still profoundly shocking more than 70 years after the event. Even counsel who had read detailed accounts of the atrocities were horrified.

Many preferred to watch the reaction of the defendants rather than the film. Ribbentrop, von Papen and Schacht turned away. Doenitz covered his eyes. Hess seemed to be mesmerized, while the virulent anti-

Semite Streicher watched avidly, nodding his head. Goering remained calm, but by the end he was seen repeatedly wiping his sweaty palms.

When the film was over, the room remained in a stunned silence until one journalist murmured: 'Why can't we shoot the swine now?' Then a soldier said: 'God, this makes me feel like killing the first German I meet.'

Hess was the first of the defendants to speak.

'I don't believe it,' he said. Goering silenced him.

Frank sat in silence for ten minutes until the guard came to take him back to his cell.

Prison psychiatrist

Dr Gustav Gilbert, the prison psychiatrist, visited the defendants in their cells to judge their reaction. Goering, who had previously told Gilbert that all the atrocities had been carried out by Himmler and 'his chosen psychopaths', was trying to pull himself together. That morning, he had revelled in the limelight when the transcript of his telephone call directing the march into Austria was read out.

'Everyone was laughing with me,' Goering said, 'and then they showed that awful film and it just spoiled everything.'

'It was those dirty SS swine,' said Keitel, who insisted he would never have let his son join the SS if he had known. Nevertheless, he managed to eat a hearty supper that night.

Sauckel said: 'I'd choke myself with these hands if I thought I had the slightest thing to do with these murders.'

Jodl, Doenitz and Neurath also denied knowing anything about it. But Frank was more illuminating: 'Don't let anyone tell you that they had no idea,' he said. 'Everybody sensed that there was something horribly wrong . . . even if we didn't know all the details. They didn't want to know. It was too comfortable to live on the system, to support our families in royal style, and to believe that it was all right.'

First witness

Jackson capitalized on the impact of the film with his first witness – Major General Erwin von Lahousen. Originally with Austrian intelligence, Lahousen had been transferred after the Anschluss to the Abwehr (German military intelligence), where he had been assistant to its chief, Admiral Canaris. Not only could he talk in detail about the murder of civilians, the maltreatment of prisoners of war and the trick the Nazis had ordered to provoke war (attacking the German radio station at Gleiwitz in 1939, leaving behind the corpses of concentration camp inmates in Polish uniforms), he could also link other defendants to these crimes.

Lahousen directly implicated Keitel, Ribbentrop and various officers in the High Command in drawing up the orders to kill all commandos, issuing instructions to the *Einsatzkommando* and the maltreatment of captured Soviet soldiers.

Before he took the stand, Gilbert had already asked Lahousen about his motives for testifying. Lahousen pointed out that Canaris and his immediate circle had been summarily executed after the failed July Plot to kill Hitler on 20 July 1944. 'I have to speak for those they murdered,' he said. 'I am the only one left.'

Keitel and Jodl were furious that such 'treacherous statements' should come from a serving officer. Goering said: 'That traitor – that's one we forgot on 20 July.' Concerned only for his own skin, Ribbentrop trembled as he said: 'What shall I do?'

Keitel's attorney, Otto Nelte, said the defendants had not been warned that Lahousen would be called, even though the press had been informed. Jackson argued that the tactic of pulling a rabbit from a hat was common in American courts. Besides, the case was being tried in a hotbed of Nazism and prosecution witnesses were in danger of their lives.

The best the defence could do was to ask Lahousen why, if he thought the orders Keitel was issuing were 'murderous' and thus criminal, he did not go to the police. Goering was exasperated by this inept line of questioning. His attorney Dr Stahmer asked whether the defendants could question the witness. The request was denied.

CHAPTER 20
'No Mere Willing Tools'

Sir Hartley Shawcross' opening statement for the British dealt with the charges of waging aggressive war. He directly addressed the argument that this had not been a crime under international law prior to the trial. He cited the Covenant of the League of Nations, which spoke of 'the acceptance of obligations not to resort to war', together with the Geneva Protocol of 1924 and the Kellogg–Briand Pact of 1928 which sought to outlaw war, along with numerous agreements between individual nations, many of which Germany had signed.

The Nazis had also signed the German-Soviet Non-Aggression Pact, which they had then cynically broken. Rudenko insisted that Stalin had seen through Hitler's double-dealing all along. Jackson remarked that the Russians 'didn't mind being called knaves as long as they weren't called fools'. Clearly the crime of aggressive war mentioned in the London Charter was not retroactive, Shawcross maintained, but filled 'a gap in criminal procedure'. He went on to argue that the responsibility of waging an aggressive war lay not only with Hitler. The defendants were 'no mere willing tools'.

After his opening speech, Shawcross had to return to London. Maxwell Fyfe took over, and introduced the various treaties. US prosecutor Sidney Alderman then outlined the case that, in collaboration with Italy and Japan, the Germans had waged aggressive war against the United States.

The Nazi plan

The viewing of captured German films illustrating the Nazi Plan occupied almost all of the 17th day of the trial. The screening was divided into four parts: The Rise of the NSDAP, 1921–33; Acquiring Control of Germany, 1933–35; Preparation for Wars of Aggression, 1935–39; and Wars of Aggression, 1939–44.

These films implicated the defendants individually. Hess was shown making a speech, crying

> *They were the men whose support built Hitler up into the position of power he occupied. These are the men whose initiative and planning often conceived and certainly made possible the acts of aggression done in Hitler's name; and these are the men who enabled Hitler to build up the army, the navy, the air force, the war economy, the political philosophy, by which these treacherous acts were carried out.'*
>
> *Sir Hartley Shawcross*

out: 'The party is the Führer and the Führer is Germany.' Goering relished seeing himself on screen and shouted out the names of pilots and aircraft he recognized. Doenitz joined in, with names of seamen.

In a sequence showing the German economic recovery, Schacht beamed and said: 'Can you see anything wrong with that?' Schirach became excited when he saw the Hitler Youth marching past a parade stand. And when Hitler was shown in a full frenzy of oration, Goering dug Hess in the ribs and said: 'Justice Jackson will want to join the party now.'

However, they fell silent during a sequence showing the suspects in the 20 July Plot being physically dragged before a people's court, with the army officers struggling to hold up their beltless trousers. When one tried to describe murders he had seen in Poland, Judge Roland Freisler screamed: 'Are you collapsing under the stress of your own vulgarity, you filthy rogue?'

Some of the July Plot suspects had been tried in the very room in which the defendants were now sitting, before being hustled out to be shot, beheaded or hanged, often slowly, using piano wire. The contrast between Nazi justice and that being exercised by the tribunal could not have been more vividly portrayed.

Forced labour

The US prosecutors then turned to the conspiracy charges concerning crimes against humanity and federal prosecutor Thomas Dodd made a two-day presentation on the use of forced labour. He quoted a letter from Sauckel to Rosenberg, dated 20 April 1942, saying: 'The aim of this new gigantic labour mobilization is to use all the rich and tremendous sources conquered and secured for us . . . for the armament of the Armed Forces and also for the nutrition of the homeland. The raw materials as well as the fertility of the conquered territories and their human labour power are to be used completely and conscientiously to the profit of Germany and her allies.'

Dodd presented evidence that some 4,795,000 people had been enslaved in the most brutal fashion. He read the speech of Erich Koch, Reichskommissar of Ukraine, to a party meeting in 1943, in which he had said: 'I will draw the very last out of this country. I did not come to spread bliss. I have come to help the Führer. The population must work, work and work again. . . . We are the master race, which must remember that the lowest German worker is racially and biologically a thousand times more valuable than the population here.'

In March 1944, Sauckel had told the Central Planning Board that he had trained French men and women to hunt for workers. They were then paid to ply candidates with liquor and dupe them, 'just as it was done in olden times for shanghaiing'. And in his diary, Frank, governor-general of Poland, wrote that he had 'no objections to all the rubbish, capable of work yet often loitering about, being snatched from the streets'. People were simply seized and taken to camps. Their families and friends rarely knew what had happened to them.

Dodd showed that the daily rations in a typical arms factory were a cup of tea at 4 a.m., with a bowl of soup and two slices of bread at the end of a 14-hour shift. An affidavit signed by a doctor at one of Krupp's labour camps, in Essen, said workers were fed 1,000 calories a day – less than the minimum prescribed for a German. They were fed condemned meat infected with tuberculosis, and they were riddled with fleas and lice. If they fell ill, there were few medical supplies. Even so, the conditions there were better than in SS labour camps where Himmler had decreed that Jews, Gypsies, Poles, Russians and Ukrainians must suffer 'extermination through work'.

Dodd also presented evidence of mass executions and the use of gas vans and gas chambers. He presented Eichmann's reporting of the death of four million Jews in concentration camps, plus another two million at the hands of the police in the east. The death books from Mauthausen concentration camp were presented. They showed that, on one day in March 1945, 203 people had died at regular intervals from 'heart attacks'.

Concentration camps

Then Dodd changed tack and held up the shrunken head of a Polish officer which camp commandant Karl Koch had used as a paperweight. The victim had apparently been hanged for a sexual encounter with a German woman. Dodd also showed the skin of prisoners which had been tattooed, then flayed from them and handed over to Koch's wife, Ilse, to make lampshades. This was supported by an affidavit from Koch.

Kaltenbrunner now joined the others in the dock and, Kaufmann, his counsel, objected. The prosecution had failed to mention that Koch had already been executed by firing squad. But it transpired that this had been for embezzlement and the murder of a camp doctor and medical orderly who had treated him for syphilis. His wife, Ilse Koch – 'the Bitch of Buchenwald' – was captured by the Americans in 1945. Sentenced to life in 1947, she was released, but re-arrested and sentenced to life again by a German court. She hanged herself in prison in 1967.

More German footage was shown. This time it was amateur film shot by an SS guard that showed naked girls running, and naked men and women being kicked and beaten by German soldiers while the SS looked on.

Colonel Storey

In the week before Christmas, US counsel Colonel Robert Storey took over again. He introduced the 39 volumes of photographs of the works of art which had been seized by Rosenberg's 'special task force'.

It then fell to Storey to present evidence against the Leadership Corps of the Nazi party. He did this with a blizzard of documents. Lawrence and Biddle could not see the relevance of many of them. When Storey conceded that one 'might be considered strictly cumulative', he was told: 'Well, if it's cumulative, we don't really want to hear it.'

Storey's case against the Reich cabinet should have proved more promising as all the defendants – apart from Fritzsche, Sauckel, Schirach and Streicher – were members. However, it had not met after 1937 and was not relevant to the crimes they had been charged with.

Storey then presented the case against the SA. However, after the 'Night of the Long Knives' in June 1934, the SA had ceased to play any major political role in Nazi affairs.

Storey returned to lay the basis of the case against the Gestapo and the SD.

Hermann Graebe

Following the Christmas recess, Storey resumed his address on 2 January 1946 with an affidavit given by Hermann Graebe, a German engineer in charge of a building firm in Ukraine, who had witnessed a massacre in Dubno on 2 October 1942. Part of it read:

> I drove to the site . . . and saw near it great mounds of earth, about 30 metres long and 2 metres high. Several trucks stood in front of the mounds. Armed Ukrainian militia drove the people off the trucks under the supervision of an SS man. The militia men acted as guards on the trucks and drove them to and from the pit. All these people had the regulation yellow patches on the front

and back of their clothes, and thus could be recognized as Jews . . . . My foreman and I went directly to the pits. Nobody bothered us. Now I heard rifle shots in quick succession from behind one of the earth mounds.

The people who had got off the trucks – men, women and children of all ages – had to undress upon the order of an SS man who carried a riding or dog whip. They had to put down their clothes in fixed places, sorted according to shoes, top clothing and undergarments. I saw heaps of shoes of about 800 to 1,000 pairs, great piles of under-linen and clothing. Without screaming or weeping these people undressed, stood around in family groups, kissed each other, said farewells, and waited for a sign from another SS man, who stood near the pit, also with a whip in his hand.

During the fifteen minutes I stood near, I heard no complaint or plea for mercy. I watched a family of about eight persons, a man and a woman both of about fifty, with their children of about twenty to twenty-four, and two grown-up daughters about twenty-eight or twenty-nine. An old woman with snow-white hair was holding a one-year-old child in her arms and singing to it and tickling it. The child was cooing with delight. The parents were looking on with tears in their eyes. The father was holding the hand of a boy about ten years old and speaking to him softly; the boy was fighting his tears. The father pointed to the sky, stroked his head and seemed to explain something to him.

At that moment the SS man at the pit started shouting something to his comrade. The latter counted off about twenty persons and instructed them to go behind the earth mound. Among them was the family I have just mentioned. I well remember a girl, slim with black hair, who, as she passed me, pointed to herself and said, 'Twenty-three years old.' I walked around the mound and found myself confronted by a tremendous grave. People were closely wedged together and lying on top of each other so that only their heads were visible. Nearly all had blood running over their shoulders from their heads. Some of the people shot were still moving. Some were lifting their arms and turning their heads to show that they were still alive. The pit was nearly two-thirds full.

I estimated that it already contained about a thousand people. I looked for the man who did the shooting. He was an SS man, who sat at the edge of the narrow end of the pit, his feet dangling into the pit. He had a tommy-gun on his knees and was smoking a cigarette. The people, completely naked, went down some steps, which were cut in the clay wall of the pit, and clambered over the heads of the people lying there to the place to which the SS man directed them. They lay down in front of the dead or wounded people; some caressed those who were still alive and spoke to them in a low voice.

Then I heard a series of shots. I looked into the pit and saw that the bodies were twitching or the heads lying already motionless on top of the bodies that lay beneath them. Blood was running from their necks. The next batch was approaching already. They went down into the pit, lined themselves up against the previous victims and were shot.

This testimony was used again in the *Einsatzgruppen* trial that followed. There again, it proved crucial.

Otto Ohlendorf

SS Lieutenant General Otto Ohlendorf was brought in to give testimony against Kaltenbrunner, having served under him in the Reich Main Security Office (RSHA), the principal body of Himmler's state security apparatus. During Operation Barbarossa, the invasion of the Soviet Union, Ohlendorf had been in command of *Einsatzgruppe* D. Asked how many his death squad had killed, he replied: 'In the year between June 1941 to June 1942 the *Einsatzkommandos* reported 90,000 people liquidated.'

The counsel for the SS, Ludwig Babel, asked: 'Was the legality of the orders explained to those people under false pretences?'

Ohlendorf was puzzled.

> *'. . . to me it is inconceivable that a subordinate leader should not carry out orders given by the leaders of the state.'*
>
> Lieutenant General Otto Ohlendorf

'I do not understand your question,' he said, 'since the order was issued by the superior authorities, the question of legality could not arise in the minds of these individuals, for they had sworn obedience to the people who had issued the orders.'

He had no scruples about carrying out orders and sent some men home because he did not consider them 'emotionally suitable' to execute these tasks. No one could disobey – 'the result would have been a court martial with a corresponding sentence'.

Ohlendorf was tried and convicted in the *Einsatzgruppen* trial in 1948 and hanged in 1951.

Dieter Wisliceny

SS Captain Dieter Wisliceny had been Eichmann's deputy. Given the task of transporting Slovakian Jews to Auschwitz, he requested verification of the order. Eichmann took a letter from his safe, written by Himmler. It said: 'The Führer has ordered the final solution of the Jewish question.' Wisliceny was then asked what 'final solution' meant.

'Eichmann told me that the words "final solution" meant the biological extermination of the Jewish race,' Wisliceny said. 'I was so much impressed with this document which gave Eichmann authority to kill millions of people that I said at the time: "May God forbid that our enemies should ever do anything similar to the German people." He replied: "Don't be sentimental – this is a Führer order." . . . The programme of extermination was already under way and continued until late 1944. There was no change in the programme during Kaltenbrunner's administration.'

Eichmann was cold-blooded about the outcome. According to Wisliceny: 'He said to me on the occasion of our last meeting in February 1945, at which time we were discussing our fates upon losing the war: "I laugh when I jump into the grave because of the feeling that I have killed five million Jews. That gives me great satisfaction and gratification."'

Wisliceny was so frank in the testimony he had given in his affidavit that neither the prosecutors nor the defence counsels could find any questions to ask him. He was tried in Czechoslovakia and hanged in February 1948.

Erich von dem Bach-Zelewski

Colonel Telford Taylor presented the case against the German General Staff and High Command. He concentrated on the Barbarossa Order issued by Keitel to German forces shortly before the invasion of the Soviet Union. One of its directives was: 'Guerrillas should be disposed of ruthlessly by the military.'

Taylor called to the stand SS Obergruppenführer Erich von dem Bach-Zelewski, whose ruthlessness Hitler had praised. Biddle said he looked like 'a mild and rather serious accountant'.

'My principal task was fighting partisans,' said Bach-Zelewski.

At the end of 1942, he had been appointed chief of anti-partisan combat units for the entire Eastern Front. Most of the anti-partisan operations were not undertaken by SS fanatics, but by ordinary army units. Bach-Zelewski confirmed that orders were issued by the highest authorities, but German soldiers committing excesses were not to be punished in the military courts.

This caused consternation among the defendants. Goering called Bach-Zelewski 'the bloodiest murderer of the whole damn set-up'. When Rosenberg's counsel asked for an explanation of the reasons for this widespread barbarity, Bach-Zelewski replied: 'If for years, for decades, a doctrine is preached to the effect that the Slav race is an inferior race, and that Jews are not even human beings, then an explosion of this sort is inevitable.'

> *The general staff and high command group planned and carried through manifold acts of aggression which turned Europe into a charnel house and caused the armed forces to be used for foul practices, foully executed, of terror, pillage, and wholesale slaughter.'*
>
> Colonel Telford Taylor

The responsibility was not his alone, he argued, but was spread throughout the Wehrmacht. Everyone had taken part.

Bach-Zelewski said he had disapproved of Himmler's plan to exterminate 30 million Slavs. He said he had tried to temper policies where he could and could not have resigned as 'if someone else had been in my position the disaster would have been greater'.

He was never prosecuted for war crimes and did not serve time in prison until 1958, when he was given four-and-a-half years for murdering an SA officer on the 'Night of the Long Knives' in 1934. He was later given an additional ten years for murdering ten German communists in the 1930s.

He died in prison in 1972.

The Women Who Lent a Hand

In the wake of the German offensive to the east in 1941 more than half-a-million young women followed the victorious Wehrmacht and SS death squads into Poland, Ukraine, Lithuania, Latvia, Estonia and Belarus, in their capacity as administrators, nurses, secretaries, guards, girlfriends and wives. Some of these women carried out terrible acts, demonstrating that cruelty, brutality, ignorance and arrogance are not exclusively male traits.

In Poland in 1942, Vera Wohlauf, the pregnant wife of Captain Julius Wohlauf, witnessed several killing operations at her husband's side. She also helped him round up 11,000 Jews for transportation to Treblinka.

Liesel Willhaus, wife of an SS official, saw nothing wrong in allowing her three-year-old son to watch her shoot at the Jews who were working in her garden in Poland.

In Ukraine, Johanna Altvater herded men, women and children into a truck like a cattle drover. Witnesses recalled how she cleared a makeshift children's hospital ward by throwing its tiny occupants out of the window to their deaths on the pavement below.

In occupied Poland (now Belarus), Liselotte Meier, personal assistant to an SS officer, took an active interest in shooting parties where the prey was human beings.

In southern Germany, nurse Pauline Kneissler toured mental institutions collecting up to 70 patients a day for use in gassing experiments. She did not like the deception involved in the euthanasia programme and said the relentless killing got on her nerves. Nevertheless she killed more patients than any other nurse. An estimated 5,000 mentally disabled children were murdered in this way before Hitler ordered an end to the programme.

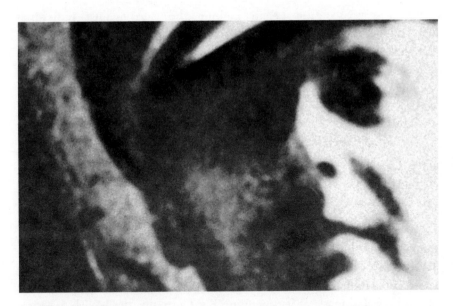

CHAPTER 21
Presenting the Evidence

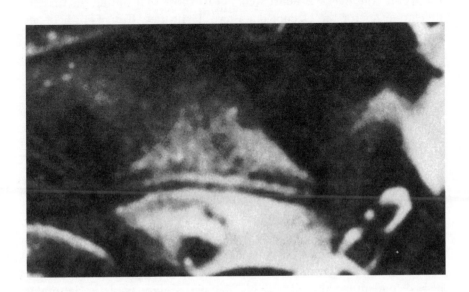

When the prosecution began making the case against individual defendants, they excluded Kaltenbrunner, Sauckel and Speer. It was felt that the guilt of these men had been sufficiently established by the evidence given in the general charges.

The American delegation began with Goering, presenting documents on his participation in the Munich Putsch of 1923 and the use of concentration camp inmates in his aircraft factories. Then they moved on to Alfred Rosenberg.

Rosenberg

The son of a Lithuanian father and Estonian mother, Rosenberg had already been implicated in the wholesale looting of artworks. The main emphasis of the submission made by US assistant prosecutor Walter W. Brudno concerned Rosenberg's establishment of the Institute for the Exploration of the Jewish Question. Brudno read the statement Rosenberg had made at its opening: 'For Germany, the Jewish question is only then solved when the last Jew has left the Greater German space. Since Germany with its blood and its folkdom has now broken for always this Jewish dictatorship for all Europe and has seen to it that Europe as a whole will become free from the Jewish parasitism once more, we may, I believe, also say for all Europeans: For Europe the Jewish question is only then solved when the last Jew has left the European continent.' Brudno went on to show that during his time as Reichminister for the Occupied Eastern Territories, Rosenberg had put these policies into action.

Frank and Streicher

Hitler's personal lawyer, Hans Frank, had handed over to his American captors 42 leather-bound volumes of his personal diaries thinking that his criticism of Hitler contained within would exonerate him. Instead they were offered as evidence for the prosecution. One extract reads: 'Before the German people suffer starvation, the occupied territories and their people shall be exposed to starvation. This means a six-fold increase over that of last year's contribution. . . . It must be done cold-bloodedly and without pity.' Evidence about the ill-treatment and murder of Jews during the time he was governor-general of Poland was also entered.

The British delegation outlined the case against Julius Streicher. Again he had condemned himself with his own pen. In January 1937, Himmler had written that future history would state: 'that Julius Streicher and his weekly *Der Stürmer* would have contributed a great deal towards the enlightenment regarding the enemy of humanity (the Jews).'

Schacht and Funk

As president of the Reichsbank and minister of economics, Hjalmar Schacht had put an end to runaway inflation. The case against him was that he had helped Hitler to power, known of his aggressive aims and organized the foreign loans that financed rearmament. But the prosecution case was thin: Schacht had distanced himself from the Nazi regime after 1937 and, following the July Plot in 1944, had been arrested and sent to Ravensbrück concentration camp.

His successor, Walther Funk, had organized the funding of the Nazi party and, as president of the Reichsbank, arranged for the gold extracted from the teeth of murdered Jews and money raised from other stolen valuables to be paid into false accounts.

Dr Franz Blaha

At this point, the first former inmate of a concentration camp was called. Dr Franz Blaha, a Czech, was interned at Dachau from April 1941 until the camp was liberated in April 1945. When he refused to perform operations on 20 healthy patients, he was sent to the autopsy room where he performed 12,000 post-mortems. He was examined on his affidavit, which stated:

> *From the middle of 1941 to the end of 1942 some 500 operations on healthy prisoners were performed. These were for the instructions of the SS medical students and doctors and included operations on the stomach, gall bladder and throat. These were performed by students and doctors of only two years' training, although they were very dangerous and difficult. Ordinarily they would not have been done except by surgeons with at least four years' surgical practice. Many prisoners died on the operating table and many others from later complications. I performed autopsies on all of these bodies. . . .*
>
> *During my time at Dachau I was familiar with many kinds of medical experiments carried out there on human victims. These*

persons were never volunteers but were forced to submit to such acts. Malaria experiments on about 1,200 people were conducted by Dr Klaus Schilling between 1941 and 1945. Schilling was personally ordered by Himmler to conduct these experiments. The victims were either bitten by mosquitoes or given injections of malaria sporozoites taken from mosquitoes. . . . Thirty to forty died from the malaria itself. Three hundred to four hundred died later from diseases which were fatal because of the physical condition resulting from the malaria attacks. In addition there were deaths resulting from poisoning due to overdoses of neosalvarsan and pyramidon. . . .

In 1942 and 1943, experiments on human beings were conducted by Dr Sigmund Rascher to determine the effects of changing air pressure. As many as 25 persons were put at one time into a specially constructed van in which pressure could be increased or decreased as required. . . . Most of the prisoners used died from these experiments, from internal haemorrhage of the lungs or brain. The survivors coughed blood when taken out. It was my job to take the bodies out and as soon as they were found to be dead to send the internal organs to Munich for study. About 400 to 500 prisoners were experimented on. The survivors were sent to invalid blocks and liquidated shortly afterwards.

Rascher also conducted experiments on the effect of cold water on human beings. This was done to find a way for reviving airmen who had fallen into the ocean. The subject was placed in ice cold water and kept there until he was unconscious. . . . Some men stood it as long as 24 to 36 hours. The lowest body temperature reached was 19 degrees centigrade, but most men died at 25 or 26 degrees. When the men were removed from the ice water attempts were made to revive them by artificial sunshine, with hot water, by electro-therapy, or by animal warmth. For this last experiment prostitutes were used and the body of the unconscious man was placed between the bodies of two women. Himmler was present at one such experiment. . . . About 300 persons were used in these experiments. The majority died. Of those who survived, many became mentally deranged. Those who did not die were sent to invalid blocks and were killed just as were the victims of the air pressure experiments. . . .

Liver puncture experiments were performed by Dr Brachtl on healthy people and on people who had diseases of the stomach and gall bladder. For this purpose a needle was jabbed into the liver of a person and a small piece of the liver was extracted. No anaesthetic was used.

The catalogue of barbarity continued throughout Blaha's testimony. Healthy men – usually Polish, Czech or Dutch priests – were injected with pus from diseased people. Half were treated, some having limbs amputated, though Blaha's autopsies revealed that chemical treatments were also harmful. Between 600 and 800 people died; others became permanent invalids and were later killed.

'It was common practice to remove the skin from dead prisoners,' said Dr Blaha. 'Human skin from human backs and chests . . . was chemically treated and placed in the sun to dry. After that it was cut into various sizes for use as saddles, riding breeches, gloves, house slippers, and ladies' handbags. Tattooed skin was especially valued by SS men. Russians, Poles, and other inmates were used in this way, but it was forbidden to cut out the skin of a German. This skin had to be from healthy prisoners and free from defects. Sometimes we did not have enough bodies with good skin and Rascher would say, "All right, you will get the bodies." The next day we would receive 20 or 30 bodies of young people. They would have been shot in the neck or struck on the head so that the skin would be uninjured.'

Skeletons and skulls, particularly those with good teeth, were in demand by SS men. Blaha would have to boil off the flesh and bleach the bones. There was evidence of cannibalism in the transports that brought fresh inmates. Blaha's autopsies showed that the victims had died from suffocation or lack of water. Sometimes a transport would be left in a siding until everyone starved to death.

Blaha also performed autopsies on the victims of the gas chamber at Dachau. He also told of the appalling treatment of prisoners of war and their deliberate murder, the epidemics and the insanitary conditions. The sick were just shot in the neck, though after the camp was liberated he found plenty of medicine in the SS hospital.

Consternation in the dock

This testimony caused consternation in the defendants' box, particularly when Blaha described visits to the camp by Bormann, Frick, Rosenberg,

Funk, Sauckel and Kaltenbrunner. He picked out those he had seen personally from among the defendants in the dock.

The defence tried to trip Dr Blaha up over precise dates, but he had a remarkable memory and could not be faulted. What's more, the guilt extended beyond those in the dock.

'In my opinion, the people who lived in the neighbourhood of Munich must have known of all these things, because the prisoners went every day to various factories in Munich and the neighbourhood; and at work they frequently came into contact with the civilian workers,' he said. 'Moreover, the various suppliers and consumers often entered the fields and the factories of the German armament works and they saw what was done to the prisoners and what they looked like.'

Dr Franz Blaha, Dachau survivor

Soldiers, sailors and diplomats

The British presented cases against the soldiers, sailors and diplomats. The case against Doenitz focused on war crimes. The submission included calling two former German captains of U-boats who testified that an order from Doenitz had encouraged the killing of shipwrecked crew. It was alleged that Doenitz 'was an extreme Nazi who did his utmost to indoctrinate the Navy and the German people with the Nazi creed'.

In his capacity as grand admiral and commander-in-chief of the German navy until 1943, Raeder had overseen the rebuilding of the Kriegsmarine in the 1930s. Documentary evidence showed that he had urged Hitler to invade and occupy Norway. He had also passed on the Commando Order, which had led to the execution of British commandos by a German navy firing squad.

Foreign minister von Neurath had been at the Hossbach Conference in 1937, where Hitler outlined his expansionist plans. As Reichsprotektor of occupied Bohemia and Moravia, he had dissolved the Czech parliament, closed the universities, taken control of the press and instituted the Nuremberg Laws. The case against Ribbentrop was largely a recapitulation of evidence already heard. And little fresh could be said against von Papen apart from that as ambassador to Vienna he had assisted Hitler in the annexation of Austria.

JOSEF MENGELE

THE ANGEL OF DEATH

'It would be a sin, a crime . . . and irresponsible not to utilize the possibilities that Auschwitz had for twin research . . . there would never be another chance like it.'

The children were screaming. They didn't know if they would ever see their parents again. Many were too young to know where they were or what was happening to them. The shouting of the men at the ramp had frightened them as they were herded off the cattle wagons, but after they were told they didn't have to have their hair cut off like the other children and would be allowed to keep their own clothes, they stopped crying. When they were told they had been singled out for 'special treatment' and ordered to line up, they must have thought they were going to a new kindergarten. And once they had been shepherded into a special barracks by the *Zwillingsvater* (Twins Father) and given white bread and milk and assured they wouldn't have to work like the other children, they dried their eyes.

UNCLE MENGELE

Later that day, they had a visitor. A handsome, dark-haired man; he was flicking a riding crop to the left and right to indicate which line the new arrivals were destined for. He called out 'Zwillinge heraus!' (Twins out!) and 'Zwillinge heraustreten!' (Twins step forward!) and the twins went to him like obedient pupils on their first day at a new school. Some mothers hid their twins beneath their clothes and smuggled them through the other line. They were never seen again.

The dark-haired man was smiling and handing out candy and chocolates to the children he had picked out of the line. He was dressed immaculately and talked softly. They called him 'Uncle Mengele'.

Mengele was also known as 'Uncle Pepi'

Dr Josef Mengele's barbaric experiments on children, including newborn babies, served no scientific purpose and were indefensible under any circumstances, but what made his crimes so shocking was the fact that he carried out his sadistic experiments not in secret but in full view of his superiors and with their tacit consent.

Auschwitz survivor Alex Dekel described him as a sadist: 'I have never accepted the fact that Mengele himself believed he was doing serious work – not from the slipshod way he went about it. He was only exercising his power. Mengele ran a butcher shop – major surgeries were performed without anaesthesia. Once, I witnessed a stomach operation – Mengele was removing pieces from the stomach, but without any anaesthetic. Another time, it was a heart that was removed, again without anaesthesia. It was horrifying. Mengele was a doctor who became mad because of the power he was given.'

EARLY SIGNS OF EVIL

Mengele's upbringing may have contributed to his depravity. His family were prosperous and devoutly religious. His father owned a manufacturing business in Bavaria, but was a reserved, unfeeling man and his wife was an ill-tempered harpy who terrorized her husband and his employees. But her three sons, of whom Josef was the eldest, were cheerful, bright and well behaved. However, Josef soon exhibited a degree of fastidiousness in his appearance that indicated an obsessive hygiene fetish. He took to wearing white cotton gloves and became passionate about the spurious science of eugenics, the study of inherited disease and deformity. It has been argued that Mengele's extravagant fastidiousness was consistent with withdrawal and that the lack of empathy he exhibited is frequently seen as 'evil'.

Mengele was not the typical sadist who began by pulling the wings off insects and torturing small animals. His psychosis was an extreme intellectual conceit in which he saw himself as superior to other people and therefore above moral laws and normal codes of conduct. He was obsessed with his own omnipotence, or the illusion of such power, and he deliberately sought out a situation in which he could exercise the power of life and death.

EDUCATION OF A MONSTER

During his first term at Munich University in 1930, he fell under the spell of Social Darwinist Dr Ernst Ruedin, who indoctrinated Mengele and his fellow students with the idea that mentally disabled and physically deformed people were unworthy of life. It was a doctor's duty, he said, to end that life to save the state the expense and their families the burden of caring for them. Ruedin's extreme views brought him to the attention of Hitler who in 1934 invited him to draw up the Protection of Hereditary Health Act, which called for the forced sterilization of persons who exhibited a range of imperfections, including simple-mindedness, epilepsy, manic depression and even alcoholism.

Ruedin's absurd theories appealed to Mengele, who saw them as scientific confirmation of his own superiority and a licence to experiment on 'inferior' human beings should he ever get the opportunity to do his own 'research'. When the National Socialists adopted Social Darwinism and eugenics to support their belief in the Aryan Master Race, Mengele became a fanatical convert to the new cult. But it was only after he had completed his PhD and was appointed research assistant at the University of Frankfurt that Mengele found the mentor who would encourage him to pursue his obsession with racial purity.

Professor Verschuer impressed on his pupils the necessity for studying twins who, he believed, held the secret of heredity. If twins shared the same genetic make-up, he argued, it should be possible to conduct experiments which demonstrated that heredity rather than environment determined an individual's psychological and physical development. Verschuer petitioned for Mengele to be awarded a grant to fund his research and encouraged him to request a posting to Auschwitz. On his arrival Mengele was appointed physician to the sub-camp of Birkenau, and quickly took to his new role with energy and enthusiasm.

MORBID OBSESSIONS

According to Professor Robert Lifton, professor of psychiatry and psychology at the City University of New York, it was as if Mengele had found his calling. In addition to his obsession with twins, Mengele had a morbid fascination with a condition known as heterochromia, which creates eyes of different colours in one person. When he found individuals with this condition he removed the eyes and sent them to Professor Verschuer to study and preserve in his new post at the Berlin-Dahlem Institute of Racial Biology. Mengele saw no ethical reason why he should not try to replicate the effect in living subjects by injecting methylene blue into the eyes of child prisoners.

Ironically, by indulging in these inhumane experiments and performing unnecessary surgery and spinal injections on healthy human beings without anaesthetic, Mengele revealed himself to be the deviant.

TWO DISTINCT SELVES

Professor Lifton believes he has identified the process by which intelligent individuals like Mengele justify their aberrant behaviour. He calls it 'doubling' and it involves the individual unconsciously creating 'a new self' to adapt to their 'evil environment'. Lifton acknowledges that Mengele possessed 'unusually intense destructive potential', but feels he exhibited no signs of aberrant behaviour before he was assigned to the camp and given authority to conduct his experiments.

These inner divisions were reflected in what one inmate described as his 'dead eyes'. Several former prisoners recalled that Mengele avoided eye contact. One inmate doctor referred to Mengele as 'the double man' who appeared to possess 'all the human feelings, pity and so on', but also an 'impenetrable, indestructible cell, which is obedience to the received order'. It is Professor Lipton's contention that Mengele's apparent affection for the children was genuine and part of his former self, but that when it came time to carry out his official function he had no hesitation in killing and dissecting the still warm bodies of the infants he had only moments before patted on the head and even played with. Mengele's behaviour resembled an extreme form of the public and private face of a politician or celebrity. Had he lived to face the enormity of his crimes, he would no doubt have seen nothing odd in acting in this way.

It was mannered and narcissistic, like the flamboyant display of a celebrity flaunting their omnipotence before the mass of lesser mortals, and it was most evident when Mengele appeared for the daily selection process.

He stood smiling and whistling a cheerful melody in his white physician's coat, his arms outstretched to separate those who would live and those who were to be dispatched to the gas chambers. His appearance earned him the name the 'Angel of Death', but to the youngest of the twins he played the protective parent, isolating them from the horrors of the main camp, although they could hear the screams and smell the fumes from the crematoria.

> 'It was the coming together of the man and the place, the "fit" between the two, that created the Auschwitz Mengele.'
>
> Professor Robert Lifton

Professor Lifton concluded: 'The psychological traits Mengele brought to Auschwitz exist in many of us, but in him they took exaggerated form. His impulse toward omnipotence and total control of the world around him were means of fending off anxiety and doubt, fears of falling apart – ultimately, fear of death. That fear also activated his sadism and extreme psychic numbing. He could quiet his fears of death in that death-dominated environment by performing the ultimate act of power over another person: murder.'

CHAPTER 22

War Crimes

On 17 January 1946, six weeks after the beginning of the trial, François de Menthon rose to make his opening statement on behalf of the French delegation. He, too, cited the Kellogg–Briand Pact – initially signed by US Secretary of State Frank B. Kellogg and French Foreign Minister Aristide Briand – as a precedent. His case was heartfelt: three times in 50 years France had been invaded by Germany.

> *The conscience of the peoples, who only yesterday were enslaved and tortured both in soul and body, calls upon you to judge and to condemn the most monstrous attempt at domination and barbarism of all times, both in the persons of some of those who bear the chief responsibility and in the collective groups and organizations which were the essential instruments of their crimes.*

> *France, which was systematically plundered and ruined; France, so many of whose sons were tortured and murdered in the jails of the Gestapo or in concentration camps; France, which was subjected to the still more horrible grip of demoralization and return to barbarism diabolically imposed by Nazi Germany, asks you, above all in the name of the heroic martyrs of the Resistance, who are among the greatest heroes of our national legend, that justice be done.*

De Menthon concentrated on war crimes, which he categorized as economic looting, forced labour, crimes against persons and crimes against humankind. He concluded by expressing the hope that their judgment would be a decisive act in the history of international law and the foundation of a peaceful order. If that was the case, he said, 'the need for justice of the martyred peoples will be satisfied, and their sufferings will not have been useless to the progress of mankind'.

Looting and forced labour

The French delegation then began presenting evidence of looting and forced labour, not just in France but also in Norway, Denmark, the Netherlands, Belgium and Luxembourg – countries whose cases had so far been under-represented.

The taking of forced labour was in violation of the Franco-German Armistice signed after the Nazi invasion in 1940 and the Hague

Conventions, which were agreements on the conduct of war signed in 1899 and 1907. Documents from the Nazi archives showed that by March 1943, some 250,000 civilians had been forced to build the Atlantic Wall in an attempt to prevent an anticipated Anglo-American invasion (it would occur on D-Day the following year). More than 875,000 French labourers were sent to work in Germany, along with 430,000 Dutch and 150,000 Belgians.

Assistant French prosecutor Jacques B. Herzog cited a report in which Sauckel admitted that there were five million foreign workers in Germany, of whom just 200,000 were volunteers. Production facilities in the occupied countries were also exploited. A report was read in which one German officer wrote: 'I attach the greatest importance to the proposition that the factories in the occupied territories, Holland, Belgium and France, be utilized as much as possible to ease the strain on the German armament production and to increase war potential.'

Illegal seizures

Article 52 of the Convention on Laws and Customs of War on Land signed in The Hague in 1899 said: 'Neither requisitions in kind nor services can be demanded from communes or inhabitants except for the necessities of the army of occupation.'

This plainly had not been the case in the Second World War. From France alone, the maximum the Germans could have legally demanded for the maintenance of their army of occupation was 74,000 million francs. They had taken more than ten times that amount. In Belgium, the illegal seizure amounted to 130,000 Belgian francs; in Denmark, 8,000 million crowns and 70 million crowns' worth of agricultural production had been seized each month.

The Netherlands lost 875,000 farm animals, 28,950 freight cars, one million bicycles and 600,000 radios, plus 1,100 million guilders' worth of machinery and oil. Norway was down 300,000 tons of hay and straw, 13,000 tons of soap, 30,000 tons of meat, 61,000 tons of dairy produce, 26,000 tons of fish, 112,000 tons of fats and 68,000 tons of fruit and vegetables.

The average daily consumption in France fell from 3,000 calories a day at the beginning of the war to 900 calories a day later on. In the Netherlands, it fell to 400 calories a day. Also entered as evidence was a speech by Goering who had boasted: 'If famine is to reign, it will not reign in Germany.'

Partisan suspects being arrested in Brittany under the 'Night and Fog' decree

Nacht und Nebel

French civilians disappeared without warning and with no indication of what had happened to them. Some 29,000 hostages were shot. Thousands were tortured in 'protective custody'. Mass fines and reprisals were imposed for sabotage. In Denmark, Hitler ordered that five Danes be killed for every German. Between the beginning of 1944 and the end of the war, 267 prominent Danes were killed in their homes and offices or on the street. Where the police caught the perpetrator, the killer got a letter of congratulation from Himmler.

In 1941, Keitel signed the *Nacht und Nebel* – 'Night and Fog' – decree. Under this, persons in occupied territories engaging in activities intended to undermine the security of German troops were to be brought to Germany 'by night and fog' for trial by special courts, thus circumventing military procedure and various conventions governing the treatment of prisoners. Keitel's counsel objected on the grounds that the decree was not the words of his client. Deputy French prosecutor Charles Dubost responded by saying: 'I knew that the accused Keitel had signed it, but that Hitler had conceived it. Therefore, I made allusion to the military honour of this general, who was not afraid to become the lackey of Hitler.'

It was estimated that 6,000 Luxembourgers, 5,200 Danes, 5,400 Norwegians, 12,000 Dutch and 37,000 Belgians were sent to concentration camps in this manner. Of the 250,000 French deported, only 35,000 returned home. Up to 25 per cent died on the transports on the way to the camps.

Maurice Lampe

The French called Maurice Lampe, a former inmate at the Mauthausen concentration camp, to testify to the conditions at the camp. After two-and-a-half years' internment in France, he was transported with 104 others in an unventilated cattle truck. Although it was 12 degrees below zero, they travelled naked. The journey took three days.

When they arrived at Mauthausen, an SS officer told the convoy of some 1,200 Frenchmen: 'Germany needs your arms. You are, therefore, going to work; but I want to tell you that you will never see your families again. When one enters this camp, one leaves it by the chimney of the crematorium.'

Lampe detailed some scenes he found particularly horrible. Forty-seven British, American and Dutch airmen were made to undress. One American officer asked that he should be allowed to meet his death as a soldier. He was beaten with a whip. They were then marched to a quarry. 'At the bottom of the steps they loaded stone on the backs of these poor men and they had to carry them to the top,' said Lampe. 'The first journey was made with stones weighing 25 to 30 kilos and was accompanied by blows. Then they were made to

> 'I saw these Soviet officers lined up in rows of five in front of my block. They were called one by one, and there was a sort of human chain between the group which was awaiting its turn and that which was in the stairway listening to the shots which killed their predecessors. They were all killed by a shot in the neck.'
>
> Maurice Lampe, Mauthausen concentration camp survivor

run down. For the second journey, the stones were still heavier; and whenever the poor wretches sank under their burden, they were kicked and hit with a bludgeon, even stones were hurled at them.

'This went on for several days. In the evening when I returned from the gang with which I was then working, the road which led to the camp was a bath of blood. I almost stepped on the lower jaw of a man. Twenty-one bodies were strewn along the road. Twenty-one had died on the first day. The twenty-six others died the following morning.'

Lampe testified that Himmler had visited Mauthausen to witness the shooting of 50 Soviet prisoners of war. Another 400 prisoners were killed because the camp was overcrowded. They had survived a convoy on which 800 had died, only to be stripped naked and left outside when the temperature was 18 degrees below zero. When they did not die fast enough, they were drenched with freezing water. The last survivors were finished off with axes.

Madame Vaillant-Couturier

Picked up by the Vichy police, Marie-Claude Vaillant-Couturier was sent to Auschwitz in 1942. She described a roll call on 5 February 1943:

In the morning at 3.30 the whole camp was awakened and sent out on the plain, whereas normally the roll call was at 3.30 but inside the camp. We remained out in front of the camp until five in the afternoon, in the snow, without any food. Then when the signal was given we had to go through the door one by one, and we were struck in the back with a cudgel, each one of us, in order to make us run. Those who could not run, either because they were too old or too ill, were caught by a hook and taken to Block 25, 'waiting block' for the gas chamber. On that day, ten of the French women of our convoy were thus caught and taken to Block 25.

When all the internees were back in the camp, a party to which I belonged was organized to go and pick up the bodies of the dead which were scattered over the plain as on a battlefield. We carried to the yard of Block 25 the dead and the dying without distinction, and they remained there stacked up in a pile . . . from time to time a hand or a head would stir among the bodies, trying to free itself. It was a dying woman attempting to get free and live. The rate of mortality in that block was even more terrible than elsewhere because, having been condemned to death, they received food or drink only if there was something left in the cans in the kitchen; which means that very often they went for several days without a drop of water.

One of our companions, Annette Epaux, a fine young woman of 30, passing the block one day, was overcome with pity for those women who moaned from morning till night in all languages, 'Drink. Drink. Water!' She came back to our block to get a little herbal tea, but as she was passing it through the bars of the window she was seen by the Aufseherin [guard], who took her by the neck and threw her into Block 25. All my life I will remember Annette Epaux. Two days later I saw her on the truck which was taking the internees to the gas chamber. She had her arms around another French woman, old Line Porcher, and when the truck started moving she cried, 'Think of my little boy, if you ever get back to France.' Then they started singing 'The Marseillaise'.

Medical experiments

Dr Victor Dupont described the interrogations at Buchenwald. There was 'every imaginable kind of beating, immersion in bathtubs, squeezing of testicles, hanging, crushing of the head in iron bands, and the torturing of entire families in each others' sight. I have . . . seen a wife tortured before her husband; and children were tortured before their mothers.'

There were medical experiments and mass murders, particularly of Jews and Gypsies. Their ashes were thrown in the excrement pit or used to fertilize the surrounding fields.

Towards the end of the war, as the Allies advanced, the camp commandant promised to hand over the keys of the camp. 'I do not want any atrocities,' he said.

When the Allied advance was held up, a delegation of prisoners went to see the commandant to remind

> 'In Block 25, in the courtyard, there were rats as big as cats running about and gnawing the corpses and even attacking the dying who had not enough strength left to chase them away.'
>
> Marie-Claude Vaillant-Couturier, Auschwitz survivor

him that he had given 'his word of honour as a soldier'. 'He seemed acutely embarrassed,' said Dr Dupont, 'and explained that Sauckel, the governor of Thuringia, had given orders that no prisoner should remain in Buchenwald.'

Dr Alfred Balachowsky also testified about the medical experiments at Buchenwald: 'The human beings subjected to experiments were recruited, not only in the Buchenwald camp, but also outside the camp. They were not volunteers; in most cases they did not know that they would be used for experiments until they entered Block 46,' he said. 'For the greater part they were of no service to science. Therefore, they can hardly be called experiments.'

Proved over and over again

Norwegian Hans Cappelen testified about being tortured by the Gestapo in Oslo. He was beaten with rubber bludgeons and iron cable ends until he fainted and then revived with ice-cold water.

Then they started to beat me again, but it was useless to beat a man like me who was so swollen up and looking so bad. Then they started in another way, they started to screw and break my arms and legs. And my right arm was dislocated. . . . Then they placed a sort of home-made – it looked to me like a sort of home-made – wooden thing, with a screw arrangement, on my left leg; and they started to screw so that all the flesh loosened from the bones. I felt an awful pain and fainted away again.

> 'The men were used for observing the effects of drugs, poisons, bacterial cultures, etc. . . . They were literally murdered to keep typhus germs alive.'
>
> Dr Alfred Balachowsky, Buchenwald camp survivor

The French continued to present witnesses until *The Times* newspaper complained that the trial was 'being surfeited by the most murderous and revolting record of all time'. Judge Norman Birkett said that 'from the point of view of the trial it is a complete waste of time. The case has been proved over and over again. Neither does the world need it any more, for all over the world the evidence has been published . . . but it seems impossible to stop it, or to check the volume of it.'

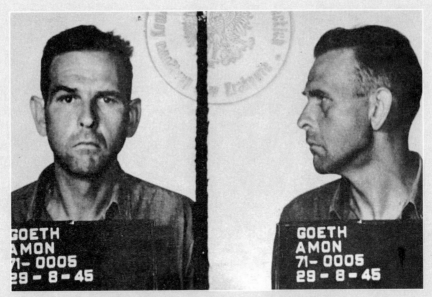

Holocaust survivor Anna Duklauer Perl said of Goeth: 'One day he hanged a friend of mine just because he had once been rich. He was the devil.'

AMON GOETH

THE NAZI BUTCHER

'When you saw Goeth, you saw death.'

Poldek Pfefferberg, Krakow-Plaszów survivor

Many of the Nazi hierarchy committed their crimes from behind a desk. Very few of the leadership bloodied their own hands. But Amon Goeth enjoyed killing and as commandant of the Krakow-Plaszów forced labour camp in Poland he had a licence to kill with impunity.

MURDER FOR PLEASURE

An early convert to the Nazi cause, Austrian-born Goeth rose in the ranks of the SS until he was assigned to Operation Reinhard in the summer of 1942 and given responsibility for rounding up and transporting Jews to the extermination camps at Treblinka, Belzec and Sobibor. For his efficiency and unstinting dedication he was appointed commandant of the newly constructed Krakow-Plaszów labour camp in the spring of 1943, which was populated with the survivors of the liquidated Krakow ghetto.

German soldiers rounding up Polish Jews in 1943

Until the camp was upgraded to a concentration camp and staffed by the SS, Goeth was permitted to do as he wished, which meant indulging his mania for dispensing death like a depraved despot. His favourite amusement was picking off prisoners at random with a high-powered rifle from the upper window of his villa, which overlooked the compound, but he also got a special thrill from setting his two vicious dogs on prisoners indiscriminately and watching as they tried in vain to fend them off. When he finally called off his dogs he looked down at the lifeless bloodied flesh with a smirk that betrayed a pride in his well-trained pets, as if they had dragged in a slaughtered rabbit for their master's approval.

SADISTIC KILLER

Goeth was a textbook psychopath who relished the power over life and death that his post had given him. But he didn't merely murder those who stood helpless before him, he took a sadistic delight in their suffering.

A Polish prisoner, Wladyslaw Kopystecki, testified that he had personally witnessed Goeth shooting a starving female prisoner who had been found eating a potato in the kitchen. Goeth then ordered her to be thrown into a cauldron of boiling water while evidently still alive. When he saw that she was thrashing about, he ordered other inmates to cover the pot and then walked away as if nothing untoward had occurred.

Escape attempts were punished by summary execution. In the event that a prisoner succeeded, members of their work detail would be shot arbitrarily by Goeth until he had vented his rage. But even minor infractions of the rules were dealt with unmercifully.

He shot his own batman because the man had saddled the wrong horse for his morning ride and he shot one of his two Jewish maids because he was embarrassed at having flirted with her the night before while drunk. He killed others for displeasing him – for meeting his gaze when they should have been looking down to show true deference, for serving his soup too hot or for failing to scrub a ring of grime from his bathtub.

As one of his two Jewish maids later testified, 'Never would I, never, believe that any human being would be capable of such horror, of such atrocities.'

KILLINGS WITHOUT REASON

When the camp was upgraded and the SS installed to take over its management, Goeth continued to dispense death on a whim. On Yom Kippur, 1943, the holiest day in the Jewish calendar, he ordered 50 inmates to be taken out and shot. No reason was given. His sadism seemed to know no limits. No justification was needed if Goeth got it into his mind that fun could be had from humiliating his victims. He took particular pleasure in tormenting them – forcing them to thank him after they were beaten, restarting the beating if they begged for mercy and making them believe they were safe before he murdered them.

On one occasion, Goeth saw a six-year-old boy scrambling from the back of a truck and assumed he had been hiding something. He called to the boy, 'Come, come, don't be afraid!' The boy stopped to empty his pockets of some toys and trinkets thinking that he would be allowed to go. Goeth took the toys, smiled reassuringly then shot the child dead.

Moshe Bejski – a Schindler Jew who survived to become an Israeli High Court judge – recalled the day Goeth refused to spare a 15-year-old boy by the name of Haubenstock, whose only crime had been to sing a Russian song: 'The boy was hanged and something happened which occurs once in many thousands of cases – the rope broke. The boy stood there, he was again lifted on to a high chair which was placed under the rope, and he began to beg for mercy. An order was given to hang him a second time. And then he was raised a second time to the gallows, and hanged, and thereafter that same Amon Goeth, with his own hands, also fired a shot.'

MENTALLY ILL

Goeth had assembled 15,000 prisoners to witness the execution, so he clearly did not expect to escape justice when the war was over. Eventually his superiors turned against him when they discovered he had been hoarding valuables stolen from the inmates, valuables to which the state had prior claim. In September 1944 he was charged with depriving prisoners of adequate food, as well as various infractions of the regulations governing the administration of the camp and the treatment of prisoners, and was subjected to a mental health examination by SS doctors. They determined that he was mentally ill and ordered him to be confined to an asylum, where he was arrested by the Allies after Germany's capitulation. He was tried by the new Polish authorities, found guilty as a war criminal, and hanged not far from the Krakow camp.

CHAPTER 23

Opening for the Defence

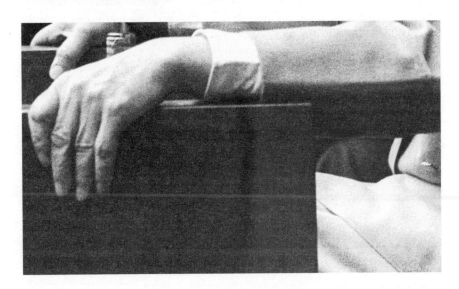

Naturally, Goering was going to be the lead for the defence. The first witness called by Stahmer, Goering's defence counsel, was General Karl Bodenschatz, liaison officer between the Luftwaffe and Hitler's headquarters. He testified that on Goering's instruction he had helped between 10 and 20 Jews who had been arrested or were threatened with arrest, and that Goering had opposed war against Britain and the Soviet Union.

It was noted that Bodenschatz was reading his testimony from a prepared statement. Jackson objected, but Lawrence allowed Bodenschatz to continue because he was with Hitler in the Wolf's Lair on 20 July 1944 and had been injured in the bomb blast. According to Bodenschatz, Goering knew nothing about the attacks on Jews and their property on Kristallnacht – 9–10 November 1938. Nor was he aware of conditions in the concentration camps or the extermination of the Jews.

Jackson tore into Bodenschatz, making the point that two days after Kristallnacht Goering had promulgated the order fining Jews one billion Reichsmarks. He had also confiscated their insurance payments and passed a new decree excluding them from economic life.

When asked how he knew about a meeting he said had taken place, Bodenschatz said: 'Dr Stahmer told me so.' This produced laughter in the courtroom. Bodenschatz began to sweat profusely. Then he was asked about Goering's boast, early in the war, that his Luftwaffe would keep Germany safe from air attack. Goering was beside himself. A reporter from the *Evening Standard* noted: 'He gnashed his teeth and his eyes blazed with fury.'

Milch and von Brauchitsch

Next came Secretary of State for the Air Ministry Erhard Milch, who maintained that Goering had built up the Luftwaffe for defensive purposes only; but he was forced to admit that, with a roughly equal number of fighters and bombers at the outbreak of war, it had been designed to support the army in the *blitzkrieg* form of warfare.

Milch was easy to undermine. He insisted that the foreign workers in Germany had been volunteers. However, he had been a member of the Central Planning Board and was present at a meeting in which Sauckel had presented figures showing that only 200,000 out of five million were volunteers. He also attended another meeting in which Speer said that slackers should be sent to concentration camps.

The minutes of the Central Planning Board showed that Milch knew about the forced labour of prisoners of war. Records showed he knew about the prosecution of an aggressive war, because he had attended a planning meeting about Poland on 23 March 1939, more than five months before the invasion had taken place. His correspondence with Himmler showed he knew about experiments on prisoners in concentration camps, including the investigation of the effects of low air pressure at high altitude, and of exposure. When Milch left the stand, the *New York Times* reported he was: 'a confused and wilted witness who had contributed as much to the prosecution case as he tried to detract from it'. A subsequent military tribunal in Nuremberg sentenced him to life imprisonment. The sentence was later commuted and he was released in 1954.

Goering's adjutant, Bernd von Brauchitsch, admitted his boss had transmitted Hitler's orders that Allied 'terror-fliers' should be lynched, but said he hoped they would not be put into practice. A former secretary of state in the Prussian state ministry, he claimed that Germany had increased the efficiency of agriculture in the occupied territories and was therefore entitled to a share of the surplus.

Kesselring

Appearing in his Luftwaffe uniform, Field Marshal Albert Kesselring made more of an impression. Jackson's cross-examination barely dented his defence. But Maxwell Fyfe confronted Kesselring with evidence that he had ordered the bombing of Rotterdam after negotiations for its surrender had begun.

Then there were the orders he had given on 17 June 1944, concerning partisans, when he was in command in Italy. They said: 'It is the duty of all troops and police in my command to adopt the severest measures. . . . Wherever there is evidence of considerable numbers of partisan groups, a proportion of the male population of the area will be arrested; and in the event of an act of violence being committed, these men will be shot.'

Maxwell Fyfe read a UN War Crimes Commission report of what happened in Italy a week later:

Two German soldiers were killed and a third wounded in a fight with partisans in the village of Civitella.

Fearing reprisals, the inhabitants evacuated the village, but when the Germans discovered this, punitive action was postponed.

On June 29, when the local inhabitants were returning and were feeling secure once more, the Germans carried out a well-organized reprisal, combing the neighbourhood. Innocent inhabitants were often shot on sight. During that day 212 men, women and children in the immediate district were killed. Some of the dead women were found completely naked.

In the course of investigations, a nominal roll of the dead has been compiled and is complete with the exception of a few names whose bodies could not be identified. Ages of the dead ranged from one year to eighty-four years. Approximately one hundred houses were destroyed by fire. Some of the victims were burned alive in their homes.

'Now, witness, do you really think that military necessity commands the killing of babies of one and people of 84?' asked Maxwell Fyfe. *The Times* said that Maxwell Fyfe's demolition of Kesselring was 'as masterly a piece of cross-examination as the court has heard'. A British military tribunal sitting in Venice sentenced Kesselring to death for ordering the execution of Italian hostages. But his sentence was commuted and he was released in 1954.

The Last Attempt

Goering's last witness was the Swedish businessman and amateur diplomat, Birger Dahlerus. He had tried to broker peace in August 1939. Goering had arranged a meeting for him with Hitler. Why would a man hell-bent on war do such a thing? asked Stahmer.

Dahlerus had written a book about his efforts called *The Last Attempt*. Goering had read a copy in his cell. Maxwell Fyfe had a copy, too, and quoted liberally from it. In the book, Dahlerus noted Goering's 'obsequious humility' towards Hitler, who ranted and screamed about 'planes, planes . . . tanks, tanks' and 'exterminating the enemy'.

The book also claimed that Goeing had demanded huge chunks of the Polish Corridor. On 1 September, as the invasion of Poland was going ahead, Goering seemed to be 'in some crazy state of intoxication', said Dahlerus.

Dahlerus' book and testimony not only served to damage Goering. He also accused Ribbentrop of trying to sabotage his plans and showed that, as foreign minister, Ribbentrop had done everything in his power to prevent the success of the negotiations.

As the cross-examination continued, Goering fumed and pulled at the cord on his headphones until a guard took them out of his hands. That evening, Ribbentrop turned to Kaltenbrunner and said: 'I don't know who to trust now.'

Goering's testimony

The defence witnesses had done little to help Goering's cause. Finally, on 13 March 1946, it was his turn to take the stand. Although he believed he was going to hang, Goering was determined to go down fighting. He had always been physically imposing. But now he had been weaned off paracodeine and slimmed down by the prison diet, he was mentally agile and the documents presented in evidence against him were largely in German, which the prosecutors had to read in translation. And the tales of his self-indulgence – his drug addiction, painted nails, made-up face and love of colourful uniforms – made him all too easy to underestimate.

Goering was nervous when he took the stand, but under the gentle questioning of Dr Stahmer he soon relaxed. Given the rift between the Soviets and the West following Churchill's Fulton speech, he was eager to emphasize that his disagreement with Hitler over the invasion of the Soviet Union was only over its timing.

He was also happy to help his co-defendants, especially over the charge of conspiracy. Only he was close enough to Hitler to have conspired with him, he maintained. He also gave them the shelter of the *Führerprinzip* – this was the principle that all decisions came from the leader, who had no time for cabinet meetings or the opinions of his generals.

Goering's jibes at his accusers also struck home. Hitler had made himself head of state, head of the government and head of the armed forces, he said, 'following the example of the United States'. While Germany was accused of using Soviet resources for its own ends, it had not transported away the entire economy 'down to the last bolt and screw' as the Russians had been doing in the German territories they occupied. Criticism of Germany's need for living space did not sit well in the mouths of the Four Powers who 'call more than three-quarters of the globe their own'. And, in defending Germany against charges that it had broken the Hague Conventions, he quoted Churchill, saying: 'In the struggle for life and death there is in the end no legality.'

Faith in their leaders

Goering stated that concentration camps had been established for 'protective custody'; and only military targets in Poland had been bombed. In the Netherlands, the bombing was intended to end the campaign as quickly as possible, thereby saving lives. Yugoslavia was attacked because she was mobilizing. Leningrad was the only Russian city to suffer starvation – and that was because it was under siege. Otherwise the Germans had not destroyed, but rather built up Russian agriculture and industry.

Goering said he knew nothing about the lynching of 'terror-fliers', nor the summary execution of the prisoners of war from Stalag Luft III at Sagan after the 'Great Escape' – as he had been on leave at the time. (The celebrated escapes by tunnelling from the Stalag Luft III camp near modern Zagan, Poland, were later dramatized in the films *The Wooden Horse* (1950) and *The Great Escape* (1963).) The workers in the Luftwaffe's underground factories here were better off than those in the camps – 'given what is known now'. The Russian anti-aircraft gunners were volunteers. When it came to looting, the artworks he had taken had been deserted by their owners. He was protecting them from destruction, though perhaps 'my collector's passion got the better of me'. However, he had intended to pay for the objects he wanted to keep. The others were to be sold to help French war victims.

After this bravura performance, the *Daily Express* said: 'The handshakes and plaudits, the bright eyes and smiles of his comrades in the dock, happier than they have been for months, are proof that he is winning them over to this last ditch stand of the Nazi regime in history.'

Goering had spent 12 hours in the witness box, almost uninterrupted by the bench. Birkett was horrified. 'It will have done much to restore German faith in their leaders,' he said.

Cross-examination

After Goering had taken the weekend to recuperate, Jackson opened the cross-examination on 18 March. The questions began with the early history of Nazism. Jackson sought to show that the crimes the Nazis had committed were implicit in the origins of the party. But this approach simply gave Goering an opportunity to warm up.

Soon he was parrying every question. Instead of giving the 'yes' or 'no' answers Jackson required, he seized the opportunity to make long-winded speeches of exculpation. When Jackson appealed to judges to impose some limits on the witness, they said they wanted to hear what Goering had to say.

According to Berlin SA leader Karl Ernst, Jackson stated, Goering and Goebbels had provided the liquid phosphorus and petroleum for the attempt to burn down the Reichstag on 27 February 1933. This provided the pretext that allowed Hitler to seize dictatorial powers. Goering said that Ernst had been shot on 30 June 1934, because together with Roehm he planned to overthrow the government and had plotted against the Führer. Besides, the accusation of Goering's complicity came from the foreign press.

'From the artistic point of view I did not at all regret that the assembly chamber was burned; I hoped to build a better one,' he said. What he did regret was that the parliament had to meet in the Kroll Opera House instead. 'The opera seemed to me much more important than the Reichstag.'

At the end of the first day of cross-examination, it was clear that Goering had the prosecution on the back foot.

Mistranslation

The second day went no better. When Jackson produced a document referring to 'preparation for the liberation of the Rhine' nine months earlier than Goering had claimed, the defendant said the document had been mistranslated. It read 'preparation for the *clearing* of the Rhine' – the river, not the Rhineland – and referred only to clearing the Rhine of civilian traffic in the event of war. Nevertheless, Jackson insisted, plans for the armed occupation of the Rhineland had been kept secret.

'I do not think I can recall reading beforehand the publication of the mobilization preparations of the United States,' Goering jibed.

Jackson complained of Goering's 'arrogant and contemptuous attitude toward the tribunal which is giving him the trial which he never gave a living soul'.

Lawrence ruled that Goering's remark about the mobilization of the United States was irrelevant. Nevertheless Goering continued to run rings around Jackson, who struck back with a litany of crude anti-

Goering in his heyday, as commander-in-chief of the Luftwaffe

Semitic remarks reputedly made by Goering which dented his image as a suave and sophisticated man. And documents showing Goering's complicity in the Holocaust could not be refuted, no matter how much he cavilled about mistranslations.

Goering had no pat answers to give when the records of his stolen art treasures were introduced – nor was he forthcoming when details of the stripping of Russian resources were presented. But then Jackson faltered. He turned his attention to the comparatively trivial matter of the destruction of the American ambassador's house in Warsaw. Seeking to prove it had been deliberately targeted by the Luftwaffe, he produced what he said were aerial photographs. Goering had been a pilot in the

First World War and knew a great deal about aerial photography. The picture, he demonstrated, had been taken from the top of a church steeple. On the back there was no date or departmental stamp. Then he said, almost contemptuously: 'However, let us assume that they were taken by the Luftwaffe, so that further questions will be facilitated.'

Jackson was floored.

British onslaught

Cross-examination then passed to the British, but most of the prosecution's ammunition had been spent. The tribunal ruled that ground already covered could not be touched on again. However, Maxwell Fyfe was a skilled trial lawyer. He showed that Goering had not been on leave when the Great Escape prisoners were shot. As time was short that day, Fyfe moved on to the Luftwaffe policy of sending all escapers, except British and Americans, to be killed at Mauthausen. Goering was rattled.

The following morning, Fyfe returned to the Stalag Luft III killings. Remorselessly, he established Goering's involvement. When Goering sought to dissemble, Fyfe cut him short.

At first Goering said that Ribbentrop had known nothing about the negotiations with Dahlerus, then that he had resented them. So which was it?

Goering could do no more than bluster over his prior knowledge of the invasion of Poland, the deliberate violation of the neutrality of Belgium and the Netherlands and the attack on Yugoslavia.

A barrage of documents about Auschwitz and the use of forced labour showed that Goering had known about it or was guilty of criminal negligence over crimes committed in his name. And he was also implicated in atrocities against partisans.

The *Daily Telegraph* said his face became 'strained and congested'. *The Times* said: 'Goering's denials sounded far less plausible than at any time . . . he ever sounded less sure of himself.'

Unshakeable loyalty

Goering's only defence was his unshakeable loyalty to Hitler. He insisted that the Führer had known nothing about the Holocaust. His policy was 'emigration not liquidation'. Himmler had kept the death camps secret, Goering said. In response, Maxwell Fyfe read from the record of a discussion between Hitler and the Regent of Hungary, Admiral Horthy. In it, Hitler said: 'In Poland, this state of affairs had been fundamentally cleared up. If the Jews there did not want to work, they were shot. If they could not work, they had to perish. They had to be treated like tuberculosis bacilli, with which a healthy body may become infected. This was not cruel – if one remembers that even innocent creatures of nature, such as hares and deer, have to be killed so that no harm is caused by them.'

When Horthy asked what he should do with the Jews in Hungary, Hitler replied: 'The Reich minister for foreign affairs declared that the Jews should be exterminated, or taken to concentration camps. There was no other possibility.'

Goering said he had not known about this. So Maxwell Fyfe read another document in which Goering had been told: 'There are only a few Jews left alive. Tens of thousands have been disposed of.'

Goering subsequently rallied slightly during Rudenko's cross-examination, but left the witness stand – according to the *New York Times* – 'with a wilted and bedraggled air'.

CHAPTER 24

Hitler's Henchmen

Hess decided not to take the witness stand in his own defence. He told Gilbert that he did not want to suffer the embarrassment of not being able to answer the prosecution questions, though his counsel, Dr Alfred Seidl, said it was because he didn't recognize the jurisdiction of the court other than in the matter of war crimes. As Hess had been in British custody since May 1941, there was little for him to answer for on that score. Again, the tribunal pointed out that the Charter prohibited any dispute over its authority.

Seidl tried to introduce a collection of press cuttings and speeches criticizing the Versailles Treaty. Biddle asked Seidl if the provisions of the treaty – no matter how unjust they were said to be – and their infraction by others could justify the war and the horrors perpetrated in it. When Seidl failed to make a cogent argument to that effect, the evidence was ruled inadmissible.

Seidl also attempted to cause discord by introducing in evidence the secret protocol to the Molotov–Ribbentrop Pact that had carved up Poland between Germany and the Soviet Union, but this was also thwarted. An affidavit from Hess' former secretary confirmed her assertion that Hess had flown to Britain with the sole desire of promoting peace.

Seidl then called Ernst Bohle, who had worked for Hess as head of the Auslands-Organization – the Nazi party's foreign wing. He claimed that Germans living abroad had never been ordered to commit any illegal act in their country of residence, either by Hitler or Hess. It was easy to show that the organization had provided the Nazi regime with military intelligence.

Hess was prepared to admit his role in the Nazi party and accept responsibility for his acts as part of the government – while challenging the tribunal's right to judge their legality. Maxwell Fyfe decided to list them and get Seidl to confirm or deny the accuracy of his account. Hess had joined the embryonic Nazi party in 1920 and introduced the concept of *Lebensraum*, to be taken from the Slavic people in the east. In Landsberg prison, he had taken dictation for Hitler's autobiographical manifesto *Mein Kampf* and edited it. Photographs were introduced to show that Hess was Hitler's constant companion, and that he had been made deputy Führer in 1933. Two years later, he signed the Nuremberg Laws for Blood and Honour, formalizing the persecution of the Jews, and the decree for compulsory military service, significantly contributing to preparations for war. He had also signed laws incorporating Austria, Danzig and Poland into the Reich. And when he flew to Britain, he already knew that preparations were being made for an attack on the

Soviet Union. The prosecution contended that Hess had come to Britain in an effort to secure peace so that Germany would have to fight on one front only.

The evidence against Hess for war crimes and crimes against humanity was thinner. He had made a statement about sending Waffen-SS units into the eastern territories because of their 'intensive National Socialist training' – implying they would be used for pogroms. There was also a complaint from the Ministry of Justice in 1941 over Hess urging the corporal punishment of Poles.

The case for the defence lasted barely a day. Hess spent much of his time making comments to his fellow defendants and was twice seized with inexplicable laughter.

Ribbentrop

Dr Martin Horn, Ribbentrop's counsel, had a more formidable task. While minutes of one meeting showed that Ribbentrop was against the lynching of enemy pilots who had attacked civilians, elsewhere he suggested that all captured airmen should suffer instant execution. Documents showed that he had urged foreign governments to exterminate Jews and that his ministry had looted artwork and colluded in the deportation of foreign workers to Germany.

When his turn came, on 25 March, Ribbentrop announced he was too ill to attend. But the prison doctor could find nothing wrong with him and he was compelled to attend the following day.

Horn began by trying to enter into evidence a huge number of documents, many of which had not been translated, were copies or had no proof of authenticity. The tribunal ruled more than half of them inadmissible.

The first witness for the defence was Baron Gustav Steengracht von Moyland, who had been Ribbentrop's adjutant before being promoted to State Secretary at the Foreign Ministry in 1943. Steengracht said: 'The foreign policy, not only on its basic lines, but also usually down to the most minute details, was determined by Hitler himself. Ribbentrop frequently stated that the Führer needed no foreign minister.'

Himmler, Goebbels, Bormann and Goering had a certain influence; Ribbentrop had none. Nevertheless, he had somehow managed to check Hitler's excesses and stayed on in office to prevent someone worse taking over. Steengracht read his testimony from a prepared sheet and was admonished for doing so.

Admiration and veneration

Then Ribbentrop's secretary Margarete Blank was called. She managed to undermine much of Steengracht's testimony, saying: 'Herr von Ribbentrop always showed the greatest admiration and veneration for Adolf Hitler. To enjoy the Führer's confidence, to justify it by his conduct and work was his chief aim.'

Ribbentrop's interpreter was the final witness for his defence. Questioned by Maxwell Fyfe, he confirmed what he had said in his affidavit: 'The general objectives of the Nazi leadership were apparent from the start, namely, the domination of the European continent, to be achieved, first, by the incorporation of all German-speaking groups in the Reich, and secondly, by territorial expansion under the slogan of "*Lebensraum*".'

Sunken and pallid

According to the *Daily Telegraph* newspaper, as Ribbentrop took his place in the witness box: 'his face was drawn, his cheeks were sunken and pallid. . . . His gait was halting as he walked to the witness stand clutching a file of papers.'

He began reading a prepared statement in a lifeless voice, rambling on about the iniquities of the Versailles Treaty and the horrors of Germany's economic collapse. Then came his first meeting with Hitler in 1932 where he thought: 'This man, if anyone, would save Germany from these great difficulties and that distress.'

The following morning, Lawrence reminded the court that both the Versailles Treaty and the history of the Nazi party had already been dealt with. Further discussion of these matters was inadmissible. Nevertheless, Ribbentrop continued a meandering diatribe on how the other nations had ganged up on Germany. The *Daily Telegraph* called it 'a nebulous apologia which only narrowly escaped the stigma of cowardice'. To *The Times*, Ribbentrop's waffle explained why it was impossible to have any diplomatic dealing with Germany before the war. His fellow defendants, who had expected some robust defence of German foreign policy, were in despair.

Ribbentrop and Goering even had a row about it in the dock until they were called to order. Like Hess, Goering then started to read a book. But Andrus would not have it, telling him to stop reading as it was an insult to the tribunal.

'We want war'

Maxwell Fyfe went in for the kill with the minutes of meetings and other documents. Ribbentrop had maintained in his testimony that he did not want war, but when Italian foreign minister Count Gian Galeazzo Ciano had asked him in 1939 whether Germany wanted the Polish Corridor or Danzig, he replied: 'Not any more; we want war.' Then when war had begun he said he was glad about the turn of events because it would be a good thing if the conflict was finished in the lifetime of the Führer.

When Ribbentrop dismissed his discussions with Ciano as 'nothing but diplomatic talk', Maxwell Fyfe asked: 'Don't you think there is any requirement to tell the truth in a political conversation?'

Ribbentrop claimed to have been only an honorary member of the SS, because as an ambassador and later as foreign minister he was considered by Hitler to warrant a uniform and rank. But evidence was entered showing he had applied to join the SS – and was accepted – three years before he became an ambassador. He was presented with a ring and a dagger as a member of the Death's Head Division.

It was established that Ribbentrop had done very well out of becoming a Nazi and had no fewer than six houses. The one at Fuschl was near the group of camps at Mauthausen, shown on a map in the courtroom. There were 33 separate units at the camp, housing 100,000 people. Ribbentrop must have flown over them several times when he went to visit his house. He could hardly maintain he knew nothing about concentration camps.

Fyfe went on to the harsh treatment of partisans. Ribbentrop denied involvement in such things, but the documents recorded him saying 'partisan gangs had to be exterminated, including men, women, and children' and urging 'merciless action' in Norway, Italy and Greece. After Fyfe's cross-examination, Ribbentrop collapsed and had to be helped back to his cell.

Then it was the turn of Edgar Faure, French counsel for the prosecution, to conduct the cross-examination. He reminded Ribbentrop of the testimony which Maxwell Fyfe had read to Goering. In it, the Hungarian leader Miklós Horthy remembered Hitler saying: 'The Reich minister for foreign affairs' – that is, Ribbentrop – 'declared that the Jews should be exterminated, or taken to concentration camps. There was no other possibility.'

All Ribbentrop could say was that he had not used those words.

Keitel

Keitel saw himself as a Prussian officer, though Goering described him as having 'a sergeant's mind inside a field marshal's body'. A lifelong military man, he believed a soldier's job was to obey. His colleagues called him 'Lackeitel' – the lackey. Others knew him as 'Nickesef' – a toy donkey with a constantly nodding head. Two shorthand writers who attended military conferences said they never bothered to write down Keitel's first sentence – it was always identical to Hitler's last.

Throughout the trial, he was immaculately turned out for the occasion and made no apologies for his actions. The Wehrmacht and the soldier were tools of the politicians, he said: 'they are not qualified in my opinion to decide or to judge whether these military operations did or did not constitute a war of aggression.'

Although orders sent out bore Keitel's signature, they were in fact Hitler's orders. These included plans of invasion, orders to seize food and loot in occupied areas, to seize and execute hostages, to lynch commandos and commissars, to deport workers to Germany as slave labour and to maltreat prisoners of war – along with the notorious *Nacht und Nebel* decree. He disapproved and his conscience was clear.

'The traditional training and concept of duty of the German officers, which taught unquestioning obedience to superiors who bore responsibility, led to an attitude – regrettable in retrospect – which caused them to shrink from rebelling against these orders and these methods even when they recognized their illegality and inwardly refuted them,' he said.

Everything was Hitler's fault because he 'abused his authority . . . in an irresponsible way in respect to use'.

There was no opportunity to question an order. At a military conference, 'the Führer arrived, spoke and went out. No one in such a situation could have found an opening to say anything.'

But still Keitel was enamoured of Hitler who he described as self-taught in military matters and, consequently, 'a genius'.

'I was the pupil not the master,' said Keitel.

When Canaris protested about the inhuman treatment of Russian prisoners of war, Keitel wrote: 'These objections arise from the military conception of chivalrous warfare. We are dealing here with the destruction of an ideology and I therefore approve such measures and I sanction them.' In his *Nacht und Nebel* decree, he said: 'Effective and lasting intimidation can only be achieved whether by capital punishment or by means which leave the relatives and the population in the dark about the fate of the culprit. Deportation to Germany serves this purpose.'

And he had issued an order to suppress insurrection in the occupied eastern territories in 1941, saying: 'In order to nip in the bud any conspiracy, the strongest measures should be taken at the first sign of trouble in order to maintain the authority of the occupying power and to prevent the conspiracy from spreading . . . one must bear in mind that in the countries affected, human life has absolutely no value and that a deterrent effect can be achieved only through the application of extraordinarily harsh measures.'

The document demanded the death penalty of 50 or 100 communists for every one German soldier killed. Keitel insisted he had originally written five to ten, but Hitler had changed it, and the German document said: 'in the countries affected human life frequently has no value'.

Only Maxwell Fyfe made any dent in Keitel's haughty demeanour. When Keitel talked of handing a prisoner over to the SD, he implied it was like putting the prisoner into police custody. Fyfe responded: 'You have been at this trial too long to think that handing people over to the SD means police custody. It means concentration camps and a gas chamber, does it not?'

When Keitel proffered a kind of apology for his orders to punish families of Frenchmen found fighting alongside the Russians, and expressed regret that these relatives had been held responsible for 'the misdeeds of their sons', Maxwell Fyfe interjected: 'If you think that is a misdeed, it is not worth our discussing it further.'

The *New York Times* reported that Keitel began to stammer, and was forced to agree that his orders were cruel and despicable. As further blows rained down, he was seen 'leaning back groggily in his chair, groping for words'.

Fyfe aimed one last savage kick at his Prussian pride.

'You were a field marshal, standing in the boots of Blücher, Gneisenau and Moltke.' These were Keitel's military heroes. 'How did you tolerate all these young men being murdered, one after another without making any protest?'

All Keitel could say was that he could add nothing to the statement he had made earlier. His testimony had done nothing to rebut the charges made against him. Witnesses called in his defence were of little help. Dr. Hans Lammers, chief of the Reichschancellery from 1933 to 1945, said that, in his opinion, no programme for the extermination of Jews had ever been set up, though it was possible that Jewish people had been shot in some town or other in wartime. In a subsequent trial, he was sentenced to 20 years, but was released in 1951.

Keitel tried to drop two further defence witnesses – General Adolf Westhoff, chief of prisoners of war, and Max Wielen, the SS chief of police in Bresau. But the tribunal called them to question on affidavits they had given on the Stalag Luft III murders. Their testimony further implicated Goering and Keitel. To the prosecution's frustration, the case against Keitel had lasted seven days.

WILHELM KEITEL

HITLER'S LACKEY

'How in heaven's name can they accuse me of conspiring to wage aggressive war when I was nothing but the mouthpiece to carry out the Führer's wishes? As chief of staff I had no authority whatsoever – no command function – nothing.'

Field Marshal Keitel, the eldest son of a middle-class landowner, was a battle-hardened professional soldier who considered it his duty to obey his commander-in-chief, be he Kaiser or Führer. But the man behind the medals was not a born soldier and he was scorned by his fellow senior officers as a sycophantic toady to Hitler. He was nicknamed '*Lakeitel*' (a pun on the German word for a lackey) and his judgement, both strategic and political, was poor.

UNREALISTIC
Prior to the invasion of Poland, Keitel had rebutted the advice given by the other commanders who warned Hitler that the invasion was certain to ignite a world war. The British, said Keitel, were too decadent, the Americans too apathetic and the French too degenerate to oppose the Wehrmacht.

Some of the generals considered his assessment of the military situation to be so unrealistic that they ignored his orders, at the risk of being reported to Hitler. Others objected to what they saw as his endorsement of the notorious Barbarossa and *Nacht und Nebel* directives to kill captured commandos, POWS, resistance fighters and Russian commissars on sight, in violation of the rules of war. Their objections brought a response from Keitel that was to

Keitel: he served Hitler's purpose as a weak general in a powerful position

count against him at Nuremberg, implicating him in atrocities that brought shame on the Wehrmacht: 'These anxieties belong to the concept of chivalrous warfare. Here we are engaged in the destruction of an ideology. For this reason I approve of the measures and stand by them.'

He also signed the infamous Decree on the Exercise of Military Jurisdiction, which declared, 'For acts committed by members of the Wehrmacht against enemy civilians, there is no obligation to prosecute, even when the act constitutes a military crime or offence.'

Those who knew him as Hitler's 'Yes Man', refused to believe Keitel's assertion that he had 'the sharpest and harshest clashes with Hitler'. Nor could they swallow the notion that he had considered suicide rather than carry out the Führer's murderous orders.

WHAT WAR CRIMES?

Hitler himself complained that Keitel had the brain of a 'cinema usher' and said he had only appointed him chief of staff because he was the ideal 'office manager'.

After signing the surrender of the German armed forces in May 1945, Keitel was taken to Nuremberg to await trial for war crimes. Keitel's jailers soon had the measure of him, now stripped of his insignia and his medals.

They joked that he would have made a fine first sergeant, meaning he was a smug arrogant exhibitionist, incapable of leadership but suited to repetitive drilling and discipline.

The prison psychologist, Leon Goldensohn, found Keitel ingratiating, insincere and highly indignant that he, a military officer of the old school, should be accused of war crimes: 'I was field marshal in name only. I had no troops, no authority – only to carry out Hitler's orders. I was bound to him by oath. One of Hitler's prime ideas was that each minister and functionary was to mind his own business. That's why I learned about some of the [war-crime] business for the first time in this court.

> 'Had I taken my life, I wouldn't have improved things, because this demon [Hitler] went ahead with whatever he wanted and succeeded. . . . He was a demon-like man, possessed of inordinate willpower, who, whenever he had something in his mind, had to accomplish it.'
>
> Wilhelm Keitel

The Fritsch Scandal

In January 1938, Keitel was promoted chief of staff of OKW, the Armed Forces High Command, after his predecessor, General Fritsch, was falsely accused of committing homosexual acts in a public place. The conspiracy to blackmail the general had been cooked up by Himmler and Goering, who hoped to succeed Fritsch.

It was only after the general was exonerated by an army court, and the one eyewitness exposed as a known criminal, that it was discovered there had been a case of mistaken identity. The real blackmail victim was a cavalry officer with a similar-sounding surname, Frisch. But by then the general's reputation had been irreparably damaged. The affair threatened to see the overthrow of the Nazi dictatorship by the outraged generals, but fortunately for Hitler the successful annexation of Austria followed shortly afterwards, appeasing their anger.

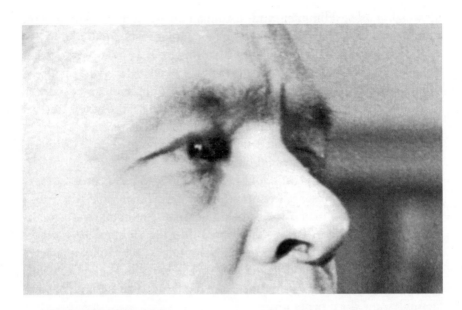

CHAPTER 25

Architects of the Holocaust

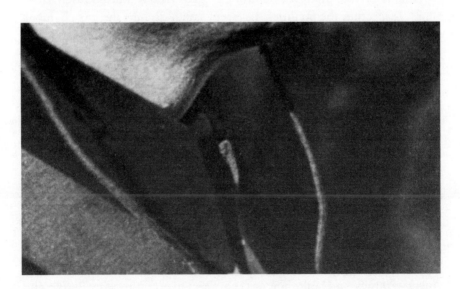

Although Hitler, Himmler and Eichmann were not at Nuremberg, a number of the principal architects of the Holocaust were on hand.

Kaltenbrunner was every inch a Nazi thug, but as he took the stand he appeared pale and nervous. As head of the Reich Security Main Office (RSHA), he had a massive list of charges against him and was also to be tried as a representative of the Gestapo. He denied none of the crimes of which the RSHA and the Gestapo – and the SD under its control – were accused. He simply maintained that he had nothing to do with them. Himmler, he said, had bypassed him.

Kaltenbrunner was cross-examined by American prosecutor Colonel John Amen, who presented damning testimony. First came the orders Kaltenbrunner had issued for British and American commandos to be shot, for SD members to be conscripted into the *Einsatzkommandos*, for anti-Jewish measures to be begun in Denmark, for Hungarian Jews to be worked to death and for 65,000 prisoners to be worked to death in Mauthausen. Kaltenbrunner denied everything. The signatures were facsimiles, the documents forged.

The only camp he had seen was Mauthausen – and it was a quarry, providing stone for the pavements of Vienna. The first he had heard of Auschwitz was in 1943; Himmler told him it was an armaments factory. He had never seen a gas chamber and had never heard of any policy to exterminate Jews – though minutes earlier he had claimed to have stopped the extermination.

Affidavits said that Kaltenbrunner had visited Mauthausen three times. Inspecting the facilities, he 'went laughing into the gas chamber. Then the people were brought from the bunker to be executed, and then all three kinds of executions: hanging, shooting in the back of the neck and gassing, were demonstrated'.

'Not a single word of these statements is true,' said Kaltenbrunner.

He later complained: 'For a whole year I have had to submit to this insult of being called a liar.'

Hoess

Kaltenbrunner's chief witness for the defence was Rudolf Hoess, the commandant of Auschwitz. Hoess admitted to killing more than two million men, women and children, and took a certain pride in his work: Auschwitz was much more efficient than Treblinka, for example; Treblinka's gas chambers only accommodated 200 at a time, while at Auschwitz they had built their gas chambers to accommodate 2,000; and the Zyklon B they used at Auschwitz was much better than Treblinka's carbon monoxide gas.

Colonel Amen read parts of Hoess' affidavit:

It took from three to fifteen minutes to kill the people in the death chamber, depending upon climatic conditions. We knew when the people were dead because their screaming stopped. We usually waited about one half hour before we opened the doors and removed the bodies. After the bodies were removed our special Kommandos took off the rings and extracted the gold from the teeth of the corpses.

'Is that true and correct, witness?' he asked.

Hoess said 'Yes' and Amen continued:

Children of tender years were invariably exterminated since by reason of their youth they were unable to work. Still another improvement we made over Treblinka was that at Treblinka the victims almost always knew that they were to be exterminated and at Auschwitz we endeavoured to fool the victims into thinking that they were to go through a delousing process. Of course, frequently they realized our true intentions and we sometimes had riots and difficulties due to that fact. Very frequently women would hide their children under their clothes, but of course when we found them we would send the children in to be exterminated. We were required to carry out these exterminations in secrecy but of course the foul and nauseating stench from the continuous burning of bodies permeated the entire area and all of the people living in the surrounding communities knew that exterminations were going on at Auschwitz.

'Is that all true and correct, witness?'

Hoess said, 'Yes.' He was equally frank about the medical experiments that were carried out. This shocking testimony was received in silence. Over lunch the defendants were also silent, though Goering and Doenitz said that Hoess must be from southern Germany: no Prussian could have done such things.

'I read only a few decrees signed by Kaltenbrunner; most of them were signed by Müller,' said Hoess. 'All mass executions through

The gates of Auschwitz, bearing the now infamous slogan 'Work Sets You Free'

gassing took place under the direct order, supervision and responsibility of RSHA. I received all orders for carrying out these mass executions directly from RSHA.'

It was easy for Amen to get Hoess to admit that Müller was simply signing the orders as the representative of Kaltenbrunner, who was head of the RSHA.

At his trial in Warsaw, Hoess was accused of murdering 3.5 million people. He protested: 'No, only two-and-a-half – the rest died from disease and starvation.' He was hanged.

Rosenberg

Jackson was furious when Rosenberg requested copies of documents, some 25,000 sheets in all. Paper, Jackson pointed out, was 'a scarce commodity today'. His counsel also asked for 260 extra copies of Rosenberg's book of documents to be printed for the press.

'The United States cannot be acting as press agent for the distribution of anti-Semitic literature,' Jackson protested.

While Rosenberg was one of the chief theoreticians of anti-Semitism, the charges against him focused on his time as minister for the occupied eastern territories. Under cross-examination, Dodd confronted him with his own order that 'all inhabitants of the occupied eastern territories are subject to the public liability for compulsory work.'

Then there was a speech he had delivered in 1941, in which he said: 'The job of feeding the German people stands this year, without doubt, at the top of the list of Germany's claims on the East. . . . We see absolutely no reason for any obligation on our part to feed also the Russian people with the products of that surplus-territory. We know that this is a harsh necessity, beyond feelings. A very extensive evacuation will be necessary, without any doubt, and it is sure that the future will hold very hard years in store for the Russians.'

Rosenberg pointed out that Russia had not signed the Geneva Convention and argued that the Hague Conventions did not apply to the Soviet Union since it was 'considered dissolved'.

As Rosenberg had no real defence against the charges against him, he was allowed a little latitude.

'For hours he maundered on,' the *Manchester Guardian* reported. 'It was no more possible to grasp what he was saying than to seize a handful of cloud. Those who could went to get coffee or took an early lunch; others such as guards and messengers had to fall asleep.'

Hans Frank

The 42 volumes of Frank's diary were enough to hang him. A former counsellor for Hitler, he was a slick operator in the courtroom. Asked by Seidl, his counsel: 'Did you ever participate in the annihilation of Jews?' Frank replied: 'I say "yes"; and the reason why I say "yes" is because, having lived through the five months of this trial, and particularly after having heard the testimony of the witness Hoess, my conscience does not allow me to throw the responsibility solely on these minor people. I myself have never installed an extermination camp for Jews, or promoted the existence of such camps; but if Adolf Hitler personally has laid that dreadful responsibility on his people, then it is mine, too, for we have fought against Jewry for years; and we have indulged in the most horrible utterances. My own diary bears witness against me. Therefore, it is no more than my duty to answer your question in this connection with "yes". A thousand years will pass and still this guilt of Germany will not have been erased.'

His admission of guilt won Frank no friends in the dock, nor were the court swayed by this semblance of contrition.

Wilhelm Frick

As minister of the interior from 1933 to 1943, Frick put in place much of the apparatus of repression and went on to become 'protector' of Bohemia and Moravia. But although he was a lawyer, he declined to go in the witness box to defend himself. The suspicion was that he wanted to avoid questions about stolen money, which he had hidden away for his wife and children.

Frick's counsel, Dr Otto Pannenberg, called Hans Bernd Gisevius, a former peacetime Gestapo officer who had been sacked and had compiled dossiers of others' crimes. With the help of Canaris, he had escaped to Switzerland. He was also going to be a witness for Schacht.

Gisevius' contribution to Frick's defence was to say that he was 'a minister with no personal executive power'. Himmler overrode him; he had no access to Hitler and no influence over him. But Frick had signed the decree legitimizing the murder of Roehm and the others on the 'Night of the Long Knives'. He had also been in charge of the running of the concentration camps and was fully informed of the abuses that went on there.

With Gisevius on the stand, Jackson was free to cross-examine him about the other defendants. Ribbentrop, Jodl and Funk had wielded more influence over Hitler than they let on; Neurath and Papen had been fully aware of the activities of the Gestapo, while Keitel had known about the atrocities carried out by the Wehrmacht and the SS, the use of slave labour and the extermination of the Jews.

But, according to Gisevius, Goering was the biggest crook of all. Not only had he planned the Reichstag fire, he had arranged the murder of one of the perpetrators who had spoken to a magistrate when he had not been paid. What's more, Goering – along with Himmler and Hitler – had drawn up the list of those to be murdered during the Roehm purge (another name for the 'Night of the Long Knives'). Goering was so angry at this testimoney that he stood up in the dock haranguing all and sundry until he was manhandled away to the lift.

Streicher

The case against Streicher was weak. Although the anti-Semitism stirred up by his newspaper *Der Stürmer* had led to the Holocaust, he had killed no one. He had fallen from favour in 1938 and in 1940 had been stripped of his office and retired to private life. But instead of leaving his counsel to argue that there was no case to answer, Streicher insisted on taking the stand.

He began with an attack on his own counsel, Dr Hans Marx, saying he had been intimidated by the communist press. Streicher then alleged that he had been kept naked in his cell, though Fritzsche had fashioned a pair of shorts for him to prevent him doing his morning exercises in the nude. He refused to wear them. He also claimed he had been made to 'kiss a negro's feet' and, when he had asked for a drink of water, had been made to drink from a latrine.

'These are the sort of things the Gestapo has been blamed for,' said Streicher.

Then he began a rant about how the Jews had seized power in Germany in 1918. He had begun his own movement in Franconia but, three years later, when he saw Hitler speak in Munich 'drenched in perspiration, radiant', he handed it over, allowing the Nazi party to expand outside Bavaria. Various allegations made against him for rape and indecent behaviour were dismissed.

Streicher admitted organizing a boycott of Jewish businesses and claimed to have contributed indirectly to the Nuremberg Laws. On Kristallnacht, the main synagogue in Nuremberg had been burned down. He justified this on architectural grounds and submitted a photograph in evidence. He even gave a diatribe on the subject of Jews being responsible for ritual murder.

'A statement of fact'

None of the other defence counsels wished to cross-examine Streicher. The task fell to Lieutenant Colonel J. M. G. Griffith-Jones. He did not even look at Streicher, who continued his anti-Semitic rants. In 1943 Streicher had referred to Hitler's promise to 'free the world from its Jewish tormentors', writing: 'How wonderful it is to know that this great man and leader is following up this promise with practical action.' Yet he denied knowing of any organized killing of Jews. He claimed to have been a subscriber to the Swiss publication *Israelitisches Wochenblatt* ('Israeli Weekly'), but could not recall any of the articles it carried about the dispossession and murder of Jews. In the press he continued to demand the 'annihilation' of the Jews. In *Der Stürmer* he referred to Jews as 'a nation of bloodsuckers and extortionists'.

Asked, 'Do you think that's preaching racial hatred?' he answered: 'No. It is not preaching racial hatred. It is just a statement of fact.'

There were arguments over what he meant when he used the word *vernichtet* – 'annihilate'.

Griffith-Jones read another extract from *Der Stürmer*: 'A punitive expedition must come against the Jews in Russia. A punitive expedition which will provide the same fate for them that every murderer and criminal must expect. Death sentence and execution. The Jews in Russia must be killed. They must be exterminated root and branch.'

Streicher denied writing this. But he had been the editor of the newspaper and was forced to take responsibility for printing it.

Maxwell Fyfe decided it was best not to cross-examine Streicher's witnesses, but rather to treat them with disdain. In the hands of Dr Marx, they did more harm than good anyway. One of them was Streicher's wife, who testified that her husband had spent the war on his farm, editing the newspaper, and had had no contact with Hitler. She was an attractive blonde woman, twenty years his junior. As she left the stand, Jodl remarked: 'Wondrous are the ways of love.' Lawrence ruled that Streicher's vast collection of pornography was no business of the tribunal.

RUDOLF HOESS

THE DEVOTED FATHER WHO MURDERED CHILDREN

'It is tragic that, although I was by nature gentle, good-natured, and very helpful, I became the greatest destroyer of human beings who carried out every order to exterminate people no matter what.'

Behind the metal gate the children played in the garden, squealing with delight as they rode their pedal cars on the paved paths around the flowerbeds. There were five: Klaus, his younger brother Hans-Rudolf, their two sisters Ingebrigitt and Heidetraut and the baby, Annegret, cradled in her mother's arms.

SEPARATING HOME AND WORK
It was an idyllic life. The house was a miniature villa in the Bavarian style, there were maids to tidy up their toys and every evening their father came home

Hoess: mild-mannered family man?

from work to sit with them at the dinner table, to play hide-and-seek, to read to them and tuck them into bed at night. There was only one time they could remember him being angry with them and they still didn't fully understand why. Their Polish maid Janina had sewn patches on their clothes and made an armband with the word 'capo' (trustee) on it for the older boy, after they had asked her to make them cloth 'badges' like the 'others' wore so they could play 'us' and 'them'. But when their father saw them, he flew into a rage, ushered them inside and tore off the armband and badges.

Every morning 'papa' would button up his tunic, straighten his cap and kiss their mother before going off to work. There were only two rules he insisted upon. No one talked about his work – they only knew it was a job requiring great responsibility and that it was 'important' – and none of the children was permitted to go beyond the garden gate.

However, Klaus was old enough to guess what was going on. From an upper window he could see the chimneys that rose into the sky on the other side of the high wall surrounding their garden and he knew what the black ash was that spewed from those chimneys. He didn't say anything, but when his mother said they should wash the 'dust' from their freshly picked strawberries before they ate them, he made sure his younger brothers and sisters did as they were told.

PROUD BOAST

Rudolf Hoess was personally responsible for the deaths of an estimated 2.5 million people at Auschwitz, the extermination camp in Galicia, Poland. He had been made camp commandant in 1940 after he had proved his usefulness and efficiency, first at Dachau and then at Sachsenhausen.

Hoess proudly boasted that he could 'get rid of 10,000 people in 24 hours' and saw nothing criminal in supervising the most notorious of the Nazi death factories, where the sadistic Dr Mengele carried out his perverse medical experiments on living prisoners, many of them women and children. Hoess excused his actions by reminding himself that the victims had already been condemned to death by the Gestapo. From time to time, the dreaded secret police would send consignments of condemned prisoners to be killed by lethal injections of benzene, which the camp doctors administered as casually as if they were conventional inoculations.

CHILDREN KILLED FIRST

Hoess also oversaw the actions of subordinates such as Wilhelm Boger, who was seen torturing inmates by beating their genitals until they lost consciousness or died as they lay naked on a metal contraption of his own devising. Sometimes the SS guards didn't wait to process the victims, but killed them indiscriminately.

Boger was seen by another observer beating a little boy to death by banging his head repeatedly against a brick wall, then casually eating the apple the child had been holding. Hoess was not ignorant of such horrors, as he coolly admitted on the stand at Nuremberg.

CHOOSING THE BEST METHOD

Hoess placed great faith in duty, which had been instilled in him from an early age by his father, a pious Catholic shopkeeper who had served as an army officer in German East Africa and who had wanted his son to become a priest.

So when his superior, SS Reichsführer Heinrich Himmler, ordered Hoess to initiate the liquidation of the prisoners in 1941, he obeyed. The order had come from the highest authority and it was not for him to question it. Hitler had given orders 'for the Final Solution of the Jewish question' and had 'chosen the Auschwitz camp for this purpose'. It was more than duty, it was an honour.

> The 'Final Solution' of the Jewish question meant the complete extermination of all Jews in Europe. I was ordered to establish extermination facilities at Auschwitz in 6/1941 . . . I visited Treblinka to find out how they carried out their exterminations. The camp commandant at Treblinka told me that he had liquidated 80,000 in the course of one half year. . . . He used monoxide gas, and I did not think that his methods were very efficient. So when I set up the extermination building at Auschwitz, I used Zyklon B, which was a crystallized prussic acid which we dropped into the death chamber from a small opening. It took from 3–15 minutes to kill the people in the death chamber, depending upon climatic conditions. . . . Another improvement we made over Treblinka was that we built our gas chamber to accommodate 2,000 people at one time, whereas at Treblinka their 10 gas chambers only accommodated 200 people each.

Hoess took a keen personal interest in the process, observing the effects to satisfy his own curiosity.

> The gassing was carried out in the detention cells of Block 11. Protected by a gas mask, I watched the killing myself. In the crowded cells, death came instantaneously the moment the Zyklon B was thrown in. A short, almost smothered cry, and it was all over. . . . I must even admit that this

gassing set my mind at rest, for the mass extermination of the Jews was to start soon, and at that time neither Eichmann nor I was certain as to how these mass killings were to be carried out. It would be by gas, but we did not know which gas and how it was to be used. Now we had the gas, and we had established a procedure.

DEDICATION TO DUTY

In 1943 Hoess was rewarded for his dedication by being appointed chief inspector of the camps in Poland and was praised for being a 'true pioneer' in an SS report which commended him for his 'new ideas and educational methods'. He admitted to only one failing, his reluctance to force screaming children into the gas chambers while they begged for their lives.

I did, however, always feel ashamed of this weakness of mine after I talked to Adolf Eichmann. He explained to me that it was especially the children who have to be killed first, because where was the logic in killing a generation of older people and leaving alive a generation of young people who can be possible avengers of their parents and can constitute a new biological cell for the re-emerging of this people?

After his capture he was interviewed by a Polish psychiatrist, Professor Batawia, who observed that Hoess' childhood was: 'stamped with principles of military discipline and religious fanaticism, accompanied by constant emphasis of sin and guilt and the need to do penance. Hoess grew up in a family atmosphere in which expressions of love, freedom from worry, spontaneity, and humour were paralyzed; where everything the child did was judged by strict moral standards, where the word "duty" had almost mystical significance and disobedience in trifles was almost a crime.'

Nazi ideology became Hoess' new religion and he considered it a mortal sin to question an order. In his prison memoirs, he claimed that his greatest fear was that any lack of resolve on his part would be seen as cowardice, unworthy of a member of the Aryan Master Race, so he cultivated an attitude of icy indifference. He had nothing personally against the Jews, he declared, but duty demanded that he should obey without recourse to his own conscience.

After being found guilty, Hoess was taken back to Auschwitz in April 1947 and hanged on a specially erected gallows within sight of the villa he had shared with his family.

CHAPTER 26

The Final Statements

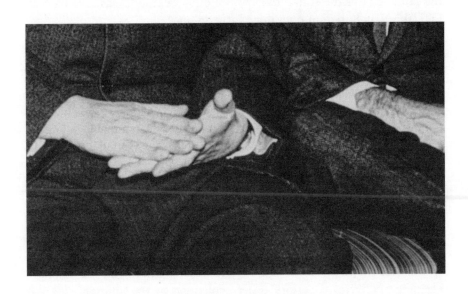

The court had now been sitting for more than 170 days and the bench was anxious to bring proceedings to a speedy conclusion. To avoid needless repetition, defence counsels were limited to half a day for their closing arguments. These were to be handed over in advance, so they could be cut if necessary. Steinbauer was asked to remove a page and a half on the influence of Beethoven and Brahms on the cultural life of Vienna. In the courtroom Lawrence said: 'I think it is possible for the tribunal to become acquainted with the history of Austria without having it read to them as a part of your argument.'

Sections entitled 'The Development of the History of the Intellectual Pursuit' and 'Renaissance, Subjectivism, the French Revolution and National Socialism' were cut from Kaufmann's speech.

Lawrence chastised him further in court, saying: 'Dr Kaufmann, the tribunal proposes, as far as it can, to decide the cases which it has got to decide in accordance with law and not with the sort of very general, very vague and misty philosophical doctrine with which you appear to be dealing in the first twelve pages of your speech, and, therefore . . . they would very much prefer that you begin on page thirteen.'

Nevertheless, Kaufmann was able to get away with a passage that began: 'The deepest and at the same time most fatal reason for the Hitler phenomenon lies in the metaphysical domain . . .'

Rebecca West declared: 'The courtroom was a citadel of boredom.' She also described it as 'water-torture, boredom falling drop by drop on the same spot of the soul'; 'the symbol of Nuremberg was a yawn' and that 'this was boredom on a huge historic scale'.

Professor Hermann Jahrreiss, assistant counsel for Jodl, was also allowed to address general legal matters brought up by the defence. Firstly, he argued that the tribunal could hardly be impartial, because the judges represented the victors while the defendants were the vanquished. But the Charter prohibited any challenge to the validity of the tribunal.

Secondly, the waging of aggressive war had not previously been a crime. The Kellogg–Briand Pact had condemned but not outlawed it. This issue had been addressed in the prosecution's opening speeches. Further laws were supposed to be applied in general, not devised for a single special case, nor was there a precedent in international law for individuals being held responsible for acts committed by a state.

Then there was the *Führerprinzip* – the Nazi leadership system whereby all orders emanated from Hitler. Reading the advanced copy of Jahrreiss' speech, Maxwell Fyfe said that the *Führerprinzip* was merely the disguised pleading of obeying superiors' orders, ruled out by the Charter.

The resurrection of Jackson

Jackson was still smarting from the mauling that Goering had given him. But in his closing statement for the prosecution, he returned to the rhetorical heights he had scaled at the outset.

'In eight months – a short time as state trials go – we have introduced evidence which embraces as vast and varied a panorama of events as has ever been compressed within the framework of a litigation,' he said. 'It is impossible in summation to do more than outline with bold strokes the vitals of this trial's mad and melancholy record, which will live as the historical text of the twentieth century's shame and depravity.'

He dismissed any challenge to the legitimacy of the proceedings.

'The defendants denounce the law under which their accounting is asked. Their dislike for the law which condemns them is not original. It has been remarked before that "No thief e'er felt the halter draw with good opinion of the law."

'Of one thing we may be sure. The future will never have to ask, with misgiving, what could the Nazis have said in their favour. History will know that whatever could be said, they were allowed to say. They have been given the kind of a trial which they, in the days of their pomp and power, never gave to any man.'

Summarizing the case, he showed that the defendants were joined in a conspiracy by the way they seized power and subjugated Germany, turning it into a police state. Jackson seized the opportunity to take a swing at Goering, who had announced publicly in 1933: 'Whoever in the future raises a hand against a representative of the National Socialist movement or of the State must know that he will lose his life in a very short while.'

Their enemies were legion. 'Therefore, the concentration camps have been created, where we have first confined thousands of communists and social democrat functionaries,' Goering had said the following year.

They began their preparations to wage wars of aggression in contravention of the Versailles Treaty as soon as they seized power. And four days after Japan had attacked without warning at Pearl Harbor, Germany declared war on the United States without provocation.

The defendants had deliberately breached both the Hague and Geneva conventions to which Germany was party, violating the rules of war. They had plundered the countries they had occupied and enslaved their people. And they had persecuted and murdered Jews and Christians: Jackson detailed some of the crimes, then quoted the defendants condemning themselves out of their own mouths. 'These, then, were the five great substantive crimes of the Nazi regime,' Jackson said. 'Their commission, which cannot be denied, stands admitted.'

Criminals

Jackson then turned his attention to the defendants in the dock.

'Goering was half militarist and half gangster,' he said. 'He stuck his pudgy finger in every pie . . .

'The zealot Hess, before succumbing to wanderlust, was the engineer tending the party machinery, passing orders and propaganda down to the Leadership Corps, supervising every aspect of party activities, and maintaining the organization as a loyal and ready instrument of power . . .

'The duplicitous Ribbentrop, the salesman of deception . . . was detailed to pour wine on the troubled waters of suspicion by preaching the gospel of limited and peaceful intentions.

'Keitel, the weak and willing tool, delivered the armed forces, the instrument of aggression, over to the party and directed them in executing its felonious designs.

'Kaltenbrunner, the grand inquisitor, took up the bloody mantle of Heydrich to stifle opposition and terrorize compliance, and buttressed the power of National Socialism on a foundation of guiltless corpses.

'It was Rosenberg, the intellectual high priest of the "master race", who provided the doctrine of hatred which gave the impetus for the annihilation of Jewry, and who put his infidel theories into practice against the eastern occupied territories. His woolly philosophy also added boredom to the long list of Nazi atrocities.

'The fanatical Frank, who solidified Nazi control by establishing the new order of authority without law, so that the will of the party was the only test of legality, proceeded to export his lawlessness to Poland, which he governed with the lash of Caesar and whose population he reduced to sorrowing remnants.

'Frick, the ruthless organizer, helped the party to seize power, supervised the police agencies to ensure that it stayed in power, and chained the economy of Bohemia and Moravia to the German war machine.

'Streicher, the venomous Bulgarian, manufactured and distributed obscene racial libels which incited the populace to accept and assist the progressively savage operations of "race purification".

'As minister of economics Funk accelerated the pace of rearmament, and as Reichsbank president banked for the SS the gold teeth-fillings of concentration camp victims – probably the most ghoulish collateral in banking history.

'It was Schacht, the facade of starched respectability, who in the early days provided the window dressing, the bait for the hesitant, and whose wizardry later made it possible for Hitler to finance the colossal rearmament programme, and to do it secretly.

'Doenitz, Hitler's legatee of defeat, promoted the success of the Nazi aggressions by instructing his pack of submarine killers to conduct warfare at sea with the illegal ferocity of the jungle.

'Raeder, the political admiral, stealthily built up the German navy in defiance of the Versailles Treaty, and then put it to use in a series of aggressions which he had taken a leading part in planning.

'Sauckel, the greatest and cruellest slaver since the pharaohs of Egypt, produced desperately needed manpower by driving foreign peoples into the land of bondage on a scale unknown even in the ancient days of tyranny in the kingdom of the Nile.

'Jodl, betrayer of the traditions of his profession, led the Wehrmacht in violating its own code of military honour in order to carry out the barbarous aims of Nazi policy.

'Von Papen, pious agent of an infidel regime, held the stirrup while Hitler vaulted into the saddle, lubricated the Austrian annexation, and devoted his diplomatic cunning to the service of Nazi objectives abroad.

'Von Schirach, poisoner of a generation, initiated the German youth in Nazi doctrine, trained them in legions for service in the SS and Wehrmacht and delivered them up to the party as fanatic, unquestioning executors of its will.

'Seyss-Inquart, spearhead of the Austrian fifth column, took over the government of his own country only to make a present of it to Hitler, and then, moving north, brought terror and oppression to the Netherlands and pillaged its economy for the benefit of the German juggernaut.

'Von Neurath, the old-school diplomat, who cast the pearls of his experience before Nazis, guided Nazi diplomacy in the early years, soothed the fears of prospective victims, and, as Reich Protector of Bohemia and Moravia, strengthened the German position for the coming attack on Poland.

'Speer, as minister of armaments and production, joined in planning and executing the programme to dragoon prisoners of war and foreign workers into German war industries, which waxed in output while the labourers waned in starvation.

'Fritzsche, radio propaganda chief, by manipulation of the truth goaded German public opinion into frenzied support of the regime and anaesthetized the independent judgement of the population so that they did without question their masters' bidding.

'And Bormann, who has not accepted our invitation to this reunion, sat at the throttle of the vast and powerful engine of the party, guiding it in the ruthless execution of Nazi policies, from the scourging of the Christian Church to the lynching of captive Allied airmen.'

The Führer principle

Jackson also dismissed the defence of the *Führerprinzip* effortlessly:

> *I admit that Hitler was the chief villain. But for the defendants to put all blame on him is neither manly nor true. We know that even the head of the state has the same limits to his senses and to the hours of his days as do lesser men. He must rely on others to be his eyes and ears as to most that goes on in a great empire. Other legs must run his errands; other hands must execute his plans. On whom did Hitler rely for such things more than upon these men in the dock? Who led him to believe he had an invincible air armada if not Goering? Who kept disagreeable facts from him? Did not Goering forbid Field Marshal Milch to warn Hitler that in his opinion Germany was not equal to the war upon Russia? . . . Who led Hitler, utterly untravelled himself, to believe in the indecision and timidity of democratic peoples if not Ribbentrop, von Neurath and von Papen? Who fed his illusion of German invincibility if not Keitel, Jodl, Raeder and Doenitz? Who kept his hatred of the Jews inflamed more than Streicher and Rosenberg? Who would Hitler say deceived him about conditions in concentration camps if not Kaltenbrunner, even as he would deceive us?*

Jackson went on to demolish whatever other arguments they had put up on their defence.

> *Besides outright false statements and double talk, there are also other circumventions of truth in the nature of fantastic explanations and absurd professions. Streicher has solemnly*

maintained that his only thought with respect to the Jews was to resettle them on the island of Madagascar. His reason for destroying synagogues, he blandly said, was only because they were architecturally offensive. Rosenberg was stated by his counsel to have always had in mind a 'chivalrous solution' to the Jewish problem. When it was necessary to remove Schuschnigg after the Anschluss, Ribbentrop would have had us believe that the Austrian chancellor was resting at a 'villa'. It was left to cross-examination to reveal that the 'villa' was Buchenwald concentration camp. The record is full of other examples of dissimulations and evasions. Even Schacht showed that he, too, had adopted the Nazi attitude that truth is any story which succeeds. Confronted on cross-examination with a long record of broken vows and false words, he declared in justification – and I quote from the record: 'I think you can score many more successes when you want to lead someone if you don't tell them the truth than if you tell them the truth.'

This was the philosophy of the National Socialists. When for years they have deceived the world, and masked falsehood with plausibilities, can anyone be surprised that they continue their habits of a lifetime in this dock? Credibility is one of the main issues of this trial. Only those who have failed to learn the bitter lessons of the last decade can doubt that men who have always played on the unsuspecting credulity of generous opponents would not hesitate to do the same, now.

Jackson concluded with a Shakespearean flourish, saying:

It is against such a background that these defendants now ask this tribunal to say that they are not guilty of planning, executing or conspiring to commit this long list of crimes and wrongs. They stand before the record of this trial as bloodstained Gloucester stood by the body of his slain king. He begged of the widow, as they beg of you: 'Say I slew them not.' And the Queen replied, 'Then say they were not slain. But dead they are . . . ' If you were to say of these men that they are not guilty, it would be as true to say that there has been no war, there are no slain, there has been no crime.

Sir Hartley Shawcross

Returning from his duties as attorney general in Britain, Sir Hartley Shawcross gave the closing address for the British delegation.

While Shawcross admitted that they were there to determine the legal guilt of the defendants, there were wider considerations.

'That these defendants participated in and are morally guilty of crimes so frightful that the imagination staggers and reels back at their very contemplation is not in doubt,' he said. 'Let the words of the defendant Frank, which were repeated to you this morning, be well remembered:

> *Thousands of years will pass and this guilt of Germany will not be erased. Total and totalitarian war, waged in defiance of solemn undertakings and in breach of treaties; great cities, from Coventry to Stalingrad, reduced to rubble, the countryside laid waste and now the inevitable aftermath of war so fought – hunger and disease stalking through the world; millions of people homeless, maimed, bereaved.*

> *And in their graves, crying out, not for vengeance but that this shall not happen again: ten million who might be living in peace and happiness at this hour, soldiers, sailors, airmen and civilians killed in battles that ought never to have been.*

> *Nor was that the only or the greatest crime. In all our countries when perhaps in the heat of passion or for other motives which impair restraint some individual is killed, the murder becomes a sensation, our compassion is aroused, nor do we rest until the criminal is punished and the rule of law is vindicated. Shall we do less when not one but on the lowest computation twelve million men, women and children, are done to death? Not in battle, not in passion, but in the cold, calculated, deliberate attempt to destroy nations and races, to disintegrate the traditions, the institutions and the very existence of free and ancient states. Twelve million murders. Two-thirds of the Jews in Europe exterminated, more than six million of them on the killers' own figures. Murder conducted like some mass production industry in the gas chambers and the ovens of Auschwitz, Dachau, Treblinka, Buchenwald, Mauthausen, Majdanek and Oranienburg.*

And is the world to overlook the revival of slavery in Europe, slavery on a scale which involved seven million men, women and children taken from their homes, treated as beasts, starved, beaten and murdered?

Acts of aggression

Shawcross went on to list the acts of aggression committed by Nazi Germany up to and including the invasion of the Soviet Union in 1941:

In no single case did a declaration of war precede military action. How many thousands of innocent, inoffensive men, women and children, sleeping in their beds in the happy belief that their country was and would remain at peace, were suddenly blown into eternity by death dropped on them without warning from the skies? In what respect does the guilt of any one of these men differ from the common murderer creeping stealthily to do his victims to death in order that he may rob them of their belongings?

In every single case, as the documents make clear, this was the common plan.

Then quoting the documents, he said:

The attack must be 'blitzartig schnell' – without warning, with the speed of lightning – Austria, Czechoslovakia, Poland – Raeder repeating Keitel's directive for 'heavy blows struck by surprise' – Denmark, Norway, Belgium, Holland, Russia. As Hitler had said in the presence of a number of these men: 'Considerations of right or wrong or treaties do not enter into the matter.' . . .

Every one of these men knew of these plans at one stage or another in their development. Every one of these men acquiesced in this technique, knowing full well what it must represent in terms of human life. How can any one of them now say he was not a party to common murder in its most ruthless form?

Shawcross again addressed Jahrreiss legal arguments. But the real point was that the defendants were common murderers. To reinforce this he reread the testimony of Hermann Graebe on the massacre of local Jews he had witnessed in the Ukraine. Rebecca West recorded that at this point, 'all the defendants wriggled on their seats, like children rated at by a schoolmaster, while their faces grew old'.

Shawcross continued:

In one way the fate of these men means little: their personal power for evil lies for ever broken; they have convicted and discredited each other and finally destroyed the legend they created round the figure of their leader. But on their fate great issues must still depend, for the ways of truth and righteousness between the nations of the world, the hope of future international co-operation in the administration of law and justice are in your hands. This trial must form a milestone in the history of civilization, not only bringing retribution to these guilty men, not only marking that right shall in the end triumph over evil, but also that the ordinary people of the world – and I make no distinction now between friend and foe – are now determined that the individual must transcend the state.

Not to be outdone by Jackson quoting Shakespeare, Shawcross concluded with a few words from Goethe:

You will remember when you come to give your decision the story of Graebe, but not in vengeance – in a determination that these things shall not occur again. The father – do you remember? – pointed to the sky, and seemed to say something to his boy.

Last words

On 31 August, the defendants were permitted to give short speeches, which were to be their final statements to the German people. Goering said: 'I wish to state expressly that I condemn these terrible mass murders to the utmost, and cannot understand them in the least. But I should like to state clearly once more before the high tribunal that I have never decreed the murder of a single individual at any time, and neither did I decree any other atrocities or tolerate them, while I had the power and the knowledge to prevent them . . .

'I did not want a war, nor did I bring it about. I did everything to prevent it by negotiations. After it had broken out, I did everything to assure victory. Since the three greatest powers on Earth, together with many other nations, were fighting against us, we finally succumbed to their tremendous superiority. I stand up for the things that I have done, but I deny most emphatically that my actions were dictated by the desire to subjugate foreign peoples by wars, to murder them, to rob them, or to enslave them, or to commit atrocities or crimes.'

Later, at lunch, von Papen asked him simply: 'Who in the world is responsible for all this destruction if not you?'

Everyone was surprised that Hess wanted to speak. He had a five-page statement that he read seated. It was rambling and incoherent. Lawrence cut him short, insisting that these final pleas should last for no more than 20 minutes.

Hess concluded: 'I was permitted to work for many years of my life under the greatest son whom my people has brought forth in its thousand-year history. Even if I could, I would not want to erase this period of time from my existence. I am happy to know that I have done my duty, to my people, my duty as a German, as a National Socialist, as a loyal follower of my Führer. I do not regret anything.'

Ribbentrop did his case little good when he read a telegram from Stalin received in 1939 after the invasion of Poland, saying: 'The friendship of Germany and the Soviet Union, based on the blood which they have shed together, has every prospect of being a firm and lasting one.'

Keitel said: 'I believed, but I erred, and I was not in a position to prevent what ought to have been prevented. That is my guilt.'

Kaltenbrunner complained: 'I am accused here because substitutes are needed for the missing Himmler . . .'

Rosenberg claimed that he had done 'honest service' for his ideology and said: 'I understood my struggle, just as the struggle of many thousands of my comrades, to be one conducted for the noblest idea.'

Frank regretted that Hitler had left no final statement – 'Amid the deepest distress of his people, he found no comforting word.'

Frick insisted that he had a clear conscience. 'My entire life was spent in the service of my people and my fatherland,' he said.

Streicher said that in *Der Stürmer* he had advocated Zionism. 'I did not want the Jewish problem to be solved by violence.'

In tears, Funk admitted that he had made many mistakes. 'I, too, have let myself be deceived in many things and I frankly acknowledge . . . that I have let myself be deceived all too easily, and in many ways have been too unconcerned and too gullible. Therein I see my guilt,' he said.

'To be sure, I erred politically,' said Schacht. 'I never claimed to be a politician. . . . My political mistake was not realizing the extent of Hitler's criminal nature at an early enough time. But I did not stain my hands with one single illegal or immoral act.'

Doenitz maintained his justification of submarine warfare and stuck up for the Führer principle that brought 'a feeling of happiness such as the entire nation had never known before'. However, in retrospect the *Führerprinzip* must be wrong 'because apparently human nature is not in a position to use the power of this principle for good, without falling victim to the temptations of this power'.

Raeder said: 'I have done my duty as a soldier because it was my conviction that this was the best way for me to serve the German people and fatherland, for which I have lived and for which I am prepared to die at any moment.'

Schirach made an appeal on behalf of German youth – that it 'be declared free of guilt. Joyfully it will grasp the hand which is stretched out to it across the ruins and debris,' he said.

Sauckel also cried when he said: 'I have been shaken to the very depths of my soul by the atrocities revealed in this trial . . . I dedicated myself to socialist love and justice toward those whose only wealth is their labour and, at the same time, to the destiny of my nation.'

Jodl, too, was unrepentant, saying: 'I believe and avow that a man's duty toward his people and fatherland stands above every other. To carry out this duty was for me an honour, and the highest law. May this duty be supplanted in some happier future by an even higher one, by the duty toward humanity.'

'When I examine my conscience,' said von Papen, 'I do not find any guilt where the prosecution has looked for it and claims to have found it. But where is the man without guilt and without faults?' He explained: 'The power of evil was stronger than the power of good and drove Germany inevitably into catastrophe.'

To Seyss-Inquart, Hitler was still the messiah: 'To me he remains the man who made Greater Germany a fact in German history. I served this man. And now? I cannot today cry "Crucify him," since yesterday I cried "Hosanna."'

Speer sounded a warning against the dangers posed by the weapons developed during the war. 'In five or ten years the technique of warfare will make it possible to fire rockets from continent to continent with uncanny precision. By atomic power it can destroy one million people in the centre of New York in a matter of seconds with a rocket operated,

Wedding rings removed from the victims of the concentration camps

perhaps, by only ten men, invisible, without previous warning, faster than sound, by day and by night.'

Von Neurath claimed to have 'a clear conscience not only before myself, but before history and the German people'. But were he to be found guilty, he would 'take it upon myself as a last sacrifice on behalf of my people'.

After 216 days of testimony, the tribunal was adjourned to consider its judgement. It would take a month.

After escaping to Brazil, Stangl was finally tracked down in 1967 by Nazi hunter Simon Wiesenthal. He was sentenced to life imprisonment in 1970, but died of heart failure in 1971

FRANZ STANGL

THE MAN WHO LOVED HIS WORK

'There is something the world has never understood; how perfect the machine was. It was only lack of transport . . . that prevented them from dealing with far vaster numbers than they did; Treblinka alone could have dealt with the 6,000,000 Jews and more besides.'

Richard Glazar, survivor of Treblinka concentration camp

Not all concentration camp commandants were psychopaths or sadists – far from it, if statements made by Franz Stangl, commandant of Sobibor and Treblinka, are to be believed. 'My conscience is clear. I was simply doing my duty,' he said. Stangl had overseen the extermination of more than 900,000 men, women and children at Sobibor (March–September 1942) and Treblinka (September 1942–August 1943) and was one of the few Nazis to grant lengthy interviews during his imprisonment after the war.

He did so in the hope that by being candid and co-operative he might curry favour with the judges who were then considering his appeal against a life sentence. Ironically, he died of natural causes just hours after giving Austrian journalist Gitta Sereny a faltering but unequivocal admission of guilt.

THE MIND OF A MASS MURDERER?

Interviewed at length over the course of several weeks in the spring of 1971, Stangl gave the impression of a man reluctant to face up to the enormity of the crimes in which he had taken part. His repeated attempts at evasion and denial suggested that, even at the end, he was still attempting to distance himself from the ruthless cruelty of the regime he had served so well. Although he protested that he had been a mere functionary, it is undeniable that his organizational skills and earnest desire to please his superiors ensured that the extermination process became more efficient than his Nazi masters could ever have imagined.

Stangl considered himself to be nothing more than an administrator whose duty, as he saw it, was to carry out his orders without question and with as little 'unpleasantness' as possible. 'This was my profession. I enjoyed it. It fulfilled me. And yes, I was ambitious about that. I won't deny it.'

He was an educated, cultured man and a devout Catholic. As the war progressed, he was ordered to speed up the killing and disposal of the trainloads of Polish Jews being transported to Treblinka in cattle trucks – several thousand at a time – and he remained wilfully blind and chillingly indifferent to the genocide he was participating in. In his defence he could only say that he had allowed himself to be persuaded that the victims were racially inferior and as such deserved to die. He became immune to their suffering and didn't view them as individuals, but as cattle to be slaughtered: 'they were cargo. . . . It had nothing to do with humanity – it could not have. It was a mass – a mass of rotting flesh... I rarely saw them as individuals. It was always a huge mass.'

Stangl claimed to have considered applying for a transfer when he realized what was being planned at Treblinka, but persuaded himself that it was better to comply than risk being summarily executed. And what good would that serve? They'd only appoint someone else to do the job the next day.

FAMILY MAN

Besides, he had his family to consider. If he refused to carry out his orders there was a chance that his wife and daughters would also be killed, although there is no evidence that this fate ever befell anyone other than those who actively conspired to overthrow the dictatorship.

After setting aside his initial reservations, Stangl began to take a perverse pride in his work and boasted of his aptitude for organization and improving efficiency, as if he had been presiding over a meat processing factory with productivity quotas to be met.

After the war he defended his role in the regime by claiming he had been uncommonly humane under the circumstances. The Jews and other 'undesirables' were deemed to have no place in the New Order. It would not do to question the methods used to achieve their removal. Stangl had been a policeman in his native Austria before the war and saw his new role as an extension of his previous duties. It was not his place to question the law, but to enforce it.

Stangl wanted his place of work to look attractive, so he ordered the paths to be paved and flowers planted along the sides of Seidel Street near the camp headquarters and the SS living quarters. He also went to lengths to deceive new arrivals that Treblinka was a stopover en route to resettlement camps in the east. He ordered the construction of a fake railway station platform with painted clocks, a 'hospital' and other buildings, as if constructing the back lot for a movie. He planted shrubs and flowers – primarily to avoid panic, but also to make it easier on his own men, who then only had to herd the incoming 'shipment' through the selection process and on to the gas chambers.

SIMPLY OBEYING ORDERS

With his mellifluous voice and courteous manners, Stangl challenged the stereotypical image of the arrogant SS officer. Stripped of his white hunting outfit and riding crop and dressed casually in grey flannel trousers, grey sweater, white shirt and tie, he presented a deceptively amiable figure to those who visited him in prison after the war. The only intimidating aspect was his physical stature – an imposing 1.83 metres (6 feet). But it was clear, even in the sterile waiting room in Düsseldorf remand prison, that Stangl had been and remained a dominant personality. But four years in solitary confinement took the edge off his arrogance. He admitted to suffering bouts of depression, though he rallied at the thought of attending a literature class and joining the chess club to take his mind off the numbing routine of prison life.

He appeared unconcerned about the outcome of his impending appeal, but it may simply have been relief that, at the age of 63, he would at last have the opportunity to justify his actions and 'clear his name'. When the court heard that he had simply been obeying orders they would surely let him go. Only by living such an illusion could he avoid facing the facts and his part in the killings. He maintained the illusion of normality with a daily routine of exercise and reading to 'improve his mind'. It was the last in a long line of lies, deceit and deception that he had unconsciously constructed to insulate himself against meeting the monster in the mirror.

NOTHING WRONG WITH MURDER

Stangl's journey from man to murderer began the day he added his name to a list of Nazi sympathizers to avoid being shot by the Germans when they marched into Austria in 1938. His fellow Linz police officers were being rounded up by the Germans for having imprisoned Austrian Nazis when the party was declared illegal in the run-up to annexation. Franz saved his neck by posing as an illegal Nazi, but his wife Theresa felt it was a betrayal of all that they believed in. He later admitted he should have killed himself in 1938, but didn't have the courage and didn't see why he and his family should be punished for something that was none of their doing.

Having aligned himself with the enemy, he then agreed to the Nazis' next demand by ending his affiliation with the Church, a requirement made of every Austrian official who wished to continue in their profession. For his wife, a regular churchgoer, this was an act of betrayal for which she could never forgive her husband or the party.

'They do it so subtly you see,' Stangl explained to his interrogator. 'They persuade you to give up all you hold dear one piece at a time – never too much at once – so that it is only later that you realize how far down you have allowed yourself to slide.'

While he felt that hiding the truth from his family was permissible under the circumstances, he had a harder time convincing himself that participation in mass murder was justifiable. The turning point appears to have come shortly after he was assigned to the Nazi euthanasia department known as T4 at Schloss Hartheim, in November 1940.

Stangl visited an institution for severely handicapped children where he claimed that the Mother Superior pointed out a 16-year-old boy curled up in a basket on the floor and said, 'Just look at him. No good to himself or anyone else. How could they refuse to deliver him from this miserable life?' A priest who was in attendance nodded approval. Stangl claimed that this affected him profoundly. 'Here was a Catholic nun, a Mother Superior, and a priest. And they thought it was right. Who was I then to doubt what was being done?'

As Stangl saw it, this endorsement of Nazi 'mercy killing' let him off the hook, for if his Catholic role models sanctioned such practices, they must be morally justified.

CLINICAL DETACHMENT

When interviewed by journalist Gitta Sereny, Stangl recalled such significant events in his career with clinical detachment. He only seemed to show emotion when he described having deceived his wife and realizing that each lie he told had lost more of her trust and brought him deeper into debt with the regime.

Once he had told one lie, it was easier to tell another and another. In the end he couldn't tell genuine memories from false. In 1942, when his wife asked about his promotion to Sobibor, he assured her he was only involved in the construction of the buildings and that it was a forced labour camp.

Simon Wiesenthal (with moustache), the Austrian-Jewish Nazi hunter, observes the proceedings at Stangl's trial in 1970

She only found out the truth when one of his colleagues made a drunken confession. Stangl then assured her that the deaths in the camp could be counted in dozens and were the unavoidable consequence of disease and bad conditions caused by Allied bombing!

IGNORED REALITY

Stangl avoided facing reality by immersing himself in a series of additions to the site: 'I repressed it all by trying to create a special place: gardens, new barracks, new kitchens, new everything; barbers, tailors, shoemakers, carpenters. There were hundreds of ways to take one's mind off it; I used them all.' His principal tactic was denial. He persuaded himself that the prisoners were nothing more than animals: 'When I was on a trip once, years later in Brazil, my train stopped next to a slaughterhouse. The cattle in the pens, hearing the noise of the train, trotted up to the fence and stared at the train. They were very close to my window, one crowding the other, looking at me through that fence. I thought then, "Look at this, this reminds me of Poland; that's just how the people looked, trustingly, just before they went into the tins. . . . Those big eyes which looked at me not knowing that in no time at all they'd all be dead."'

All the while Stangl was aware that if he didn't carry out his orders he would be sent back to his former posting in the police force where he would have to work under a superior he detested. It didn't seem to occur to him that this disagreeable situation would be infinitely preferable to living with the knowledge that he had facilitated the murder of tens of thousands of innocent people. In his mind, he had managed to disconnect his actions from the consequences.

THE JEWS WERE TO BLAME

The extermination of the Jews and other prisoners was seen as a necessary evil and the first stage in creating a New Order in Europe. According to Nazi thinking, it wasn't murder, it was ethnic cleansing, and comparable to a surgeon who cuts out a tumour in order that a patient can live.

Stangl refused to take responsibility. The Jews weren't blameless, he argued. They weren't all innocent. The wealthier ones could have saved the poor ones had they shared their possessions; the trustees could have refused to participate in the processing of new arrivals. It was everyone's fault but his. He didn't hate the Jews, but despised them for submitting to their fate so meekly.

He had never hurt anyone, he protested. The Holocaust wasn't committed out of hatred. It was to remove the Jews' wealth and influence. It was all about money. And Stangl himself was an expert on this topic. He had stolen the possessions of those he had hounded into the gas chambers; his haul amounted to 145 kilograms of gold and 4,000 carats in diamonds by the time he left Treblinka. The loot was deposited in SS bank accounts.

> *They were so weak; they allowed everything to happen, to be done to them . . . that is how contempt is born. I could never understand how they could just give in as they did.'*
>
> Franz Stangl's view on the Jews he 'processed' at Treblinka concentration camp

CHAPTER 27
The Judgement

On 1 October 1946, the verdict was handed down. Hans Frank, the governor-general of Poland; Wilhelm Frick, minister of internal affairs; Alfred Jodl, Hitler's strategic adviser; Ernst Kaltenbrunner, head of the RSHA; Field Marshal Wilhelm Keitel; Joachim von Ribbentrop, Hitler's foreign minister; Alfred Rosenberg, minister for the occupied territories; Fritz Sauckel, organizer of forced labour; Julius Streicher, anti-Semitic propagandist and *gauleiter* in Franconia; and Arthur Seyss-Inquart, commissioner for the occupied Netherlands, were all sentenced to death and hanged in the early morning of 16 October 1946 in the old gymnasium of Nuremberg prison. The bodies were cremated in Munich and the ashes were strewn in an estuary of the Isar river.

The head of the Luftwaffe, Hermann Goering, was also sentenced to death, but committed suicide before he could be executed. And Nazi party organizer Martin Bormann was sentenced to death *in absentia*, although he was officially declared dead in 1973 after a body identified as his was unearthed in Berlin.

Walther Funk, minister for economic affairs and president of the German central bank, was sentenced to life imprisonment, but was released in 1957 because of ill-health. He died in 1960. Erich Raeder, commander-in-chief of the German navy, received a life sentence, but was released in 1955, again on grounds of ill-health, and died in 1960. Rudolf Hess was also sentenced to life imprisonment. He committed suicide in 1987 in Spandau prison in Berlin where the other Nuremberg detainees had been held.

Karl Doenitz, admiral of the fleet and Hitler's successor, was sentenced to ten years' imprisonment. He was released in 1956 and died in 1980. Albert Speer, minister for weapons and munitions, was sentenced to 20 years in prison. Released in 1966, he died in 1981. Baldur von Schirach, head of the ministry for youth and *gauleiter* of Vienna, was also sentenced to 20 years. He was released in 1966 and died in 1974. And Konstantin von Neurath, protector of Bohemia and Moravia, was sentenced to 15 years' imprisonment. Released in 1954 because of ill-health, he died in 1956.

Hans Fritzsche, head of the news service section in the ministry of propaganda and essentially a stand-in for Goebbels (who had committed suicide) was acquitted, but in the subsequent de-Nazification procedures a German court sentenced him to nine years' imprisonment. He was released in 1950 and died in 1953. Franz von Papen, vice-chancellor in Hitler's first cabinet, was also acquitted. In de-Nazification procedures, he was sentenced to eight years' imprisonment. Released in 1949, he died in 1969. Also acquitted was Hjalmar Schacht, president of the Reichsbank and minister of economics who had been imprisoned in the concentration camp at Flossenbürg since 1944. The German authorities imprisoned him until 1948. He died in 1970.

Guilty verdicts were also handed down on the leadership corps of the NSDAP, the SS, the SD and the Gestapo.

Epilogue

Although it was originally planned for the International Military Tribunal to sit again, the Cold War had started and there was no further co-operation among the participants. Nevertheless, further military tribunals sat in the separate French, British, American and Soviet zones of occupation. The US tribunals sat at Nuremberg and on 9 December 1946 proceedings began against 23 German doctors accused of participating in the Nazi euthanasia programme to murder the mentally deficient and of conducting medical experiments on concentration camp inmates. The trial lasted 140 days: 85 witnesses appeared and 1,500 documents were introduced in evidence; 16 of the doctors were found guilty, of whom seven were sentenced to death and executed on 2 June 1948.

In the 12 subsequent proceedings at Nuremberg, 175 Germans were convicted. In all, 10,000 Germans were convicted and 250 sentenced to death.

In 1960, Adolf Eichmann was found in Argentina. He was kidnapped by Mossad, the Israeli intelligence agency, and taken to Israel to stand trial. He was convicted and hanged two years later. Josef Mengele was also found in South America. Escaping capture, in 1979 he suffered a stroke while swimming and drowned.

Japanese war trials

The Potsdam Declaration of July 1945 called for the trial of those who had 'deceived and misled' the Japanese people into war. As commander of the occupation, General Douglas MacArthur arrested 39 suspects, most of them members of General Tojo's war cabinet. Tojo himself tried to commit suicide, but was resuscitated by American doctors.

In Manila, MacArthur had already held war crimes trials which had resulted in the executions of generals Yamashita and Homma, but there were doubts about the legitimacy of such proceedings.

Nevertheless, on 6 October MacArthur was given the authority to try suspects under three broad categories. Class A charges alleging 'crimes against peace' were to be brought against Japan's top leaders who had planned and directed the war. Class B and C charges, which could be levelled at Japanese of any rank, covered 'conventional war crimes' and 'crimes against humanity' respectively. In early November, MacArthur was also given authority to purge other wartime leaders from public life.

On 19 January 1946, the International Military Tribunal for the Far East was established with 11 judges. Sir William Webb, an Australian, was the tribunal's president and US assistant attorney general Joseph Keenan was named chief prosecutor.

The Tokyo trials began on 3 May 1946, and lasted two-and-a-half years. By 4 November 1948, all of the remaining defendants had been found guilty. Seven were sentenced to death, 16 to life terms and two to lesser terms. Two had died during the trials and one had been found insane. After reviewing their decisions, MacArthur praised the work of the tribunal and upheld the verdicts.

On 23 December 1948, General Tojo and six others were hanged at Sugamo prison. Afraid of antagonizing the Japanese people, MacArthur defied the wishes of President Truman and banned photography. Instead, four members of the Allied Council were present as official witnesses.

The Tokyo trials were not the only forum for the punishment of Japanese war criminals. The Asian countries that had suffered under Japan's war machine tried an estimated 5,000 suspected war criminals, executing as many as 900 and sentencing more than half to life in prison.

ADOLF EICHMANN

THE HOLLOW MAN

I will gladly jump into my grave in the knowledge that five million enemies of the Reich have already died like animals.'

Smartly dressed in a plain suit and tie, the balding man with thick, black-framed spectacles sat impassively in the glass booth. His face betrayed no emotion as the first of more than a hundred witnesses took the stand just a few feet away from him to relive the nightmares that would haunt them to their graves. He might have been an official in a government department, rubber-stamping documents as they passed across his desk, instead of a notorious war criminal on trial for genocide.

As the television cameras broadcast the day's proceedings from the stifling heat of the Jerusalem courtroom, one witness described Adolf Eichmann's demeanour as a 'block of ice'.

SMILING AT DEATH

Eichmann made careful notes with the air of a man who wanted to be sure everything was in order, but otherwise he appeared detached from the proceedings as if recording the fortunes of another defendant. He seemed to be resigned to his fate that it was now too late for Germany to order his extradition and save him from the death penalty. Only once did he betray his true feelings. When the court lights were dimmed and newsreel film of the liberation of Bergen-Belsen was projected on to a screen, a young television technician caught a close-up of the defendant on a monitor. He was smiling.

The former Obersturmbannführer (lieutenant-colonel) had been indicted on 15 counts including Crimes Against Humanity and Crimes Against the Jewish People, all of which he denied. He was accused of co-ordinating the deportation of Jews from all over Europe to extermination camps and confiscating the property and assets of those he had sent to their deaths.

NO PERSONALITY

Even in the glare of worldwide publicity, Eichmann remained an enigma; not because he exuded an air of mystery, but because he projected no personality at all. He was a colourless, two-dimensional man, blank, expressionless and seemingly disconnected from reality. When he did speak it was to deny all responsibility and to claim that he had never been an anti-Semite. After all, hadn't he once had a Jewish mistress?

It was common knowledge among Eichmann's colleagues in the Gestapo's Bureau of Jewish Affairs in Berlin that he had cheated on his wife with a series of mistresses, one of whom he had taken on a 'working holiday' to Hungary, where he supervised the rounding up and deportation of Jews to Dachau and Auschwitz. Witnesses testified that he often strutted before his intended victims, assuring them that Auschwitz was a 'holiday camp' which only married couples were eligible to enter. He then suggested that they had better marry if they didn't want to lose their place. He even penned postcards for inmates to sign and send to their relatives, urging them to hurry up and join the rest of their family.

'To sum it all up, I must say that I regret nothing' – the colourless
Adolf Eichmann in the dock

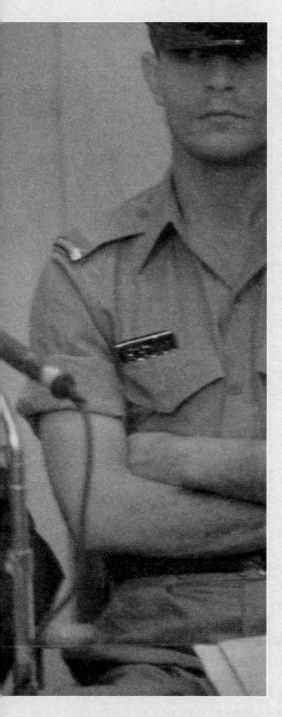

CUNNING COVER-UP

In Argentina, not long before his abduction by Mossad in 1960, Eichmann had entertained Willem Sassen, an ex-member of the Waffen SS, and agreed to talk at length about his crucial role in the Holocaust. The so-called 'Sassen tapes' reveal that Eichmann and his superiors were not only exceptionally callous but also cunning and devious in covering up the nature and enormity of their crimes: 'We had words for the concealment of annihilation such as "special treatment" or "expulsion to the east" or "the final solution to the Jewish question".' It was Orwellian doublespeak taken to hideous extremes.

Eichmann justified whatever atrocities he had presided over by quoting the SS oath, which demanded unquestioning obedience and loyalty. When asked if that meant he would murder his own father if ordered to do so, he didn't hesitate to reply 'yes'.

ENJOYED HIS WORK

Eichmann told Sassen that he enjoyed his work and was proud of having been an efficient administrator. 'I must confess I did not greet this assignment with the apathy of an ox. I was fascinated by it.' Later, on the witness stand he declared, 'My heart was light and joyful in my work, because the decisions were not mine.'

Eichmann attempted to portray himself as nothing more than a 'transportation officer' whose duties were confined to logistics. He was the man who had made the trains run on time. It was immaterial to him that these engines pulled cattle trucks loaded with human cargo bound for the death camps. And when he was admonished by his superiors for packing twice as many people into one particular train than was usual, he explained that it was of no concern because many of them were children and didn't take up so much space.

In private, Eichmann had shared his colleagues' pride in facilitating the eradication of the Jews from Germany and the conquered territories to the east. He boasted to Sassen that he had dictated Goering's letter to Heydrich on 31 July 1941, ordering the genocide of the Jews.

As a functionary he was commendably thorough and methodical. His own colleagues had described him as a 'tyrant', which he took as a compliment saying, 'It wasn't my business to be loved.'

Not a single Jew was to escape his trap. Whenever he received an appeal urging him to make an exception because a particular individual was of use to another department, Eichmann would refuse point blank to release them.

He told Sassen, 'One of these officers was a certain Obergruppenführer Wolff, whom I once wanted to challenge to a duel because he made a swine of me over the telephone. He wanted to grant a particular Jew an extraordinary status, and this I could not allow under any circumstances. If I were to make exceptions which were not covered by the Reichsführer's instructions, it would have started an avalanche.'

HISTORY RE-WRITTEN

When not in court, Eichmann spent the long hours of solitude in his cell writing his memoirs in which he absolved himself of all blame and expressed the hope that he might persuade the judges to be lenient. But after handing down the verdict of 'Guilty' on all counts and passing the sentence of death, the judges ordered the papers to be locked away where they remained unseen for 40 years. Adolf Eichmann was hanged just after midnight on 31 May 1962.

His memoirs portray a vain, arrogant, unrepentant personality with a weakness for self-aggrandizement and a habit of rewriting history – casting himself in the role of a courageous man of principle. When offered false papers to aid his escape at the end of the war, he claimed to have spat on them in disdain and waved his revolver as the only 'certificate' he would need to show his captors.

An unabashed fantasist, he confided to Sassen that he had offered to lead a last stand against the Allies in the Alpine stronghold around Berchtesgaden. And that SS General Ernst Kaltenbrunner had commended him for his selfless gesture and sacrifice: 'Now [Himmler] can talk to Eisenhower differently in his negotiations, for he will know that if Eichmann is in the mountains he will never surrender . . . '

Sensing that he had the ear of a gullible admirer, Eichmann added, 'My immediate superior, General Müller, said to me, "If we had 50 Eichmanns we could have won the war!!"'

This recasting of himself as a man of action was disputed by SS Captain Dieter Wisliceny, a key figure in the deportation and liquidation of Hungarian Jews, who described Eichmann as 'a cowardly man, who was at great pains to protect himself from responsibility'.

INSTIGATED 'DEATH MARCH'

Eichmann's capacity for self-deception, however, was limitless. After witnessing a mass execution, he asked the readers of his memoirs to see him as a 'sensitive man' forced to steel himself into committing 'unpalatable' acts: 'At heart I am a very sensitive man. I simply can't look at any suffering without trembling myself. Even if today I see someone with a deep cut, I have to look away.'

But the earlier confession captured on the Sassen tapes had Eichmann bragging that it was he who suggested the camps use Zyklon-B gas instead of carbon monoxide to speed up the killings. He is alleged to have said, 'It has proven efficient at exterminating lice, so it should be good for exterminating human vermin.'

And it was Eichmann who had instigated the 'Death March' of 50,000 Jews from Hungary to the Austrian border in 1944, in defiance of Himmler's express orders. Eichmann was not prepared to allow the advancing Russians to thwart his plans. After having repeatedly denied knowing anything about the forced 220-km (137-mile) march of starving men, women and children, Eichmann finally identified his signature on a document produced by the Israeli prosecutors, which ordered the march in defiance of Himmler's directive. Pride and arrogance had proved to be his undoing: 'I was responsible for the march. I admit it. As it turned out, the march was more trouble than if I had sent a hundred trains to Auschwitz. I wanted to show the Allies my hand, as it were, to tell them, "You smashed our transportation routes, but we will carry on in the most elegant manner."'

Never once during his detention did Eichmann express remorse. 'They were old people,' he said. 'It is clear when you chop wood, chips will fall.'

His only regret was that he hadn't completed the programme: 'We didn't do our job properly. We could have done more. I didn't just take orders. If I had been that kind of person, I would have been a fool. Instead, I was part of the thinking process, I was an idealist.'

The rail entrance to Auschwitz-Birkenau concentration camp

Timeline

1889 ~ 20 April
Adolf Hitler born near Linz, Austria
✦
1918 ~ 11 November
First World War ends
Germany defeated
✦
1919 ~ 28 June
Signing of the Versailles Treaty
✦
1921 ~ 29 July
Adolf Hitler elected leader of National
Socialist German Workers' party
✦
1923 ~ 9 November
The Munich Beer Hall Putsch fails
Hitler imprisoned
✦
1925 ~ 18 July
Mein Kampf published
✦
1929 ~ 29 October
Wall Street stock market crash ushers
in the Great Depression. Results in
widespread inflation and high
unemployment in North America
and Europe
✦
1930 ~ 14 September
Nazis become the second-largest
political party in Germany
✦
1933 ~ 30 January
Adolf Hitler becomes
chancellor of Germany
✦
27 February
Arson attack on the Reichstag building
in Berlin
✦
24 March
As a result of the Reichstag fire,
Hitler invokes emergency powers
✦

1 April
Nazis encourage boycott of Jewish
businesses
✦
10 May
Ritual book-burning in German cities
✦
14 July
Nazis outlaw opposition parties
✦
1934 ~ 30 June
Night of the Long Knives
✦
25 July
Nazis murder Chancellor Dollfuss
✦
2 August
Death of German President von
Hindenburg
✦
19 August
Adolf Hitler is confirmed as Führer
✦
1935 ~ 15 September
Nuremberg Race Laws deny Jews
equal rights
✦
1936 ~ 7 March
German troops occupy the Rhineland
unopposed
✦
18 July
Civil war in Spain. Fascists under
Franco receive military aid from
Germany
✦
1 August
Olympic Games open in Berlin
✦
1937 ~ 11 June
Soviet army severely weakened and
demoralized after Stalin instigates
purge of senior Red Army officers
✦

1938 ~ 12 MARCH
Germany's Anschluss (union)
with Austria
+

30 SEPTEMBER
British Prime Minister Neville
Chamberlain signs Munich
Agreement guaranteeing that Britain
and her Allies will not intervene if
Hitler 'reclaims' the Sudetenland.
Chamberlain claims he has secured
'peace in our time' by appeasing Hitler
and preventing a European war
+

15 OCTOBER
German troops occupy the
Sudetenland
+

9 NOVEMBER
Kristallnacht (Night of Broken Glass).
Throughout Germany, Nazi thugs and
their supporters smash the windows of
Jewish businesses and set synagogues
on fire
+

1939 ~ 15–16 MARCH
Nazis take Czechoslovakia
+

28 MARCH
Spanish Civil War ends. Franco's
fascists take power
+

22 MAY
Nazis sign 'Pact of Steel' with Italy
+

21 AUGUST
Nazis and Soviets sign
Non-Aggression Pact, leaving
Germany free to attack the west
without fear of a second front being
opened up to the East
+

25 AUGUST
In response, Britain and Poland sign
a Mutual Assistance Treaty
+

1 SEPTEMBER
Nazis invade Poland
+

3 SEPTEMBER
Britain, France, Australia and New
Zealand declare war on Germany
+

17 SEPTEMBER
Soviet army invades Poland
Ten days later, Poland surrenders
+

29 SEPTEMBER
Nazis and Soviets divide up Poland
+

OCTOBER
Nazis instigate euthanasia policy
The sick and disabled are exterminated
+

8 NOVEMBER
Assassination attempt on Hitler fails
+

30 NOVEMBER
Soviets invade Finland. On 12 March,
Finland signs a peace treaty
+

1940 ~ 9 APRIL
Nazis invade Denmark and Norway
+

10 MAY
Blitzkrieg! Nazis invade France,
Belgium, Luxembourg and the
Netherlands. Winston Churchill
appointed British prime minister
+

15 MAY
Holland surrenders. Belgium
capitulates on 28 May
+

26 MAY
Evacuation of Allied troops from
Dunkirk (ends 3 June)
+

10 JUNE
Norway surrenders; Italy declares war
on Britain and France
+

14 JUNE
German troops enter Paris

✦

16 JUNE
Marshal Pétain becomes French prime minister

✦

18 JUNE
Hitler and Mussolini form alliance
Soviets occupy the Baltic states

✦

22 JUNE
Hitler humiliates France by forcing its leaders to sign an armistice in the same railway carriage in which Germany signed the surrender in 1918

✦

28 JUNE
Britain recognizes the exiled General Charles de Gaulle as the leader of the Free French. In France, the 'puppet' Vichy government collaborates with the Nazis

✦

1 JULY
German U-boat campaign begins in the Atlantic, harassing merchant convoys bringing vital supplies to the British Isles

✦

10 JULY
Battle of Britain begins. Throughout August, German bombers target British airfields and factories. The British respond by bombing Berlin – the first long-range raid of the war

✦

13 SEPTEMBER
Italians invade Egypt

✦

15 SEPTEMBER
German air raids extend to Southampton, Bristol, Cardiff, Liverpool and Manchester

✦

27 SEPTEMBER
Axis formed when Germany, Italy and Japan sign the Tripartite Pact

✦

7 OCTOBER
German troops invade Romania

✦

12 OCTOBER
Germans cancel Operation Sealion

✦

28 OCTOBER
Italian army invades Greece

✦

20 NOVEMBER
Hungary joins the Axis, followed three days later by Romania

✦

9–10 DECEMBER
British North African campaign begins against the Italians

✦

1941 ~ 22 JANUARY
British and Australians take strategically vital North African port of Tobruk, which will change hands several times after Rommel's Afrika Korps enter the desert theatre on 12 February

✦

27 MARCH
A coup in Yugoslavia overthrows the pro-Axis government

✦

6 APRIL
Nazis invade Greece and Yugoslavia
The latter surrenders on 17 April
Greece surrenders ten days later

✦

10 MAY
Deputy Führer Rudolf Hess flies to Scotland and is arrested

✦

27 MAY
Nazi flagship, the *Bismarck*, sunk by the British navy

✦

JUNE
Nazi SS *Einsatzgruppen* begin programme of mass murder in Latvia

✦

22 JUNE
German invasion of the Soviet Union, codenamed Operation Barbarossa

✦

3 JULY
Stalin orders a scorched earth policy in the face of the advancing Germans

✦

12 JULY
The British and Soviets sign Mutual Assistance Agreement

✦

31 JULY
Goering instructs Heydrich to instigate the Final Solution – the mass extermination of the Jews in Germany

✦

1 SEPTEMBER
Nazis order Jews to wear yellow stars

✦

3 SEPTEMBER
First experimental use of gas chambers at Auschwitz

✦

2 OCTOBER
Operation Typhoon – the German advance on Moscow – begins
Four days later, the Soviet army launches a major counter-offensive

✦

5 DECEMBER
German retreat from Moscow begins

✦

7 DECEMBER
The Japanese bomb Pearl Harbor

✦

19 DECEMBER
Hitler takes complete command of the German army

✦

1942 ~ 20 JANUARY
SS leader Heydrich holds the Wannsee Conference to co-ordinate the 'Final Solution'

✦

30 MAY
First thousand-bomber British air raid (against Cologne)

✦

JUNE
Mass murder of Jews begins at Auschwitz

✦

4 JUNE
Heydrich dies after assassination attempt in Prague
Nazis liquidate Lidice in reprisal

✦

11 JUNE
Himmler orders the destruction of Jewish ghettos in Poland

✦

1–30 JULY
First Battle of El Alamein

✦

SEPTEMBER
Battle of Stalingrad begins

✦

1943 ~ 14–24 JANUARY
At Casablanca, Churchill and Roosevelt demand the unconditional surrender of Germany

✦

27 JANUARY
First American bombing raid on Germany

✦

2 FEBRUARY
Encircled Germans surrender at Stalingrad

✦

18 FEBRUARY
Nazis arrest White Rose resistance leaders in Munich

✦

19 APRIL
Waffen SS launch assault on Jewish resistance group in the Warsaw ghetto. Resistance holds out until 16 May

✦

13 MAY
German and Italian troops surrender in North Africa

✦

9–10 JULY
Allies land in Sicily

✦

25–26 JULY
Mussolini arrested and replaced by Marshal Badoglio. He is rescued six weeks later by the Germans

✦

1 OCTOBER
Allies enter Naples, Italy

✦

1944 ~ 22 JANUARY
Allies land at Anzio

✦

27 JANUARY
The siege of Leningrad is lifted after 900 days

✦

15–18 FEBRUARY
Allies bomb the monastery of Monte Cassino

✦

4 MARCH
First major daylight bombing raid on Berlin by the Allies

✦

5 JUNE
Allies enter Rome

✦

6 JUNE
D-Day landings

✦

13 JUNE
First German V1 rocket attack on Britain

✦

22 JUNE
The Soviet summer offensive begins the rout of the German invaders

✦

3 JULY
'Battle of the Hedgerows' in Normandy
A week later, Caen is liberated

✦

20 JULY
Hitler survives assassination attempt at the 'Wolf's Lair' HQ

✦

24 JULY
Soviet troops liberate first concentration camp at Majdanek

✦

25 AUGUST
Paris is liberated

✦

13 SEPTEMBER
US troops reach the Siegfried Line

✦

17 SEPTEMBER
Operation Market Garden begins (Allied airborne assault on Holland)

✦

2 OCTOBER
Polish Home Army forced to surrender to the Germans in Warsaw after weeks of heroic resistance

✦

14 OCTOBER
Allies liberate Athens
Rommel commits suicide on Hitler's orders for his part in the July Plot

✦

16–27 DECEMBER
Battle of the Bulge in the Ardennes. Retreating Waffen SS murder 81 US POWs at Malmedy

✦

26 DECEMBER
The 'Battling Bastards of Bastogne' are relieved by General Patton

✦

1945 ~ JANUARY
The Germans withdraw from the Ardennes

✦

26 JANUARY
Soviet troops liberate Auschwitz

✦

4–11 FEBRUARY
Roosevelt, Churchill and Stalin meet at Yalta and plan the partition of post-war Germany

✦

13–14 FEBRUARY
Dresden is destroyed by a firestorm after Allied bombing raids

✦

APRIL
Allies recover stolen Nazi art hidden in salt mines

✦

1 APRIL
US troops encircle remnants of German army in the Ruhr

✦

12 APRIL
Allies uncover the horrors of the 'Final Solution' at Buchenwald and Belsen concentration camps
President Roosevelt dies
Truman becomes US president

✦

16 APRIL
Americans enter Nuremberg

✦

18 APRIL
German army surrenders at the Ruhr

✦

21 APRIL
Soviet army enters Berlin

✦

28 APRIL
Mussolini hanged by Italian partisans

✦

29 APRIL
US 7th Army liberates Dachau

✦

30 APRIL
Adolf Hitler and Eva Braun commit suicide in the Berlin bunker, followed by Goebbels and his wife, who kill their children before taking their own lives

✦

7 MAY
The unconditional surrender of the German forces is signed

✦

8 MAY
VE (Victory in Europe) Day

✦

9 MAY
Hermann Goering surrenders to US 7th Army

✦

23 MAY
SS Reichsführer Himmler commits suicide

✦

5 JUNE
Allies partition Germany and divide Berlin into sections
The Cold War begins

✦

20 NOVEMBER
Nuremberg war crimes trials begin
Goering will commit suicide almost a year later, two hours before his scheduled execution

Index

Picture Credits